Oracle Forms

INTERACTIVE WORKBOOK

ISBN 0-13-015808-9

90000

9 780130 158086

BOOKS IN THIS SERIES

- Baman Motivala
  "Oracle Forms Interactive Workbook"
  0-13-015808-9

- Benjamin Rosenzweig & Elena Silvestrova
  "Oracle PL/SQL"
  0-13-015743-0

- Alex Morrison & Alice Rischert
  "Oracle SQL Interactive Workbook"
  0-13-015745-7

Oracle Forms

INTERACTIVE WORKBOOK

BAMAN MOTIVALA

Prentice Hall PTR
Upper Saddle River, New Jersey 07458
www.phptr.com

Editorial/Production Supervision: *Wil Mara*
Acquisitions Editor: *Tim Moore*
Development Editor: *Russ Hall*
Marketing Manager: *Bryan Gambrel*
Manufacturing Manager: *Alexis Heydt*
Buyer: *Maura Goldstaub*
Cover Design Director: *Jerry Votta*
Cover Designer: *Nina Scuderi*
Art Director: *Gail Cocker-Bogusz*

Prentice Hall books are widely used by corporations and government agencies for training, marketing, and resale. The publisher offers discounts on this book when ordered in bulk quantities. For more information, contact Prentice Hall's Corporate Sales Department—phone: 1-800-382-3419; fax: 1-201-236-7141; email: corpsales@prenhall.com; address: Corp. Sales Dept., Prentice Hall PTR, 1 Lake Street, Upper Saddle River, NJ 07458

Printed in the United States of America
10 9 8 7 6 5 4 3 2 1

ISBN 0-13-015808-9

Prentice-Hall International (UK) Limited, *London*
Prentice-Hall of Australia Pty. Limited, *Sydney*
Prentice-Hall Canada Inc., *Toronto*
Prentice-Hall Hispanoamericana, S.A., *Mexico*
Prentice-Hall of India Private Limited, *New Delhi*
Prentice-Hall of Japan, Inc., *Tokyo*
Pearson Education Asia P.T.E., Ltd.
Editora Prentice-Hall do Brasil, Ltda., *Rio de Janeiro*

for maria.

FROM THE EDITOR

Prentice Hall's Interactive Workbooks are designed to get you up and running fast, with just the information you need, when you need it.

We are certain that you will find our unique approach to learning simple and straightforward. Every chapter of every Interactive Workbook begins with a list of clearly defined Learning Objectives. A series of labs make up the heart of each chapter. Each lab is designed to teach you specific skills in the form of exercises. You perform these exercises at your computer and answer pointed questions about what you observe. Your answers will lead to further discussion and exploration. Each lab then ends with multiple-choice Self-Review Questions, to reinforce what you've learned. Finally, we have included Test Your Thinking projects at the end of each chapter. These projects challenge you to synthesize all of the skills you've acquired in the chapter.

Our goal is to make learning engaging, and to make you a more productive learner.

And you are not alone. Each book is integrated with its own "Companion Website." The website is a place where you can find more detailed information about the concepts discussed in the Workbook, additional Self-Review Questions to further refine your understanding of the material, and perhaps most importantly, where you can find a community of other Interactive Workbook users working to acquire the same set of skills that you are.

All of the Companion Websites for our Interactive Workbooks can be found at http://www.phptr.com/phptrinteractive.

Timothy C. Moore
V.P., Executive Editor
Prentice Hall PTR

CONTENTS

Introduction   xi
Acknowledgments   xvii
About the Author   xix

Chapter 1 Concepts and Objects   1
LAB 1.1 Oracle Forms Concepts   2
    1.1.1 Explain How Oracle Forms Works   4
LAB 1.2 Mandatory Forms Objects   11
    1.2.1 Identify Items and Their Types   17
    1.2.2 Identify Canvases and Frames   18
    1.2.3 Define Base-table Blocks   19
    1.2.4 Understand Modules   20
    1.2.5 Relate the Mandatory Forms Elements 20
CHAPTER 1 Test Your Thinking   30

Chapter 2 Wizards and Files   31
LAB 2.1 The Data Block and Layout Wizards   32
    2.1.1 Use the Data Block and Layout Wizards 42
    2.1.2 Reentering the Wizards   43
LAB 2.2 Oracle Forms Files   53
    2.2.1 Differentiate Between Source
    and Executable Files   54
    2.2.2 Compile Binary Files into Executable Files 55
    2.2.3 Run Executable Files   57
CHAPTER 2 Test Your Thinking   63

Chapter 3 The Development Environment   65
LAB 3.1 The Object Navigator   66
    3.1.1 Open and Identify Objects   68
    3.1.2 Create and Delete objects   69
    3.1.3 Drag & Drop and Cut & Paste Objects 70
    3.1.4 Run and Save Forms   72
    3.1.5 View Database Objects   72

viii *Contents*

LAB 3.2 The Property Palette 84
    3.2.1 View Properties 86
    3.2.2 Change Properties 86
LAB 3.3 The Layout Editor 93
    3.3.1 Create and Format Objects 95
    3.3.2 Arrange and Size Objects 97
CHAPTER 3 Test Your Thinking 105

Chapter 4 Master-Detail Forms **107**
LAB 4.1 Master-Detail Forms 108
    4.1.1 Create a Master-Detail Form 110
    4.1.2 Work with Master-Detail Forms
    and Relations 112
CHAPTER 4 Test Your Thinking 124

Chapter 5 Items **125**
LAB 5.1 Text Items and Display Items 126
    5.1.1 Create and Define Text Items Without
    the Wizard 127
    5.1.2 Create and Define Display Items 131
LAB 5.2 Buttons, List Items, Radio Groups,
  and Check Boxes 143
    5.2.1 Create Buttons 147
    5.2.2 Put Simple Code Behind Buttons 148
    5.2.3 Create List Items 150
    5.2.4 Create Radio Groups 153
    5.2.5 Create Check Boxes 155
CHAPTER 5 Test Your Thinking 169

Chapter 6 Triggers & Built-ins **171**
LAB 6.1 Trigger Basics 172
    6.1.1 Use PL/SQL and SQL in Triggers 175
    6.1.2 Understand Trigger Scope 176
    6.1.3 Categorize Triggers 178
LAB 6.2 Creating Triggers of Various Types 187
    6.2.1 Create Query Triggers 189
    6.2.2 Create Validation Triggers 192
    6.2.3 Create Transactional Triggers 195
    6.2.4 Create Key Triggers 197
LAB 6.3 Forms Built-ins 213
    6.3.1 Use Forms Built-ins 216
CHAPTER 6 Test Your Thinking 223

Chapter 7 LOVs and Alerts — **225**

LAB 7.1 Lists of Values (LOVs) — 226
   7.1.1 Create LOVs — 228
   7.1.2 Display LOVs — 233
LAB 7.2 Alerts — 248
   7.2.1 Create and Display Alerts — 251
CHAPTER 7 Test Your Thinking — 259

Chapter 8 Canvases and Windows — **261**

LAB 8.1 Canvas and Window Concepts — 262
   8.1.1 Understand Windows — 267
   8.1.2 Understand Canvases — 269
LAB 8.2 Content Canvases and Windows — 277
   8.2.1 Create a Content Canvas and Window — 278
LAB 8.3 Stacked Canvases — 287
   8.3.1 Create and Display Stacked Canvases — 289
LAB 8.4 Toolbars — 298
   8.4.1 Create a Toolbar Canvas — 299
   8.4.2 Use the Toolbar in Another Form — 302
CHAPTER 8 Test Your Thinking — 311

Chapter 9 Reusable Objects — **313**

LAB 9.1 Subclassing — 314
   9.1.1 Subclass Objects — 315
LAB 9.2 Visual Attributes and Property Classes — 323
   9.2.1 Create and Apply Named Visual Attributes — 325
   9.2.2 Create and Apply Property Classes — 327
LAB 9.3 Object Groups and Object Libraries — 336
   9.3.1 Create and Reuse Object Groups — 338
   9.3.2 Create and Utilize Object Libraries — 341
LAB 9.4 Template Forms — 348
   9.4.1 Create and Use Template Forms — 349
CHAPTER 9 Test Your Thinking — 352

Chapter 10 Reusable Code — **353**

LAB 10.1 Program Units — 354
   10.1.1 Create a Program Unit — 357

LAB 10.2 PL/SQL Libraries | 362
    10.2.1 Create and Attach PL/SQL Libraries | 364
    10.2.2 Use Indirect References in Library Code | 366
LAB 10.3 Stored PL/SQL Objects | 374
    10.3.1 Use Stored PL/SQL Objects | 375
CHAPTER 10 Test Your Thinking | 379

Chapter 11 Multiple-Form Applications   381

LAB 11.1 Calling One Form from Another | 382
    11.1.1 Open Multiple Forms | 385
    11.1.2 Create a Parameter List and Pass
    It to a Form | 387
CHAPTER 11 Test Your Thinking | 400

Chapter 12 Oracle Forms and Oracle Reports   403

LAB 12.1 Running Oracle Reports from Forms | 404
    12.1.1 Run an Oracle Report with run_product | 406
    12.1.2 Run an Oracle Report
    with run_report_object | 407
LAB 12.2 Passing Parameters to Reports | 414
    12.2.1 Pass Parameters to a Report | 416
CHAPTER 12 Test Your Thinking | 420

Chapter 13 Forms Menus   421

LAB 13.1 Menu Modules | 422
    13.1.1 Create Menus and Menu Items | 426
LAB 13.2 Menu Security | 435
    13.2.1 Implement Menu Security | 436
CHAPTER 13 Test Your Thinking | 443

Appendix A   445

Appendix B   455

Index   461

INTRODUCTION

The *Oracle Forms Interactive Workbook* presents Oracle Forms in a unique and highly effective format. It challenges you to learn Oracle Forms by using it rather than by simply reading about it.

Just as a grammar workbook would teach you about nouns and verbs by first showing you examples and then asking you to write sentences, the Oracle Forms workbook teaches you about Forms, triggers, and items by first showing you examples and then asking you to create these objects yourself.

WHO THIS BOOK IS FOR

This book is intended for anyone who needs a quick but detailed introduction to building applications with Oracle Forms. The ideal readers are those with some experience with relational databases, specifically Oracle, but little or no experience with Oracle Forms or application development.

You should be comfortable with relational database concepts, as well as SQL and PL/SQL. If you are unfamiliar with any of these subjects, refer to the other books in the Prentice Hall Interactive Oracle Series.

The content of this book is based on the material that is taught in an Introduction to Oracle Forms class at Columbia University's CTA program in New York City. The student body is rather diverse in that there are some students who have years of experience with IT and programming, but no experience with Oracle Forms, and then there are those with absolutely no experience in IT or programming. The content of the book, like the class, is balanced to meet the needs of both extremes.

HOW THIS BOOK IS ORGANIZED

The intent of this workbook is to teach you about Oracle Forms by presenting you with a series of challenges followed by detailed solutions to those challenges. The basic structure of each Chapter is as follows:

Chapter

    Lab

        Exercises

Exercise Answers with Detailed Discussion

Self-Review Questions

Lab...

Test Your Thinking Questions

Each Chapter contains interactive Labs that introduce topics about Oracle Forms. The topics are discussed briefly and then explored through Exercises, which are the heart of each Lab.

Each Exercise consists of a series of steps that you will follow to perform a specific task, along with questions that are designed to help you discover important things about Forms on your own. The answers to these questions are given at the end of the Exercises, along with more in-depth discussion of the concepts explored.

The Exercises are not meant to be closed-book quizzes to test your knowledge. On the contrary, they are intended to act as your guide and walk you through a task. You are encouraged to flip back and forth from the Exercise question section to the Exercise answer section so that if need be, you can read the answers and discussions as you go along.

At the end of each Lab is a series of multiple-choice self-review questions. These are meant to be closed-book quizzes of sorts to test that you have absorbed the Lab material. The answers to these questions appear in Appendix A. There are also additional self-review questions at this book's companion Web site, found at http://www.phptr.com/phptrinter-active/. (The companion Web site will be explained in the next section of this introduction.)

Finally, at the end of each Chapter you will find a "Test Your Thinking" section, which consists of a series of projects designed to solidify all of the skills you have learned in the Chapter. If you have successfully completed all of the Labs in the Chapter, you should be able to tackle these projects with few problems. There are not always "answers" to these projects, but where appropriate, you will find guidance and/or solutions at the companion Web site.

The Chapters should be completed in sequence because the material builds on itself as you go along. Additionally, many of the files you create and save in earlier Chapters will be required in later Chapters. In the end, all of the skills you have acquired and files you have created will come together in Chapter 13, "Forms Menus," where you will create a menu system to manage your completed and working application.

ABOUT THE COMPANION WEB SITE

The companion Web site is located at:

```
http://www.phptr.com/motivala
```

Here you will find two very important things:

1)   Files you will need ***before*** you begin reading the workbook.
2)   Answers to the Test Your Thinking questions.

All of the Exercises and questions are based on a sample database called STUDENT. The files required to create and install the STUDENT schema are downloadable from the Web site. Additionally, many of the Exercises require that you work with pre-created Forms files. For example, in Exercise 1.1.1, you will be required to open and answer questions about a file called EX01_01.fmb. This file and all the rest you will need for the workbook are downloadable from the Web site.

The answers to the "Test Your Thinking" sections will also be found at the Web site. These answers will be textual or in the form of downloadable files.

In addition to required files and "Test Your Thinking" answers, the Web site will have many other features like additional review questions, a message board, and periodically updated information about the book.

You should visit the companion Web site and download the required files before starting the Labs and Exercises.

WHAT YOU'LL NEED

There are software programs as well as knowledge requirements necessary to complete the exercise sections of the workbook.

SOFTWARE

Oracle Developer 6.0

Oracle8

Access to the WWW

Windows 95/98 or NT 4.0

ORACLE DEVELOPER 6.0: Oracle Developer 6.0 is Oracle's application development tool suite that contains a number of different components. The *Oracle Forms Interactive Workbook* is concerned only with Oracle Forms. Oracle Forms Version 6.0.5.0.2 was used to create the Exercises, but subsequent versions should be compatible.

Since Oracle frequently improves and changes its products, new versions are released all the time. However, the concepts covered in this book are fundamental to the Oracle Forms product and are unlikely to change significantly in the near future. So, even if your version of Oracle Forms is different than the one listed here, you should still be able to make use of this book.

ORACLE8: Oracle8 is Oracle's RDBMS and its flagship product. You can use either Oracle Personal Edition or Oracle Enterprise Edition. If you use Oracle Enterprise Edition, it can be running on a remote server or locally on your own machine. Oracle 8.0.5 Enterprise Edition running locally was used to create the Exercises for this book, but subsequent versions of Oracle should be compatible.

Additionally, you should have access to and be familiar with SQL*Plus.

WINDOWS 95/98 OR NT 4.0: The Oracle Forms development environment is available on a number of different operating system platforms, including Microsoft Windows and various flavors of UNIX. The Exercises, screenshots, and examples in this workbook were created using Microsoft Windows NT 4.0 with Service Pack 3. Therefore, it is geared more toward those working in a Windows environment.

But, as mentioned before, most of the Forms concepts in this book are rather fundamental and, therefore, apply to all operating systems. So, even if you are developing on a UNIX platform, this book can still be of use to you. If you are using UNIX or another non-Windows OS, keep in mind that the screenshots will not match what you see on your screen and that Appendix B, "Windows Registry," does not apply to you.

ACCESS TO THE WWW: You will need access to the Internet and WWW so that you can reach the companion Web site, `http://www.phptr .com/ phptrinteractive/`

Here you will find the files that are necessary for completing the Exercises.

It is important that you visit this site and download the necessary files before you start working through the Chapters in this book.

KNOWLEDGE

To complete the Exercises, you should be familiar with relational databases as well as Oracle database concepts. You should be comfortable using SQL to access and manipulate database objects such as tables, constraints, sequences, and so on. You should also be able to write simple PL/SQL procedures that include, among other things, local variables, conditional logic, and cursors. If you are not familiar or comfortable with these subjects, it is recommended that you refer to the other books in the Oracle series. These are listed earlier in this Introduction.

Finally, you should be reasonably comfortable with accessing and configuring the Windows Registry. This will be necessary so that Oracle Forms can properly locate all of the files you create. Appendix B, "Windows Registry," provides a brief description of the Registry and all of the information you will need to configure it for Oracle Forms.

 You should read and complete the tasks in Appendix B before starting the Labs and Exercises.

ABOUT THE SAMPLE SCHEMA

The STUDENT schema contains tables and other objects meant to keep information about a registration and enrollment system for a fictitious university. There are ten tables in the system that store data about students, courses, instructors, and so on. In addition to storing contact information (address and telephone number) for students and instructors, and descriptive information about courses (cost and prerequisites), the schema also keeps track of the sections for particular courses, and the sections that students have enrolled in.

The SECTION and ENROLLMENT tables are two of the most important in the schema. The SECTION table stores data about the individual sections that have been created for each course. Each of these section records also stores information about where and when the section will meet, and which instructor will teach the section. The SECTION table is related to the COURSE table and INSTRUCTOR table.

The ENROLLMENT table is equally important because it keeps track of which students have enrolled in which sections. Each enrollment record also stores information about the student's grade and enrollment date. The ENROLLMENT table is related to the STUDENT table and SECTION table.

The schema also has a number of other tables that manage grading for each student in each section.

CONVENTIONS USED IN THIS BOOK

There are several conventions that are used in this book to try and make your learning experience easier. These are explained here.

This icon is used to flag notes or advice from the author to you, the reader. For instance, if there is a particular topic or concept that you really need to understand for the exam, or if there's something that you need to keep in mind while working, you will find it set off from the main text like this.

This icon is used to flag tips or especially helpful tricks that will save you time or trouble. For instance, if there is a shortcut for performing a particular task or a method that the author has found useful, you will find it set off from the main text like this.

Computers are delicate creatures and can be easily damaged. Likewise, they can be dangerous to work on if you're not careful. This icon is used to flag information and precautions that will not only save you headaches in the long run, they may even save you or your computer from harm.

This icon is used to flag passages with a reference to the book's companion Web site, which once again is located at `http://www.phptr.com/phptrinteractive/`.

ACKNOWLEDGMENTS

Many people were instrumental in helping me complete this project. I'm glad to have the opportunity to acknowledge them here.

I'd like to thank Michael Stowe for serving as technical editor. He provided valuable insight and suggestions, and caught a number of ghastly errors. Also, thanks to Gayle Conarello, Matt Portnoy, Tom Ziek, and Mehli Motivala (my dad) for making many helpful comments after working through the Exercises in the early Chapters of the book.

On the publishing side, I am indebted to Ralph Moore and Russ Hall, who deftly handled the developmental process as well as my unceasing questions. Tim Moore of Prentice Hall was also a great help in handling things on the acquisitions side.

I would also like to acknowledge the other authors in the Oracle Series for making this a team effort. I am especially indebted to Douglas Scherer, first for offering me the opportunity to be one of the authors, then for acting as coordinator and general problem-solver for the whole series.

I am lucky to have two caring families, one in Sweden and one in the U.S., who offered their constant support and encouragement. My mom and dad deserve very special thanks for teaching me to speak and write properly, and for always standing behind me no matter what I choose to do.

Finally, I'd like to acknowledge the two women in my life. Olivia, my four-legged companion, who took me for long walks when I was tired of thinking about Forms and triggers, and Maria, my fiancée.

One night in December of 1998, I announced to Maria that I had been asked to write a book about Oracle Forms. I had planned to follow this announcement with a dozen reasons and excuses as to why I couldn't do it. But before I could continue, she had thrown her arms around my neck and showered me with such a torrent of enthusiastic encouragement, congratulations, and questions that it was impossible to introduce any negativity. This project would not even have been started, let alone completed, without her belief in me, and her unyielding optimism.

ABOUT THE AUTHOR

In years past, Baman Motivala has worked as an English teacher in Japan and an underpaid editorial assistant in New Jersey. Seeking a change from the rigors of proofreading, he enrolled in Columbia University's CTA program, where he was introduced to Oracle and its products. After finishing at Columbia, he became a Sales Consultant in the Tools Division at Oracle Corporation's Manhattan office, where he focused on Oracle Developer and Oracle Designer. While working at Oracle, he returned to Columbia University to spend a few evenings a week teaching a class in Oracle Forms.

He now lives in Stockholm, Sweden, with Maria, his fiancée, and Olivia, their basset hound.

L A B   1 . 1

ORACLE FORMS CONCEPTS

LAB OBJECTIVES

After this Lab, you will be able to:

- Explain How Oracle Forms Works

Oracle Forms belongs to a larger product called Oracle Developer, which has close to 20 individual components. Oracle Forms, Oracle Reports, and Oracle Graphics are the core components of the development environment. Supporting this environment are sub-components and utilities, including a project manager, debugger, database schema builder, and many others.

The primary focus of this interactive workbook is Oracle Forms. The purpose of this Lab is to get you acquainted with how Oracle Forms applications (forms) work.

HOW DOES ORACLE FORMS WORK?

In the following sections, you will learn what an event-driven model is and how it forms the basis of event-driven programming. You will also be introduced to items and triggers, two of the most common Forms objects, as well as events, a fundamental Forms concept. In the Exercises, you will get an opportunity to explore the Form Builder.

EVENTS AND TRIGGERS

Oracle Forms applications are event-driven, meaning an event occurs and the application responds to it. An event is either an *interface event*, which corresponds to a user action, or an *internal processing event*, which corresponds to a system action. Clicking a button, tabbing from one item to another, and opening or closing a window are typical examples of interface events.

Validating an item is an example of an internal processing event. It is one of the events that occurs after a user has changed the value of an item (either by entering a new value or changing one queried from the database) and then left that item either by tabbing or navigating with the mouse. The Validate Item event tells Forms to make sure that the value in the item conforms to whatever validation rules have been defined. Events are important because they drive Forms applications. They are also important because they give you, the programmer, a tremendous amount of control over an application because for every event that occurs, you have the opportunity to write code to respond to it.

The code objects that respond to events are called *triggers*. A trigger *fires,* or numerous triggers fire, whenever an event occurs. For example, if a user wants to close an application window on a Windows platform, he will click the Close button at the upper right-hand corner of the window. This is an event. In response to this event, Forms fires the WHEN-WINDOW-CLOSED trigger. You, the programmer, have written code inside this trigger to tell the application what to do. You could have the entire application close along with the window, or you could flash a message reminding the user to save his work if he intends to quit. Basically, you can have the application do anything in response to an event.

ITEMS

The Forms interface is made up of *items*. Buttons, text fields (called text items or display items in Forms), check boxes, and radio groups are typical examples of items. Items are used to present information from the database (base-table items) or to act as controls (non-base-table items). In other Forms books, you may see base-table items referred to as data items and non-base-table items referred to as control items.

Most item types, like display items, are flexible so that they can be used as base-table items or non-base-table items.

■ FOR EXAMPLE:

You may create a display item to present information pulled directly from the database, such as a student's name or address. This would be considered a base-table item because the display item is based on a column in the database. Or, you may create a display item to present the number of students enrolled in a certain section. This would be considered a non-base-table item because its value must be calculated instead of retrieved from the database.

EVENTS, TRIGGERS, AND ITEMS WORKING TOGETHER

It is quite common for an item to have a trigger associated with it, so that when an event occurs that involves the item, its trigger will fire.

■ *FOR EXAMPLE:*

You have created a base-table item in a form called ZIP that is based on the zip column in the STUDENT table of the STUDENT schema. There is also a ZIPCODE table in the schema that stores all of the valid Zip Codes. When the user enters or changes values in the ZIP item in the form, you want to validate the value she has entered by checking that it exists in the ZIPCODE table. The following would occur:

1. The user changes the ZIP item's value from 10011 to 07652.
2. The user presses the TAB key, which is an interface event.
3. The interface event causes a number of internal processing events to occur. One of them is the Validate Item event.
4. The Validate Item event fires the WHEN-VALIDATE-ITEM trigger.
5. The code in the WHEN-VALIDATE-ITEM trigger validates the value in ZIP.

It can be said, with only a hint of drama, that this series of occurrences represents the essence of a Forms application. In the Exercises that follow, you will explore the Form Builder to discover more about items, events, and triggers.

LAB 1.1 EXERCISES

1.1.1   EXPLAIN HOW ORACLE FORMS WORKS

Open the Form Builder. You will see a dialog titled "Welcome to the Form Builder." Ignore this dialog and simply click the Cancel button.

The earlier section titled "About the Companion Web Site" explained how to download required files from the companion Web site at http://www.phptr.com/phptrinteractive. *The sample database and some Oracle Forms files available at the site are*

required to complete the Exercises in this Chapter and in almost all of the Chapters that follow. Please read the entire Introduction now and then visit the Web site to learn more about what you must download.

Also note that in many of the Exercises, reference is made to the "audit columns." These columns are in each table in the STUDENT *schema and are named* CREATED_BY, CREATED_DATE, MODIFIED_BY, *and* MODIFIED_DATE. *If you are unfamiliar with the* STUDENT *schema, please read the Introduction before continuing.*

You will not be able to insert new records into the tables in the STUDENT *schema until after you have completed Chapter 6, "Triggers & Built-ins." This is not a problem because you will not be required to insert records before then.*

From the Main Menu, select File | Open and open the file named EX01_01.fmb, which should be in the \guest\forms\exercises directory on your local machine.

In the upper left-hand corner, you will see a window titled "Object Navigator." Here, you will find a hierarchical tree that lists all of the objects in a particular form.

The first node on the list is Forms, under which you will see that there is a Forms object named EX01_01. Looking down the list, you will see nodes called Triggers, Alerts, Attached Libraries, and so on.

Continue looking down the list until you come to the node named Canvases. Click the small plus sign to the left of the word "Canvases" to expand this node. The Object Navigator behaves like the Windows Explorer with regard to expanding and collapsing nodes.

Once the Canvases node is expanded, you will see a small, colorful icon with the word "STUDENT" next to it. Double-click this canvas icon. You have just opened the Layout Editor and are getting a WYSIWYG view of a form. Refer to Figure 1.1 to see how the Form Builder should look after taking these steps.

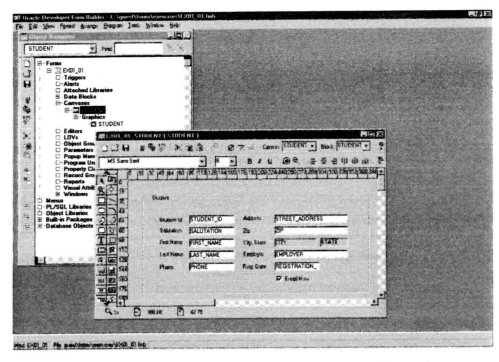

Figure 1.1 ■ The Form Builder with the Object Navigator's Canvases node expanded and the Layout Editor open.

a) What type of Forms object is the button labeled "EXIT"? In Forms terminology, what is the result when a user clicks this button?

_____

_____

b) If the EX01_01.fmb form were running, describe what would happen behind the scenes in Forms if a user clicked the EXIT button?

_____

_____

c) By expanding objects in the Object Navigator, try to locate the code associated with this button. What is the code called? Does this particular piece of code have a name? What language is it written in?

_____

_____

On the bottom right-hand side of the screen, there is a check box labeled "Enroll Now." Right now there is no trigger associated with this item. So, if a user tries to change the value of the check box, no code will respond.

> **d)** Based on the information provided in this Exercise, try to guess the name of the trigger you would use if a user were to change the value in the check box. If you feel up to it, explore the Form Builder and try to find the correct name to see if you are right.

LAB 1.1 EXERCISE ANSWERS

1.1.1 ANSWERS

> **a)** What type of Forms object is the button labeled "EXIT"? In Forms terminology, what is the result when a user clicks this button?
>
> *Answer: The button is an item. The result of clicking this button is an interface event.*

All Forms applications are driven by responses to interface events and internal processing events. When a user clicks something, this results in an interface event. When a user moves the cursor from one item to another, this results in an event. When a user inserts, updates, deletes, or queries records from the database, these are also events.

> **b)** If the EX01_01.fmb form were running, describe what would happen behind the scenes in Forms if a user clicked the EXIT button?
>
> *Answer: A Forms trigger would fire in response to this event. If the trigger code were written properly, the application would exit.*

> **c)** By expanding objects in the Object Navigator, try to locate the code associated with this button. What is the code called? Does this particular piece of code have a name? What language is it written in?
>
> *Answer: The code is called a trigger. This particular trigger is called* WHEN-BUTTON-PRESSED. *The* WHEN-BUTTON-PRESSED *trigger is written in PL/SQL as are all triggers, procedures, and functions in Oracle Forms.*

If you were unable to locate the WHEN-BUTTON-PRESSED trigger in the Object Navigator, take the following steps and then look at Figure 1.2:

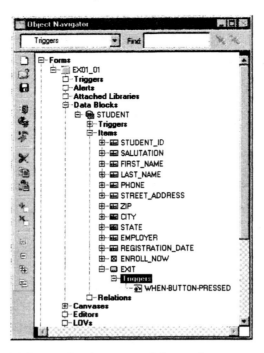

Figure 1.2 ▪ The Object Navigator with nodes expanded to show the EXIT button's WHEN-BUTTON-PRESSED trigger.

1) Look in the Object Navigator for the Data Blocks node and expand it. Remember, to *expand* a node, you simply click the small plus sign next to the node name.

2) Expand the data block named STUDENT.

3) Expand the Item named EXIT.

4) Expand the Triggers node.

For almost every conceivable interface event and system event, there exists a corresponding Forms trigger. For the user event of clicking a button, you have already seen the WHEN-BUTTON-PRESSED trigger. You will learn about other user events and their corresponding triggers in Chapter 6, "Triggers & Built-ins."

As a Forms programmer, you put your own code inside a trigger. This gives you the power to have Forms respond to any event in any way that you would like.

d) Based on the information provided in this Exercise, try to guess the name of the trigger you would use if a user were to change the value in the check box. If you feel up to it, explore the Form Builder and try to find the correct name to see if you are right.

Answer: The name of the trigger is WHEN-CHECKBOX-CHANGED.

Until you become very comfortable with Forms, you will find yourself wanting to respond to an event, but not knowing the name of the corresponding trigger. In Exercise 1.1.1.d, you knew you needed the application to respond to the changing of a check box, but you had to guess what the trigger name might be. Of course there is a list of all available triggers, but it is rather long. Being able to make educated guesses will help you sift through the list to find the trigger you need more quickly.

You will delve into events and their corresponding triggers in Chapter 6, "Triggers & Built-ins," but for now, here are three quick ways to find the name of the trigger you need in the Form Builder:

1) In the Object Navigator, right-click the ENROLL _NOW item and select Smart Triggers. This will give you a short list of trigger suggestions.

2) In the Object Navigator, expand the ENROLL_NOW item to reveal the Triggers node. Double-click on the Triggers node. A window titled Triggers will open with a list of triggers that you can scroll through.

3) Select Help | Form Builder Help Topics from the Main Menu. Select the Index tab and search for Triggers, alphabetical list of.

Forms triggers are quite different from Oracle database triggers. Forms triggers are stored inside an Oracle Forms application, while Oracle database triggers are stored in the database. Forms triggers fire because a user event or system event has occurred in a Forms application. Oracle database triggers fire when there is an attempt to insert, update, or delete data from an Oracle database table.

LAB 1.1 SELF-REVIEW QUESTIONS

In order to test your progress, you should be able to answer the following questions:

1)   Oracle Forms triggers fire in response to which of the following?
   a) _____ Oracle database triggers
   b) _____ Interface events
   c) _____ Internal processing events
   d) _____ b & c

2)   Forms triggers are written in which of the following languages?
   a) _____ C
   b) _____ PL/SQL
   c) _____ ActiveX
   d) _____ a & c

3)   The result of clicking a button is considered which of the following?
   a) _____ An interface event
   b) _____ A trigger
   c) _____ An internal processing event
   d) _____ An item

4)   Radio groups and check boxes are examples of which of the following?
   a) _____ Text items
   b) _____ Triggers
   c) _____ Events
   d) _____ Items

5)   Non-base-table items can be used for which of the following?
   a) _____ Insertable values
   b) _____ Updatable values only
   c) _____ Displaying non-database values
   d) _____ a & b

Quiz answers appear in Appendix A, Section 1.1.

L A B   1 . 2

MANDATORY
FORMS OBJECTS

LAB OBJECTIVES

After this Lab, you will be able to:

- Identify Items and Their Types
- Identify Canvases and Frames
- Define Base-table Blocks
- Understand Modules
- Relate the Mandatory Forms Elements

In this Lab, you will be introduced to the five mandatory Forms objects: items, canvases, windows, blocks, and modules. Items, canvases, and windows are *physical* interface objects, while blocks and modules are *logical* container objects. In the text and Exercises, you will focus on understanding the individual roles of these objects and how they relate to each other.

MORE ON ITEMS

Items are the interface objects (buttons, text items) that allow Forms users to interact with Forms applications.

"Interface object" is a fancy term for an object whose purpose is rather simple. Put plainly, items allow applications and users to communicate. An application can communicate with a user by presenting database data in a text item. A user can communicate with an application by clicking a button item.

Items are defined by their properties. Properties include physical attributes such as Height, Width, X Position and Y Position, and so on; examples of data attributes are `Column Name`, `Primary Key`, `Insert Al-lowed`, and so on. By adjusting properties, you can change the look, feel, and behavior of an item. Properties are listed and accessed in a window called the Property Palette, which you will explore in Chapter 3, "The Development Environment." There are two ways to adjust the properties of items: at design-time and at run-time.

At design-time, you can change properties in the Property Palette simply by clicking them and making adjustments. You can also use the Layout Editor to change properties at design-time. The Layout Editor is a graphical WYSIWYG (what you see is what you get) tool that lets you position and size screen objects by dragging and dropping. You will get your first peek at the Layout Editor in the Exercises in this Lab and then explore it more completely in Chapter 3.

To change properties at run-time requires changing them programmatically. What that means is that while the application is running, the values of many properties can be changed by code within the form. For example, a trigger can be written to change the `Background Color` property of an item if that item's value is negative. This is a very powerful feature because it allows you to change the look or behavior of an application in response to what the user has done, the data that has been returned to the form, or virtually any Forms event.

You adjust an item's type depending on the kind of information you'd like to communicate to users or depending on the kind of control you'd like to give them. For example, if you'd like the user to view a value retrieved from the database but not have the ability to change it, you would set the item type to display item. Or, if you'd like to give them the ability to open another window, you may use a button item.

You can determine an item's type in one of three ways:

1. By looking at the `Item Type` property in the Property Palette.
2. By looking at the item itself in the Layout Editor.
3. By looking at the icon to the left of the item's name in the Object Navigator.

There are 15 different item types in Forms. You will explore six of the most important types in the Exercises.

CANVASES

For items to be visible to users, they must be positioned on canvases. Similar to a painter's canvas, a Forms canvas is the surface on which you position, size, and color different objects. The parallel between programmer and painter should end there, for, as a programmer, it is wise to rein in your creative energy with regard to object positioning and color schemes. A user should be able to work with an application without being distracted by bright colors or acrobatic widgets. The best-designed user interfaces are those that the user hardly notices.

Layout, positioning, coloring, and so on are done in the Layout Editor— the tool in the Form Builder that gives you a WYSIWYG view of the canvas and its items. Canvases, like items, have properties that can be viewed and manipulated in the Property Palette at design-time or programmatically at run-time.

Graphical objects called frames are contained in canvases, and although frames are not mandatory Forms objects, they are worth mentioning here because they can be rather helpful in controlling the positioning of a group of items. You can put a group of items in a frame and then set properties for that frame which affect the entire group.

Figure 1.3 shows a typical canvas in the Layout Editor with two frames and items of varying types.

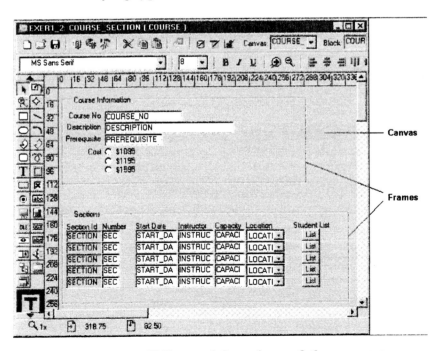

Figure 1.3 ■ The Layout Editor with a view of the COURSE canvas, COURSE and SECTION frames, and multiple items.

WINDOWS

Windows are the physical containers of canvases. This also makes them the ultimate physical containers of all the visual objects on canvases, such as items and graphics. As with other objects in Forms, windows have properties that can be changed at design-time and run-time.

The windows you create for your Forms applications are similar to the windows you have seen in typical Microsoft Windows applications. They have titles, icons, and sizable borders. They can be opened and closed manually by the user or programmatically by the application.

BASE-TABLE BLOCKS AND NON-BASE-TABLE BLOCKS

Canvases serve as physical containers of items. Blocks, on the other hand, serve as logical containers of items. There are two types of blocks: *base-table blocks* and *non-base-table blocks*. In other Forms books, you may see base-table blocks referred to as data blocks and non-base-table referred to as control blocks.

Base-table blocks, as their name implies, are based on a database table or view and must contain at least one item that is based on a column in that database table or view. If you create a block based on the STUDENT table, at least one of its items must be based on a column in the STUDENT table, such as STUDENT_ID, LAST_NAME, or one of the other columns. It is quite common to build base-table blocks that include items for each column in the base table. However, while this is common, it is not mandatory since the block can contain as many or as few items as you'd like.

Additionally, not all of the items in a base-table block have to be based on columns in the table. Display items and other non-base-table items can be included also.

■ *FOR EXAMPLE:*

The form in Figure 1.4 shows the layout of items from the INSTRUCTOR base-table block, which is based on the INSTRUCTOR table. The INSTRUCTOR block contains items based on most of the columns in the INSTRUCTOR table, like INSTRUCTOR_ID, SALUTATION, FIRST_NAME, and so on. It also contains CITY and STATE, which are non-base-table items. There are no columns in the INSTRUCTOR table for city and state values. These are retrieved from the ZIPCODE table using trigger code. If you were looking at the Object Navigator, you would see that CITY and STATE are included in the INSTRUCTOR block. They were put there because of their function, which is to provide more information about the INSTRUCTOR record.

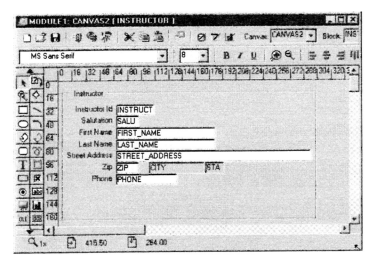

Figure 1.4 ■ Items in the INSTRUCTOR block on a canvas. CITY and STATE are non-base-table display items in the INSTRUCTOR block.

Typically, base-table blocks are based on database tables or views. It is possible, however, to base a block on an Oracle stored procedure. This is an advanced topic that will not be covered in this interactive workbook. For more information, refer to the on-line help in the Form Builder's help topics.

Non-base-table blocks are not based on any database object, nor are any of their items. They typically contain non-base-table items such as buttons. Sometimes they contain display items that show non-database information, such as the time or perhaps the user's name.

All blocks, whether they are base-table or non-base-table blocks, are regarded as logical because they do not have physical properties like X Position, Y Position, Height, Width, and so on. They serve a purely functional purpose in that they allow you to group items without regard to physical location. Therefore, you can easily perform programmatic operations on a block no matter where the items in the block are physically positioned.

■ FOR EXAMPLE:

Figure 1.5 shows a screenshot of a running form. You can see that there are two windows, one called Student and one called Record History. By clicking the Record History button, the user has the option to view the record's history information. This form has one block that is based on the STUDENT table and includes all of its columns as items. Some of the

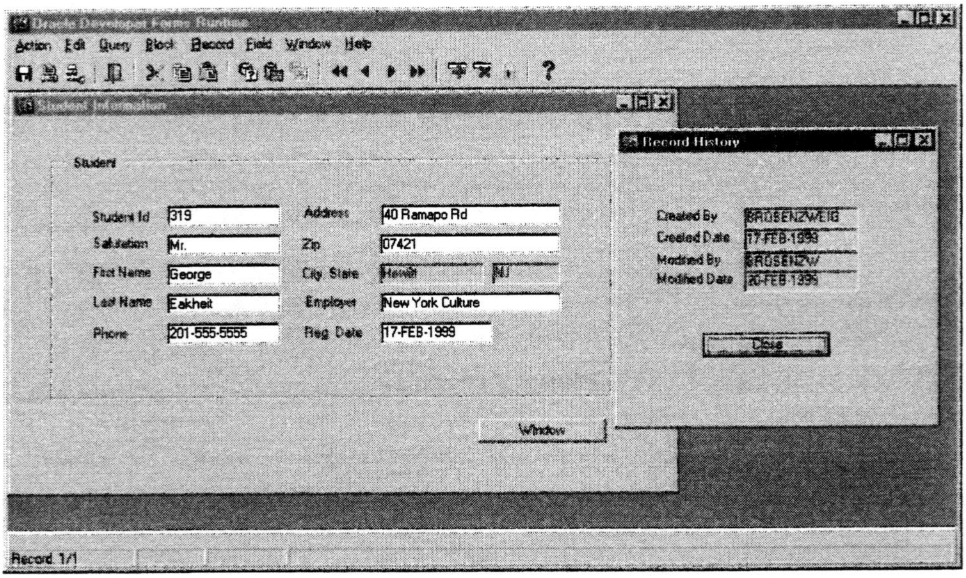

Figure 1.5 ▨ Items can be logically contained by one block, but physically positioned across multiple canvases and windows.

items are on a canvas in the `Student` window, while the rest of the items are on a canvas in the `Record History` window.

Forms will still automatically coordinate and manage the querying and record status of the block even though its items are *not* positioned together physically.

MODULES

Although "forms module" is the proper term, these objects are commonly referred to simply as "forms." These terms will be used interchangeably throughout this workbook.

Modules are logical containers of all the objects in a form, which means they serve as the highest-level object in the hierarchy of a single form. In Figure 1.5, what you can see are the physical objects that are contained within a forms module called COURSE.fmb. A typical application is made up of a group of modules. Depending on the complexity of the application, there could be tens or hundreds of modules.

HOW ARE ALL OF THESE MANDATORY FORMS OBJECTS RELATED?

You have already learned that blocks contain items; items can be positioned on canvases, and windows contain canvases. In Exercise 1.2.5, you will learn more about the relationships between objects by exploring a form in the Form Builder.

LAB 1.2 EXERCISES

1.2.1 IDENTIFY ITEMS AND THEIR TYPES

Open the Form Builder. If you have any forms or modules open, close them by going to the Main Menu and selecting `File | Close`.

Now, open the form file titled `EX01_02.fmb`, which should be in your `\guest\forms\exercises` directory. If you cannot find it, read the information on how to download this file and other files from the companion Web site.

a) Locate the items in `EX01_02.fmb` in the Object Navigator. What purpose do items serve in a Forms application?

_____

_____

From the Main Menu, select `Tools | Layout Editor`. The Layout Editor will open, and you will see the layout for a canvas named COURSE_SECTION.

b) There are six different types of items on the COURSE_SECTION canvas. Identify one item for each of these six types. Can you briefly describe each type (e.g., COURSE_NO is a text item. Text items are used . . .)?

_____

_____

c) Which items have properties associated with them? Which items in the COURSE block have triggers associated with them, and what are the names of these triggers?

_____

_____

d) What are two ways a Forms programmer can manipulate and control the look, feel, and behavior of items?

_____

_____

1.2.2   IDENTIFY CANVASES AND FRAMES

As in the previous Exercise, have the Form Builder open to form EX01_02 . fmb.

a) Identify the name and canvas type of each canvas in form EX01_02 . fmb. What purpose do canvases serve in a Forms application?

_____

_____

b) Identify the frames associated with this canvas.

_____

_____

c) What is the value of the SECTION frame's Layout Data Block property?

_____

_____

d) Are there any triggers associated with this canvas? How do you know?

_____

_____

1.2.3   DEFINE BASE-TABLE BLOCKS

As in the previous two Exercises, we will continue working in the Form Builder with EX01_02.fmb.

a) What are blocks and what purposes do they serve?

_____

_____

b) Name the blocks in EX01_02.fmb. Are they non-base-table blocks or base-table blocks?

_____

_____

c) Explore the Object Navigator to determine if these blocks are related. What is the name of the relation?

_____

_____

d) Can a Forms user see or interact with a block? Why or why not?

_____

_____

e) Why does Forms need blocks at all? Why can't items simply be grouped by canvas?

_____

_____

f) Which block property would you change if you wanted to control the order of the records returned?

_____

_____

1.2.4   UNDERSTAND MODULES

Once again, you will complete this Exercise in the Form Builder using `EX01_02.fmb`.

**LAB
1.2**

> **a)** Make a list of the objects that are owned or contained by a form. Are there any instances of these objects in `EX01_02.fmb`? What are they called (e.g., Alerts - DEMO_OBJECTS; Triggers - ON-...)?

_____

_____

From the Main Menu, select `File | New | Form` and observe what happens.

> **b)** What did Forms name the new module? Did the Form Builder create any default objects for this form? If so, what kinds of objects are they and what are they called?

_____

_____

_____

> **c)** Can you assign a menu to a form (module)? How do you know?

_____

_____

1.2.5   RELATE THE MANDATORY FORMS ELEMENTS

> **a)** Which Forms objects contain items? Can an item stand by itself or be self-contained?

_____

_____

b) Where do you put an item if you want it to be visible to a Forms user?

_____

_____

c) How do blocks relate to canvases?

_____

_____

d) Can a form have more than one block? canvas? module?

_____

_____

e) Which objects can have triggers associated with them in the Object Navigator?

_____

_____

f) Of the objects you've learned so far, which are visible to the Forms user?

_____

_____

LAB 1.2 EXERCISE ANSWERS

1.2.1 ANSWERS

a) Locate the items in EX01_02.fmb in the Object Navigator. What purpose do items serve in a Forms application?

Answer: Items are the interface objects that allow a Forms user to interact with a Forms application.

To locate the items, take the following steps in the Object Navigator:

1. Expand the `Data Blocks` node. You will see two blocks, `COURSE` and `SECTION`.

2. Expand the `COURSE` and `SECTION` blocks. You will see three sub-nodes beneath each block: `Triggers`, `Items`, and `Relations`.

3. Expand the `Items` node. You will see a list of the items that belong to this block.

b) There are six different types of items on the `COURSE_SECTION` canvas. Identify one item for each of these six types. Can you briefly describe each type?

Answer: `COURSE_NO` *is a text item. Text items are used to display database data or derived values in characters, numbers, or a mixture of both. Users can navigate to a text item and edit its value.*

`COST` *is a radio group. Radio groups are used to present a series of mutually exclusive choices to the user. One value is always selected.*

`SECTION_ID` *is a display item. Display items are used to display database data or derived values in characters, numbers, or a mixture of both. Users cannot navigate to a display item and edit its value.*

`LOCATION` *is a list item. List items are used to display a drop-down list of choices to the user.*

`AUTHORIZATION` *is a check box. Check boxes have two states, checked and unchecked. Very often they are used when the value must be either Yes/No, On/Off, Accept/Decline, etc.*

`LIST` *is a push button. Push buttons are used for many different things, but usually they initiate some kind of action like a query, save, exit, show list, and so forth. Push buttons are usually referred to simply as buttons.*

As described in the Lab, there are three ways to determine an item's type: you can look in the Property Palette, the Object Navigator, or the Layout Editor. The Property Palette will give you the surest answer because it shows the actual name of the item type, while the Object Navigator and Layout Editor show graphical representations of the item's type.

As you may have already realized, the Object Navigator, Layout Editor, and Property Palette are synchronized. So, if you select an item, or any object for that matter, in the Object Navigator, its property list will appear in the Property Palette and it will be selected in the Layout Editor. By the same token, if you select any object in the Layout Editor, its properties will also appear.

There are other item types in Oracle Forms, but the six identified are the most common. There are some rules of thumb for choosing item types, but in general, item types and their uses are pretty straightforward. In Chapter 5, "Items," you will learn how to create, edit, and manipulate different items. You will also learn when it may be appropriate to use one item type over another.

c) Which items have properties associated with them? Which items in the COURSE block have triggers associated with them, and what are the names of these triggers?

*Answer: **All** items have properties associated with them.* AUTHORIZATION *has a* WHEN-CHECKBOX-CHANGED.

Not only do all items have properties, but all other types of objects created in Forms have properties also.

d) What are two ways a Forms programmer can manipulate and control the look, feel, and behavior of items?

Answer: A programmer can manipulate and control items at design-time by manually editing them in the Layout Editor or by adjusting their properties in the Property Palette. Items can also be manipulated at run-time by changing their properties programmatically with triggers or procedures.

Using the Property Palette and Layout Editor at design-time are obvious and rather easy ways to manipulate non-base-table items. You will learn more about how to use these tools in Chapter 3, "The Development Environment." Controlling items programmatically at run-time is a bit more complicated, but also extremely powerful. For example, you may want to have the application change the color of an item depending on its value. Let's say that you want to color the SECTION_ID red for all classes that are overbooked, meaning the enrollment is greater than the capacity. You would do this programmatically by writing a trigger that uses Forms built-ins to check enrollment and capacity, then change or SET the color of the SECTION_ID for the overbooked courses. You will learn how to use triggers and built-ins to change properties at run-time in Chapter 6, "Triggers & Built-ins."

1.2.2 ANSWERS

a) Identify the name and canvas type of each canvas in form EX01_02.fmb. What purpose do canvases serve in a Forms application?

Answer: The canvas name is COURSE_SECTION. *It has a canvas type of content. Canvases are the physical surfaces upon which items are positioned, sized, and colored.*

By now you should be accustomed to looking in the Object Navigator and Property Palette for answers. Both would have told you that the canvas name is COURSE_SECTION.

Canvas types were not discussed in the Lab, but you probably guessed that, like items, a canvas' type can be found in the Property Palette. There are four different canvas types: Content, Stacked, Toolbar (vertical and horizontal), and Tab. For the first couple of Chapters, you will work only with content canvases. Canvas types are discussed in more detail in Chapter 8, "Canvases and Windows."

b) Identify the frames associated with this canvas.

Answer: There are two frames, COURSE and SECTION, associated with this canvas. To find them, expand the COURSE_SECTION canvas. You will see a node called Graphics. Expand the Graphics node and you will see the two frame names.

c) What is the value of the SECTION frame's Layout Data Block property?

Answer: The SECTION frame's Layout Data Block property is set to SECTION.

Again, you should have been able to find this easily by selecting the SECTION frame in the Object Navigator or Layout Editor and then looking at its properties in the Property Palette.

By setting the Layout Data Block property to SECTION, you are telling Forms that you want all the items in the SECTION block to be within the SECTION frame. If you add items to the block later on, they will automatically be laid out in that frame.

Frames can be either annoying or helpful in that they will automatically adjust the layout of a group of items even if you don't want them to. To see this illustrated, take the following steps:

1) Open the Form Builder to form EX01_02.fmb. Open the Layout Editor.
2) Select the PREREQUISITE item and drag it outside the COURSE frame.
3) Select the COURSE frame and drag it slightly to the right.

You will see that, after dragging the frame, the PREREQUISITE item was automatically repositioned back inside it. There will be cases in which you will want to intentionally drag items outside their frames or otherwise manually position items yourself. To prevent a frame from automatically updating the layout, set the frame's Update Layout property to Locked.

d) Are there any triggers associated with this canvas? How do you know?

Answer: No, there are no triggers associated with this canvas. In the Object Navigator, there is no Trigger node under Canvases.

Canvases never have triggers directly associated with them. The only objects that can have triggers associated with them are items, blocks, and modules. Item, block, or module triggers can *affect* canvases, but triggers cannot belong to, be contained by, or be owned by canvases.

1.2.3 ANSWERS

a) What are blocks and what purposes do they serve?

Answer: Blocks are logical containers of like items. Blocks fall into one of two types, base-table or non-base-table.

A base-table block is based on a table and its items are based on the columns in that table. In a non-base-table block, the items are not based on any objects in the database.

b) Name the blocks in EX01_02.fmb. Are they non-base-table blocks or base-table blocks?

Answer: There are two blocks named COURSE and SECTION. They are both base-table blocks.

c) Explore the Object Navigator to determine if these blocks are related. What is the name of the relation?

Answer: Yes, they are related. The relation is named COURSE_SECTION. The relation object is under the COURSE block's Relations node.

Relations are similar to joins in SQL queries in that they allow you to join or create a relationship between two blocks. In Forms, this is called a master-detail relation. In the form EX01_02.fmb, the relation COURSE_SECTION has COURSE as the master block and SECTION as the detail block. For each COURSE record returned, Forms will return and display the corresponding SECTION records. Master-detail forms are very common, and you will learn more about them in Chapter 4, "Master-Detail Forms."

d) Can a Forms user see or interact with a block? Why or why not?

Answer: No, a user cannot see or interact with a block. Blocks are logical containers, not physical ones, so they are not displayed to the user.

Examples of physical objects in Oracle Forms are items, canvases, windows, lists of values, and alerts. These objects are physical because they have physical properties such as Height and Width, which make them visible to the user. Blocks do not have any physical properties to make them visible. Blocks do not need physical properties because their purpose is functional and perhaps sometimes organizational.

e) Why does Forms need blocks at all? Why can't items simply be grouped by canvas?

Answer: Because sometimes it is convenient to perform operations on a logical group of items rather than on a physical group of items.

f) Which block property would you change if you wanted to control the order of the records returned?

Answer: You would change the Order By property.

1.2.4 ANSWERS

a) Make a list of the objects that are owned or contained by a form. Are there any instances of these objects in EX01_02.fmb? What are they called?

Answer: The list is displayed in the following table:

Object	Instances
Triggers	ON-CLEAR-DETAILS WHEN-NEW-FORM-INSTANCE
Alerts	DEMO_OBJECTS
Attached Libraries	None
Data Blocks	COURSE SECTION
Canvases	COURSE_SECTION
Editors	None
LOVS	None
Object Groups	None
Parameters	None
Popup Menus	None
Program Units	CHECK_PACKAGE_FAILURE CLEAR_ALL_MASTER_DETAILS DEMO_ALERT QUERY_MASTER_DETAIL
Property Classes	TABLE_ITEM_PROMPT_ALIGNMENT
Record Groups	None
Reports	None
Visual Attributes	None
Windows	COURSE_INFORMATION

From the Main Menu, select `File | New | Form` and observe what happens.

b) What did Forms name the new module? Did the Form Builder create any default objects for this form? If so, what kinds of objects are they and what are they called?

Answer: Forms named the module MODULE2 *(the number may be different for you). Forms created a window called* WINDOW1.

Whenever you create a module in Forms, it is named MODULE# by default. This is also true for how Forms initially names all objects you create. Whenever you create a new form or module, Forms creates WINDOW1 by default. A single module can have multiple windows.

c) Can you assign a menu to a form (module)? How do you know?

Answer: Yes you can. Each module object has a Menu Module *property.*

So far you have only explored single forms. A typical Forms application will be made up of many forms. It is common to employ a menu system to control all of the forms that make up a single application. Menus are built in the Form Builder and then assigned to forms using the Menu Module property. In Chapter 13, "Forms Menus," you will build your own menu using the Form Builder and a tool within it called the Menu Editor.

1.2.5 ANSWERS

a) Which Forms objects contain items? Can an item stand by itself or be self-contained?

Answer: Blocks contain items. No, an item cannot stand by itself. It must be contained by a block.

b) Where do you put an item if you want it to be visible to a Forms user?

Answer: You put an item on a canvas if you want it to be visible to a Forms user.

c) How do blocks relate to canvases?

Answer: Items from a block can be positioned on a canvas, but there is no direct relationship between blocks and canvases themselves.

This means that at no time do you specify that a block is *on* a certain canvas. Nor at any time do you specify that a canvas *belongs to* or *is owned by* a certain block.

d) Can a form have more than one block? canvas? module?

Answer: Yes, a form can have more than one block and more than one canvas. However, a form can only have one module.

Remember, "form" and "module" are interchangeable terms, so the latter part of this question was a bit deceiving. However, it does help to illustrate that a module (form) is a single application component that cannot be contained or owned by any other application component. It can, however, be associated with other form or module components as you will learn later on.

e) Which objects can have triggers associated with them in the Object Navigator?

Answer: Forms, blocks, and items can have triggers associated with them in the Object Navigator.

Other objects, such as alerts and canvases, can be controlled and manipulated by triggers, but only modules, blocks, and items can have triggers associated with them.

Later, as you work more with triggers, you will find that they are sometimes referred to as *form-level* triggers, *block-level* triggers, or *item-level* triggers.

f) Of the objects you've learned so far, which are visible to the Forms user?

Answer: Canvases, frames, windows, and items are visible to the user.

In passing, you have learned about alerts and lists of values (LOVs), which are also visible to the user.

LAB 1.2 SELF-REVIEW QUESTIONS

In order to test your progress, you should be able to answer the following questions:

1) All but which of the following are physical objects?
   a) _____ Buttons
   b) _____ Canvases
   c) _____ Items
   d) _____ Blocks

2) Which two of the following are logical containers?
   a) _____ Frames
   b) _____ Blocks
   c) _____ Radio buttons
   d) _____ Modules
   e) _____ b & d

3) Blocks are contained by which of the following?
  a) _____ Modules
  b) _____ Triggers
  c) _____ Canvases
  d) _____ Nodes

4) Canvases are best described as which of the following?
  a) _____ Physical surfaces for laying out items
  b) _____ Logical structures similar to a painter's canvas
  c) _____ Associated with one frame
  d) _____ Containers of windows and items

5) Which of the following is not a type of item?
  a) _____ Check boxes
  b) _____ Text items
  c) _____ Java Beans
  d) _____ Frames
  e) _____ Buttons

6) Which of the following are owned by modules?
  a) _____ All objects
  b) _____ Forms
  c) _____ Only canvases
  d) _____ Items in the master block

7) How can you manipulate properties?
  a) _____ In the Property Palette
  b) _____ In the Layout Editor
  c) _____ Programmatically
  d) _____ All of the above

8) Which of the following is true of base-table blocks?
  a) _____ Can be related to each other
  b) _____ Are owned by canvases
  c) _____ Are indirectly related to canvases through frames
  d) _____ a & c

Quiz answers appear in Appendix A, Section 1.2.

C H A P T E R   1

TEST YOUR THINKING

This Chapter is introductory, so this section contains only one question. In future Chapters, you will complete projects in this section that will review the skills you learned in the Labs for the Chapter. The projects will usually involve creating or modifying forms. It is important to complete these questions as you go along because the files you create in one Chapter will often be edited or updated in a later Chapter.

1) Which columns in the STUDENT schema might be suitable candidates for radio group items? list items? display items? check box items?

C H A P T E R 2

WIZARDS
AND FILES

CHAPTER OBJECTIVES

In this Chapter, you will learn about:

✔ The Data Block and Layout Wizards   Page 32
✔ Oracle Forms Files   Page 53

It is now time to try your hand at creating some simple applications. The Form Builder has a vast and versatile interface that you will continue to uncover throughout the rest of this book and throughout your relationship with the tool. Lab 2.1 will bring you through the wizards that provide an extremely friendly environment in which to start your acquaintance with the Form Builder.

Once you have used the wizards to create some simple applications, you will want to know what to do with the files that store them. Lab 2.2 will lead you through some of the files you will encounter when using the Form Builder and illustrate how you can run and compile them.

L A B   2 . 1

THE DATA BLOCK AND LAYOUT WIZARDS

LAB OBJECTIVES

After this Lab, you will be able to:

- Use the Data Block and Layout Wizards
- Reenter the Wizards

Having sat patiently through two introductory Labs, you are now ready to start creating objects and simple applications. Despite your limited experience with the Form Builder interface, you will be able to quickly and easily create a block and assign its items to a canvas by employing the Data Block and Layout Wizards.

The initial part of this Lab will walk you through the pages of the wizards. This will be interactive and will require that you read and work in the Form Builder simultaneously. The Exercises will push you a bit further in using the wizards and test the skills you learned in the Lab.

Throughout this Lab and the Exercises, try to think about the concepts you have already learned. What are the mandatory Forms objects that you are creating with the wizards? Can you see how they are related? Can you identify possible events in your new applications and anticipate which triggers you might use to respond to them?

THE WIZARDS

The Data Block Wizard and Layout Wizard are usually used in sequence, meaning you walk through the Data Block Wizard to create a block, then you go straight to the Layout Wizard to create a canvas and frame.

Each screen in a wizard is referred to as a page. The creators of Oracle Forms have given each page a specific name, and it is these names that will be used here. Each page will be described briefly in the Lab and will be accompanied by a screenshot. You should have the Form Builder open and follow along with each step in the Lab.

You will start by using the Data Block Wizard to create a block based on the STUDENT table.

Each wizard has a Welcome! page. These will not be discussed in the Lab.

To set the environment, take the following steps:

1) Open the Form Builder.
2) From the Main Menu, select File | New | Form to create a new form.
3) From the Main Menu, select File | Connect to connect to the database.
4) From the Main Menu, select Tools | Data Block Wizard to open the Data Block Wizard.

THE DATA BLOCK WIZARD

The Data Block Wizard has three pages:

1) Type page (Figure 2.1).
2) Table page (Figure 2.2).
3) Finish page.

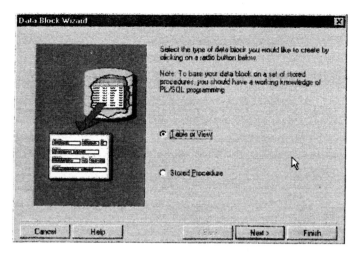

Figure 2.1 ■ The Data Block Wizard's type page.

TYPE PAGE

Here you have one task—to select the type of database object your block will be based upon. Throughout most of this book, you will base your blocks on tables.

So, here you should leave this page set to Table or View (the default) and click the Next button.

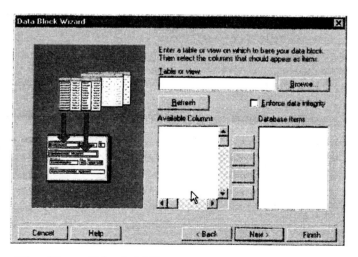

Figure 2.2 ■ The Data Block Wizard's table page.

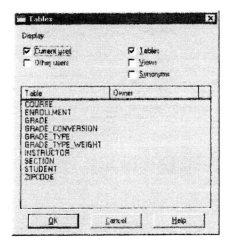

Figure 2.3 ■ The Database Wizard's Tables window.

TABLE PAGE

Here you have three tasks:

1) Choose the base table.
2) Select the database columns to include as block items.
3) Decide whether or not to enforce data integrity.

There are two ways to choose the base table. You can either type the table name directly into the Table or view field, or you can click the Browse button to choose the table name from a list. If you click Browse, Forms will peer into the database's data dictionary and present you with a Tables window with a list of tables and views like the one in Figure 2.3.

Double-click the STUDENT table to select it. This brings you back to the table page, which will now look like Figure 2.4.

Now you are on to the second task on this page, which is to select the database columns to include as items in this block. You do not have to include all of them, but it is wise to always include the primary-key columns and foreign-key columns. To select columns, simply move them from the Available Columns text list to the Database Items text list. There are two ways to do this:

1) Use the arrow buttons positioned between the two text lists.
2) Double-click individual items.

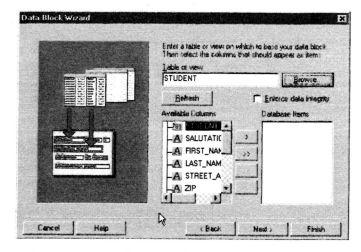

Figure 2.4 ■ The Database Wizard's table page with the STUDENT table selected.

Windows multi-select functions also work here so that you can move more than one column at a time. Move all of the columns in the STU-DENT table to the Database Items list.

Check Enforce data integrity for your STUDENT block. The table page should now resemble Figure 2.5. Click the Next button to move on.

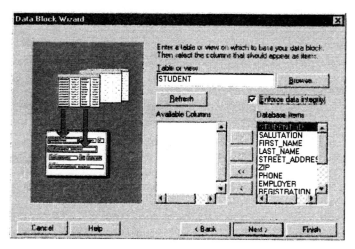

Figure 2.5 ■ Completed table page.

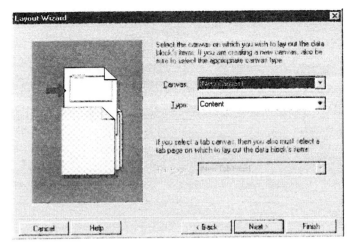

Figure 2.6 ▪ The Layout Wizard's canvas page.

FINISH PAGE

This page is self-explanatory, so no screenshot has been included. All you have to do is decide whether or not to continue on to the Layout Wizard.

Select the Create the Block and then Call the Layout Wizard radio button (the default) and click the Finish button to move on to the Layout Wizard.

THE LAYOUT WIZARD

The Layout Wizard has six pages:

1) Canvas page (Figure 2.6).
2) Data block page (Figure 2.7).
3) Items page (Figure 2.8).
4) Style page.
5) Records page (Figure 2.9).
6) Finish page.

CANVAS PAGE

Here you have two or three tasks that you will accomplish by making selections from three list items:

1) Choose the canvas.
2) Choose the canvas type.
3) Choose the tab page.

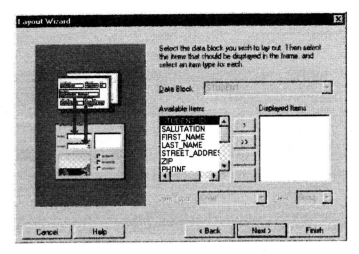

Figure 2.7 ■ The Layout Wizard's data block page.

In this case, you are starting a new form, so your only choice is to select New Canvas from the Canvas list item. However, if you were working with an existing form and had already created a canvas, you would see its name in the Canvas list. Also, because this is a new form, you will leave the Type list item set to Content.

Had you chosen Tab from the Type list, the Tab Page list would have become enabled, and you would have been able to select from a list of available tab pages.

Click the Next button to move on to the data block page.

DATA BLOCK PAGE

Here you have three tasks:

1) Select the items to be displayed.
2) Order the items.
3) Select the item types.

As you can see, this page is nearly identical in layout to the Data Block Wizard's table page. It behaves the same way as well, so you already know how to move items from the Available Items list to the Displayed Items list. Use whichever method you prefer to move all of the items to the Displayed Items list. It is possible and common to display only a few of the items that are available. It all depends on how you want your canvas to look.

Your next task is to order the items. The Layout Wizard will lay the items out on the screen in the order in which they appear in the Displayed

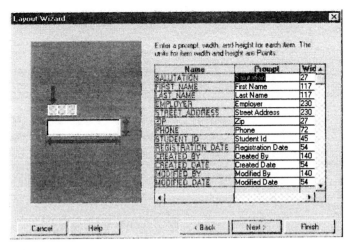

Figure 2.8 ■ The Layout Wizard's items page.

`Items` text list. To reorder items, simply drag and drop in the list to get them into the proper positions. Put the items in the following order:

1)	SALUTATION	8)	STUDENT_ID
2)	FIRST_NAME	9)	REGISTRATION_DATE
3)	LAST_NAME	10)	CREATED_BY
4)	EMPLOYER	11)	CREATED_DATE
5)	STREET_ADDRESS	12)	MODIFIED_BY
6)	ZIP	13)	MODIFIED_DATE
7)	PHONE		

Your next task is to set the item type for each item. To do this, take the following steps:

1) Select an item in the `Displayed Items` list.
2) Change its type using the `Item Type` drop-down list.

Change the following items to type `Display Item`:

- CREATED_BY.
- CREATED_DATE.
- MODIFIED_BY.
- MODIFIED_DATE.

Once you have completed this task, click the `Next` button to move on to the items page.

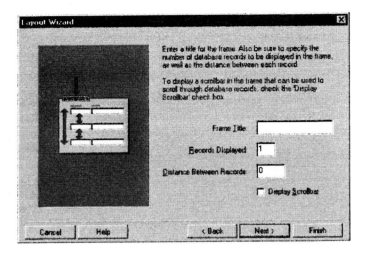

Figure 2.9 ■ The Layout Wizard's records page.

ITEMS PAGE

Here you have two tasks:

1)   Adjust the Prompt values.

2)   Adjust the Height and Width values.

To complete this task, simply position the cursor on the value that you'd like to change and edit it. Make the following adjustments:

1)   Change the Width of CREATED_BY to 117.

2)   Change the Width of MODIFIED_BY to 117.

After you have made these changes, click the Next button to continue to the style page.

STYLE PAGE

No screenshot is necessary here as this is a rather simple page. Your task is to decide how you would like the items to be laid out. In form style, the items are laid out so that the screen will resemble a paper-based form. In tabular style, the items are laid out in a grid. Look at the images on the left-hand side of the wizard page to see examples of how each style will look.

Select the Form style. Click the Next button to move on to the records page.

RECORDS PAGE

Here you have four tasks:

1)   Choose a Frame Title.

2) Indicate the number of Records Displayed.

3) Set the Distance Between Records.

4) Include a scrollbar.

Because this is a new form and because you have chosen Form as the layout style, you will only have to complete the first task on this page. You will leave the rest as their default values. Type the name Student into the Frame Title field; this will be displayed on the canvas. Because the items will be laid out in form style, it is common to display only one record. Therefore, there is no need to change the value in the Records Displayed field. For the same reason, there is no need to change the value in the Distance Between Records field or the Display Scrollbar check box. In this Lab's Exercises, you will have to create some forms with a tabular style, which lends itself to displaying multiple records at one time with a scrollbar.

Click the Next button to move on to the finish page. You could also simply click the Finish button here as the finish page is purely informational.

FINISH PAGE

No screenshot has been included, as there are no tasks on this page for you to complete. It is purely an informational page.

Click the Finish button and the Layout Wizard will close and your new canvas will be displayed in the Layout Editor. It should resemble Figure 2.10.

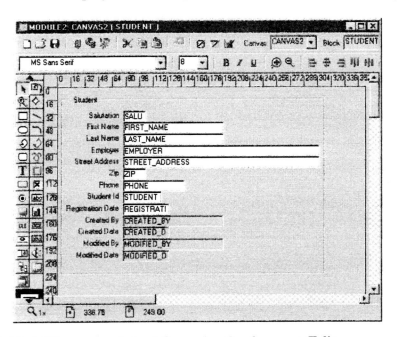

Figure 2.10 ■ The completed form in the Layout Editor.

Now that your form is complete, you should save it. From the Main Menu, select File | Save and save it to your \guest\forms\exercises directory as R_WIZARD.fmb.

Now that the wizards are complete, you are free to edit the form. You can do this manually using the Layout Editor and Property Palette, or you can use the wizards again by reentering them.

In this Lab's Exercises, you will practice creating forms with the wizards and then you will edit one of your forms by reentering both the Data Block Wizard and Layout Wizard.

LAB 2.1 EXERCISES

2.1.1   USE THE DATA BLOCK AND LAYOUT WIZARDS

Explore the Form Builder and find at least four different ways to access the Data Block Wizard.

a) What are the four ways you discovered to open the Data Block Wizard?

_____

_____

Open the R_WIZARD.fmb form, which you created in the previous Lab. Expand the Data Blocks node, expand the STUDENT block, and then expand the STUDENT block's trigger node.

b) What is the name of this trigger?

_____

_____

Double-click the icon to the right of the trigger to open the PL/SQL Editor and view the trigger code.

c) What function will this trigger code perform?

_____

_____

d) Where did the Data Block Wizard get the information needed to write this trigger?

_____

_____

e) What did you do to make the Data Block Wizard create this trigger?

_____

_____

f) Have any triggers been created for other objects in this block? Fully expand the block and its items to find out.

_____

_____

View the properties for the STUDENT_ID item.

g) What are the values for the Data Type and Required properties?

_____

_____

h) How did the Data Block Wizard know to set them this way?

_____

_____

2.1.2 REENTERING THE WIZARDS

Select File | Close from the Main Menu to close the R_WIZARD.fmb form.

Select File | New | Form from the Main Menu to create a new form.

Use the wizards to quickly create a form based on the SECTION table. In the Data Block Wizard, include all of the SECTION table's columns in the block except CREATED_BY and MODIFIED_BY. Enforce data integrity should be **unchecked.**

In the Layout Wizard, display all of the items. Do not make any changes to Prompt, Width, or Height on the items page. Choose Form as the layout style. Display one record and do not include a scrollbar. Click the Finish button when you are done so that control returns to the Form Builder. Use the Name property in the Property Palette to rename the canvas SECTION and its frame SECTION. Select File | Save from the Main Menu and save the form to \guest\forms\exercises as R_SECTION.fmb.

a) Try to reenter the Data Block Wizard for the SECTION block using the Object Navigator. How did you do it?

_____

_____

b) How does the reentered Data Block Wizard look different from the wizard you are used to using?

_____

_____

c) Which tab page should you select to add CREATED_BY and MODIFIED_BY to the block? How did you add them?

_____

_____

Click the Finish button.

d) Have CREATED_BY and MODIFIED_BY been added to the block? How about the canvas?

_____

_____

Select the SECTION canvas in the Object Navigator and right-click to open the Layout Wizard.

e) Does it look like you have *reentered* the Layout Wizard? How can you tell that you haven't?

_____

_____

f) Which object should you select in the Object Navigator to reenter the Layout Wizard for the items in the SECTION block? Why? Hint: This is a physical object that helps you group and arrange items.

_____

_____

Position the reentered wizard in the upper right-hand corner of the screen so that you get a partial (or whole, depending on the size of your monitor) view of the Layout Editor.

Select the Data Block tab page in the wizard and move CREATED_BY and MODIFIED_BY to the Displayed Items list. Click the Apply button.

g) Between which items did they appear on the canvas? How can you use the wizard to position them so that they appear after CAPACITY and before CREATED_DATE?

_____

_____

Change the style of the form to Tabular and display five records. Click the Apply button to view the changes.

h) What steps did you take to accomplish this? List the tab page names as well as a brief description of what you did on each page.

_____

_____

After you apply the changes and exit the wizard, the layout will have changed and will not look very pleasing. Ignore this. The purpose of this Exercise is to experiment with reentering the wizard. Look and feel is not important here.

LAB 2.1 EXERCISE ANSWERS

2.1.1 ANSWERS

a) What are the four ways you discovered to open the Data Block Wizard?

Answer: There are actually at least six ways to access the Data Block Wizard. They are as follows:

1) From the Main Menu, select Tools | Data Block Wizard.
2) In the Object Navigator, double-click the Data Blocks node. (Note: This will only work for the first block of each module.)
3) In the Object Navigator, select the Data Blocks node and click the Create button. The Create button has a green plus sign as its icon.
4) In the Object Navigator, select the Data Blocks node and right-click. Select Data Block Wizard.
5) In the Layout Editor, click the Data Block Wizard button. The Data Block Wizard button is situated in the middle of the Layout Editor's horizontal toolbar. It has a gray cylinder and a magic wand as its icon.
6) On the Form Builder Welcome dialog, in the section labeled Designing, select Use the Data Block Wizard, and click the OK button.

It is certainly not necessary to memorize these six ways now. However, as you become more familiar with the Form Builder, you will become anxious to speed your programming by learning different ways to accomplish the same tasks. As a beginner, it is wise to use the toolbars because they are visual and intuitive. Right-clicking is also very easy because you will be presented with a descriptive, context-sensitive list of choices.

b) What is the name of this trigger?

Answer: The name of this trigger is KEY-DELREC.

Double-click the icon to the right of the trigger to open the PL/SQL Editor and view its code.

c) What function will this trigger code perform?

Answer: It will prevent the user from deleting STUDENT records if ENROLLMENT records exist.

d) Where did the Data Block Wizard get the information needed to write this trigger?

Answer: It queried the database's data dictionary to see if there were any integrity constraints defined for the table and its columns.

e) What did you do to make the Data Block Wizard create this trigger?

Answer: You should have checked `Enforce data integrity` *on the Data Block Wizard's table page.*

f) Have any triggers been created for other objects in this block? Fully expand the block and its items to find out.

Answer: Yes, `WHEN-VALIDATE-ITEM` *triggers have been created for many of the items in the block.*

As you have learned through these Exercises, checking `Enforce data integrity` results in the Form Builder writing a series of triggers in the form to enforce the integrity constraints that are stored at the database level. Had there been check constraints against the STUDENT table, triggers to enforce them would have been written as well. By checking `Enforce data integrity`, you are helping to insure that the data going to the database is valid.

■ FOR EXAMPLE:

Re-open the R_WIZARD.fmb form if you have already closed it.

Double-click the icon next to the WHEN-VALIDATE-ITEM trigger for the STUDENT.ZIP item. Note that the code has two sections. If you study the code for the first section, you can see that it is based on the STU_ZIP_FK foreign-key constraint. The trigger code is analogous to the constraint in that it will compare the ZIP value that a user has entered in the form with the ZIP values in the ZIPCODE table. If it does not find the value in the ZIPCODE table, the trigger will return an error. This corresponds to what you know about foreign-key constraints; a ZIP value cannot be inserted or updated into the STUDENT table unless that value already exists in the ZIPCODE table.

Well, you say, the database would have done this anyway: *that's* what the constraint is for. True, but the database would not have checked until the user had tried to commit the record. The user would have tabbed out of the ZIP item and would have had to navigate back to fix it. But, it is unlikely that the user would know which item to fix because the database would not have returned an intelligible error message. By putting the validation logic at the item level within the application itself, the user is alerted to his mistake immediately and is given a message he can understand.

g)   What are the values for the Data Type and Required properties?

Answer: The Data Type *is* Number *and* Required *is set to* Yes.

h)   How did the Data Block Wizard know to set them this way?

Answer: It inherited information from the data dictionary tables in the database. The Data Type *of* STUDENT_ID *in the* STUDENT *table is* Number *and it is a not-null column.*

The Data Block and Layout Wizards set many properties for items based on what they read in the data dictionary tables. The values for Prompt, Height, and Width are other examples of properties set by what is defined for the columns in the data dictionary tables. Keep in mind, however, that it is often necessary to adjust these properties after the wizard has set them.

■ *FOR EXAMPLE:*

By default, the wizard uses the column names in the database to create the prompts for the items. In the sample STUDENT schema, most of the column names are in near-plain English, so in most cases, there really isn't any need to change the default prompts that the wizard assigns. In many database systems, column and table names will not be in plain English, or they may be prefixed with some kind of system codes like ST_STUD_NAM. In cases like these, it is wise to use the items page of the Layout Wizard to change the prompts. You can certainly change the prompts later, but if you do it on the items page, the Layout Wizard will create the default layout with these prompts in mind. That is, it will adjust the layout automatically depending on the lengths of the prompts. If you choose to set the prompts manually in the Layout Editor, which is certainly possible, you may have to manually adjust more than just the prompt name to keep the layout neat and organized. This could cost you some time and considerable effort.

The length of an item is expressed in points. Forms makes each item approximately five points wide for each character. So, if a column in the database is set to be VARCHAR(5), Forms will make its corresponding item approximately 25 points wide. These values are set for each module in the Coordinate System property. To view the Coordinate System settings, take the following steps:

1)   Open R_WIZARD.fmb in the Form Builder.
2)   In the Object Navigator, select the R_WIZARD module and view its properties.

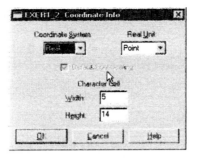

Figure 2.11 ■ The Coordinate Info dialog displaying the coordinate system information for the form.

3) Scroll down in the Property Palette window until you see the property named Coordinate System.
4) Select the Coordinate System property and click the More button.
5) You will see a window like the one in Figure 2.11.

You can reset the coordinate values here if you wish. The Coordinate System pop-up list lets you choose between Real and Character coordinates. Real gives you a finer grain of control over the positioning of items, while Character positions items by character cell. What you select here depends on how you plan to deploy the application. The Forms help system provides a small chart that explains which Coordinate System setting to choose for some of the more common deployment strategies.

If you choose the Real coordinate system you can choose which real unit you'd like to use and the size of each character cell. The Character Cell values determine the size of each character cell, expressed in the Real Unit you have chosen.

All of this is quite a mouthful and not worth worrying about now. It is certainly possible that at some point, depending on the deployment strategy, you will have to reset these values. For now you should understand the concepts behind the different coordinate systems, but stick with the default values.

2.1.2 ANSWERS

a) Try to reenter the Data Block Wizard for the SECTION block using the Object Navigator. How did you do it?

Answer: You should have selected the SECTION block, then right-clicked and selected the Data Block Wizard.

b) How does the reentered Data Block Wizard look different from the wizard you are used to using?

Answer: It has tabbed pages instead of standard wizard pages.

The point of these two questions is to illustrate that it is necessary to have the proper block or one of its items selected in the Object Navigator to reenter the Data Block Wizard. If you had selected the Blocks node or some other object, the Form Builder would have assumed that you were trying to start a new block, not edit an existing one.

c) Which tab page should you select to add CREATED_BY and MODIFIED_BY to the block? How did you add them?

Answer: The Table tab. They were added by moving them from the Available Columns list to the Database Items list.

The reentered wizard's interface behaves in the same way as the regular Data Block Wizard.

Click the Finish button.

d) Have CREATED_BY and MODIFIED_BY been added to the block? How about the canvas?

Answer: Yes, they have been added to the block; no, they have not been added to the canvas.

They will not be added to the canvas or its frame until you reenter the Layout Wizard.

Interestingly, the Data Block Wizard does not seem to allow you to *remove* items from a block. You can go through the motions of removing an item in the Data Block Wizard, but when you click the Apply button, the item is not actually removed from the block. Luckily, it is easy to remove items simply by selecting them in the Object Navigator or Layout Editor and then deleting them manually by clicking the DELETE key.

Select the SECTION canvas in the Object Navigator and right-click to open the Layout Wizard.

e) Does it look like you have *reentered* the Layout Wizard? How can you tell that you haven't?

Answer: No it doesn't. The pages aren't tabbed. It looks like the regular Layout Wizard.

f) Which object should you select in the Object Navigator to reenter the Layout Wizard for the items in the SECTION block? Why? Hint: This is a physical object that helps you group and arrange items.

Answer: You should select the SECTION *frame.*

When the Layout Wizard creates and positions items on canvases, it also lays them out within frames. As described before, these frames are graphical objects that belong to canvases. They make it easier to control the layout of multiple groups of items.

■ *FOR EXAMPLE:*

In Chapter 4, "Master Detail Forms," you will learn how to create forms, which will allow you, among other things, to have two groups of items on a single canvas. One of those groups will be laid out in form style, while the other will be laid out in tabular style. Each group of items will be in a frame. Having two frames will let you reenter the Layout Wizard for each group (frame) individually.

Select the Data Block tab page in the Wizard and move CREATED_BY and MODIFIED_BY to the Displayed Items list. Click the Apply button.

g) Between which items did they appear on the canvas? How can you use the wizard to position them so that they appear after CAPACITY and before CREATED_DATE?

Answer: It depends on which item was selected in the Displayed Items *list when you moved* CREATED_BY *and* MODIFIED_BY *over. You can drag the items up and down in the* Displayed Items *list to position them.*

Change the style of the form to Tabular and display five records. Click the Apply button to view the changes.

h) What steps did you take to accomplish this? List the tab page names as well as a brief description of what you did on each page.

Answer: On the style page, you must select the radio button labeled Tabular. *On the rows page, you should set* Records Displayed *to 5 and check the check box labeled* Display Scrollbar.

Reentering the wizard can be fast and efficient for adding items to the Displayed Items list or changing the layout style from Form to Tabular, or vice versa. However, it can sometimes be more trouble than it is worth. In the example, it stretched the layout far beyond the width of the canvas. As your proficiency with the Form Builder improves, you may find it easier to make adjustments manually in the Layout Editor rather than reentering the Layout Wizard.

LAB 2.1 SELF-REVIEW QUESTIONS

In order to test your progress, you should be able to answer the following questions:

1) Which of the following is true of all of the settings in the Layout Wizard?
   a) _____ They are final
   b) _____ They are subclassed to the block
   c) _____ They are based on frames and their widths
   d) _____ They contribute to the first cut of a canvas

2) Which of the following is true of the Data Block Wizard?
   a) _____ It associates blocks with tables
   b) _____ It creates display items for non-null columns
   c) _____ It has canvas properties
   d) _____ Both b & c

3) Where do the prompts set in the Layout Wizard become editable?
   a) _____ In the database
   b) _____ By reentering the wizard
   c) _____ In the Object Navigator
   d) _____ b & c

4) The wizards never do which of the following?
   a) _____ Write triggers
   b) _____ Access the database
   c) _____ Change module names
   d) _____ Create frames

Quiz answers appear in Appendix A, Section 2.1.

L A B   2 . 2

ORACLE FORMS FILES

LAB OBJECTIVES

After this Lab, you will be able to:

- Differentiate Between Source and Executable Files
- Compile Binary Files into Executable Files
- Run Executable Files

In the previous three Labs, you learned how Forms works, what its mandatory objects are, and how to create those objects quickly and easily using wizards. With this knowledge, you have been able to create some simple applications. Now you will learn how Forms stores the applications you create, how it readies those applications for deployment, and how it runs those readied files.

BINARY AND EXECUTABLE FILES

When you work in the Form Builder, you are creating binary files, and when you run an application, you are executing executable files. Forms stores its binary files with an .fmb extension and its executable files with an .fmx extension. You were already exposed to .fmb files when you were asked to open them in the Form Builder.

The .fmx files are the compiled version of .fmb files. To run a form for testing or deployment, it must first be compiled into an .fmx file. The .fmx files are the files that ultimately make it to your users.

Oracle Developer, and therefore Oracle Forms, is a multi-platform product. It can run on Windows systems as well as UNIX systems. It is possible to develop applications on one platform and then run them on another. This is because the .fmb files are platform-independent. They can be created on one platform and then edited or compiled on another.

The `.fmx` files, on the other hand, are platform-dependent. An `.fmx` file compiled on Windows NT cannot run on UNIX, and vice versa.

COMPILING

It is possible to compile `.fmb` files into executable `.fmx` files directly in the Form Builder. This creates an `.fmx` file and then allows you to continue working in the Form Builder. You may choose to do this if you'd simply like to check your form for errors. If there are any errors, the compilation will fail and the Form Builder will alert you to the existence and location of these errors.

However, you do not have to be in the Form Builder to compile a form. Installed with the Form Builder and the rest of the application components is a utility called the Form Compiler. If you are using a Windows platform, you may have seen it when you navigated through the `Start` menu to start the Form Builder.

You will get an opportunity to practice compiling using the Form Builder and Form Compiler in this Lab's Exercises.

RUNNING

It is common to want to test your forms as you are building them. You finish the wizard, make a few changes to the layout, add a couple of triggers, and then you want to test the form and see how it looks and operates. You can do this by running the form directly from the Form Builder.

You do not have to be in the Form Builder to run a form. Along with the Form Builder and Form Compiler, another utility called the Forms Runtime is available.

In the Exercises, you will get the opportunity to run forms from the Form Builder, as well as from the Forms Runtime.

LAB 2.2 EXERCISES

2.2.1 DIFFERENTIATE BETWEEN SOURCE AND EXECUTABLE FILES

a) What are the differences between `.fmb` files and `.fmx` files?

_____

_____

b) Which file do you work with in the Form Builder?

_____

_____

c) Do both files get distributed to application users? If not, which one does?

_____

_____

_____

2.2.2   COMPILE BINARY FILES INTO EXECUTABLE FILES

Open `EX02_02.fmb` in the Form Builder. Select `File | Administration | Compile File` from the Main Menu.

a) How can you tell that a form compiled successfully?

_____

_____

b) What can you assume was created and written to the filesystem?

_____

_____

Expand the Triggers node for the module and double-click the icon for the `WHEN-NEW-FORM-INSTANCE` trigger. Delete the semi-colon after the word `Null`. Compile the file again using the steps for Question a.

c) Did the form compile successfully? How do you know?

_____

_____

Replace the semi-colon and compile the form a third time.

Select `Program` from the Main Menu and view the compilation options you see.

d) These options are for compilation, but they do not create `.fmx` files. What do you think they compile?

_____

_____

From the Windows `Start` menu, locate and run the Form Compiler. You will find it just below the Form Builder in the menu system. Once the Form Compiler has opened, use its `Browse` button to locate the file `EX02_02`.

e) Which should you compile, the `.fmx` file or `.fmb` file?

_____

_____

Enter your `User ID`, `Password`, and `Database alias` and click the `OK` button.

f) What happened?

_____

_____

g) Why can you develop your applications on a Windows NT workstation but then deploy them to a UNIX server?

_____

_____

h) What steps would you take to accomplish 2.2.2.g? Assume that the UNIX machine is running Solaris 2.6.

_____

_____

2.2.3   RUN EXECUTABLE FILES

Open EX02_02.fmb in the Form Builder.

a) Which button on the Object Navigator should you use to run the form?

_____

_____

b) What *has* to be happening by default when you run a module from the Form Builder?

_____

_____

_____

From the Windows Start menu, locate and run the Forms Runtime. You will find it just below the Form Compiler in the menu system. Once the Forms Runtime is open, use the Browse button to locate the file EX02_02.

c) Which should you run, the .fmx file or the .fmb file?

_____

_____

A running form can be in one of three modes: Normal, Enter Query, or Fetch mode.

d) Which button on the default toolbar can you use to put the form into Enter Query mode?

_____

_____

e) In which mode should the form be to insert records?

_____

_____

LAB 2.2 EXERCISE ANSWERS

2.2.1 ANSWERS

a) What are the differences between .fmb files and .fmx files?

Answer: .fmb files are binary files; .fmx files are executable files. .fmb files are platform-independent, while .fmx files are platform-dependent.

b) Which file do you work with in the Form Builder?

Answer: You work with .fmb files in the Form Builder.

That is, you work with .fmb's in the Form Builder when you are creating forms modules. Later you will learn how to create menus and libraries in the Form Builder, in which case you will work with .mmb and .pll files.

c) Do both files get distributed to application users? If not, which one does?

Answer: No, both do not. Only .fmx files get distributed to application users.

2.2.2 ANSWERS

a) How can you tell that a form compiled successfully?

Answer: The message Module Built Successfully *will appear in the Form Builder's hint line.*

You can also tell that it has compiled successfully when no error messages are reported.

b) What can you assume was created and written to the filesystem?

Answer: You can assume that an .fmx file was created since the result of a successful compilation is an executable.

When the Form Builder creates .fmx files, it names them after the .fmb files. So, if you look in the filesystem, you will now find a file called EX02_02.fmx.

Compile the file again using the steps for Question a.

c) Did the form compile successfully? How do you know?

Answer: No, a Compilation Errors *window opened.*

Note that the message in the window is very descriptive. It tells you where in the form it encountered the error and supplies an error number.

> *Answer: Under the* Program *selection from the Main Menu, there are options for* Compile *and* Compile Selection.

d) These options are for compilation, but they do not create . fmx files. What do you think they compile?

> *Answer: They compile the PL/SQL in the form, but do not create an* . fmx *file.*

As your forms get more complicated, you will add more PL/SQL objects such as triggers, program units, and PL/SQL libraries. You can use the Compile and Compile Selection commands to compile these PL/SQL objects.

e) Which should you compile, the . fmx file or . fmb file?

> *Answer: The* . fmb *file. The compiled version of the* . fmb *is saved as an* . fmx *file.*

Enter your User ID, Password and Database alias and click the OK button.

f) What happened?

> *Answer: Next to nothing. There was a pause, then the Form Compiler closed.*

If the module compiles successfully, the Form Compiler will not give you any confirmation of success; it will simply close. You can confirm the compilation by looking for the . fmx file in the filesystem.

If there are any errors during compilation, they will be displayed in a Forms Compilation Error window and written to a text file. This text file will have the same name as the . fmb file and will have an . err extension. So, in this case, if there had been an error, you would have seen it listed in an error window and would have been able to find an EX02_02.err file in the filesystem.

g) Why can you develop your applications on a Windows NT workstation but then deploy them to a UNIX server?

> *Answer: Because* . fmb *files are platform-independent and therefore portable from platform to platform.*

The current release of Oracle Developer is supported on Windows 95, 98, and NT, as well as a host of UNIX and other platforms. For a complete list of supported platforms, visit www.oracle.com.

It is very common for application developers to develop their applications on a Windows workstation and then port them to a UNIX environment for deployment.

This is especially true when Oracle Forms will be deployed in a Web environment with a browser or applet viewer interface. In these cases, the applications are developed on Windows workstations and then transferred to powerful middle-tier servers. If these servers are not Windows NT servers, then the application will have to be recompiled for the appropriate operating system.

h) What steps would you take to accomplish 2.2.2.g? Assume that the UNIX machine is running Solaris 2.6.

Answer: To do this, you would take the following steps:

1) Develop a module using a Windows NT workstation.
2) Save the .fmb file.
3) FTP or somehow copy the .fmb file from the NT workstation to the Solaris machine.
4) Compile the .fmb on the UNIX machine using the Solaris version of the Form Compiler.
5) You will now have an .fmx that is runnable on Solaris.

Cross-platform development is a large topic, though it is not covered within the scope of this book. However, it is worth noting that it is one of the features that has made Oracle Forms such a popular product.

2.2.3 ANSWERS

Open EX02_02.fmb in the Form Builder.

a) Which button on the Object Navigator should you use to run the form?

Answer: From the Object Navigator's vertical toolbar or the Layout Editor's horizontal toolbar, click the Run Form Client/Server *button. This button has a traffic light as its icon.*

b) What *has* to be happening by default when you run a module from the Form Builder?

Answer: By default, the Form Builder has to be compiling the .fmb *file and creating an* .fmx *file.*

Remember, in the Form Builder you are working with .fmb files, which are binary files and therefore not executable. Only executables, .fmx files, can be run.

When you click Run, Forms automatically compiles the form before running it. If there are any errors during compilation, they will be displayed to you in a Compilation Errors window. If the form can run despite these errors, it will. If it can't, you will have to fix the errors in the Form Builder before continuing.

c) Which should you run, the .fmx file or .fmb file?

Answer: You should run the .fmx file, which is the executable.

A running form can be in one of three modes: Normal, Enter Query, or Fetch mode.

d) Which button on the default toolbar can you use to put the form into Enter Query mode?

Answer: The Enter Query *button, which has a question mark in front of a cylinder as its icon.*

When a form first opens, the default behavior is for it to be in Normal mode, which means it is capable of accepting new records or updating existing ones. By putting the form in Enter Query mode, it is set to accept a query by example.

■ FOR EXAMPLE:

Run the EX02_02 form from the Form Builder. Click the Enter Query button. Type 101 into the INSTRUCTOR ID item. Click the Execute Query button. Note that only the record for Instructor 101 was returned to the form. You can add more than one parameter in Enter Query mode and you can also use wildcards. So, what would you do to get all of the instructors whose Zip Code is 10025 and whose FIRST NAME begins with "T?" Put the form into Enter Query mode, enter T% in the FIRST NAME item and 10025 in the ZIP item, and click the Execute Query button.

There are certain restrictions that apply to writing code in Enter Query mode, which you will learn in later Chapters as you begin to write more complicated logic and utilize built-ins.

e) In which mode should the form be to insert records?

Answer: The form should be in Normal mode.

You can always get out of Enter Query mode and back to Normal mode by clicking the Cancel Query button on the toolbar.

Shortcut keys in the Form Builder can be very helpful for running and compiling forms. Use CTRL-R to run the form. Use CTRL-T to compile the form without running it.

LAB 2.2

LAB 2.2 SELF-REVIEW QUESTIONS

In order to test your progress, you should be able to answer the following questions.

1) Which of the following can be used to compile binary files?
   a) _____ The Forms Runtime
   b) _____ The Form Builder
   c) _____ The Form Compiler
   d) _____ b & c

2) Which of the following is not true about .fmx files?
   a) _____ Distributed to users
   b) _____ Platform-dependent
   c) _____ Binary files
   d) _____ Runnable from the Layout Editor

3) To run an .fmx client/server, the user would need which of the following?
   a) _____ The Forms Runtime
   b) _____ Access to a database
   c) _____ Module files for the button icons
   d) _____ The .fmx to be compiled for their operating system
   e) _____ a, b, & d

4) Which of the following can be used to compile .fmb's?
   a) _____ The Form Compiler
   b) _____ The Run button on the Object Navigator
   c) _____ Program/Compile/All from the Form Builder's Main Menu
   d) _____ CTRL+T in the Form Builder

Quiz answers appear in Appendix A, Section 2.2.

C H A P T E R   2

TEST YOUR THINKING

Use the wizards to create several forms based on the following criteria. It is important to complete these now as you will be required to enhance some of these forms in later Chapters. Save all of the forms to your \guest\forms\exercises directory.

1) Create a form based on the STUDENT table. Include all of the columns as items in the block. Do not enforce data integrity. Display all of the items in the frame on the canvas except for the audit columns. Select Form for the layout style and display only one record. Give the frame a suitable name. Save the form as R_STUDENT.fmb.

2) Create a form based on the INSTRUCTOR table. Include all of the columns as items in the block. Do not enforce data integrity. Display all of the items in the frame on the canvas except for the audit columns. Select Form for the layout style and display only one record. Give the frame a suitable name. Save the form as R_INSTRUCTOR.fmb.

3) Create a form based on the ENROLLMENT table. Include all of the columns as items in the block. Do not enforce data integrity. Display all of the items in the frame on the canvas except for the audit columns. Select Tabular for the layout style and display five records. Include a scrollbar and give the frame a suitable name. Save the form as R_ENROLLMENT.fmb.

4) Create a form based on the GRADE table. Include all of the columns as items in the block. Do not enforce data integrity. Display all of the items in the frame on the canvas except for the audit columns. Select Tabular for the layout style and display five records. Include a scrollbar and give the frame a suitable name.

Reenter the wizard and adjust some of the item widths so that all of them fit neatly on the canvas. Shorten some of the prompt values to make this easier. Try to make the frame smaller using the Layout Editor.

Save the form as R_GRADE.fmb.

CHAPTER 3

THE DEVELOPMENT ENVIRONMENT

CHAPTER OBJECTIVES

In this Chapter, you will learn about:

✔	The Object Navigator	Page 66
✔	The Property Palette	Page 84
✔	The Layout Editor	Page 93

The Oracle Forms development environment is a simple one to navigate. The three main tools within in it are designed to make development intuitive and easy. The Exercises and Labs in this Chapter will walk you through the basic ins and outs of the Object Navigator, Property Palette, and Layout Editor. Along the way you will also learn more about how to configure the mandatory Forms objects that you learned about in Chapter 1, "Concepts and Objects."

 Some of the Exercises in this Chapter may seem elementary if you already have experience with a graphical development tool. You should still complete the Chapter since it will teach you many features and functions that are specific to the Form Builder and that may not be in the other tools to which you are accustomed.

Chapters 1, 2, and 3 are meant to prepare you for the more complicated and interesting lessons that lay ahead.

L A B   3 . 1

THE OBJECT NAVIGATOR

LAB OBJECTIVES

After this Lab, you will be able to:

* Open and Identify Objects
* Create and Delete Objects
* Drag & Drop and Cut & Paste Objects
* Run and Save Forms
* View Database Objects

In the preceding Chapters, you learned about the fundamentals of Forms behavior and Forms objects, as well as how to create simple forms with the help of wizards. In doing so, you were exposed to the Object Navigator. In this Lab, you will take what you have learned about objects and apply it to working with those objects in the Object Navigator.

The Object Navigator gives you a hierarchical view of all the objects in a form. It organizes these objects by *node* and lets you *expand* or *collapse* nodes to view objects.

Within the Object Navigator, you can create, delete, move, and manipulate objects in other ways. You can name an object in the Object Navigator, but you cannot define it any further. To adjust the specific characteristics of an object, you must use the Property Palette or Layout Editor, which are discussed later in the Chapter.

Figure 3.1 shows a screenshot of a single form open in the Object Navigator.

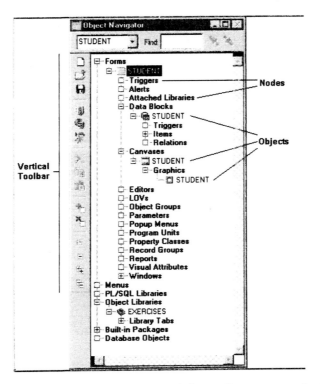

Figure 3.1 ■ The Object Navigator with nodes expanded to show Data Blocks and Canvases.

Along the left-hand side is the vertical toolbar, and in the center is the hierarchy itself. Note that the `Data Blocks` and `Canvases` nodes are expanded to reveal their objects. Also note that below both the `Data Blocks` and `Canvases` nodes there are sub-nodes that are collapsed.

In this Lab's Exercises, you will be exposed to copying and moving objects from node to node and even from form to form within the Object Navigator. This powerful feature paves the way for object reusability, which you will learn about in later Chapters.

You may have noticed that `Forms` is not alone as the highest node in the hierarchy. At the bottom there are five other nodes: `Menus`, `PL/SQL Libraries`, `Object Libraries`, `Built-ins`, and `Database Objects`, which are also at the top level of the hierarchy. In this Lab's Exercises, you will experiment with the `Database Objects` node only, but the rest will come in later Chapters.

As you would expect, the `Database Objects` node lets you view and in some cases edit database objects.

The Object Navigator is an extremely friendly tool and does not need much explanation. You will be able to complete the Exercises by simply exploring it on your own.

Many of the Exercises ask you to click a specific button on the toolbar. The buttons have icons that indicate their function. However, if the meaning of an icon is not clear, note that all of the buttons have Tool Tips to further explain their purposes.

LAB 3.1 EXERCISES

3.1.1   OPEN AND IDENTIFY OBJECTS

Open the Form Builder, but close all Forms modules.

Use a button on the Object Navigator's toolbar to open `EX03_01.fmb`.

a) Which button did you use to open `EX03_01.fmb`?

_____

_____

b) Does this form have any alerts? How about LOVs? How could you tell without even touching the mouse or keyboard?

_____

_____

Use the expand and collapse buttons on the Object Navigator's **vertical toolbar** to answer Questions c–g

c) How many blocks does this form have?

_____

_____

d) Are there any block-level triggers? Name them.

_____

_____

e) Do both blocks have items?

_____

_____

f) Are there any item-level triggers? Name them.

_____

_____

In the top left-hand corner of the Object Navigator window there is a Find feature. Use this to find the object QUERY_MASTER_DETAILS.

g) What kind of object is it?

_____

_____

3.1.2 CREATE AND DELETE OBJECTS

Open form EX03_01.fmb in the Form Builder.

Use the buttons on the Object Navigator's toolbar to complete the tasks in this Exercise. If you have not already done so, familiarize yourself with all of the buttons in the toolbar by reading their Tool Tips.

Create an alert and change its name to NEW_ALERT.

a) What did you have to do to change the alert's name?

_____

_____

b) How can you create a block **manually?** Change its name to CONTROL.

_____

_____

Create two items in the CONTROL block. Name one SAVE and the other EXIT. Select Tools | Property Palette from the Main Menu to open the Property Palette. Change the Item Type property of the SAVE and EXIT items to Push Button.

c) Why can't you see these buttons in the Layout Editor?

_____

_____

Delete NEW_ALERT.

d) Which button did you use to delete it?

_____

_____

3.1.3 DRAG & DROP AND CUT & PASTE OBJECTS

Open form EX03_01.fmb in the Form Builder as in the previous two Exercises.

Drag the button CONTROL.SAVE to the INSTRUCTOR block. Position it after the INSTRUCTOR.ZIP item.

a) How did the Object Navigator indicate that you were positioning CONTROL.SAVE after INSTRUCTOR.ZIP?

_____

_____

Using the buttons on the Object Navigator's vertical toolbar, copy the button CONTROL.EXIT to the SECTION block. Position it after the SECTION.CA-PACITY item.

b) Which buttons did you use and how were you able to position the button item properly this time?

_____

_____

Leave EX03_01.fmb open, and then open form EX03_03.fmb. You will be working with both of them.

Drag the following objects from EX03_01.fmb to EX03_03.fmb:
    Form Trigger - WHEN-NEW-FORM-INSTANCE.
    Alert - DEMO_OBJECTS.
    Program Unit - DEMO_ALERT.

> *If you have trouble locating any of these objects, use the Object Navigator's Find feature.*

c) What happened as you tried to drag these objects from one form to the other?

_____

_____

d) What do you think the relationship will be between the objects in EX03_01.fmb and EX03_03.fmb if you choose Subclass?

_____

_____

e) What if you choose Copy?

_____

_____

Choose Copy for each object. If you already chose Subclass, simply delete all of the objects you dragged into EX03_03.fmb. Drag them over again, but this time choose Copy. Keep form EX03_03.fmb open for the next Exercise.

3.1.4   RUN AND SAVE FORMS

The purpose of this Exercise is to run a form from the Form Builder. You will also check that the objects from EX03_01.fmb in the previous Exercise were dragged over successfully.

Using the buttons in the Object Navigator's vertical toolbar, run the form EX03_03.fmb in Client/Server mode. Note the horrible layout. You will be fixing it in Exercise 3.3.1.

a) Which button did you choose to run EX03_03.fmb?

_____

_____

b) What message did you receive when you ran this form?

_____

_____

Use the buttons on the Object Navigator's vertical toolbar to save the changes to the form. Make sure you save it to the \guest\forms\exercises directory.

3.1.5   VIEW DATABASE OBJECTS

Open the Form Builder. It is not necessary to have any forms open, but it will not hurt if you do. Make sure you are connected to the database. If you are unsure, reconnect from the Main Menu by selecting File | Connect.

Open and view the STUDENT schema under the Database Objects node.

a) What types of objects are visible to you? (Give the object types like Synonyms, Rollback Segments, and so forth.)

_____

_____

b) Can you rename the STUDENT table to ST_STUDENTS?

_____

_____

c) Can you add columns to the STUDENT table?

_____

_____

d) Does the STUDENT table have any triggers?

_____

_____

e) Are you able to create and edit database triggers?

_____

_____

LAB 3.1 EXERCISE ANSWERS

3.1.1 ANSWERS

a) Which button did you use to open EX03_01.fmb?

Answer: You should use the Open *button and navigate the filesystem to find* EX03_01.fmb. *The* Open *button has a small file folder as its icon.*

You could also have opened the form by going to the Main Menu and selecting File | Open. As in most Windows-based applications, both methods have the same outcome.

b) Does this form have any alerts? How about LOVs? How could you tell without even touching the mouse or keyboard?

Answer: Yes, this form does have some alerts, but it does not have any LOVs. You can tell because there is a small plus sign (+) to the left of the Alerts *node, but only an empty box next to the* LOVs *node.*

This is nearly identical to the interface for the Windows 95/98/NT Explorer or File Manager and should be very familiar to you.

c) How many blocks does this form have?

Answer: This form has two blocks.

If you had trouble with this, take the following steps:

1)   Select the Data Blocks node.

2)   Click the Expand button on the Object Navigator's toolbar.
     The Expand button has a single black plus sign as its icon.

Of course, you could have done this by simply clicking the small plus
sign to the left of the Data Blocks node. Or, you could have even
double-clicked the text of the node. However, it is good to become familiar with all of the GUI features of the Object Navigator and Form Builder.

d)   Are there any block-level triggers? Name them.

Answer: Yes, there are three block-level triggers: POST-QUERY, ON-POPULATE-
DETAILS, *and* ON-CHECK-DELETE-MASTER.

If you had trouble with this, take the following steps:

1)   Select the Data Blocks node.
2)   Click the Expand All button on the Object Navigator's toolbar.
     The Expand All button has two black plus signs as its icon.

In this case, it is best to use the Object Navigator's toolbar buttons instead of going straight for the node or the objects themselves. The Expand All button expands all of the blocks and all of the items as well,
giving you a complete view. In this case, it lets you answer the question
in two steps instead of three, four, or maybe more.

e)   Do both blocks have items?

Answer: Yes, they both have items. If you used the Expand All *button as described
in 3.2.2.d, you would not have had to take any steps to find this out.*

f)   Are there any item-level triggers? Name them.

Answer: No, there are no item-level triggers. If you used the Expand All *button as
described in 3.2.2.d, you would not have had to take any steps to find this out.*

You may have been skeptical about the value of Expand All in Exercise
3.2.2.d. One click, two clicks, what's the difference? Here, the value of
Expand All should be quite clear. There will often be times when you
will want to see all of the trigger objects for all of your items. To click
through each item individually would be tedious and annoying.

While Expand All is convenient, it can also make the Object Navigator a
bit messy. Luckily there are two other buttons, Collapse and Collapse
All, on the Object Navigator that reduce what has been expanded to
make the Navigator more readable.

g)   What kind of object is it?

Answer: QUERY_MASTER_DETAILS *is a Program Unit.*

If you had trouble with this, take the following steps:

1) Position the cursor in the Find text field, which is in the top right-hand corner of the Object Navigator.

2) Start typing QUER ... You don't have to type the whole thing. In fact, it should have been found after you typed the first character. The Form Builder will automatically begin searching as soon you begin typing.

The Find feature is helpful as your forms get more involved, and it is especially helpful for finding triggers.

3.1.2 ANSWERS

Create an alert and change its name to NEW_ALERT.

a) What did you have to do to change the alert's name?

Answer: To change the name of an object in the Object Navigator, you have to first select it, then click it again to put it into an editable mode.

This is a rather simple concept, but it does deserve some discussion for it can lead to some frustration if you are a beginner. There are three states for objects in the Navigator: deselected, selected, and name-editable. Again, this follows the same behavior as the Windows 95/98/NT Explorer.

In this Exercise, you are focusing on the Object Navigator. Later on, you will learn how you could have changed the object name in the Property Palette instead. Both achieve the same result; the one you choose depends on where you are in the Form Builder at the time, or which method you prefer.

If you had trouble with this, take the following steps:

1) Select the Alerts node in the Object Navigator.
2) Click the Create button on the Object Navigator's toolbar. The Create button has a large green plus sign (+) as its icon.
3) Select the alert that was just created. It should be called ALERT14 (although the number may be different for you).
4) Click it again so that a blue box appears around the text ALERT14.
5) Change the name to NEW_ALERT.

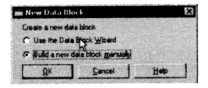

Figure 3.2 ■ New Data Block window.

When you create objects, Forms gives them a default name (object name + #), as in ALERT14. This is true for all objects.

b) How can you create a block **manually?** Change its name to CONTROL.

Answer: See discussion below.

If you had trouble with this, take the following steps:

1) Select the Data Blocks node in the Object Navigator.
2) Click the Create button.

A small window titled New Data Block opens, like the window pictured in Figure 3.2

3) Select Build a new data block manually and click the OK button.
4) Select the block that has just been created and name it CONTROL.

In Step 1, you selected the Data Blocks node and then clicked Create. Doing so in Forms positions your new block first in the list. If you had selected the INSTRUCTOR block, it would have put CONTROL second on the list.

When a form is running, the user will be able to navigate through the form by tabbing from item to item. Forms sets the default navigation order based on how the items are positioned in the Object Navigator. So, the first item in the first block listed in the Object Navigator will be navigated to first, then the next, and so on.

■ FOR EXAMPLE:

Figure 3.3 shows the Data Blocks node of the Object Navigator for a given form. Figure 3.4 shows the Layout Editor for the same form. Note the positions of the items in both the Object Navigator and Layout Editor. They are in a different order, aren't they?

Figure 3.3 ■ A block with items.

The order in the Object Navigator will take precedence over how the items are laid out on the screen. This means that when the form is run, the cursor will be positioned in STATE first because STATE is listed first in the Object Navigator. When the user tabs from text item to text item, navigation will be STATE - CITY - ZIP.

So, returning to EX03_01.fmb, because your CONTROL block is positioned first in the Navigator, whatever items you place in it will be the first that Forms navigates to. In the next Exercise, you will create a button. Depending on the requirements for the application, you may not want this button to be the first item that Forms navigates to. You will probably want Forms to navigate to the first enterable item in the INSTRUCTOR block. You can control the navigation order very easily by dragging items and blocks up and down in the Object Navigator to get them into the desired order. You will practice this in Exercise 3.1.3.

In the beginning, relying on default navigation is the easiest way to control navigation in your form. However, you are not limited to using default navigation order, and as your experience grows, you can override the defaults and control navigation by setting properties or writing triggers.

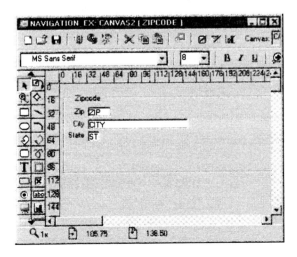

Figure 3.4 ■ The Layout Editor.

Create two button items in the CONTROL block. Name one SAVE and the other EXIT.

c)   Why can't you see these buttons in the Layout Editor?

Answer: You can't see these buttons because you have not assigned them to a canvas yet.

If you had trouble creating the buttons, take the following steps:

1) Select the Items node under the CONTROL block.
2) Click the Create button twice.
3) Rename the items SAVE and EXIT.
4) Go to the Property Palette for each item and change the Item Type property to Push Button.

Whenever you create items in the Object Navigator, they will not be visible until you go to Property Palette and set the item's Canvas property. You will also have to set the item's X Position and Y Position properties to position them properly on the canvas.

If you'd like to position these buttons on the canvas, take the following steps:

1) Select both buttons with CTRL + click.
2) In the Property Palette, change their Canvas property to INSTRUCTOR_SECTION.
3) Open the Layout Editor and you will see that they are now positioned in the upper left-hand corner of the canvas.
4) Drag them to positions below the SECTION frame.

You must have noticed also that you cannot specify an item's type in the Object Navigator. By default, the Object Navigator creates new items as text items, then it is up to you to change the properties accordingly.

Delete NEW_ALERT.

d)   Which button did you use to delete it?

Answer: The Delete button, which has a red X as its icon.

You could also have pressed the DELETE key on your keyboard.

3.1.3 ANSWERS

a) How did the Object Navigator indicate that you were positioning
CONTROL.SAVE after INSTRUCTOR.ZIP?

Answer: A horizontal black line appeared to indicate where the button item would be positioned.

If you had trouble with this, take the following steps:

1) Expand the INSTRUCTOR block and all of the items contained within it.
2) Click and hold the CONTROL.SAVE button.
3) Drag it down into the INSTRUCTOR block until the horizontal black line is below INSTRUCTOR.ZIP.

Note that dragging an object *within* a form actually moves that object from one place to another. Again, it is important to be aware of positioning in the Object Navigator. By placing the SAVE button after INSTRUCTOR.ZIP, you are indicating that you want the form to navigate from INSTRUCTOR.ZIP to INSTRUCTOR.SAVE (as it now belongs to the INSTRUCTOR block), then to INSTRUCTOR.TELEPHONE.

b) Which buttons did you use and how were you able to position the button item properly this time?

Answer: You should have used the Copy button, which has two pieces of paper as its icon, and the Paste button, which has a clipboard as its icon. You should have selected SECTION.CAPACITY before pasting to put the item in the proper position.

1) Select CONTROL.EXIT and click the Copy button.
2) Expand the SECTION block and the items below it.
3) Select SECTION.CAPACITY and click the Paste button.

Whenever you are pasting or creating objects in the Object Navigator, they will always be positioned directly below the object that is currently selected.

c) What happened as you tried to drag these objects from one form to the other?

Answer: As you tried to drop the object, a small alert should have appeared asking you whether you wanted to copy or subclass the object.

d) What do you think the relationship will be between the objects in EX03_01.fmb and EX03_03.fmb if you choose Subclass?

Answer: There will be a link between the objects. The newly created or "dragged" object will become a child of the source object.

Subclassing is a concept that will be discussed in later Chapters, but you probably have an impression of what it means and how it can be useful. When you drag objects from one form to another, you are actually creating new objects based on old ones, or if you choose to subclass, child objects (subclassed objects) based on parent objects (source objects). The subclassed object is linked to the source in such a way that if changes are ever made to the source, the subclassed object will inherit these changes. This can be extremely helpful when you want to create an object or a group of objects that you will reuse over and over and over again.

e) What if you choose Copy?

Answer: You will be making a copy of the object in the new form. However, no relationship will exist between this new object and the one it was "dragged" from.

3.1.4 ANSWERS

a) Which button did you choose to run EX03_03.fmb?

Answer: You should have used the Run button, which has the traffic light as its icon (the traffic light without the globe behind it).

If you had trouble running the form, take the following steps:

1) Put the focus of the Form Builder anywhere within the form EX03_03.fmb.

2) Click the Run button. As you already know, the Run button has a traffic light as its icon.

To "put the focus" of the Form Builder on a certain form in the Object Navigator, you select any object within that forms module. This tells the Form Builder which form you want to work with when you click Run, Close, Compile, Save, and so forth. If you have multiple forms open at one time, which is often the case, getting the proper focus is essential.

b) What message did you receive when you ran this form?

Answer: An alert saying, "A letter of approval from the director must accompany all teaching reassignments" should have appeared when you ran the form. If it did not, then you made a mistake when completing the tasks before in Exercises 3.1.3.c–e

3.1.5 ANSWERS

a) What types of objects are visible to you? (Give the object types like Synonyms, Rollback Segments, and so forth.)

Answer: Stored Program Units, PL/SQL Libraries, Tables, Views, and Types are visible.

If you had any trouble locating STUDENT's objects, take the following steps:

1)   Expand the `Database Objects` node in the Object Navigator.
2)   Expand the STUDENT schema.

b) Can you rename the STUDENT table to ST_STUDENTS?

Answer: No you cannot.

See the discussion under Question c for more details.

c) Can you add columns to the STUDENT table?

Answer: You cannot add columns to a table through the Object Navigator.

Tables, views, and columns are "read only," so you cannot change them. However, the `Database Objects` node is a handy way to examine the contents of database tables and views. It shows you table, view, and column names, as well as column data types and lengths. This can save you from having to go to SQL*Plus or another tool to view table descriptions.

d) Does the STUDENT table have any triggers?

Answer: No.

e) Are you able to create and edit database triggers?

Answer: Yes you are.

You can create and edit any stored PL/SQL object through the Form Builder. To test this out, simply select the `Triggers` node for the STUDENT table and click the Object Navigator's `Create` button. The database trigger editor will open and you will be able to set the trigger type as well as write the trigger code. You can also write PL/SQL stored procedures, packages, and functions through the Form Builder.

But, be careful! While it is convenient to be able to crank out quick functions and procedures straight from the Form Builder, it is also a bit dangerous in that you can drop PL/SQL objects from the database as well.

LAB 3.1 SELF-REVIEW QUESTIONS

In order to test your progress, you should be able to answer the following questions:

1) How does the Object Navigator organize Forms elements?
   a) ____ In a grid
   b) ____ By object ID
   c) ____ In a hierarchy
   d) ____ Arbitrarily

2) It is possible to use the Object Navigator to do which of the following?
   a) ____ Compile a form
   b) ____ Save a form
   c) ____ Delete a form
   d) ____ All of the above

3) In the Object Navigator, which of the following can you change with regard to an item?
   a) ____ The block it belongs to
   b) ____ Its name
   c) ____ Its order in the hierarchy
   d) ____ All of the above

4) Whenever you are pasting or creating objects in the Object Navigator, they will always be positioned directly below the object that is currently selected.
   a) ____ True
   b) ____ False

5) You can add columns to a table through the Object Navigator by selecting the column to the right of the column you wish to add and clicking the Create Column button.
   a) ____ True
   b) ____ False

6)   Which of the following best describes subclassing?
   a) _____ When one object is linked to another object in such a way that if changes are made to either object, both objects are updated with these changes
   b) _____ When you make a copy of an object in one form and place it into another form
   c) _____ When a source object is linked to a subclassed object in such a way that if changes are ever made to the source, the subclassed object can inherit these changes
   d) _____ Creating new objects based on old ones

7)   While you can drag objects from one form to another, you cannot drag an object from node to node within a form.
   a) _____ True
   b) _____ False

Quiz answers appear in Appendix A, Section 3.1.

LAB 3.2

THE PROPERTY PALETTE

LAB OBJECTIVES

After this Lab, you will be able to:

- View Properties
- Change Properties

In the Object Navigator, you create objects; in the Property Palette, you define objects. The Property Palette displays a list of characteristics (properties) for whichever object is currently selected in a form. The look, feel, and behavior of an object can be defined by its properties.

VIEW PROPERTIES

Figure 3.5 shows a screenshot of the Property Palette displaying the properties for a text item.

First be aware that what is shown here is not the entire Property Palette. The window is scrollable, and for an item, the list of properties is over four times as long as the list you see in the figure. Having this many configurable properties gives you a tremendous amount of control over the object.

The Property Palette is coordinated with both the Object Navigator and Layout Editor. So, if you select an object in either of these tools, its properties appear in the Property Palette.

Within the Property Palette, properties are grouped in categories like General, Physical, Database, and so on. These categories are expandable and collapsible like the nodes in the Object Navigator. Having this expand-and-collapse ability makes it much easier to view properties.

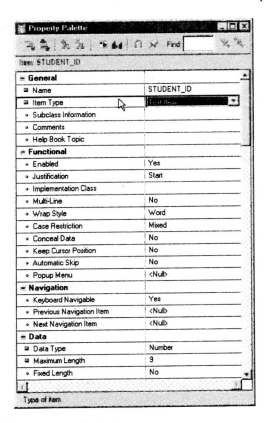

Figure 3.5 ■ The Property Palette.

CHANGING PROPERTIES

Forms objects are defined by their properties. So, if you change an object's properties, you are changing its definition.

If the changes you make affect an object's physical appearance, those changes will be immediately apparent in the Layout Editor. By the same token, any changes you make graphically in the Layout Editor will be immediately apparent in the Property Palette.

You can change properties for one object at a time, or you can do mass changes by selecting multiple objects.

■ FOR EXAMPLE:

Let's say you wanted 10 items in your form to be displayed in the font Times New Roman. To make mass property changes to these items, you would take the following steps:

1) Select the 10 items in the Object Navigator or Layout Editor.
2) Change the Font Name property to Times New Roman in the Property Palette.

LAB 3.2 EXERCISES

3.2.1 VIEW PROPERTIES

Open form EX03_02.fmb in the Form Builder.

a) Explore the Form Builder and list three different ways of opening the Property Palette for the STUDENT.PHONE item.

_____

_____

b) View the properties for the STUDENT block. Now switch to view the properties of the STUDENT canvas. What are the first three nodes in the Property Palette for the block? for the canvas?

_____

_____

View the Bevel property for the STUDENT.PHONE item. Press the FI key (for MS Windows users) to view help for the Bevel property.

c) What is the purpose of the item's Bevel property? Besides the FI key, can you see another way to get a hint about what the property is for?

_____

_____

3.2.2 CHANGE PROPERTIES

Use form EX03_02.fmb as in the previous Exercise.

For the item STUDENT.ZIP, change the following properties:

- Font Name to Arial.
- Font Weight to Demibold.

- `Insert Allowed` to No.
- `Update Allowed` to No.

a) What happened to the small icons to the left of the property names? Why is this helpful?

_____

_____

Go back to the properties for `STUDENT.ZIP` and select the `Insert Allowed` property. Click the `Inherit` button on the Property Palette's toolbar.

b) What happened?

_____

_____

Stay with the properties of `STUDENT.ZIP`. Click the `Freeze` button so that its icon becomes a pinhead rather than a full pin. Select `STUDENT.PHONE` in the Object Navigator. Right-click to open another Property Palette window. Drag this window to the left.

c) What can you see under the Property Palette window you just dragged away?

_____

_____

Use CTRL + click to select `STUDENT.ADDRESS`, `STUDENT.EMPLOYER`, and `STUDENT.REGISTRATION_DATE`. View the `Y Position` property for each object.

d) What are the values of these properties? Can you change them?

_____

_____

e) View the `Name` property for all of these items. Can you change that property?

_____

_____

In Question a of this Exercise, you changed the Font Name and Font Weight properties for STUDENT.ZIPCODE. Copy the font-related properties from one of these items and paste them to the remaining items in the STUDENT block.

f) Can you complete this task for all of the items at once? How?

_____

_____

LAB 3.2 EXERCISE ANSWERS

3.2.1 ANSWERS

a) Explore the Form Builder and list three different ways of opening the Property Palette for the STUDENT.PHONE item.

Answer: There are actually five ways to access the palette from the Form Builder:

1) From the Main Menu, select Tools | Property Palette.
2) In the Object Navigator, select the object whose properties you'd like to see and right-click.
3) In the Object Navigator, double-click on the icon to the left of the object whose properties you'd like to see (this does not work for canvases).
4) In the Layout Editor, select the object whose properties you'd like to see and right-click.
5) Press F4.

Because the Property Palette is a tool you will access frequently, it is helpful to familiarize yourself with all of the methods listed here.

b) View the properties for the STUDENT block. Now switch to view the properties of the STUDENT canvas. What are the first three nodes in the Property Palette for the block? for the canvas?

Answer: For the block, the first three nodes are General, Navigation, *and* Records. *For the canvas, they are* General, Functional, *and* Physical.

This illustrates two important points: first, that there is coordination between the Object Navigator and Property Palette; second, that the properties for each type of object can vary greatly.

c) What is the purpose of the item's `Bevel` property? Besides the F1 key, can you see another way to get a hint about what the property is for?

Answer: For an item, setting the `Bevel` property changes the appearance of the item's border. Besides pressing F1, you can find this out by looking at the Property Palette's hint line.

The help system has a lot of information to offer about a property. Obviously, you can get a description of the property. In addition, the help system lists restrictions for using the property and the Forms *built-in* you would have to use to change this property programmatically. A *built-in* is a pre-written sub-program that you can use for standard application functions. To change an item programmatically, you write a trigger that calls a built-in.

■ FOR EXAMPLE:

Let's say you want to create a button that changes the foreground color (font color) of the `STUDENT_ID` item. You would write a `WHEN-BUTTON-PRESSED` trigger that would include the following command:

```
SET_ITEM_PROPERTY('STUDENT.STUDENT_ID', foreground_color, 'red');
```

The built-in is `SET_ITEM_PROPERTY`. There are hundreds of built-ins available in Forms, and as you get deeper into this workbook, you will learn more of them.

3.2.2 ANSWERS

a) What happened to the small icons to the left of the property names? Why is this helpful?

Answer: They have changed from small dots to small green squares. This is helpful because it shows which properties have been changed and which still have their original value.

In later Chapters when you experiment with visual attributes, property classes, and subclassing, you will see even more changes to the icons in the Property Palette.

b) What happened?

Answer: The property has been returned to its default value.

In this case, the property was returned to its default value. Think of this as an undo-like feature for properties.

c) What can you see under the Property Palette window you just dragged away?

Answer: You can see the frozen Property Palette, which is listing the properties for STUDENT.PHONE.

Usually, you will only be viewing one object at a time. But in some cases, you will want to view the properties of two or three objects side-by-side to make comparisons.

The Freeze/Unfreeze button on the Property Palette's toolbar gives you this capability. This button has a pin as its icon. It can be especially helpful when you wish to compare X and Y positions of multiple objects. You can continue to pin and open additional instances of the Property Palette as many times as you'd like.

d) What are the values of these properties? Can you change them?

Answer: The values are ****. Yes, you can change them.

Figure 3.6 shows the font properties for the four items that have been selected.

Note that Font Name and Font Weight have question marks next to the property name and asterisks where the property's value should be. Here, Forms is indicating that the objects you have selected have different values for this property. On the other hand, note that each of the objects selected has the same value for the Font Size, Font Style, and Font Spacing properties.

e) View the Name property for all of these items. Can you change that property?

Answer: No you cannot.

▦ Font	
? Font Name	xxxxx
▣ Font Size	8
? Font Weight	xxxxx
▣ Font Style	Plain
▣ Font Spacing	Normal

Figure 3.6 ▪ The Property Palette when more than one object has been selected.

Not all properties are available for mass changes. The purpose of mass changes is to give more than one object the same value for a certain property. Therefore, Forms will not allow you to do mass changes on the Name property of items because all items within a block must have a unique name.

Also, Forms will not allow you to do mass changes to the Subclass Information property.

f) Can you complete this task for all of the items at once? How?

Answer: Yes you can. Copy the properties for STUDENT.ZIPCODE, *then select all of the items in the* STUDENT *block. Click any property in the Property Palette to put the focus there, then click the* Paste Property *button.*

As you can see, there are many ways to change the properties for multiple items at once.

LAB 3.2 SELF-REVIEW QUESTIONS

In order to test your progress, you should be able to answer the following questions:

1) The Property Palette has which of the following?
   a) _____ A list of configurable properties
   b) _____ Height and width information
   c) _____ a & b

2) What feature can you use to view two instances of the Property Palette simultaneously?
   a) _____ The Paste Property Window feature
   b) _____ The Navigator
   c) _____ The Freeze/Unfreeze button
   d) _____ The Inherit feature

3) Which of the following are possible in the Property Palette?
   a) _____ Mass edits of properties
   b) _____ Running multiple forms
   c) _____ Copying properties
   d) _____ a & c

4) How are changes to properties indicated in the Property Palette?
   a) _____ The changed property's value is highlighted
   b) _____ The changed property's value is grayed out
   c) _____ There is no indication
   d) _____ The changed property has a green box as its icon

5) Which of the following have properties that can be viewed in the Property Palette?

a) _____ Triggers

b) _____ Items

c) _____ Record Groups

d) _____ All of the above

6) What does the inherit feature do?

a) _____ Returns a property to its default value

b) _____ Copies properties from other objects

c) _____ Creates a new version of the property

d) _____ None of the above

7) How will properties appear in the Property Palette if two objects are selected in the Object Navigator?

a) _____ If the property value is the same for both of the objects, ***** will be displayed

b) _____ If the property value is different for both of the objects, **** will be displayed

c) _____ The Property Palette will be blank

d) _____ Both values will appear separated by commas

Quiz answer appear in Appendix A, Section 3.2.

L A B   3 . 3

THE LAYOUT EDITOR

LAB OBJECTIVES

After this Lab, you will be able to:

*   Create and Format Objects
*   Arrange and Size Objects

The Layout Editor complements the Object Navigator and Property Palette in that it allows you to give faces to the objects you create and configure. Here you will visually position, arrange, size, and color your objects.

In the Object Navigator, you can create any object, be it logical or physical. In the Layout Editor, you can only create *physical* objects that can appear on a canvas, such as items, other canvases, and graphics. Graphics include frames and any other non-item objects like rectangles, circles, lines, and static text.

The Layout Editor has three toolbars that provide utility, formatting, and create functions. Figure 3.7 shows the Layout Editor and its toolbars.

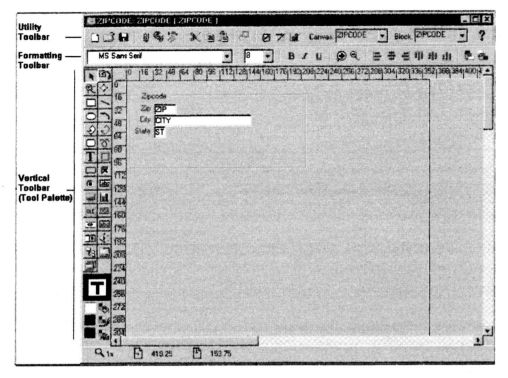

**LAB
3.3**

*Utility
Toolbar*

*Formatting
Toolbar*

*Vertical
Toolbar
(Tool Palette)*

Figure 3.7 ■ The Layout Editor and its three toolbars.

The Forms help system does not use these names for the toolbars. They are used in this text for the sake of the explanations and Exercises.

A brief introduction to the toolbars will provide a good starting point for understanding the Layout Editor.

UTILITY TOOLBAR

From the Utility toolbar, you can open, save, and run forms, as well as cut and paste and so on. As these functions are shared with the Object Navigator, there is no reason to explain them in detail.

The Utility toolbar also lets you coordinate which block or canvas you are working with, as well as gain access to the wizards.

FORMATTING TOOLBAR

The first half of the Formatting toolbar is for formatting text and is similar in look and function to the equivalent toolbar you see in word processors. It also provides tools for positioning and arranging text. The more tidy a form is, the easier it will be on the user's eyes. The Exercises will walk you through the Formatting toolbar so that you can quickly and easily position objects in an orderly manner.

VERTICAL TOOLBAR OR TOOL PALETTE

The Tool Palette lets you

- Select, rotate, and reshape objects.
- Create graphic objects.
- Create items.
- Color objects.

You will explore each of these functions in this Lab's Exercises.

The most powerful feature of the Tool Palette is that it provides an alternative to creating items in the Object Navigator.

LAB 3.3 EXERCISES

3.3.1   CREATE AND FORMAT OBJECTS

Open EX03_03.fmb in the Form Builder. Open the Layout Editor and Property Palette.

The objective of this set of Exercises is to learn the functions of the Layout Editor by cleaning up EX03_03.fmb.

Use the Layout Editor to create a button item and position it anywhere within the Student frame. Change its name to EXIT and change its label to Exit.

a) Which toolbar did you use to create the EXIT button?

_____

_____

b) Which block was EXIT assigned to?

_____

_____

In the Object Navigator, create a block manually and name it CONTROL. Drag EXIT from the STUDENT block into the CONTROL block. Your objective is to create two more buttons for the CONTROL block. Before doing so, answer the following questions.

c) Which feature on the Utility toolbar can you use to ensure that these new buttons are assigned to the CONTROL block?

_____

_____

Select the Button tool on the Tool Palette by clicking it once. The button will appear inset as if it has been "pressed." Now, double-click it until an icon appears.

d) What icon has appeared on the Button tool?

_____

_____

Drag the mouse pointer into the canvas area on the Layout Editor and click once in one spot, then click again in another spot.

e) What has "pinning" the Button tool allowed you to do?

_____

_____

f) How do you think you can get out of the Pinning mode?

_____

_____

Rename and label these new buttons Save and Print. Arrange them neatly below the STUDENT frame.

Using the Layout Editor's horizontal toolbar, change the font of the STUDENT_ID item to Ms Sans Serif, 8 pt.

g) Can you repeat the font change you just made by selecting all of the remaining items and prompts on the canvas?

_____

_____

There are three buttons at the bottom of the Tool Palette that deal with color.

h) What are the Tool Tips for each of these buttons, and which property do you think each corresponds to?

_____

_____

i) Can you change the background color for all of the text items to white? Be sure to do this simultaneously for all items. Do not include the button items.

_____

_____

j) How about the foreground color? How would you change the foreground color for all of the items so that they are blue?

_____

_____

k) Have the prompt background colors changed, too? Can you change their background colors to gray without affecting the text items?

_____

_____

3.3.2 ARRANGE AND SIZE OBJECTS

Select all of the text items on the canvas. Do not include the buttons. Use the Layout Editor's Formatting toolbar to arrange all of the text items on the canvas so that they are flush-left (meaning their left-hand edges are all in a line). *Hint: You may have trouble aligning if you select both the item and its prompt.*

a) Which button on the Formatting toolbar did you choose?

_____

_____

There are some Layout Editor functions that are not available on the toolbars. From the Main Menu, select `Arrange | Size Objects` to open the `Size Objects` dialog.

b) Which options would you select to give the objects a height of 14 points?

_____

_____

Again, have only the text items selected and from the Main Menu, select `Arrange | Align` objects.

c) Which options should you choose to stack the objects vertically?

_____

_____

Select the `STUDENT` frame and change its `Update Layout` property to `Automatically`. Move three or four of the items so that they are misaligned by dragging them out of their current positions. Select the `STUDENT` frame in the Layout Editor. Click the `Update Layout` button on the Utility toolbar.

d) What has the `Update Layout` button done?

_____

_____

e) Does this button update the layout of a canvas or frame?

_____

_____

f) What must the frame's `Update Layout` property be set to for it to work?

_____

_____

LAB 3.3 EXERCISE ANSWERS

3.3.1 ANSWERS

a) Which toolbar did you use to create the `EXIT` button?

Answer: The Tool Palette and the button, too.

If you had trouble with this, take the following steps:

1. On the Layout Editor's Tool Palette, click the `Button` tool so that it appears to be inset. As you would imagine, the `Button` tool has a button as its icon!
2. Move the mouse pointer into the layout area and it will change into a crosshair.
3. When you have chosen a position, click once and the button will be created.
4. Upon clicking, the crosshair indicates where the button's upper left-hand corner will be positioned. This is true for the creation of other items as well.

For graphical objects such as items, stacked canvases, and frames, it is common to use the Layout Editor for creation. This way, you get to create, position, and size the object all at once.

In this question, you single-clicked to create the button, which gave it the default size. Had you clicked and held the mouse button, you would have been able to drag out the size of the button as you were creating it. Create another button in `EX03_03.fmb` and try to size it upon creation.

The upper left-hand corner of an object is what indicates its position. What this means is that if the `X Position` and `Y Position` properties are set to `10, 10`, the object's upper left-hand corner is at the coordinates `10, 10`. This is true for items, frames, canvases, windows, and all other graphical objects.

Go into the Layout Editor and slowly drag the mouse pointer in circles. Look at the Layout Editor's hint line and you will see two numbers changing rapidly. These indicate the current X, Y position, in points, of the mouse pointer relative to the current canvas. The rules you see on the edge of the Layout Editor are also given in points, one of the standard units of measure for graphical objects.

b)   Which block was EXIT assigned to?

Answer: It was assigned to the STUDENT block.

c)   Which feature on the Utility toolbar can you use to ensure that these new buttons are assigned to the CONTROL block?

Answer: On the Utility toolbar, use the drop-down list labeled Block.

When you begin to work with multi-block forms, it will be common for you to have objects from more than one block on the same canvas. When creating additional objects for these blocks in the Layout Editor, it will be important that you adjust the Block drop-down list accordingly. But, if you do forget to adjust it and you end up creating an item in the wrong block, you can use the Object Navigator to drag the item to the correct block.

d)   What icon has appeared on the Button tool?

Answer: A small pin icon.

e)   What has "pinning" the Button tool allowed you to do?

Answer: Pinning allows you to create more than one button at once.

Pinning works for all the objects that you can create from the Tool Palette, including graphical objects and canvases. It was extremely helpful in this case, when you needed to create multiple buttons, and it will come in handy in future Exercises when you will need to quickly create more than one display item.

f)   How do you think you can get out of the Pinning mode?

Answer: Click the Select tool in the upper right-hand corner of the Tool Palette, or any other tool in the Tool Palette.

g)   Can you repeat the font change you just made by selecting all of the remaining items and prompts on the canvas?

Answer: Yes you can.

Selecting deserves a bit of attention. The Windows select functions work here, so you could CTRL + click items individually to select them.

However, in this case, because you are selecting many items, it is best to "rubber-band" them. To do so, you would follow these steps:

1. Position the mouse pointer above and to the left of all the items.
2. Click and drag so that you are creating a rectangular band.
3. Stretch this band around all of the items and release to select them. The entire object must be within the band for it to be included in the selection.

You can now start formatting and setting properties for all of the items and objects that you have selected. You can also move them as a group. If you were to single-click and drag one of the selected objects, all of the other objects would move with it.

To perform an operation on everything on a canvas, go to the Main Menu and select Edit | Select All.

h) What are the Tool Tips for each of these buttons, and which property do you think each corresponds to?

Answer: Listed from top to bottom: Fill Color *corresponds to* Background Color, Line Color *corresponds to* Edge Foreground *color, and* Text Color *refers to* Foreground Color.

Ignore Line Color since it only applies to frame edges and other graphical objects. Fill Color and Text Color are the tools you will use most frequently since they are what will alter the color of the text in a text or display item and the color of, obviously, its background.

i) Can you change the background color for all of the text items to white? Be sure to do this simultaneously for all items. Do not include the button items.

Answer: Yes you can.

If you had trouble with this, try these simple steps:

1) Select all of the items, *but not* their prompts. The best way to do this is to rubber-band everything then deselect the prompts.
2) Click the Fill button and choose white to change the background color. The Fill button has a paint can as its icon.

j)   How about the foreground color? How would you change the foreground color for all of the items so that they are blue?

Answer: Multi-select all of the items, click the `Text Color` *button, and select blue.*

k)   Have the prompt background colors changed, too? Can you change their background colors to gray without affecting the text items?

Answer: Yes, some of them have probably changed to blue. CTRL + click all of the discolored prompts and use the `Fill` *button to change their background color to gray.*

3.3.2   ANSWERS

a)   Which button on the Formatting toolbar did you choose?

Answer: The button with `Align Left` *as its Tool Tip.*

As you experienced in some of the questions in Exercise 3.2.3, it is often necessary to deselect the prompts when performing group operations like coloring or arranging. In this case, you do not want the prompts to be included in the aligning function. You only want to align the text items and the prompts will follow.

b)   Which options would you select to give the objects a height of 14 points?

Answer: Under `Width`, *select* `No Change`. *Under* `Height`, *select* `Custom`, *and then type* `14` *into the text item. Under* `Units`, *select* `Points`.

The `Size Objects` window lets you enter custom measurements as you did in Question b, and it also lets you size objects based on other objects.

c)   Which options should you choose to stack the objects vertically?

Answer: Under `Align`, *select* `Each Other`. *Under* `Horizontally`, *select* `None`. *Under* `Vertically`, *select* `Stack`.

d)   What has the `Update Layout` button done?

Answer: The `Update Layout` *button has automatically arranged the items on the canvas.*

e)   Does this button update the layout of a canvas or frame?

Answer: `Update Layout` *only works for items within a frame.*

Other items on the canvas that are outside the frame will not be adjusted when you click the `Update Layout` button.

f) What must the frame's Update Layout property be set to for it to work?

Answer: The Update Layout *property must be set to either* Automatically *or* Manually.

Once you have completed the Exercises in this Lab, the items in your canvas should be arranged and formatted as they are in Figure 3.8.

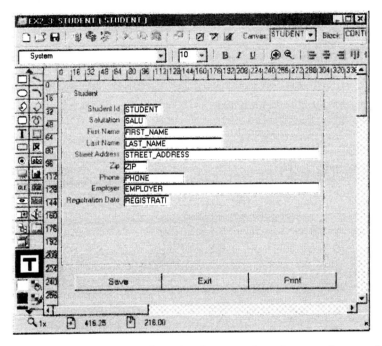

Figure 3.8 ■ **EX03_03.fmb after its layout has been cleaned up.**

LAB 3.3 SELF-REVIEW QUESTIONS

In order to test your progress, you should be able to answer the following questions:

1) Which of the following can you *not* view in the Layout Editor?
   a) _____ Radio button
   b) _____ Check box
   c) _____ Block
   d) _____ Frame

2) The Layout Editor is coordinated with which of the following?
   a) _____ The Property Palette
   b) _____ The Main Menu
   c) _____ The Forms Runtime
   d) _____ The hint line on a running form

3) All objects in the Layout Editor are which of the following?

a) _____ Items

b) _____ Physical

c) _____ Logical

d) _____ a & b

4) Which of the following *can* you do in the Layout Editor?

a) _____ Create and delete objects

b) _____ Run a form

c) _____ Change the background color of a frame

d) _____ a & b

e) _____ All of the above

5) How do the X Position and Y Position properties indicate the position of an object on a canvas?

a) _____ They indicate the position of the center of the object

b) _____ They indicate the position of the upper left-hand corner of the object

c) _____ They are not used to indicate position on the canvas

d) _____ None of the above

6) Which of the following can you do when creating objects in the Layout Editor?

a) _____ You can size them

b) _____ You can position them

c) _____ You can assign them to blocks

d) _____ All of the above

Quiz answers appear in Appendix A, Section 3.3.

CHAPTER 3

TEST YOUR THINKING

Use the wizards to quickly create a form based on the INSTRUCTOR table. Include all of the columns as items in the block. Enforce data integrity should be **unchecked**. Do not display the audit columns on the canvas. Use the Layout Editor and Property Palette to adjust the items so that they appear as they do in Figure 3.9.

What Layout Editor feature can you use to make the prompts flush left?

What Layout Editor feature can you use to group the items and their prompts together?

What property can you use to have text appear in the window's title bar?

Draw a solid white rectangle on the canvas. What Layout Editor tools can you use to position it in front of or behind other objects on the canvas? Can you position the rectangle on top of an item or a prompt? What types of canvas objects can be positioned in front of or behind the rectangle?

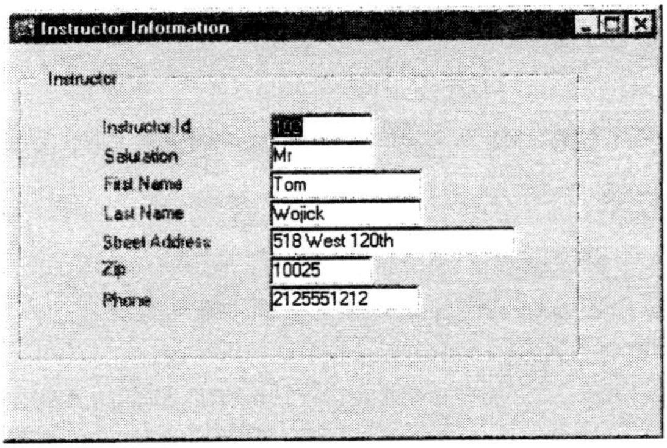

Figure 3.9 ■ **A block based on the INSTRUCTOR table with items arranged.**

C H A P T E R   4

MASTER-DETAIL FORMS

CHAPTER OBJECTIVES

In this Chapter, you will learn about:

✔ Master-Detail Forms   Page 108

In the previous Chapters, you created and worked with forms that had only one base-table block. In this Chapter, you will create a form with multiple base-table blocks and establish a relationship between them. The relationship will, among other things, allow your users to issue a query in the master block, which will cause the form to issue a corresponding query in the detail block.

You will create the master and detail blocks using wizards. This will automatically create an object called a relation. You will adjust the properties of the relation to change the behavior of the form.

L A B   4 . 1

MASTER-DETAIL FORMS

LAB OBJECTIVES

After this Lab, you will be able to:

- Create a Master-Detail Form
- Work with Master-Detail Forms and Relations

In the STUDENT schema, as in almost all schemas in relational databases, there are tables that are related. If the relationship is a primary-foreign key relationship, then one table can be considered the parent and the other can be considered the child.

■ *FOR EXAMPLE:*

In the STUDENT database, there is a table containing data about students and a table containing data about enrollments. There is a primary-foreign key relationship between the STUDENT and ENROLLMENT tables that tells you that for each student record there may be zero or many enrollment records.

In Forms, you can work with this relationship using a master-detail form like the one in Figure 4.1.

A master-detail form is powerful in that it allows you to relate two blocks in the same way that two tables are related in a database. Thus, the users can see the data from both tables in a meaningful way. For instance, when they query on a certain student record, they will see only that student's corresponding enrollment records. Not only will they be allowed to see the records, but they will be able to insert, update, and delete records in these blocks as well.

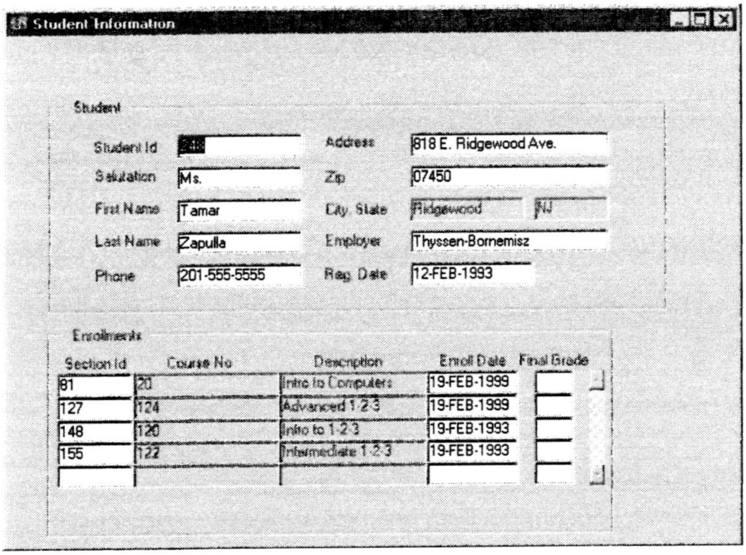

Figure 4.1 ■ A master-detail form showing a Student and her associated Enrollments.

The form in Figure 4.1 was created using wizards and then manually edited in the Layout Editor.

Note that the STUDENT items that belong to the master block are laid out in Form style with only one record displayed. The ENROLLMENT items that belong to the detail block are laid out in Tabular style with five records displayed. This single-record block to multi-record block layout style is typical for a master-detail form.

The wizards can help tremendously in creating master and detail blocks. They create blocks as they normally do, but also help you create and configure the objects that will coordinate the master and detail block.

There are a number of objects that work together to coordinate the processing of master and detail blocks. The main object is called a relation. Its job is to hold the join condition that relates the blocks.

The relation object has a number of properties that control how the master and detail blocks are coordinated. The creation of the relation object also initiates the creation of some triggers and program units. These triggers are written by the Form Builder for you.

LAB 4.1

LAB 4.1 EXERCISES

4.1.1 CREATE A MASTER-DETAIL FORM

In the following Exercises, you will create a master-detail form based on the INSTRUCTOR and SECTION tables.

a) Which table will the master block be based on? the detail? Why?

_____

_____

Create the master block and its canvas using the wizards. Include all of the columns as items in the blocks, but do **not** display the audit columns on the canvas. Leave Enforce data integrity **unchecked.** Lay the items out in Form style.

b) Did you have to do anything to indicate that this was to be a master block?

_____

_____

Start to create the detail block using the wizards. Leave Enforce data integrity **unchecked.**

c) Have you encountered a new wizard page? What will it help you do?

_____

_____

Auto-join data blocks **should be checked.** Click the Create Relationship **button.**

d) What is this List of Values dialog showing you? What happens after you click the OK button?

_____

_____

e) Because the wizard has already written the join condition for you, do you need to change the values in the `Detail Item` and `Master Item` list items?

_____

_____

Click the `Next` button and continue on to the Layout Wizard. The `SECTION` block should appear directly below the items in the `INSTRUCTOR` block.

f) Which canvas should you choose for the `SECTION` block? Is it necessary to create a new one?

_____

_____

Continue through the Layout Wizard until you get to the items page.

g) Which of these items already appears in the `INSTRUCTOR` frame? Is it necessary to display it again in the `SECTION` frame?

_____

_____

Continue through the Layout Wizard. Select `Tabular` as the display style and display five records. Click the `Finish` button when you are done.

h) If the layout of the `SECTION` items is not so pleasing, how can you make quick changes?

_____

_____

Run the form and issue a query.

i) Have the items in both frames been populated?

_____

_____

j) What happens to the records in the SECTION frame when you scroll to the next record in the INSTRUCTOR frame?

_____

_____

Save the form you have just created as R_INS_SEC.fmb.

4.1.2 WORK WITH MASTER-DETAIL FORMS AND RELATIONS

Use R_INS_SEC.fmb for all of the Exercises in this section.

a) Which block is listed first in the Object Navigator? What would be the problem if SECTION were listed first?

_____

_____

b) Has a relation object been created? What is it called? Which of the blocks owns the relation?

_____

_____

c) What is the value of the SECTION.INSTRUCTOR_ID item's Copy Value from Item property? Why has the Form Builder done this?

_____

_____

d) What form-level triggers have been created? What block-level triggers have been created?

_____

_____

e) Judging from their names, what do you think these triggers do?

_____

_____

Expand the Object Navigator so that you can see the triggers under the IN-STRUCTOR block. Change the INSTRUCTOR_SECTION relation's Delete Record Behavior property to Cascading.

f) What has happened to the triggers under the INSTRUCTOR block?

_____

_____

Double-click the new trigger that has been created and view its code.

g) Judging from the code you see and what you know about the term *cascading* from SQL, what will happen if you run the form and delete a master record?

_____

_____

Run the form. Navigate to SECTION_ID in the SECTION frame and issue a query.

h) Were the SECTION records returned to the form? How about the INSTRUCTOR records?

_____

_____

Exit the form and return to the Form Builder. Change the INSTRUCTOR_SECTION relation's Prevent Masterless Operations property to Yes. Run the form. Navigate to SECTION_ID in the SECTION frame and issue a query.

i) Were the SECTION records returned to the form this time? What does the Prevent Masterless Operations property do?

_____

_____

Exit the form and return to the Form Builder. Change the INSTRUCTOR_ SECTION relation's Deferred property to Yes and the Automatic Query property to No. Run the form and issue a query.

j) Were the items in the SECTION frame populated?

_____

_____

k) What then does the Deferred property defer?

_____

_____

Navigate to SECTION_ID in the SECTION frame and click the Execute Query button on the toolbar.

l) What happened after you issued the second query?

_____

_____

m) How could this be useful?

_____

_____

Exit the form and return to the Form Builder. Change the INSTRUCTOR_ SECTION relation's Automatic Query property to Yes. Run the form and issue a query.

n) Will you have to issue a second query this time? If not, what should you do to populate the items in the SECTION frame?

_____

_____

o) How could this be useful?

LAB 4.1   EXERCISE ANSWERS

4.1.1   ANSWERS

a) Which table will the master block be based on? the detail? Why?

Answer: The master block will be based on the INSTRUCTOR *table and the detail block will be based on the* SECTION *table.*

There is a one-to-many relationship between the INSTRUCTOR and SECTION tables. INSTRUCTOR_ID is the primary key in the INSTRUCTOR table and the foreign key in the SECTION table.

A master-detail form is used to establish and display a one-to-many (primary key-to-foreign key) relationship between blocks. The primary-key items are always in the master block and the foreign-key items are always in the detail block.

In this Exercise, you built a form that displays one instructor and one or many of the sections that this instructor teaches. Therefore, the master block will be based on the INSTRUCTOR table because it is on the "one" side of the relationship. The detail block will be based on the SECTION table because it is on the "many" side of the relationship.

Master-detail relationships in forms can also be based on REF columns, which are a type of object column that can be used if your database contains object tables. Object tables are not within the scope of this book, so you will not learn about REF columns here. Refer to the Oracle Forms Reference Manual for more details.

Create the master block and its canvas using the wizards.

b) Did you have to do anything to indicate that this was to be a master block?

Answer: No.

When you are creating the first block in a form, the wizard does not know whether or not you intend to create a master-detail form. The wizard will only prompt you with master-detail pages and questions if there is already another block in the form.

When you create the detail block, the wizard will ask if you want to create a relation object that will establish the join condition between the two blocks and manage the coordination of their records.

c) Have you encountered a new wizard page? What will it help you do?

Answer: Yes. It will help to create the relation object between the master and detail blocks.

d) What is this `List of Values` dialog showing you? What happens after you click the `OK` button?

Answer: The `Data Blocks` dialog that displays a list of base table blocks along with their foreign-key names will appear. After you click OK, the wizard writes a join condition for the two blocks and displays it in the `Join Condition` field.

The relation will be based on the join condition you see here. The relation will also initiate the creation of other objects that will assist in the coordination of the two blocks.

Before the join condition was created, you were presented with the `Data Blocks` dialog box, which displayed a list of blocks that you could choose from for establishing the relationship.

e) Because the wizard has already written the join condition for you, do you need to change the values in the `Detail Item` and `Master Item` list items?

Answer: No.

`Auto-join data blocks` was checked, so the wizard wrote the join condition for you. If you had not checked `Auto-join data blocks`, then you would have had to use the `Detail Item` and `Master Item` poplists to create the join condition yourself.

In the STUDENT schema, all of the related tables have explicit primary-foreign key constraints declared at the database level. However, you do not have to have such constraints declared to create a master-detail form. You can build a master-detail form between two blocks where there exists only a logical primary-foreign key relationship. In this case, you would not check `Auto-join data blocks` and create the join condition yourself. You would select the items that make up the logical join and the wizard would use those items to write the relation object's join condition.

f) Which canvas should you choose for the SECTION block? Is it necessary to create a new one?

Answer: You would choose INSTRUCTOR if you had already renamed it, or CAN-VAS# if it still had the default name. And you wouldn't have to create a new canvas because you want the items in both blocks to appear on the same canvas.

g) Which of these items already appears in the INSTRUCTOR frame? Is it necessary to display it again in the SECTION frame?

Answer: INSTRUCTOR_ID already appears in the INSTRUCTOR frame. No, it is not necessary to display it again.

In most master-detail forms, it would be redundant to display the join item, in this case INSTRUCTOR_ID, in both frames.

h) If the layout of the SECTION items is not so pleasing, how can you make quick changes?

Answer: Reenter the Layout Wizard and adjust some of the column widths.
Run the form and issue a query.

i) Have the items in both frames been populated?

Answer: Yes they have.

j) What happens to the records in the SECTION frame when you scroll to the next record in the INSTRUCTOR frame?

Answer: They are coordinated. If you go to the next record in the INSTRUCTOR frame, you see its corresponding records appear in the SECTION frame.

4.1.2 ANSWERS

Use R_INS_SEC.fmb for all of the Exercises in this section.

a) Which block is listed first in the Object Navigator? What would be the problem if SECTION were listed first?

Answer: It depends on what object or node you had selected in the Object Navigator when you clicked the Create button. If SECTION were listed first, the default navigation would be wrong.

This is a bit of a review from the last Chapter. Remember, when you create an object using the Object Navigator, it positions the new object directly below the object you have selected. The object's position in the Navigator will affect default navigation. So, if you had the Data Blocks node selected when you created the SECTION block, it would have been placed first, ahead of the INSTRUCTOR block. When you ran the form for Question h of Exercise 4.1.1, the cursor would have been placed in the SECTION_ID item instead of INSTRUCTOR_ID. It would have been best to select the INSTRUCTOR block, then click the Create button so that the SECTION block would have been positioned properly in the Navigator and default navigation would have been smoother.

If your blocks are positioned incorrectly, simply drag SECTION below INSTRUCTOR to fix the problem. This is a rather small point, but it can be rather annoying if not done correctly.

b) Has a relation object been created? What is it called? Which of the blocks owns the relation?

Answer: Yes, the relation object has been created. It is called INSTRUCTOR_ SECTION, *and it belongs to the* INSTRUCTOR *block.*

As described in Exercise 4.1.1, the relation object is what holds the join condition and manages the coordination between the master and detail blocks.

The master block always contains the relation object. Don't be confused by the fact that the wizards create the relation object during the creation of the detail block.

c) What is the value of the SECTION.INSTRUCTOR_ID item's Copy Value from Item property?

Answer: The value is INSTRUCTOR.INSTRUCTOR_ID.

The Copy Value from Item property is set whenever a relation gets created. The Form Builder analyzes the join condition and sets the value of the detail block's foreign-key item's Copy Value from Item property to the name of the master block's primary-key item.

In this case, the foreign-key item in the detail block is SECTION .INSTRUCTOR_ID. The primary-key item in the master block is INSTRUCTOR .INSTRUCTOR_ID. So, the value of the Copy Value from Item property of SECTION.INSTRUCTOR_ID is set to INSTRUCTOR.INSTRUCTOR_ID.

Why has the Form Builder done this?

Answer: The `Copy Value from Item` *property is what coordinates the population of the detail block.*

When the Form Builder issues a query in the master block, it needs to return corresponding rows to the detail block. This ensures that when a record is queried in the master block, the corresponding records will be brought back to the detail block.

d) What form-level triggers have been created?

Answer: An `ON-CLEAR-DETAILS` *trigger has been created.*

A description of this trigger will follow Question e.

What block-level triggers have been created?

Answer: The `ON-POPULATE-DETAILS` *and* `ON-CHECK-DELETE-MASTER` *triggers have been created.*

A description of these triggers will follow Question e.

e) Judging from their names, what do you think these triggers do?

Answer: They help the relation coordinate the population of records in the master and detail blocks and manage the deletion of records.

These three triggers, along with three program units (`CHECK_PACKAGE_FAILURE`, `CLEAR_ALL_MASTER_DETAILS`, and `QUERY_MASTER_DETAILS`), are created automatically whenever a relation object is created. This is true whether you use the wizards to create the relation or do it manually.

The `ON-CLEAR-DETAILS` and `ON-POPULATE-DETAILS` triggers work together to ensure that the records in the detail block correspond to those in the master block. This means that if you are looking at Instructor ID 101 in the master block, then in the detail block you should only see the sections Instructor 101 has taught.

The `ON-CLEAR-DETAILS` trigger fires whenever the user goes from one record in the master block to another. This could be done by scrolling to the next record with a button on the toolbar or by issuing an entirely new query. This trigger simply calls the `CLEAR_ALL_MASTER_DETAILS` procedure that flushes the records from any of this master block's detail blocks. So, in simple terms, it clears out the detail block.

The ON-POPULATE-DETAILS trigger checks to ensure that the current master record exists in the database and then calls the QUERY_MASTER_DETAILS procedure that populates the detail block. The way in which QUERY_MASTER_DETAILS populates the detail block will differ depending on the value of the Deferred property of the relation. You will experiment with the Deferred property in Question k. In short, this trigger and procedure work together to put records into the detail block.

The ON-CHECK-DELETE-MASTER trigger fires whenever a user tries to delete a record in the master block. If detail records exist, then deletion of the master record is prevented. The nature of this trigger changes depending on the value of the relation object's Delete Record Behavior property.

Chances are you will never have to change or manipulate any of the triggers and procedures that coordinate the master and detail blocks. However, it is good to have an understanding of how and when they fire.

f) What has happened to the triggers under the INSTRUCTOR block?

Answer: The ON-CHECK-DELETE-MASTER *trigger has been changed to a* PRE-DELETE *trigger.*

g) Judging from the code you see and what you know about the term *cascading* from SQL, what will happen if you run the form and delete a master record?

Answer: All the records in the detail block will be marked for deletion.

As its name suggests, the Delete Record Behavior property controls how to coordinate the deletion of a record in the master block with the corresponding records in the detail block. The effects of the three choices for Delete Record Behavior are summarized as follows:

1) Cascading will delete the master record and all corresponding detail records.

2) Isolated will delete the master record, but does not delete any of its detail records. It is important to note that if the constraints in the database do not allow the deletion of a master record when detail records exist, then it will prevent Forms from doing so as well.

3) Non-Isolated (default) will not delete the master record if detail records exist.

Run the form. Navigate to SECTION_ID in the SECTION frame and issue a query.

h) Were the SECTION records returned to the form? How about the INSTRUCTOR records?

Answer: Yes, both sets of records were returned to the form.

i) Were the SECTION records returned to the form this time? What does the Prevent Masterless Operations property do?

Answer: No, the SECTION records were not returned this time. The Prevent Masterless Operations property does not allow you to perform operations on the detail block if a master record is not in the master block.

Specifically, it will not allow the user to query or insert records into the detail block unless there is a record present in the master block.

j) Were the items in the SECTION frame populated?

Answer: No they were not.

k) What then does the Deferred property defer?

Answer: It defers or holds off on executing the query for the detail block.

In the previous questions, the master block was queried and populated immediately after the detail block was queried and populated. With the Deferred property set to Yes, the form waits for more actions from the user before querying and populating the detail block.

l) What happened after you issued the second query?

Answer: The detail records were returned to the form.

m) How could this be useful?

Answer: This can be useful if the user wants to query by example for the detail block, or if the user wants to insert detail records without querying existing records.

■ FOR EXAMPLE:

What if a user wanted to see the sections that Instructor ID 101 taught that had a capacity of 15? By setting Deferred to Yes and Auto Query to No, the user can retrieve the Instructor 101 record first, then retrieve all of the sections that had a capacity of 15. Take the following steps to test this:

1) Check that the INSTRUCTOR_SECTION relation's Deferred property is still set to Yes and Auto Query is set to No.
   Run the form.

2) Click Enter Query button on the toolbar and enter 101 in the INSTRUCTOR_ID item.

3) Click Execute Query on the toolbar. Note that only the master records have been returned.

4) Navigate to any field in the SECTION frame and click the Enter Query button on the toolbar. Enter 15 in the CAPACITY item.

5) Click the Execute Query button on the toolbar again. Note that only the records with a CAPACITY of 15 have been returned to the detail block.

n) Will you have to issue a second query this time? If not, what should you do to populate the items in the SECTION frame?

Answer: No, simply navigate to the SECTION frame to populate the items within.

In this case, the query and subsequent population of the detail records is still deferred. However, as soon as the user navigates to an item in the detail block, the query is issued and it gets populated. The user does not have to enter more query criteria or explicitly click the Execute_Query button.

o) How could this be useful?

Answer: This could be useful if the user wants to view the master records before deciding whether or not to view the details.

■ FOR EXAMPLE:

Assume that the SECTION block will cause a long-running query. The user may not always want to wait for the query to complete. Here, he can query an instructor record and view it to decide whether or not it is necessary to also see the section records. For the user, this operation is fast and flexible. Fast because the return of the instructor record is not hindered by the slowness of the query for the section records. Flexible because he has a choice of whether or not to view the section records at all.

LAB 4.1 SELF-REVIEW QUESTIONS

In order to test your progress, you should be able to answer the following questions:

1) The blocks in a master-detail form are which of the following?
   a) _____ Two non-base-table blocks linked by a relation
   b) _____ Two base-table blocks linked by a relation
   c) _____ Neither the master nor the detail block contains non-base-table items
   d) _____ The blocks are based on the same database object and coordinated by triggers

2) What can't you do with master-detail blocks?
   a) _____ Create them with a wizard
   b) _____ Create them manually
   c) _____ Edit their relation object's properties
   d) _____ Display their relation object on a different canvas

3) What database objects are relation objects analogous to?
   a) _____ Many-to-one relationships
   b) _____ Parent-child tables
   c) _____ Primary-foreign key constraints
   d) _____ Database links

4) Which of the following is not true of the data items in a detail block?
   a) _____ They are base-table items
   b) _____ They are copied from the master block
   c) _____ They can appear on the same canvas as the items in the master block
   d) _____ It is common to give them a Tabular style layout

5) Which of the following is true about the relation object?
   a) _____ It is owned by the detail block
   b) _____ It is owned by the master block
   c) _____ One of its properties can affect the way records are deleted
   d) _____ a & c
   e) _____ b & c

6) What will happen when the `Deferred` property of a relation is set to `No`?
   a) _____ The master block is populated after the detail block
   b) _____ The detail block is populated along with the master
   c) _____ The detail block is disabled
   d) _____ The master and detail blocks are put into Enter Query mode.

7) What will happen when the `Prevent Masterless` property is set to `Yes`?
   a) _____ The detail records will be deleted along with corresponding master records
   b) _____ The detail block's operations are put into Normal mode
   c) _____ The detail block cannot be queried or inserted into unless a master record is present
   d) _____ The master operations are prevented from coordinating the detail processing

Quiz answers appear in Appendix A, Section 4.1.

CHAPTER 4

TEST YOUR THINKING

1) Build a master-detail form between the ZIPCODE and STUDENT tables. On the Data Block Wizard's master-detail page, uncheck Auto-join data blocks and create the relation yourself. The items in the ZIPCODE block should be laid out in Form style. The items in the STUDENT block should be laid out in Tabular style. Display five records for the STUDENT block.

2) Build a master-detail form between the COURSE and SECTION tables. The items in the COURSE block should be laid out in Form style. The items in the SECTION block should be laid out in Tabular style. Display five records for the SECTION block. Configure the relation so that the user can enter query criteria for both blocks.

3) Build a master-detail form between the STUDENT and ENROLLMENT tables. The items in the STUDENT block should be laid out in Form style. The items in the ENROLLMENT block should be laid out in Tabular style. Display five records for the ENROLLMENT block. Configure the relation so that the detail records are returned as soon as the master block is queried.

4) Is it possible to build a master-detail-detail form between the INSTRUCTOR, SECTION, and ENROLLMENT tables? Try to build it. Choose the proper layout styles for the items in each block. Don't be overly concerned if the canvas is very long. Experiment with the Deferred and Auto Query properties of each relation.

CHAPTER 5

ITEMS

```
┌─────────────────────────────────────────────────────────────┐
│                      CHAPTER OBJECTS                          │
│                                                               │
│ In this Chapter, you will learn about:                        │
│                                                               │
│  ✔  Text Items and Display Items              Page 126        │
│  ✔  Buttons, List Items, Radio Groups,                        │
│     and Check Boxes                           Page 143        │
│                                                               │
└─────────────────────────────────────────────────────────────┘
```

Nearly all of the interaction between users and your forms will take place through items. In this Chapter, you will learn more about how to create items of various types and how to set their properties. You will create database items for items based on columns in a database and non-database items to initiate some kind of action or to represent data or information that is not based on a column in a database.

Throughout the Exercises that deal with items, you will encounter questions and answers that provide brief tips about GUI design techniques. This is by no means intended to be an exhaustive coverage of the topic. In fact, in many of the Exercises you will be encouraged to ignore layout and aesthetics in favor of concentrating on creating Forms objects. Once you have mastered the basic functions of Oracle Forms, it is recommended that you read the "Designing Visually Effective Applications" section in the Oracle Forms on-line manuals, or purchase a separate book dedicated to the subject of GUI design such as *GUI Design Essentials* by Susan Weinschenk, Pamela Jamar, and Sarah Yeo (John Wiley & Sons, 1997).

L A B   5 . 1

TEXT ITEMS AND DISPLAY ITEMS

LAB OBJECTIVES

After this Lab, you will be able to:

* Create and Define Text Items Without the Wizard
* Create and Define Display Items

In Chapters 1 through 4, you created and defined some text and display items using wizards. In this Lab, you will go a few steps further by exploring their uses and properties in more detail

Display items and text items are fairly similar and share many of the same properties. The biggest difference between the two is that a user can navigate to a text item and change its value. This is not possible with a display item. As its name implies, it merely *displays* information.

Items, especially text and display items, have by far the most properties of all the objects in Forms. It would be impractical and unnecessary to discuss all of them here. Impractical because of the sheer number and unnecessary because so many of the property names are self-explanatory. However, there are several properties in the Functional, Data, and Database property categories that are worth exploring and that you will experiment with in the Exercises.

TEXT ITEMS

Text items are usually database items, meaning they are commonly based on columns in a database. The Data Block Wizard is the easiest tool to use to create these types of items. As you have seen in previous Chapters, it automatically sets properties so that the form knows which database column the text item is based on.

Text items can serve as non-database items as well. That is, they do not always have to be based on a column in a database.

DISPLAY ITEMS

As described in Chapter 1, "Concepts and Objects," display items can be either database items or non-database items. In this Lab's Exercises, the display item you create will be a non-database item. You will use its properties to configure it to perform a calculation. In other situations, you will use display items to display data from other tables.

■ *FOR EXAMPLE:*

Assume you have a block based on the ENROLLMENT table that includes the STUDENT_ID column. Along with the enrollment information, you'd also like to display the student's last name. You could create a display item to hold the last name and use a trigger to fetch the value from the database. This will be covered in Chapter 6, "Triggers & Built-ins."

Keep in mind that not all non-database display items have to display the results of calculations or values fetched from other tables. Often, display items are used to provide simple information to the user such as the time, date, or perhaps the name of the database to which the user is connected.

LAB 5.1 EXERCISES

5.1.1 CREATE AND DEFINE TEXT ITEMS WITHOUT THE WIZARD

The purpose of this Exercise is to manually create a database text item. A second and equally important purpose is for you to become familiar with some of the more common text item properties. Incidentally, almost all of the properties you will explore here also apply to display items.

Use the wizards to quickly create a new form based on the COURSE table. Do not include the COST column in your block. Enforce data integrity should be **unchecked.** Include the audit columns in the block, but do not display them on the canvas.

Choose Form as your layout style. Name both the canvas and its frame COURSE.

Use the Object Navigator to create an item in the COURSE block. Name it COST and position it between DESCRIPTION and PREREQUISITE in the COURSE block.

a) Is COST positioned on the COURSE canvas? What one property should you change to place it there? What values has Forms assigned for X Position and Y Position?

_____

_____

b) Instead of manually dragging COST to position it between DESCRIPTION and PREREQUISITE, which of the Layout Editor's functions can you use to position it automatically?

_____

_____

Now that you have created and positioned the text item, begin exploring its properties.

c) Did you have to adjust the Item Type property when you created this item? What does this tell you about the default behavior of creating items in the Object Navigator?

_____

_____

d) How would the Item Type property have been set if you had created COST in the Layout Editor?

_____

_____

Change the COST item's Enabled property to No. Run the form and execute a query.

e) How does the appearance of the value in the COST item differ from that of the other items? Can you enter the item via the keyboard or with the mouse? When might you want to use this function?

_____

_____

Exit the form and return to the Form Builder. Change the COST item's Enabled property back to Yes. Stay in the Functional category and look at the Multi Line and Word Wrap properties.

f) Judging from the names of these properties and the description in the hint line, would it be appropriate to set Multi Line to Yes for COST? Which other item in the COURSE block might it apply to and why?

_____

_____

You will need to use the Database Objects node to answer parts of the following questions.

g) What is the data type of the course.cost column? What is the value of the COURSE.COST item's Data Type property? What does this tell you about the default behavior of creating items outside of the wizard?

_____

_____

Change the COST item's Data Type property to Number.

For the next question, you will work with the COURSE_NO item. Select COURSE_NO in the Object Navigator and set its Initial Value property to:

:SEQUENCE.COURSE_NO_SEQ.NEXTVAL

h) How will this affect the COURSE_NO item?

_____

_____

Return to the properties for the COST item. Select Format Mask in the Property Palette and press the F1 key on your keyboard. Scroll down in the help screen until you see a section titled "Numbers".

i) What should you put in the Format Mask property to format COST so that it is displayed like this: $1,195?

_____

_____

j) Is COST set to be a database item?

_____

_____

Save this form as R_COURSE.fmb as you will be using it again.

k) What are some of the things about the layout of the form in Figure 5.1 that make it attractive and easy to read?

_____

_____

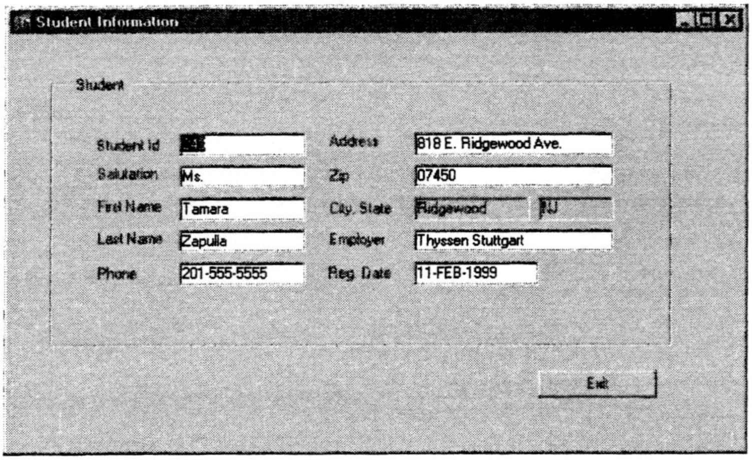

Figure 5.1 ■ Items from the STUDENT block arranged on a canvas.

5.1.2 CREATE AND DEFINE DISPLAY ITEMS

Use the wizards to quickly create a new master-detail form based on the ENROLLMENT and GRADE tables. Include the audit columns in the blocks, but do not display them on the canvas. For both blocks, Enforce data integrity should be **unchecked**.

Choose Form as the layout style for the ENROLLMENT block.

Choose Tabular as the layout style for the GRADE block and display five records.

Adjust the widths of the items in the GRADE block so that they fit neatly on the canvas.

Name the canvas ENRO_GRAD and the frames ENROLL and GRADE, respectively.

In this Exercise, you will create a display item that displays the average grade for each enrollment.

Use the Layout Editor's Tool Palette to create a display item in the GRADE block and name it GRADE_AVG. Position it below the NUMERIC_GRADE column of items.

a) How many GRADE_AVG items are displayed? Remember, GRADE_AVG must belong to the GRADE block.

_____

_____

b) Which property can you change so that the GRADE_AVG item is displayed only once, but the rest of the items in the GRADE block are displayed five times?

_____

_____

Resize GRADE_AVG to match NUMERIC_GRADE and give it a meaningful prompt.

c) Which of the Prompt properties should you change so that the GRADE_AVERAGE prompt is positioned like the prompt for ENROLLMENT.SECTION_ID?

_____

_____

You are going to make GRADE_AVG a calculated item and have it display the average NUMERIC_GRADE.

d) Which category of properties will you work with for GRADE_AVG to make it a calculated item?

_____

_____

You will be using a pre-written function to calculate the average of the grades.

e) How do you think you should set the Calculation Mode and Summary Function properties?

_____

_____

f) Which item in which block will you be summarizing? Set the associated properties accordingly.

_____

_____

g) What should the data type of the GRADE_AVG item be? Why?

_____

_____

Set the GRADE block's Query All Records property to Yes.

h) Why do you think you had to set this property?

Run the form again to test your calculation.

LAB 5.1 EXERCISE ANSWERS

5.1.1 ANSWERS

a) Is COST positioned on the COURSE canvas? What one property should you change to place it there? What values has Forms assigned for X Position and Y Position?

Answer: No, COST *is not positioned on the* COURSE *canvas. Change its* Canvas *property to position it on the canvas. Forms has assigned the value 0 for both* X Position *and* Y Position.

For an item to be visible at run-time, it must be assigned to a canvas that is visible in a window. Even if it has values for other physical properties such as Height, Width, and so on, the user will not be able to see it until it is positioned on a canvas.

This is so because it is common to create and use items that are never positioned on canvases and therefore never appear to the user. You should have noticed that the COST item's Canvas property was set to Null before you changed it. When the Canvas property of an item is set to Null, it is referred to as a *null-canvas item*. It is common to use null-canvas items as variables and assign and reference their values using PL/SQL. You can see null-canvas items in the Object Navigator, and you can configure their properties; however, they are not visible in the Layout Editor or at run-time.

Above the Canvas property in the Property Palette, you should have noticed the Visible property. This property must also be set to Yes to make an item visible on the canvas it is assigned to. You did not have to explicitly set this because whenever you create an item, its Visible property defaults to Yes. It is common to programmatically change an item's Visible property to show it and hide it at run-time. Note that when the Visible property is set to No, you will still be able to see it in the Layout Editor. However, when you run the form, it will not be visible to the user.

**LAB
5.1**

b) Instead of manually dragging COST to position it between DESCRIPTION and PREREQUISITE, which of the Layout Editor's functions can you use to position it automatically?

Answer: You can select the COURSE frame and click the Update Layout button.

c) Did you have to adjust the Item Type property when you created this item? What does this tell you about the default behavior of creating items in the Object Navigator?

Answer: No. This tells you that the default behavior of the Object Navigator is to create items as text items.

d) How would the Item Type property have been set if you had created COST in the Layout Editor?

Answer: That would depend on which item tool you selected on the Layout Editor's Tool Palette.

In the Tool Palette, you create items using the tools that correspond to their item type. If you are creating a button, you use the Button tool. If you are creating a text item, you use the Text Item tool.

e) How does the appearance of the value in the COST item differ from that of the other items? Can you enter the item via the keyboard or with the mouse? When might you want to use this function?

Answer: The COST value is grayed out and it cannot be navigated to with the mouse or the keyboard.

Setting a text item's Enabled property to No will allow you to display values in the item, but prevent the user from editing or updating those values. It will also gray them out, which will set them off from other items on the canvas. This can be useful if you want to display information to a user, but not let them change or update it.

■ FOR EXAMPLE:

The STUDENT schema contains SEQUENCES that generate values for columns such as student.student_id and instructor.instructor_id. When you display these sequence-generated values in forms, you will not want to allow the user to insert or update their values. By setting the Enabled property to No, the user will be able to view the value of student_id or instructor_id, but not change it.

Won't a display item provide the same functionality? In a way, yes, in that it will also display information in an item but will prevent the user from accessing it. However, a display item prevents access during Enter Query mode, as well as Normal mode. This means that if STUDENT_ID is a display item, a user cannot use Enter Query mode to search for a student whose ID is 101. However, a text item with Enabled set to Yes is accessible during Enter Query mode. This will allow a user to enter query criteria for the item. Note that there is no Enabled property for display items.

f) Judging from the names of these properties and the description in the hint line, would it be appropriate to set Multi Line to Yes for COST? Which other item in the COURSE block might it apply to and why?

Answer: No, it would not really be appropriate for COST. *It might apply to* DE-SCRIPTION.

As their names imply, the Multi Line and Wrap Style properties allow you to create items that can display more than one line. Because a DE-SCRIPTION can be rather lengthy, it may be appropriate to set its Multi Line property to Yes. If you set Multi Line to Yes, you must remember to manually adjust the Height property of the item if you want more than one line to be visible to the user. The Multi Line and Word Wrap properties are often used when displaying address items.

g) What is the data type of the course.cost column? What is the value of the COURSE.COST item's Data Type property? What does this tell you about the default behavior of creating items outside of the wizard?

Answer: The course.cost *column has* Number *as its data type. The* COURSE.COST *item's* Data Type *property is set to* Char. *When you create items outside of the wizard, the item does not inherit any properties from the database and sets every item's* Data Type *property to* Char.

In this case, the mismatch of data types did not prevent the form from running and functioning properly. However, it is wise to adjust the item's Data Type property to match the data type of its base column. In Question i, you will work with format masks to format the appearance of the COST item. If you had left the Data Type as Char, you would have encountered problems when trying to create a format mask.

h) How will this affect the COURSE_NO item?

Answer: When the user is creating new records, the form will populate the COURSE_NO *item with the next value in the sequence.*

In many applications, sequences will exist in the database and will be used to populate column values. Forms can make use of database sequences by setting the Initial Value property using the following syntax:

LAB 5.1

`:SEQUENCE.sequence_name.NEXTVAL`

In the STUDENT schema, there is a sequence called COURSE_NO_SEQ that you can use for COURSE_NO values. There are also sequences for the INSTRUCTOR_ID, SECTION_ID, and STUDENT_ID columns.

i) What should you put in the Format Mask property to format COST so that it is displayed like this: $1,195?

Answer: You should use $9,999.

Format Mask is a powerful and flexible property in that it lets you display information in a format that is different from how the information is stored in the database. You can use format masks to format the display of currencies, Social Security numbers, telephone numbers, product codes, dates, character strings, etc. Format masks can also be used to validate how values are entered into an item.

■ FOR EXAMPLE:

Set the COURSE.CREATED_DATE item's Canvas property to COURSE. Do not be concerned with where it is positioned on the canvas. Set the COURSE.CREATED_DATE item's Format Mask property to DY-DD-MM-YY. Set its Width property to 90. Run the form and issue a query.

Note that the date was returned and displayed as indicated in the Format Mask property. In the running form, change the CREATED_DATE value to 12-MAR-99. Tab out of the item and look at the running form's hint line. Note that the error message is indicating the proper format mask. So, not only has the format mask affected the display of the item, but it will also prevent users from entering data in invalid formats.

j) Is COST set to be a database item?

Answer: Yes it is. The Database Item *property is set to* Yes.

The Database Item property tells Forms that this item is based on a column in the database. Forms will include this item's name in whatever SQL statements it issues to the database. Take the following simple steps to get a feel for how the properties you set for an item can affect how Forms builds queries for blocks.

1) Set Database Item to No.
2) Run the form and issue a query.

What happened? Note that the COST value was not returned. This is because Forms ignored this item when it issued its SELECT statement to the database. It assumed that COST was a non-database item.

1) Set Database Item to Yes.
2) In the Object Navigator, change the name of COST to V_COST.
3) Run the form and issue a query.

What happened? You got an Unable to Perform Query error because Forms included V_COST in the SQL statement it issued to the database. Because V_COST is not a column in the COURSE table, the database returned an error.

1) Set the Column Name property to COST.
2) Run the form and issue a query.

Note that this time the query worked. The item name V_COST was overridden by the item's Column Name property. When you create data items manually, it is wise to set the Column Name property appropriately, even if you name the item after its base column. Note that the other data items in the block that were created by the wizard have this property set.

k) What are some of the things about the layout of the form in Figure 5.1 that make it attractive and easy to read?

Answer: Read the discussion below.

When using an application, it is important that the user can accomplish her tasks quickly and easily without being distracted by the interface. The user should be able to navigate from item to item quickly and smoothly and read and understand the information on the form easily.

■ FOR EXAMPLE:

In Figure 5.1, there is plenty of space between each item so that the form does not appear crowded. The items are sized similarly so that their right-hand edges are nearly flush. If they were all sized differently, the right-hand edge of all the items would not be smooth and would create a distracting, jagged edge.

The font is uniform across all of the items and is rather plain. Fancy fonts with serifs are attractive, but they are rather difficult to read and should not be used in Forms applications.

The items are arranged so that navigation starts in the upper left-hand corner with STUDENT_ID. The next navigation item is SALUTATION and from there navigation continues to flow vertically down through the items in the left-hand column. When the user tabs out of the PHONE item, the form will navigate to ADDRESS and continue through the right-hand column using the same vertical flow.

Occasionally, the Layout Wizard will lay items out in two columns when you select the Form style. The form will look similar to the one pictured in Figure 5.1. However, the navigation will go from left to right, from column to column. This can be a bit awkward as the cursor jumps in a jerky fashion from column to column. Therefore, it is sometimes necessary to rearrange items that have been positioned by the wizard so that navigation is smoother.

5.1.2 ANSWERS

a) How many GRADE_AVG items are displayed? Remember, GRADE_AVG must belong to the GRADE block.

Answer: Five GRADE_AVG items are displayed.

When the Layout Wizard sets the Number of Records Displayed, it does it for all items in the block being created. Then, all of the items in the block inherit this value. Even though you created GRADE_AVG outside the wizard, it is still inheriting this property from the GRADE block.

If only one GRADE_AVG item is displayed, then you have created it in the ENROLL block by accident. What probably happened is that you did not set the value of the Block drop-down properly in the Layout Editor's Utility toolbar. If you created GRADE_AVG in the ENROLL block, delete it and try it again using the proper tools in the Layout Editor.

b) Which property can you change so that the GRADE_AVG item is displayed only once, but the rest of the items in the GRADE block are displayed five times?

Answer: You can change the GRADE_AVG item's Number of Items Displayed *property to* 1.

As you can see, by setting an individual item's Number of Items Displayed property, you can override the block-level value for that specific item, but you will not affect the other items in the block.

c) Which of the Prompt properties should you change so that the GRADE_ AVERAGE prompt is positioned like the prompt for ENROLLMENT .SECTION_ID?

Answer: Attachment Offset.

The properties under the Prompt category in the Property Palette allow you to set the position of the prompt relative to its item. You can attach the prompt to any of the item's four edges, set how far the prompt should be from the item, set how the prompt should be aligned to the item, and so on.

At design-time, you can set the values for Prompt Alignment Offset and Prompt Attachment Offset in the Property Palette and Layout Editor. However, Prompt Attachment Edge, Prompt Alignment, Prompt Justification, and the rest of the properties in the Prompt category can only be changed in the Property Palette.

The beauty of these Prompt properties is that they will not change if you reposition an item. What this means is that if you drag an item from one position on the canvas to another, its prompt will be dragged along with it. Not only will it accompany the item across the canvas, but its position relative to the item will stay the same. This saves you from having to reposition the prompt every time you reposition an item.

d) Which category of properties will you work with for GRADE_AVG to make it a calculated item?

Answer: Calculation.

e) How do you think you should set the Calculation Mode and Summary Function properties?

Answer: Calculation Mode *should be set to* Summary *and* Summary Function *should be set to* AVG.

A calculated item gets its value from either an existing summary function, like AVG or SUM, or from a formula. Summary functions are convenient because like pre-existing database functions, the mathematical expression is already written for you.

In this example, since you wish to calculate the average of the grades for each enrollment, the Calculation Mode property should be set to Summary and the Summary Function property should be set to AVG.

In another example, you may wish to determine the total cost of all the courses taken by a single student. In that case, you would set Calculation Mode to Formula and write your own PL/SQL expression in the Formula property.

■ *FOR EXAMPLE:*

Assume you created an item called NO_OF_ENROLL that contained the number of students enrolled in a given section. You included NO_OF_EN-ROLL in a SECTION block. Now you want to create another item called SEATS_LEFT in the SECTION block. In this item you want to display the number of seats remaining in the section. You would calculate this by subtracting SECTION.NO_OF_ENROLL from SECTION.CAPACITY.

In the properties for the SEATS_LEFT item, you would set Calculation Mode to Formula and you would write the following expression in the Formula property:

```
:SECTION.CAPACITY - :SECTION.NO_OF_ENROLL
```

At run-time, the results of this formulaic expression would be displayed in the SEATS_LEFT item.

f) Which item in which block will you be summarizing? Set the associated properties accordingly.

Answer: You will be summarizing GRADE.NUMERIC_GRADE. *Therefore,* Summarized Block *should be set to* Grade *and* Summarized Item *should be set to* Numeric Grade.

g) What should the data type of the GRADE_AVG item be? Why?

Answer: The Data Type *property should be set to* NUMBER *since the calculation will produce a number value.*

If you leave GRADE_AVG as CHAR, the form will return an error.

h) Why do you think you had to set this property?

Answer: So that the average is computed for all of the records in the query's result set.

By default, Forms does not always return all of the records in a result set to the form at once. Each block has a Query Array Size property, which determines how many records will be fetched from the database at a time. The default value of this property is set by the Number of Records Displayed property. What this means is that by default, the number of records returned to a block is equal to the number of records displayed on the canvas. For instance, in the GRADE block, only 5 records are displayed on the canvas, so the Query Array Size property is also set to 5.

What if 10 or 20 records are part of the result set? Forms would not be able to calculate the average correctly because not all of the values would be returned. Therefore, when creating summary items, it is necessary to set the Query All Records property to Yes. By doing so, the Query Array Size property is overridden, all records are returned to the form, and the average is computed accurately.

In this example, it is safe to return all of the records to the form because the result sets are rather small. However, there may be cases in which the result set could be rather large. This would mean that setting Query All Records to Yes could possibly degrade the performance of the application. In these cases, you would set the properties for the GRADE block a bit differently. First, you would set Query All Records to No. Then, under the Advanced DML category in the Property Palette, you would set the Pre Compute Summaries property to Yes. This will not return all of the records to the block at once. Instead, the number of records returned to the block will be based on the number set by the Query Array Size property. But won't this mean that the average for the calculated item will be incorrect? Not in this case, because Forms will issue a second query to figure out the average. This way, the average is being computed by the database and then returned to the form. The value will be correct and the form will not have to fetch all of the rows from the database.

LAB 5.1 SELF-REVIEW QUESTIONS

In order to test your progress, you should be able to answer the following questions:

1) What is the major difference between a display item and a text item?
   a) _____ Text items can display database values, display items cannot
   b) _____ Text items are always database items while display items are always non-database items
   c) _____ Text items are navigable and editable, display items are not
   d) _____ Text items and display items are identical except for their background color

2) Why would you set the Multi Line property?
   a) _____ To display items on the canvas
   b) _____ To display more than one record in a single item
   c) _____ To display more than one line of text in a single item
   d) _____ None of the above

3) The `Format Mask` property allows you to display values in the form in a different format than they are stored in the database.

a) _____ True

b) _____ False

4) Which of the following must be true for an item to be visible?

a) _____ `Enabled` must be set to `Yes`

b) _____ It must be a database item

c) _____ The `Width` property must not exceed the length of the column in the database

d) _____ It must be assigned to a canvas with the `Visible` property set to `Yes`

5) How can you view the properties for a prompt?

a) _____ By selecting the prompt in the Object Navigator

b) _____ By viewing the properties for the prompt's item

c) _____ You can't because prompts don't have properties

d) _____ a & b

6) Which properties can you set to prevent a user from changing the value in an item?

a) _____ Set `Item Type` to `Display Item`

b) _____ Set `Enabled` to `No`.

c) _____ Set `Update Allowed` and `Insert Allowed` to `No`

d) _____ All of the above

Quiz answers appear in Appendix A, Section 5.1.

L A B   5 . 2

BUTTONS, LIST ITEMS, RADIO GROUPS, AND CHECK BOXES

LAB OBJECTIVES

After this Lab, you will be able to:

- Create Buttons
- Put Simple Code Behind Buttons
- Create List Items
- Create Radio Groups
- Create Check Boxes

The items in this Lab are different from text items and display items in that they don't simply display text to communicate their value. Instead they employ different combinations of text and graphics to display information or provide a function. As you may have noticed, there are many other item types available in Forms such as images, sounds, ActiveX Controls, and so on. In this Lab and in the rest of this book, you will focus on buttons, list items, radio groups, and check boxes. These, along with text and display items, are by far the most common Forms item types. For a complete list of all the different item types, simply look at the Item Type property in the Property Palette and refer to the help system for details on how to implement them.

BUTTONS

Buttons give users opportunities to make a form do something. This could be something simple like saying "OK," or it could be something more involved like executing a query or even opening another form. Creating and positioning buttons in Forms is easy. What's challenging is writing the code that goes behind them. As you already know, each button should have a WHEN-BUTTON-PRESSED trigger associated with it so that it can respond to the Button Pressed event. In the Exercises, you will use the help system to locate Forms built-ins to put behind your buttons.

LIST ITEMS, RADIO GROUPS, AND CHECK BOXES

List items, radio groups, and check boxes look very different, but they are similar to each other in that they present the user with a number of choices. The choices they present are often more understandable representations of the data or information stored behind them.

■ FOR EXAMPLE:

The list item in Figure 5.2 shows three choices for the SECTION table's LOCATION column. The labels are Lecture Hall One, Lecture Hall Two, and Lab One. But, they may not necessarily be this way in the database. The column values could be L210, L500 and L510, respectively. The list has been configured so that the user sees values that are more meaningful to them.

What this illustrates is that radio groups, list items, and check boxes allow you to display information in any way you'd like, regardless of how the values are stored in the database. When you configure these items, you define the values you'd like to display, along with how they should be represented in the database.

These three types of items can also handle data that they are not designed to expect.

Figure 5.2 ■ The list item elements are not necessarily how the information is stored in the database.

■ FOR EXAMPLE:

At design-time, the `Location` list item in Figure 5.2 could be configured to handle the database values L210, L500, and L510. When the user issues a query, the list item would expect that one of these three values would be returned to the form. But, what would happen if the user issued a query and the database returned the value L999? The list item is not expecting this value and would not know what to do with it. Luckily there is a list item property called `Mapping of Other Values` that can be set to handle this situation. Radio groups and check boxes have a similar property. In the Exercises in this Lab, you will explore the `Mapping of Other Values` property in more detail.

LIST ITEMS

List items are exactly what their name implies—a short list of values that the user can choose from.

List items can serve as either database or non-database items. The list item you create in the Exercise will be based on the COST column in COURSE table. You can also use list items for selection lists that are not bound to columns in the database but instead act as controls. The Form Builder makes use of list items in this way in the Layout Editor's Utility toolbar as shown in Figure 5.3.

Figure 5.3 ■ List items in the Layout Editor's toolbar.

RADIO GROUPS

Radio groups are logical containers of radio buttons. Radio buttons are the small circles that appear on the screen which the user can click to select values. Radio group selections are mutually exclusive. That is, selection of one radio button deselects the previously selected button.

The radio group you will build in the Exercises will be a database item. However, radio groups can also be non-database items.

■ FOR EXAMPLE:

You often see radio groups used in the Form Builder itself to let the user make choices. Figure 5.4 shows the `New Data Block` dialog with a radio group with two radio buttons.

Figure 5.4 ■ The New Data Block dialog with a radio group.

In this case, the radio group is acting as a control, much like a button item acts as a control. It gives a user the opportunity to choose how the application should behave. If you were to employ such a radio group in one of your Forms applications, you would have to write triggers to change the behavior of the form depending on which radio button was selected.

CHECK BOXES

Check boxes are useful for storing Yes/No, True/False, and On/Off-type values. Like radio groups and list items, they can also serve as both database items and non-database items. In the Form Builder, there are multiple examples of check boxes as non-database items. Figure 5.5 shows a check box on the welcome page of the Data Block Wizard.

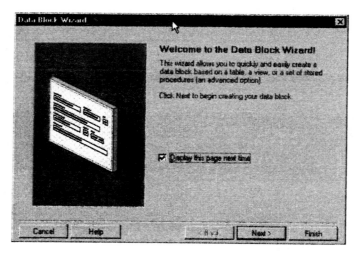

Figure 5.5 ■ The welcome page of the Data Block Wizard, which includes a check box.

LAB 5.2 EXERCISES

5.2.1 CREATE BUTTONS

Open the R_COURSE.fmb form that you created previously.

Create a block manually and name it CONTROL. The form should resemble Figure 5.6, but does not have to match it exactly.

Create three buttons using the Layout Editor's Tool Palette.

a) What should you do when you select from the Tool Palette to make the creation of the buttons easier?

_____

_____

b) What should you set on the Layout Editor's toolbar to make sure that these buttons are assigned to the CONTROL block?

_____

_____

Rename the buttons Clear, Save, and Exit.

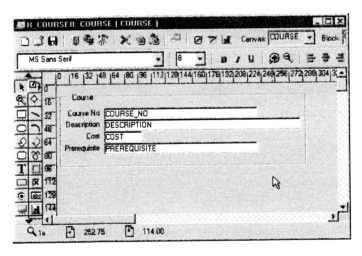

Figure 5.6 ■ Suggested layout for R_COURSE.fmb.

c) Edit the properties so that the text on the button matches its name in the Object Navigator. Which property did you use?

_____

_____

Run the form.

d) Which item has the Forms Runtime navigated to (where is the cursor)? Why is Forms doing this?

_____

_____

Exit the running form and return to the Form Builder.

e) What should you do to prevent the button from being navigated to first?

_____

_____

Save R_COURSE.fmb as you will need it in the next Exercise.

5.2.2 PUT SIMPLE CODE BEHIND BUTTONS

Open R_COURSE.fmb in the Form Builder. Right-click the Exit button in either the Object Navigator or Layout Editor and explore the Smart Triggers.

a) Which trigger should you create to respond to the event of a user clicking this button?

_____

_____

Select this trigger.

b) What is the title of the window that has just opened and what should you do in it?

You will need to use a Forms built-in to exit the form. Use the help system to determine which one you need. From the Form Builder's Main Menu, select `Help | Form Builder Help Topics`. Click the `Index` tab and type the word `Exit` into the first field.

c) What is the name of the built-in you should use to exit the form?

Type the code for the built-in into the PL/SQL Editor. Put a semi-colon after the built-in so that it compiles correctly. Click the PL/SQL Editor's `Compile` button. Close the PL/SQL Editor. Run the form and test the `Exit` button.

Create the same trigger for the `Clear` button using the `CLEAR_BLOCK` built-in as the trigger code. Click the PL/SQL Editor's `Compile` button.

The `Save` button on this form is not for saving files, but for saving changes a user has made by inserting or updating records to the database. With this in mind, answer the following questions.

d) What is the command for saving updated or inserted records to the database?

Based on the answer to the previous question, search the help system again.

e) Which built-in should you use to "save" the changes a user has made?

Type the code for the built-in into the PL/SQL Editor and click `Compile`. Close the PL/SQL Editor. Run the form and issue a query. Test the `Save` button by making a change to one of the records returned. Test the `Clear` button as well. Save the `R_COURSE.fmb` form for future Exercises.

LAB 5.2

Read the answers and discussions for Exercises 5.2.1 and 5.2.2 before continuing to the next Exercise.

5.2.3 CREATE LIST ITEMS

Use the `R_COURSE.fmb` form for the following questions. For Question a, consider the following information about the columns in the COURSE table:

`course_no` is numeric and a unique identifier of each course.

`course_description` is a textual description of each course. Each course has a different description.

`course_cost` is a numeric cost of each course. One of the STUDENT business rules is that there are only three possible costs for a course.

`course_prerequisite` is a numeric column based on `course_no`. It indicates the course that must be taken as a prerequisite.

a) Which text item(s) in the COURSE block would be better displayed as a list item(s)?

_____

_____

Change the COURSE.COST item's `Item Type` property to `List Item`. Use the `Freeze/Unfreeze` button you learned about in Chapter 3, "The Development Environment," to compare the Functional properties of COURSE.COST to those of COURSE.COURSE_NO.

b) What list-related properties have been added to the Functional category of COURSE.COST?

_____

_____

c) What happens when you click the `Elements in List` property and then click the `More` button?

_____

_____

d) If list elements are what appear to the user, what are list item values used for?

_____

_____

e) Can a list element be different from its list item value? When and why might you want them to be different?

_____

_____

Assume that there are only three possible costs for courses in the STUDENT database (1095, 1195, 1595). Use these values to populate the `List Element` and `List Item Value` fields.

f) Can you format list elements with dollar signs and commas?

_____

_____

g) Which Data property would you set so that a list item would start at 1595 during an insert?

_____

_____

Run the form and query Course Number 100.

h) Can you change the COST to 2000?

_____

_____

Exit the form and return to the Form Builder. Change the COST item's List Type property to Combo Box. Run the form and query Course Number 100 again.

i) Can you change the COST to 2000 now?

_____

_____

j) Can you change the COST to $2,000 *and* save the change? Why not?

_____

_____

Exit the form and return to the Form Builder. Change the COST item's List Type property to Tlist.

k) Does COST still look like a list item? What does it look like now?

_____

_____

Change the COST item's Height property to 34. Run the form.

l) What has happened to COST? How many of its elements are visible?

_____

_____

m) If there were 15 values for the COST item, would it still be appropriate to use a list item? What if there were 20? 30?

_____

_____

Read the answers and discussions for Exercise 5.2.3 before continuing to the next Exercise.

5.2.4 CREATE RADIO GROUPS

Use the R_COURSE.fmb form for the following questions. Before you begin, take the following steps to organize the canvas.

1) Change the COST item's Height property to 14.
2) Reposition COST after PREREQUISITE in the Object Navigator.
3) Update the layout for the COURSE frame by using the Update Layout button on the Layout Editor.
4) Reposition the buttons if they are in the way.

In this Exercise, you will use the COST item again, but this time you will implement it as a radio group item.

Change the COST item's Item Type property to Radio Group.

a) Is COST still visible on the COURSE canvas? Is it still in the COURSE block? Why isn't it still visible on the canvas?

_____

_____

b) What are the nodes under the COST item in the Object Navigator?

_____

_____

c) Can you create radio buttons in the Object Navigator? Why might it be easier to create them in the Layout Editor?

_____

_____

Select the Radio Button tool from the Layout Editor's Tool Palette and create three radio buttons. Use the pinning feature you learned in Chapter 3, "The Development Environment," to make this easier. Update the layout when you are done. Change the background color of the buttons to match the canvas.

Readjust the position of the Save, Clear, and Exit buttons if they are in the way.

d) What else did you have to decide in addition to selecting the position of the radio buttons?

_____

_____

Assume that there are only three possible costs for courses in the STUDENT database (1095, 1195, 1595). Rename the radio buttons in the Object Navigator.

e) Are you able to rename them 1095, 1195, 1595? Why?

_____

_____

f) Which radio button property should you change so that $1,095, $1,195, and $1,595 appear next to each radio button respectively?

_____

_____

g) Which radio button property should you use to indicate its value?

_____

_____

Assume that a query returns a value to the COST radio group that is not one of its pre-defined values.

h) What Functional radio group property can handle this situation?

_____

_____

i) Does the COST radio group have a property for labeling or titling the group?

_____

_____

j) Can you create a graphic object to indicate to the users that this group of radio buttons describes the course's cost? Which ones can you use?

k) If there were 6 values for the COST item, would it still be appropriate to use a radio group? What if there were 10? 20?

5.2.5 CREATE CHECK BOXES

Use the wizards to quickly create a new form based on the Grade_Type_ Weight table. Include the audit columns in the block, but do not display them on the canvas. Enforce data integrity should be **unchecked.** Choose Form as your layout style. Rename the canvas and its frame GRADE_TYPE_ WEIGHT.

The purpose of this Exercise is to learn about check boxes, so do not be overly concerned if the layout is unattractive.

Change the GRADE_TYPE_WEIGHT.DROP_LOWEST item's property to Check Box.

a) Which of the DROP_LOWEST item's Functional properties allow you to set the value that will be inserted or updated to the database?

b) If the allowable values for DROP_LOWEST are Y and N (Yes and No), what should you enter for Value When Checked? Value When Unchecked? Why?

c) What are the three values of the `Check Box Mapping of Other Values` property? Give a brief description of what you think each means.

Set the `DROP_LOWEST` item's `Check Box Mapping of Other Values` property to `Not Allowed`. Run the form.

d) What was the error you received just before the Forms Runtime started? If you were unable to see the error message, minimize the Forms Runtime and navigate to the Form Builder.

Set the `DROP_LOWEST` item's `Check Box Mapping of Other Values` property to `Checked` and run the form to confirm that the error has been corrected.

Set the `DROP_LOWEST` item's `Width` property to `90`. Set the `DROP_LOW-EST` item's `Label` property to `Drop Lowest Grade`.

e) What is the difference between the `DROP_LOWEST` item's `Prompt` property and its `Label` property?

f) Are there any check box-related triggers? Check the Smart Triggers to find your answer.

LAB 5.2 EXERCISE ANSWERS

5.2.1 ANSWERS

a) What should you do when you select from the Tool Palette to make the creation of the buttons easier?

Answer: Double-click the `Button` *tool to pin it.*

b) What should you set on the Layout Editor's toolbar to make sure that these buttons are assigned to the CONTROL block?

Answer: Set the `Block` *list item on the Layout Editor's Utility toolbar to* CONTROL.

c) Edit the properties so that the text on the button matches its name in the Object Navigator. Which property did you use?

Answer: You should have used the `Label` *property.*

The `Label` property positions text on the button itself. The button also has a `Prompt` property that, as with other items, will position text somewhere next to the item. You should always use labels for buttons. However, these labels don't always have to be textual; it is possible to put icons on buttons as well.

■ *FOR EXAMPLE:*

Select the `Save` button in `R_COURSE.fmb` and locate its `Iconic` property. Change `Iconic` to `Yes`, and change `Icon Name` to `Save`. Look at the `Save` button in the Layout Editor and note how the text has been replaced by an icon. If you were to use this icon, you would obviously have to adjust the size and position of the button to make it look better. But for now, simply leave it as it is.

When you installed Oracle Developer, a number of sample icon files were installed along with it. They should be in your `\ORACLE_HOME\tools\devdem60\bin\icon` directory. The Form Builder and Forms Runtime are able to find these icon files because an entry in the Windows Registry points to this directory. For more information about the Registry, see Appendix B.

d) Which item has the Forms Runtime navigated to (where is the cursor)? Why is Forms doing this?

Answer: Forms has navigated to the `Save` *button because it is listed first in the Object Navigator.*

Exit the running form and return to the Form Builder.

e)   What should you do to prevent the button from being navigated to first?

Answer: You should reposition the CONTROL *block after the* COURSE *block.*

This will prevent the form from navigating to these buttons before it navigates to the enterable items in the COURSE block.

You should also set the Mouse Navigate button to No. Users will still be able to click the buttons, but the cursor will not rest on a button; it will return to the previous item. If the cursor can rest on a button, it may prevent the user from performing some operations. A form, for instance, will not allow a user to issue a query if the cursor is resting on a button.

5.2.2 ANSWERS

a)   Which trigger should you create to respond to the event of a user clicking this button?

Answer: The WHEN-BUTTON-PRESSED *trigger.*

b)   What is the title of the window that has just opened and what should you do in it?

Answer: The PL/SQL Editor.

The PL/SQL Editor is the tool you will use to write trigger and procedure code in Oracle Forms. It will be discussed in more detail in Chapter 6, "Triggers & Built-ins."

c)   What is the name of the built-in you should use to exit the form?

Answer: You should use the EXIT_FORM *built-in.*

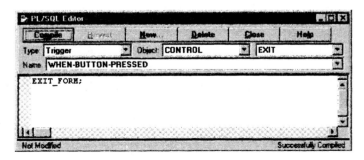

Figure 5.7 ■ The PL/SQL Editor with the EXIT_FORM built-in. Note the semi-colon following the built-in.

Forms built-ins, as stated before, will be discussed in Chapter 6. For now, simply type the built-in into the PL/SQL Editor and click the `Compile` button. If you are having problems, refer to Figure 5.7 to see how the code should look in the PL/SQL Editor.

d) What is the command for saving updated or inserted records to the database?

Answer: You commit updated or inserted records to the database.

e) Which built-in should you use to "save" the changes a user has made?

Answer: The `COMMIT_FORM` *built-in.*

Type the code for the built-in into the PL/SQL Editor and click `Compile`. Close the PL/SQL Editor. Run the form and issue a query. Test the `Save` button by making a change to one of the records returned. Test the `Clear` button as well. Save the `R_COURSE.fmb` form for future Exercises.

5.2.3 ANSWERS

a) Which text item(s) in the COURSE block would be better displayed as a list item(s)?

Answer: COURSE.COST *might be better displayed as a list item because it has only three allowable values.*

b) What list-related properties have been added to the Functional category of `COURSE.COST`?

Answer: List, List Style, *and* Mapping of Other Values *have been added to the Functional category.*

c) What happens when you click the `Elements in List` property and then click the `More` button?

Answer: You are presented with a List Elements *dialog box.*

This is the main tool for configuring a list item.

d) If list elements are what appear to the user, what are list item values used for?

Answer: The list item values are how each item in the list is represented in the database.

Each element in a list is represented in two ways: to the user as a list element and to the database as a list item value. Every list element must have a corresponding list item value. The `List Elements` dialog box lets you set both of these values.

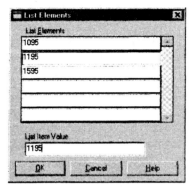

**Figure 5.8 ■ The completed List Elements dialog box for
COURSE.COST.**

■ *FOR EXAMPLE:*

For the list item COURSE.COST, you will have three list elements: 1095,
1195, and 1595. The list elements are what the user will see in the list item
at run-time. These list elements will have corresponding list item values of
1095, 1195, and 1595, respectively. The list item values are what will be inserted or updated to the database when the user makes a change. Figure 5.8
shows the completed List Elements dialog box for COURSE.COST.

Note that in Figure 5.8, the 1195 list element is selected, so its corresponding value appears in the List Item Value field. The values in both fields
are the same now, but as you move through the Exercises, they will change.

e) Can a list element be different from its list item value? When and why might
you want them to be different?

Answer: Yes.

The ability to use list items to represent elements one way and then send
and retrieve their values from the database in another is what makes list
items convenient and powerful.

■ *FOR EXAMPLE:*

The GRADE_TYPE table contains a GRADE_TYPE_CODE column. The values
in this column are FI for final, QZ for quiz, HW for homework, and so on.
If you were to create a list item based on the GRADE_TYPE_CODE column,
it would make sense to represent the values differently from how they are
stored in the database. For example, you would have Final as a list element with FI as its corresponding list item value. Refer to Figure 5.9 to see
how this would look in the List Elements dialog box.

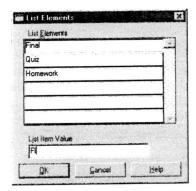

**Figure 5.9 ▪ List elements with different list item values. Note that
Final is selected.**

The Functional category has the Mapping of Other Values property. As
discussed in the Lab text, its purpose is to handle values that are returned
from the database that don't match any of those entered as list item values. That is, if a value that is not one of the list item values is returned
from the database, it will be mapped to the value indicated in the Mapping of Other Values property.

▪ FOR EXAMPLE:

Assume that in the GRADE_TYPE_CODE example, FI, QZ, and HW are the
only values entered as list item values. Also assume that the Mapping of
Other Values property is set to QZ. What would appear in the list item if
the user queried a record in the GRADE_TYPE table that had TEST as the
value for GRADE_TYPE_CODE? TEST does not match any of the list item
values. But, since Mapping of Other Values was set to QZ, the list item
would display QZ's corresponding list element. Then, when this record is
resaved to the database, the column will be updated with the QZ value.

f) Can you format list elements with dollar signs and commas?

Answer: Yes you can.

This is the same as changing FI to Final in the answer discussion for
Question e. The list element does not have to match its list item value
and can contain any combination of characters.

g) Which Data property would you set so that a list item would start at 1595 during an insert?

Answer: You would set the Initial Value *property to* 1595.

If the user is creating a new record, the value in the list item will initially be set to 1595. The value in the `Initial Value` property must be one of the list item values that were entered in the `List Elements` dialog.

LAB 5.2

h) Can you change the COST to 2000?

Answer: No you can't. There is no way to add values that are not on the list.

i) Can you change the COST to 2000 now?

Answer: Yes you can.

There are three types of list items: poplists, Tlists, and combo boxes. In Questions a through g, you worked with poplists, which are the default type. They restrict the user from selecting only from the list elements that are displayed.

A combo box is nearly identical to a poplist in look and functionality except that it allows users to enter values that are not defined on the list. For example, in this case you were able to change the COST to 2000, even though it was one of the list elements.

j) Can you change the COST to $2,000 *and* save the change? Why not?

Answer: No, because COST is a numeric column in the database and will not accept the dollar sign.

k) Does COST still look like a list item? What does it look like now?

Answer: No, it looks like a regular text item with a miniature scrollbar.

l) What has happened to COST? How many of its elements are visible?

Answer: All of its elements are visible in a list.

m) If there were 15 values for the COST item, would it still be appropriate to use a list item? What if there were 20? 30?

Answer: Yes, it would still be appropriate with 15 values, but not 20 or 30.

A good rule of thumb is to limit the number of values in a list item to 15. If the list grows much larger than 15, you should consider using a List of Values object, which you will learn about in Chapter 7, "LOVs and Alerts." For more information on the design concerns for list items, refer to the *Oracle Developer 6.0 On-line Manuals* in the section titled "Designing Effective GUI Applications."

5.2.4 ANSWERS

a) Is COST still visible on the COURSE canvas? Is it still in the COURSE block? Why isn't it still visible on the canvas?

Answer: No, it is not visible on the COURSE canvas. Yes, it is still in the COURSE block.

A radio group is a logical container of radio buttons. Therefore, the group itself is not represented on the canvas because it has no physical properties. For this radio group, you will create radio buttons that have physical properties and are visible on the canvas. The radio buttons serve as a visual representation of the choices in the radio group. In this Exercise, you have already created a radio group called COURSE.COST. Soon you will create three radio buttons to represent the values 1095, 1195, and 1595.

b) What are the nodes under the COST item in the Object Navigator?

Answer: The Triggers *and* Radio Buttons *nodes are under the* COST *item.*

The Radio Button node is positioned here in the Object Navigator's hierarchy so that the Form Builder will know which radio buttons are logically contained by which radio groups.

c) Can you create radio buttons in the Object Navigator? Why might it be easier to create them in the Layout Editor?

Answer: Yes, you can create them in the Object Navigator.

However, it would be easier to create them in the Layout Editor so that you can position them as you create them.

d) What else did you have to decide in addition to selecting the position of the radio buttons?

Answer: You had to select which radio group they would be assigned to by using the Radio Groups *dialog.*

In this case, you only had one radio group created so the choice was simple. If you had created more than one radio group in this form, they would have been listed here. Also note that you could have created a new radio group using this dialog.

e) Are you able to rename them 1095, 1195, 1595? Why?

Answer: No, because Forms will not accept numbers as names of objects.

You must prefix the numbers with something like COST_ or RB_ if you would like the numbers to be included in a radio button's name.

f) Which radio button property should you change so that $1,095, $1,195, and $1,595 appear next to each radio button respectively?

Answer: You should use the Label *property.*

Radio buttons are similar to button items in that they have both Label and Prompt properties. Again, it is customary to use Label for radio buttons rather than Prompt.

g) Which radio button property should you use to indicate its value?

Answer: You should use the Radio Button Value *property.*

h) What Functional radio group property can handle this situation?

Answer: The Mapping of Other Values *property.*

If the database returns a value that does not match one of the values for one of the radio buttons, the form will return an error. However, if the Mapping of Other Values property is set, the unmatched value will be handled by the form.

■ FOR EXAMPLE:

Assume that the radio button values are set to 1095, 1195, and 1595. Also assume that the Mapping of Other Values property is set to 1095. If the database returns a value of 9999 to the form, then the 1095 radio button will be selected as is indicated in the Mapping of Other Values property. When the user commits changes to this record, the COST column will be updated to 1095.

i) Does the COST radio group have a property for labeling or titling the group?

ANSWER: No, it does not.

j) Can you create a graphic object to indicate to the users that this group of radio buttons describes the course's cost? Which ones can you use?

Answer: You can use text or a frame.

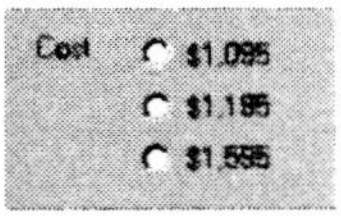

Figure 5.10 ■ **The** Cost **radio group with a textual label.**

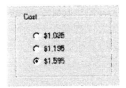

Figure 5.11 ■ The Cost radio group with a titled frame.

You can use the Tool Palette to create a textual label for the radio group as in Figure 5.10, or you can create a frame with a title around the radio group as in Figure 5.11.

In this example, the textual label probably makes more sense since the inclusion of a frame under the rest of the COURSE block's items would look strange.

k) If there were 6 values for the COST item, would it still be appropriate to use a radio group? What if there were 10? 20?

Answer: Yes, it would still be appropriate with 6 values, but not with 10 or 20.

A good rule of thumb is to have no more than six radio buttons in a radio group. If there are going to be more than six, you might want to consider using a list item, which provides similar functionality.

Radio groups are convenient because all of their choices are always visible. There is no need to display or click a radio group to view its choices like there is with a list item or a list of values. But this comes with a cost in that radio groups require a lot of real estate on the canvas. You must consider the space available on the form and the number of other items you wish to display before determining whether or not a radio group is appropriate.

5.2.5 ANSWERS

a) Which of the DROP_LOWEST item's Functional properties allow you to set the value that will be inserted or updated to the database?

Answer: The Value When Checked *and* Value When Unchecked *properties.*

The check box has two states, checked and unchecked, that correspond to the values Yes/No, True/False, and On/Off. In the checked state, the user will see a small check mark in the check box. In the unchecked state, the check box will be empty.

b) If the allowable values for DROP_LOWEST are Y and N (Yes and No), what should you enter for Value When Checked? Value When Unchecked? Why?

Answer: Y *for* Value When Checked, N *for* Value When Unchecked.

A Forms check box is analogous to the check boxes you have seen on paper-based forms. On paper-based forms, you often see check boxes for things like "Add me to your mailing list," "Insured?" "Criminal Record?", and so on, which require that you check the box if you meet the condition stated. The behavior is the same in Forms. The Value When Checked property typically corresponds to the positive or affirmative state, while Value When Unchecked corresponds to the negative state. So in this case, by checking DROP_LOWEST, the user is indicating "Yes, the lowest grade for this type should be dropped." Forms will insert a Y into the DROP_LOWEST column for this record.

c) What are the three values of the Check Box Mapping of Other Values property? Give a brief description of what you think each means.

Answer: Checked, Unchecked, *and* Not Allowed.

The Check Box Mapping of Other Values is similar to the Mapping of Other Values function in list items and radio groups. It is used to determine how to handle those values returned from the database that do not match either of the values you have assigned to the check box in the Value When Checked or Value When Unchecked properties.

■ FOR EXAMPLE:

Assume that for the DROP_LOWEST check box, the Value When Checked property and Value When Unchecked property are set to Y and N respectively. Also assume that a user using a different application has inserted an "M" for Maybe into the DROP_LOWEST column for one of the records in the GRADE_TYPE_WEIGHT table. When a user queries this record, the form will behave in the following ways depending on how the Check Box Mapping of Other Values property is set:

1) Checked—The check box will be set to the checked state when M is returned.

2) Unchecked—The check box will be set to the unchecked state when M is returned.

3) Not Allowed—The form will not be able to retrieve the record. An FRM-40301 error will be returned and appear with a message in the hint line.

In Situations 1 and 2, the form will accept the M value and let the user continue processing the record even though it does not match either of the values specified in the Value When Checked or Value When

Unchecked properties. When the record is saved, the DROP_LOWEST column will be updated with the value in the Check Box Mapping of Other Values property. In Situation 3, the form will reject the M value and not allow the user to process the record.

d) What was the error you received just before the Forms Runtime started? If you were unable to see the error message, minimize the Forms Runtime and navigate to the Form Builder.

Answer: The message reads "FRM-30188: No initial value given, and other values are not allowed (item GRADE_TYPE_WEIGHT .DROP_LOWEST)."

If you decide to set Check Box Mapping of Other Values to Not Allowed, then you must specify an Initial Value for the check box. This Initial Value must match one of the values specified in the Value When Checked or Value When Unchecked properties.

e) What is the difference between the DROP_LOWEST item's Prompt property and its Label property?

Answer: The Prompt *property's value appears to the left of the item, while the* Label *property's value appears to the right.*

As with button items and radio buttons, it is customary to use the Label property rather than the Prompt property.

f) Are there any check box-related triggers? Check the Smart Triggers to find your answer.

Answer: Yes, there is a WHEN-CHECKBOX-CHANGED *trigger.*

The following is optional. To test the behavior of the check box as it responds to a WHEN-CHECKBOX-CHANGED trigger, take the following steps:

1) Right-click on the DROP_LOWEST item.
2) Navigate to Smart Triggers and select the WHEN-CHECKBOX-CHANGED trigger.
3) The PL/SQL Editor will open. Enter the following code:

```
IF GRADE_TYPE_WEIGHT.DROP_LOWEST = 'Y' THEN
     MESSAGE('The lowest grade will be dropped');
ELSE
     MESSAGE('The lowest grade will not be dropped');
END IF;
```

4) Run the form and issue a query.

5) Toggle DROP_LOWEST and watch the Forms Runtime's status line.

LAB 5.2 SELF-REVIEW QUESTIONS

In order to test your progress, you should be able to answer the following questions:

1) How can you communicate the purpose of a button?
   a) _____ With a label
   b) _____ With a prompt
   c) _____ With an icon
   d) _____ a & c

2) How do you make a radio group visible?
   a) _____ You set the X Position and Y Position properties for the group
   b) _____ You create radio buttons for the group and make them visible
   c) _____ You use the Layout Wizard to position the group
   d) _____ None of the above

3) Which type of list item will allow the user to enter values that are not displayed in the list?
   a) _____ Combo box
   b) _____ Poplist
   c) _____ Tlist
   d) _____ List of values

4) Radio group selections are mutually exclusive.
   a) _____ True
   b) _____ False

5) Which of the following items can have triggers associated with them?
   a) _____ Radio groups
   b) _____ List items
   c) _____ Check boxes
   d) _____ All of the above

6) Which of the following is true about the Mapping of Other Values property for a list item?
   a) _____ It will handle the values that are returned to the form but not specified in the list item values
   b) _____ It will prevent the user from entering her own items to the list
   c) _____ It must be set to one of the values that are specified as list item values
   d) _____ a & c

Quiz answers appear in Appendix A, Section 5.2.

C H A P T E R   5

TEST YOUR THINKING

1) Many Windows applications provide "bubble help" or Tool Tips for fields and buttons. How can you do the same in Forms? Add Tool Tips to all the items in the R_COURSE.fmb form. Can you add Tool Tips to buttons just as easily? What is the difference between a hint and a Tool Tip?

2) Use the wizards to create a block based on the GRADE_TYPE_WEIGHT table. Set GRADE_TYPE_CODE to be a list item. Use SQL*Plus to determine all of the distinct values for GRADE_TYPE and create one list element for each. Make sure the list elements make sense to the user and are not just simple codes. For example, if the value in the database is FI, then the list element should be Final.

3) Use SQL*Plus to query the system tables to find out all of the sequences that are defined for the STUDENT schema. Go through the forms R_STUDENT, R_INSTRUCTOR, R_CRSESECT.fmb, and R_STUDENRL.fmb to see which items could be set using sequences. Adjust the appropriate property so that these items are populated by a value from the sequence when a user tries to create a new record. NOTE: Do not do this for items that belong to blocks that cannot be queried.

Go through the forms listed above, but this time, adjust the appropriate property so that all date fields are populated with the current date when a user tries to create a record. Search the help system if you need help.

CHAPTER 6

TRIGGERS & BUILT-INS

CHAPTER OBJECTIVES

In this Chapter, you will learn about:

✔ Trigger Basics   Page 172
✔ Creating Triggers of Various Types   Page 187
✔ Forms Built-ins   Page 213

Oracle Forms applications come equipped with a significant amount of default processing. That is, when events occur, there is always default code that responds. Quite often this default processing is not enough to give the application the functionality your users require. The problem is that you cannot directly access and edit the code for the default processing to make it do what you want. This is why you write triggers: to complement, augment, or replace this default processing.

In this Chapter, you will delve a bit deeper into trigger and event concepts. You will learn how and when triggers fire, and how they fire in relation to each other. You will also write triggers of your own.

PL/SQL language, syntax and structure will not be discussed here, since it is assumed that you have already had ample experience writing database stored procedures, functions, and triggers.

L A B   6 . 1

TRIGGER BASICS

> ## LAB OBJECTIVES
>
> After this Lab, you will be able to:
>
> - Use PL/SQL and SQL in Triggers
> - Understand Trigger Scope
> - Categorize Triggers

In the simplest terms, a trigger contains PL/SQL code that responds to Forms events. You have already been exposed to many triggers and the events that fire them in the previous Labs and Exercises, so you have a general idea of how they work.

One of the advantages of using Oracle Forms and an Oracle database together is that the PL/SQL programming language is used in both of them. So, if you have already written packages and procedures for the database, then you already know how to write triggers in Forms. But, before you begin writing triggers, it is necessary to understand when they fire and how they are organized.

TRIGGER SCOPE

Triggers are always attached to other objects. The level of the object in the Forms hierarchy helps determine the scope of the attached trigger(s). The ON-POPULATE-DETAILS trigger in Figure 6.1 is defined at the block level. It is attached to the COURSE block in the Object Navigator and will only fire in response to events within the scope of the COURSE block.

Triggers can be attached to items and forms as well. Triggers at the item level fire in response to events within the scope of their respective items. Form-level triggers fire in response to events within the scope of the form.

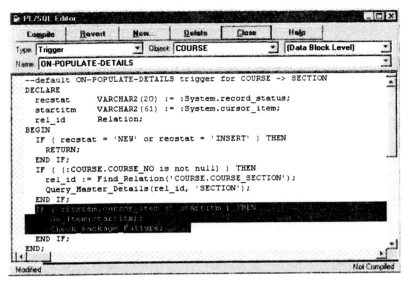

Figure 6.1 ■ **The ON-POPULATE-DETAILS trigger displayed in the PL/SQL Editor.**

Certain trigger types can be attached at the item level, the block level, or the form level. You can attach a trigger at higher levels of the Forms hierarchy to increase its scope.

■ FOR EXAMPLE:

In previous Exercises, you attached WHEN-BUTTON-PRESSED triggers to individual items. You created a button item called EXIT and attached a trigger directly to that item which fired code to exit the form. The trigger's scope was limited to the EXIT button. That is, the trigger only fired in response to the Button Pressed event of the EXIT item (button). It is possible to attach a WHEN-BUTTON-PRESSED trigger at the block or form level. What does this mean? Assume you have a CONTROL block with five buttons and you assign a WHEN-BUTTON-PRESSED trigger at the block level. When will the trigger fire? It will fire in response to a Button Pressed event for *any* of the buttons in the block. What does this mean? It means the scope of the trigger is now at the block level rather than only at the item level.

CATEGORIES OF TRIGGERS

The Forms help system categorizes triggers in two ways: by name and by functional category. Understanding the two methods of categorization will help you understand when and why certain triggers fire, which will

in turn help you decide which triggers to choose when you want to respond to Forms events.

CATEGORIZING TRIGGERS BY NAME

There are five named trigger categories. The first word in a trigger's name
will tell how it will affect Forms default processing and when it will fire
relative to Forms default processing.

The five named categories are as follows:

1) **When** event triggers, which augment Forms default processing.
2) **On** event triggers, which replace Forms default processing.
3) **Pre** event triggers, which fire just before a When event or an
   On event.
4) **Post** event triggers, which fire just after a When event or On
   event.
5) **Key** triggers, which fire when a user presses a certain key.

You would choose the appropriate trigger from one of these categories
depending on what you want your own trigger code to do and how you
want Forms to handle its own default processing.

■ *FOR EXAMPLE:*

Assume you wanted to write some code to respond to the Commit Transac-
tions event which fires each time a form tries to insert a record. There are a
number of insert-related triggers to choose from, including ON-INSERT,
PRE-INSERT, and POST-INSERT. Do you want to replace Forms default insert processing and write all of the insert logic yourself? In that case, use an
ON-INSERT trigger. Do you want to fire some of your own logic just before
Forms executes its default insert processing? In that case, you would use a
PRE-INSERT trigger. Or, you might want to use a POST-INSERT trigger to
fire just after Forms has completed its default processing.

CATEGORIZING TRIGGERS BY FUNCTION

Triggers can also be categorized by the functions to which they are related. A WHEN-BUTTON-PRESSED trigger is an Interface Event trigger because it responds to the Button Pressed event, which, as its category name
implies, is an interface event. ON-INSERT and PRE-INSERT triggers belong to the Transactional functional category because they are related to
transactions and respond when there are transaction-related events. The
Forms help system lists a number of functional trigger categories. In the
Exercises in this Lab, and in the rest of the Labs in this Chapter, you will
focus on the following functional categories:

1) **Query triggers**, which respond to events regarding queries.
2) **Validation triggers**, which respond to events regarding the validation of items and records.
3) **Transactional triggers**, which respond to events regarding inserting, updating, and committing of records.
4) **Key triggers**, which respond to Key Press events.

Each trigger falls into both a named and a functional trigger category.

■ *FOR EXAMPLE:*

The ON-UPDATE trigger falls into both the On event trigger named category and the Transactional functional trigger category.

LAB 6.1 EXERCISES

6.1.1 USE PL/SQL AND SQL IN TRIGGERS

Open the form EX06_01.fmb in the Form Builder. Open the PL/SQL Editor for the STUDENT.ZIP item's WHEN-VALIDATE_ITEM trigger.

a) What typical PL/SQL sections and constructs can you see here?

_____

_____

b) Look at the SQL statement that defines the c_val_zip cursor. How are the block and item expressed?

_____

_____

c) How would you write an SQL statement to select DESCRIPTION from the COURSE table into a DESCRIPTION display item in a SECTION block? The DESCRIPTION value you select should correspond to the COURSE_NO value that is currently in the form.

_____

_____

Look at the STUDENT.EXIT button's WHEN-BUTTON-PRESSED trigger.

d) Is this still PL/SQL? Why or why not?

_____

_____

6.1.2 UNDERSTAND TRIGGER SCOPE

Open form EX06_01.fmb in the Form Builder.

STUDENT.SALUTATION and STUDENT.ZIP both have WHEN-VALIDATE-ITEM triggers.

a) When an item needs to be validated, which of these triggers will fire? Will Forms simply fire both?

_____

_____

b) For EX06_01.fmb, at which levels within the Forms hierarchy are there WHEN-VALIDATE-ITEM triggers?

_____

_____

Run the form. Type Mr. into the SALUTATION item and then press the TAB key. Look at the status line for the Forms Runtime.

c) Which of the WHEN-VALIDATE-ITEM triggers fired? What does this tell you about the firing order of triggers?

_____

_____

Keep the form running, but go to the Form Builder.

d) Are there any WHEN-VALIDATE-ITEM triggers at the item level for FIRST_NAME and LAST_NAME?

_____

_____

Go back to the Forms Runtime. Take the following two actions and watch the status line after each. Type Joe into the FIRST_NAME item and press the TAB key. Type Smith into the LAST_NAME item and press the TAB key.

e) Which trigger fired? Why do you think this happened?

_____

_____

Exit and close the Forms Runtime and return to the Form Builder. View the properties for the SALUTATION item's WHEN-VALIDATE-ITEM trigger. Change the Execution Hierarchy property to Before. Run the form, type Mr. in the SALUTATION item and press the TAB key. Read the alert message, then click the OK button. Take note of the status line.

f) How has changing the Execution Hierarchy property affected the form?

_____

_____

Select the Triggers node under the STUDENT.SALUTATION item and click the Create button in the Object Navigator.

g) Can you create a PRE-FORM trigger here? Why not?

_____

_____

6.1.3 CATEGORIZE TRIGGERS

You will not need to open a specific form to complete this Exercise. However, you may want to have the Form Builder open in case you need to access the help system.

a) What trigger would you create to replace the default delete processing? What named category does this fall under? What functional category does it fall under?

_____

_____

b) Is it mandatory that you write triggers to respond to each event? What happens if you don't?

_____

_____

In the Exercises for Lab 6.2, you will create display items called CITY and STATE for a block based on the STUDENT table. You will also write a trigger to populate the CITY and STATE items with values that correspond to the value that has been fetched into the ZIP item.

c) When should the trigger you write populate these items? Before or after the query is issued?

_____

_____

d) Based on your answer to Question c, what trigger should you create? At what level should you attach it to the form? Search the help system if you are having trouble with this question.

_____

_____

Also in the Exercises for Lab 6.2, you will write another trigger to check that the value a user has entered into the ZIP item is valid in that it exists in the ZIPCODE table.

> **e)** Which trigger should you create? What named and functional categories does this trigger belong to?

_____

_____

In the Exercises for Lab 6.3, you will write two triggers to set the values for the audit columns. These triggers will assign values to CREATED_BY, CREATED_DATE, MODIFIED_BY, and MODIFIED_DATE so that they can be inserted or updated to the database.

> **f)** Should these triggers fire before or after the inserts and updates are issued?

_____

_____

> **g)** Based on your answer to Question f, which triggers should you choose and what are their functional and named categories?

_____

_____

LAB 6.1 EXERCISES ANSWERS

6.1.1 ANSWERS

Open the form EX06_01.fmb in the Form Builder. Open the PL/SQL Editor for the STUDENT.ZIP item's WHEN-VALIDATE-ITEM trigger.

a) What typical PL/SQL sections and constructs can you see here?

Answer: There are Declare, Begin, *and* End *statements, a cursor, and conditional logic.*

The PL/SQL blocks you write in Forms triggers are identical in structure to the code you have written for Oracle database stored procedures. The WHEN-VALIDATE-ITEM trigger includes a DECLARE section for variables, cursors, and so on and a BEGIN statement that is followed by executable commands. Although there are none here, you can also include an EXCEPTION section in your Forms triggers for error handling.

■ FOR EXAMPLE:

The WHEN-VALIDATE-ITEM could have been written a little differently, in which case, it would have had to include an exception handler. Instead of using a cursor, a simple SQL statement could have been used to fetch rows from the database. Therefore, the trigger could no longer use the cursor attribute %NOTFOUND to detect invalid records. It would have to include an exception instead. The code would look like this:

```
BEGIN
    SELECT city, state
    INTO :STUDENT.CITY, :STUDENT.STATE
    FROM zipcode
    WHERE zip = :STUDENT.ZIP;
EXCEPTION
    WHEN NO_DATA_FOUND THEN
    MESSAGE('Zipcode does not exist in Zipcode
table.');
    RAISE FORM_TRIGGER_FAILURE;
END;
```

This trigger is using the pre-defined NO_DATA_FOUND exception to handle instances in which no rows are returned for the SELECT...INTO statement. You are not restricted to pre-defined exceptions, however. You can create your own user-defined exceptions in Forms triggers just as you have in standard PL/SQL stored procedures.

b) Look at the SQL statement that defines the c_val_zip cursor. How are the block and item expressed?

Answer: The block and item are expressed as : STUDENT.ZIP.

Whenever you want to refer to an item and its block in an SQL statement in a trigger, you must express the reference using the following syntax:

```
:block.item
```

Note that this applies to the SELECT...INTO section of the SQL statement as well as the WHERE clause.

c)   How would you write an SQL statement to select DESCRIPTION from the COURSE table into a DESCRIPTION display item in a SECTION block? The DESCRIPTION value you select should correspond to the COURSE_NO value that is currently in the form.

Answer: See description below.

```
SELECT description
INTO :SECTION.DESCRIPTION
FROM course
WHERE course.course_no = :SECTION.COURSE_NO.
```

Look at the STUDENT.EXIT button's WHEN-BUTTON-PRESSED trigger.

d)   Is this still PL/SQL? Why or why not?

Answer: Yes it is.

The EXIT_FORM statement is a Forms built-in. Even though there are no BEGIN or END statements listed here, this is still PL/SQL. If there is nothing to declare in the DECLARE statement, then it is not mandatory that you include a BEGIN and an END statement. You can simply issue a series of PL/SQL executable commands. The STUDENT.EXIT button's WHEN-BUTTON-PRESSED trigger has only one line, which is a simple call to a Forms built-in. It is possible to have more involved PL/SQL triggers that still do not include a BEGIN or an END statement.

6.1.2 ANSWERS

Have form EX06_01.fmb open in the Form Builder.

STUDENT.SALUTATION and STUDENT.ZIP both have WHEN-VALIDATE-ITEM triggers.

a)   When an item needs to be validated, which of these triggers will fire? Will Forms simply fire both?

Answer: The trigger that is attached to the item that is being validated will fire.

The trigger that fires is determined by the scope of the event. The Validate Item event will occur at a specific item. Therefore, only that item's

WHEN-VALIDATE item trigger will fire. This will still be true even if other WHEN-VALIDATE-ITEM triggers are attached to other items in the form. This same rule applies to triggers attached at the block level.

b) For EX06_01.fmb, at which levels within the Forms hierarchy are there WHEN-VALIDATE-ITEM triggers?

Answer: There are WHEN-VALIDATE-ITEM *triggers at the item, block, and form levels.*

In Question a you learned that the same trigger can exist for multiple objects at the same level (i.e., WHEN-VALIDATE-ITEM triggers for each item in a block), but the only trigger that will fire is the one attached to the object. It is also possible to have the same trigger at different levels in the form. In form EX06_01.fmb, there are WHEN-VALIDATE-ITEM triggers at the item, block, and form levels. It is possible to have some or all of these triggers fire. You will explore how to control the firing order of triggers in the following questions.

Run the form. Type Mr. into the SALUTATION item and then press the TAB key. Look at the status line for the Forms Runtime.

c) Which of the WHEN-VALIDATE-ITEM triggers fired? What does this tell you about the firing order of triggers?

Answer: The item-level WHEN-VALIDATE-ITEM *has fired.*

This tells you that the default firing order of triggers is determined by the level of the object in the Forms hierarchy. The trigger that is attached to the object at the lowest level in the hierarchy will take precedence over triggers of the same name that are higher in the hierarchy. In this example, the SALUTATION item's WHEN-VALIDATE-ITEM trigger will take precedence and fire instead of the block-and-form level WHEN-VALIDATE-ITEM triggers.

Keep the form running, but go to the Form Builder.

d) Are there any WHEN-VALIDATE-ITEM triggers at the item level for FIRST_NAME and LAST_NAME?

Answer: No, there are no WHEN-VALIDATE-ITEM *triggers attached to these items.*

Go back to the Forms Runtime. Take the following two actions and watch the status line after each. Type Joe into the FIRST_NAME item and press the TAB key. Type Smith into the LAST_NAME item and press the TAB key.

e) Which trigger fired? Why do you think this happened?

Answer: The block-level WHEN-VALIDATE-ITEM *trigger fired.*

The block-level WHEN-VALIDATE-ITEM trigger fired in both of these cases because there was no WHEN-VALIDATE-ITEM trigger at the item level. The Validate Item event occurred, so Forms went searching for WHEN-VALI-DATE-ITEM triggers. It found none at the item level, so it continued to the block level. It found one there and fired it. This can be very useful if there is logic that you'd like to execute for every item in the block.

Exit and close the Forms Runtime and return to the Form Builder. View the properties for the SALUTATION item's WHEN-VALIDATE-ITEM trigger. Change the Execution Hierarchy property to Before. Run the form. Type Mr. in the SALUTATION item and press the TAB key. Read the alert message, then click the OK button. Take note of the status line.

f) How has changing the Execution Hierarchy property affected the form?

Answer: Now both the item-level and block-level WHEN-VALIDATE-ITEM *triggers have fired.*

The default firing order has been changed so that the block-level trigger is now fired as well, instead of being ignored. The item-level trigger is fired first, then the block-level trigger. As you can tell, the Execution Hierarchy property lets you determine the order in which like triggers at different levels in the Forms hierarchy should be fired. By selecting Before, you indicated that you wanted the lowest level WHEN-VALIDATE-ITEM trigger to fire before any WHEN-VALIDATE-ITEM triggers at higher levels. You can imagine what would have happened if you had set Execution Hierarchy to After.

What would happen if you were to set the block-level WHEN-VALIDATE-ITEM's Execution Hierarchy property to Before? When the Validate Item event occurred for SALUTATION, all three of this forms' WHEN-VALI-DATE-ITEM triggers would fire in the following order: item, block, form.

Select the Triggers node under the STUDENT.SALUTATION item and click the Create button in the Object Navigator.

g) Can you create a PRE-FORM trigger here? Why not?

Answer: No you cannot.

A PRE-FORM trigger is form-specific and therefore cannot be defined at the item level. That is, not all trigger types can be defined at multiple levels in the Forms hierarchy.

6.1.3 ANSWERS

a) What trigger would you create to replace the default delete processing? What named category does this fall under? What functional category does it fall under?

Answer: You would create the ON-DELETE *trigger. This is an On event trigger that falls into the Transactional category.*

Since the ON-DELETE trigger replaces the way Forms would normally delete a record, it is considered a Transactional trigger.

b) Is it mandatory that you write triggers to respond to each event? What happens if you don't?

Answer: No it is not. Forms default processing handles the event.

Form EX06_01.fmb has a number of triggers that respond to events like Validate Item, Button Pressed, and so on. But, think back to the forms you created in earlier Chapters. You did not write any triggers to respond to the Validate Item events, yet the events still occurred when you changed an item's value and then navigated to another item. Forms looked for triggers to respond to the events, but when it found none, it simply executed the default processing.

c) When should the trigger you write populate these items? Before or after the query is issued?

Answer: The trigger should populate these items after the query is issued and the results have been returned to the form.

d) Based on your answer to Question c, what trigger should you create? At what level should you attach it to the form? Search the help system if you are having trouble with this question.

Answer: You should create a POST-QUERY *trigger and attach it at the block level.*

POST-QUERY is a Post event trigger that belongs to the Query group of triggers.

As its name implies, the POST-QUERY trigger will fire each time a record is returned to the block. POST-QUERY triggers can be attached at the block or form level, but not at the item level. If you attach a POST-QUERY trigger to a STUDENT block, for example, it will only fire when records are fetched to the STUDENT block. If you attach a POST-QUERY trigger at the form level of a form that has a STUDENT and an ENROLLMENT block, it will fire whenever a record is fetched into either block.

e) Which trigger should you create? What named and functional categories does this trigger belong to?

Answer: You should create a WHEN-VALIDATE-ITEM *trigger. This is a When event trigger that belongs to the Validation functional category.*

f) Should these triggers fire before or after the inserts and updates are issued?

Answer: These triggers should fire before the inserts and updates are issued.

g) Based on your answer to Question f, which triggers should you choose and what are their functional and named categories?

Answer: You should choose PRE-INSERT *and* PRE-UPDATE *triggers. These are Pre event triggers that belong to the Transactional functional category.*

LAB 6.1 SELF-REVIEW QUESTIONS

In order to test your progress, you should be able to answer the following questions:

1) What is the scope within which triggers fire?
   a) ____ The object they are attached to
   b) ____ The PL/SQL block
   c) ____ The user's session
   d) ____ The PL/SQL Editor

2) When will a block-level WHEN-BUTTON-PRESSED trigger fire?
   a) ____ In response to Button Pressed events for buttons belonging to the block
   b) ____ For every button in the form without an item-level WHEN-BUTTON-PRESSED trigger
   c) ____ For every button in the block that has a WHEN-BUTTON-PRESSED trigger with Execution Hierarchy set to Override
   d) ____ All of the above

3) Where can a WHEN-NEW-ITEM-INSTANCE trigger be defined?
   a) ____ At the form level
   b) ____ At the block level
   c) ____ At the item level
   d) ____ All of the above
   e) ____ Only b & c

4) Which of the following are true about a POST-TEXT-ITEM trigger?
   a) ____ It is a When event trigger
   b) ____ It is a navigational trigger
   c) ____ It will replace Forms default processing
   d) ____ None of the above

5) Which of the following is true about When event triggers?
   a) _____ They augment default Forms processing
   b) _____ They replace default Forms processing
   c) _____ They only respond to interface events
   d) _____ None of the above

6) Which of the following is true about the ON-ERROR trigger?
   a) _____ It fires when you compile code that has errors
   b) _____ It replaces default Forms processing
   c) _____ It is created when the relation object is created
   d) _____ It rolls back the form when errors occur

7) What will happen if an item-level WHEN-NEW-ITEM-INSTANCE trigger's Execution Hierarchy property is set to Override?
   a) _____ All other WHEN-NEW-ITEM-INSTANCE triggers attached to other items in the block will be overriden
   b) _____ All other WHEN-NEW-ITEM-INSTANCE triggers at higher levels in the Forms hierarchy will be overridden
   c) _____ New items will be created in the block to override the old ones
   d) _____ All of the above

8) Which of the following cannot be done with a WHEN-NEW-FORMS-INSTANCE trigger?
   a) _____ It cannot be created in the same form as a PRE-FORM trigger
   b) _____ It cannot be created at the item level
   c) _____ You cannot use the SET_ITEM_PROPERTY in it
   d) _____ You cannot use it to set block properties

Quiz answers appear in Appendix A, Section 6.1.

LAB 6.2

CREATING TRIGGERS OF VARIOUS TYPES

LAB OBJECTIVES

After this Lab, you will be able to:

- Create Query Triggers
- Create Validation Triggers
- Create Transactional Triggers
- Create Key Triggers

There are hundreds of triggers in Forms, and multiple ways to use each trigger. In this Lab, you will learn to write some commonly used triggers. The code you write will be specific to the objects in the STUDENT application, but can serve as templates for triggers you write in your own applications.

QUERY TRIGGERS

The POST-QUERY is often used to populate non-base table display items in a block. These non-base table display items are sometimes referred to as "lookup" items, and are used to make one or more of the base-table items more meaningful.

■ FOR EXAMPLE:

Assume you have created a block based on the SECTION table. You are displaying all of its columns, including COURSE_NO. To make each record more meaningful, you'd like to display the course's description as well. However, the DESCRIPTION column resides in the COURSE table, so you can't include it as a base-table item in the SECTION block. You must, therefore, include it as a display item and populate it with a POST-QUERY trigger. To do this, you would create a display item, name it DESCRIPTION (or whatever you'd like), and use a POST-QUERY trigger to fetch records into the DESCRIPTION item.

The form would fetch a section record into the block and then fire the POST-QUERY trigger. The trigger would then fetch the corresponding course.description from the database and place it into the DESCRIPTION display item.

VALIDATION TRIGGERS

There are two Validation triggers that are commonly used in Forms: WHEN-VALIDATE-ITEM and WHEN-VALIDATE-RECORD. Each serves to validate data entered by a user. In the Exercises, you will write some simple Validation triggers to confirm that:

1) Values entered by a user adhere to the business rules.
2) Values entered into foreign-key items exist in the parent table.

■ *FOR EXAMPLE:*

Assume there is a business rule in the STUDENT application that states that no class can cost more than $5,000. Whenever a user enters a value into a COST item, you want the form to confirm that the value they've entered adheres to the rule. You could do so by writing a WHEN-VALIDATE-ITEM trigger that contains the following code and attach it to the COST item:

```
IF :SECTION.COST > 5000 THEN
    MESSAGE('Course costs must be less than
$5,000.');
    RAISE FORM_TRIGGER_FAILURE;
END IF;
```

The WHEN-VALIDATE-ITEM trigger will fire when both of the following two conditions have been met:

1) The user has changed the value in the item.
2) The user has navigated out of the item.

If the user enters a value greater than 5000 and navigates out of the item, the Validate Item event will occur and the WHEN-VALIDATE-ITEM trigger will fire. Since validation has failed, the user will receive a message and processing will stop.

Validation triggers can also be used to check that values entered into foreign-key items exist in the parent table.

■ *FOR EXAMPLE:*

Assume you have a form based on the ENROLLMENT table. You want the application to confirm that the value entered for SECTION_ID exists in the SECTION table. If it doesn't, the INSERT or UPDATE statement will be rejected by the database. If the database is going to reject it anyway, which is essentially validation, then why repeat the code in the application? For one thing, it makes the application a bit more user-friendly. The user will be alerted to his mistake immediately rather than later at the time of the insert. It also makes it easier to process the error. You respond to and handle validation item-by-item rather than by trying to process the error message returned by the database, which might not always be meaningful.

TRANSACTIONAL TRIGGERS

There are a number of Transactional triggers used to augment or replace Forms default transaction processing. The ON-POPULATE-DETAILS and ON-CHECK-DELETE-MASTER master-detail triggers are considered Transactional triggers. PRE-CHANGE, POST-FORMS-COMMIT, POST-DATABASE-COMMIT, and many other transaction-related triggers allow you to write your own processing logic in and around Forms-level and database-level transactions. In this Lab, you will experiment with two: the PRE-INSERT and PRE-UPDATE triggers. You will use these to set values for the audit columns.

KEY TRIGGERS

Key triggers fire whenever a user presses a corresponding key on the keyboard. If a user presses the down arrow, or the down key, then the KEY-DOWN trigger will fire. Key triggers can be used if you want to change or replace default key processing.

LAB 6.2 EXERCISES

6.2.1 CREATE QUERY TRIGGERS

Use the wizards to quickly create a form based on the STUDENT table. Enforce data integrity on the wizard's table page should be **unchecked.** Include the audit columns in the block, but do not display them on the canvas. Lay the items out in Form style. Create two display items in the STUDENT block and name them CITY and STATE. Position them after STUDENT.ZIP in the block and just to the right of STUDENT.ZIP on the canvas. Size and align them so that they are arranged neatly, but do not be overly concerned with the look of the form.

Use the code below to answer Questions a–d.

```
DECLARE
    CURSOR c_city_state IS SELECT city, state
          FROM zipcode
          WHERE zip = :STUDENT.ZIP;
BEGIN
    OPEN c_city_state;
    FETCH c_city_state INTO :STUDENT.CITY,
:STUDENT.STATE;
    CLOSE c_city_state;
END;
```

a) What two database columns is this trigger querying?

_____

_____

b) How will the POST-QUERY trigger know which record to fetch from the database?

_____

_____

c) Which items are being populated? Which line of code populates these items?

_____

_____

d) Which object should you attach the POST-QUERY trigger to?

_____

_____

Create a POST-QUERY trigger and attach it to the object that was your answer for Question d. Type the code above into the PL/SQL Editor and click the Compile button.

> **e)** Were there any errors?

_____

_____

When the POST-QUERY trigger compiles correctly, run the form and issue a query.

> **f)** Were the CITY and STATE items populated?

_____

_____

If not, look at the Forms Runtime's status line for error messages. Select Help | Display Errors from the Forms Runtime's Main Menu to see more details.

> **g)** What was the error? Why did this happen? What should you do to the display items to correct this?

_____

_____

Exit the form and fix the mistake. Run the form again and issue a query to test the POST-QUERY trigger.

> **h)** Did it populate CITY and STATE this time? What happens when you scroll from record to record?

_____

_____

> **i)** If you were to create a new form based on the ENROLLMENT table, what are some display items you could create and populate with a POST-QUERY trigger?

_____

_____

j) What would the code for the trigger be?

Save the form as R_POSTQ_VAL.fmb.

6.2.2 CREATE VALIDATION TRIGGERS

In the following Exercise questions, you will write a Validation trigger for STUDENT.ZIP in the R_POST_VAL.fmb form. The trigger will validate that the ZIP value a user wishes to insert or update exists in the Zipcode table. Use the code below to answer Questions a–e.

```
DECLARE
    v_invalid BOOLEAN;
    CURSOR c_val_zip IS SELECT city, state
    FROM zipcode
    WHERE zip = :STUDENT.ZIP;
BEGIN
    OPEN c_val_zip;
    FETCH c_val_zip INTO :STUDENT.CITY, :STUDENT.STATE;
    v_invalid := c_val_zip%NOTFOUND;
    IF v_invalid THEN
            MESSAGE('This zipcode is invalid. Re-enter
another.');
            RAISE FORM_TRIGGER_FAILURE;
    END IF;
END;
```

a) What variable are you declaring to help check the validity of the ZIPCODE value? What is its data type?

b) Which line of code assigns a value to this variable? What cursor attribute are you using to assign the value?

c) What will be the value of the `v_invalid` variable if the cursor fails to fetch a row? What will this mean about the value the user has entered?

d) What two commands will the trigger issue if the value is invalid?

e) Why is the trigger fetching values into the `CITY` and `STATE` columns if the purpose is to validate the `ZIP` item? Won't the columns be populated by the `POST-QUERY` trigger?

Create a `WHEN-VALIDATE-ITEM` trigger for the `STUDENT.ZIP` item and enter the code above. Compile the trigger. Run the form and issue a query. Change the value in the `ZIP` item to `123` and press the TAB key.

f) Has the `WHEN-VALIDATE-ITEM` trigger fired? What two things about the form's behavior indicate that it has?

g) What Forms object could you attach to this item to help the user choose a valid Zip Code?

Save the changes to form R_POSTQ_VAL.fmb.

Use the wizards to quickly create a form based on the SECTION table. En-force data integrity on the wizard's table page should be **unchecked.** Include the audit columns in the block, but do not display them on the canvas. Lay the items out in Form style.

Assume that there is a building called L5 on the STUDENT campus. The rooms in this building can only seat 15 students or less. In the SECTION table's LO-CATION column, all of the rooms in the L5 building are named L501, L502, and so on. When users are inserting or updating section records, you want to prevent them from making the CAPACITY greater than 15 for any room in the L5 building.

h) Could you write a Validation trigger to enforce this rule? What would the code be? **Write your answer on paper first.** The trig-ger code should not be overcomplicated. You should be able to do it in three simple statements.

_____

_____

i) If you use a WHEN-VALIDATE-ITEM trigger, which item could the trigger code be attached to? Do not create the trigger, simply write down your answer.

_____

_____

j) If your answer to Question i was CAPACITY, when will the WHEN-VALIDATE-ITEM trigger fire?

_____

_____

k) If the user inserted a new row, what would happen if the user set CAPACITY to 25 first and then set LOCATION to L501? Would the validation take place? Why not?

_____

_____

l) Which Validation trigger could you create to make sure that the trigger fires for each record? Which object should you attach it to? Create the trigger, enter the code, and test the form.

_____

_____

You do not need to save this form as you will not need it in future Exercises.

6.2.3 CREATE TRANSACTIONAL TRIGGERS

Use the wizards to quickly create a form based on the COURSE table. Leave Enforce data integrity **unchecked.** Include the audit columns in the block **and** on the canvas. Normally you would not include the audit columns on the canvas. You are doing it here so you can see the outcome of the trigger code. Give the canvas a Form-style layout and set the audit columns to be display items.

Set the COURSE_NO initial value property to:

> **:SEQUENCE.COURSE_NO_SEQ.NEXTVAL**

In this Exercise, you will write Transactional triggers to set the values for the audit columns.

a) Why do you have to write a trigger to set these values? Why not make the user input these values?

_____

_____

b) Should this trigger be assigned to the form or block level?

_____

_____

c) What two pieces of information will you need to get from the system to assign values for the audit columns?

_____

_____

The code for the PRE-INSERT trigger will be as follows:

```
DECLARE
    v_block         VARCHAR2(30);
    v_username      VARCHAR2(30);
    v_date          DATE;
BEGIN
  v_username := GET_APPLICATION_PROPERTY(USERNAME);
  v_date := SYSDATE;
  v_block := :SYSTEM.CURSOR_BLOCK;

  COPY(v_date, v_block||'.CREATED_DATE');
  COPY(v_username,  v_block||'.CREATED_BY');
  COPY(v_date, v_block||'.MODIFIED_DATE');
  COPY(v_username,  v_block||'.MODIFIED_BY');
END;
```

d) Which built-in is being used to get the user's name?

_____

_____

e) How is the value of v_block assigned?

_____

_____

f) What parameters are being passed to the COPY built-in?

_____

_____

Create the PRE-INSERT trigger at the form level and enter the code above. Run the form and try to insert a new record.

g) Did the trigger work? How do you know?

h) What trigger should you create to set MODIFIED_BY and MOD-IFIED_DATE every time a record is changed?

i) What will the code be for this trigger?

j) Could you reuse these triggers exactly as they are for forms with SECTION blocks? STUDENT blocks? Any block?

Save this form as R_TRANS.fmb.

6.2.4 CREATE KEY TRIGGERS

In this Exercise, you will create a simple Key trigger for response when the user clicks the Execute Query button on the keyboard.

You will also explore a Key trigger that is written by the Form Builder when you select Enforce data integrity in the Data Block Wizard. This KEY-DELREC trigger is written whenever primary-foreign key constraints exist in the database that correspond to one of the items in the block.

Open EX06_02.fmb in the Form Builder. Use the Object Navigator to create a form-level KEY-EXEQRY trigger. Add the following statement to the trigger:

MESSAGE ('You have pressed the F8 key to execute a query') ;

Run the form and press the F8 key on the keyboard to test the trigger. Exit the form after you have tested the trigger to return to the Form Builder.

**LAB
6.2**

> **a)** Did the Key trigger respond when the key was pressed? Why didn't the form execute a query?

_____

_____

Add the EXECUTE_QUERY statement to the end of the KEY-EXEQRY trigger. The trigger should now be as follows:

**MESSAGE ('You have pressed the F8 key to execute a query') ;
EXECUTE_QUERY ;**

Create a WHEN-BUTTON-PRESSED trigger for the ZIPCODE.EXECUTE_QUERY button. Add the following statement:

EXECUTE_QUERY ;

Run the form and press the F8 key on the keyboard to confirm that the query has been executed. Now click the Execute Query button.

> **b)** Was the message text issued along with the query? Why not?

_____

_____

Change the code in the WHEN-BUTTON-PRESSED trigger to the following:

DO_KEY ('EXECUTE_QUERY') ;

Run the form and test the Execute Query button.

> **c)** What function did the DO_KEY built-in provide?

_____

_____

Study the code for the ZIPCODE block's KEY-DELREC trigger.

d) What function will this trigger perform?

_____

_____

Run the form. Click the Enter Query button on the toolbar to put the form into Enter_Query mode. Issue a query for the Zip Code 06605. Click the Remove Record button on the toolbar.

e) Did the KEY-DELREC trigger fire? What built-in must the trigger associated with the Remove Record button use to make this happen?

_____

_____

LAB 6.2 ANSWERS

6.2.1 ANSWERS

a) What two database columns is this trigger querying?

Answer: It is querying the CITY and STATE columns in the ZIPCODE table.

The cursor c_city_state defines the query, which will fetch the values to populate the display items CITY and STATE. In this case, the SQL statement is rather simple. It is merely selecting two columns from the same table. Statements can be much more complicated in that they can include more columns, joins, complicated WHERE clauses, and so on.

b) How will the POST-QUERY trigger know which record to fetch from the database?

Answer: The WHERE clause indicates that the ZIP in the ZIPCODE table should correspond with the ZIP item in the STUDENT block.

Note that the item is expressed as: block.item, which is the same syntax you learned in Lab 6.1.

c) Which items are being populated? Which line of code populates these items?

Answer: The CITY and STATE items in the STUDENT block are being populated. They are populated with the following line of code:

```
FETCH c_city_state INTO :STUDENT.CITY, :STUDENT.STATE;
```

The cursor fetches the records directly into the items CITY and STATE. Instead of using a cursor, the POST-QUERY trigger can also be written using a SELECT...INTO statement like the following:

```
SELECT city, state
INTO :STUDENT.CITY, :STUDENT.STATE
FROM zipcode
WHERE zipcode = :STUDENT.ZIP;
```

d) Which object should you attach the POST-QUERY trigger to?

Answer: You should attach the POST-QUERY *trigger to the* STUDENT *block.*

In this case, the POST-QUERY trigger applies only to the STUDENT block, so it should be attached to the STUDENT block. It is possible to attach POST-QUERY triggers at the form level, but that only makes sense if you want the trigger to apply to all of the blocks in the form.

e) Were there any errors?

If there were some errors, perhaps you made a small typo. Compare your code with that in Figure 6.2. Also, take a moment to study the buttons in the PL/SQL Editor.

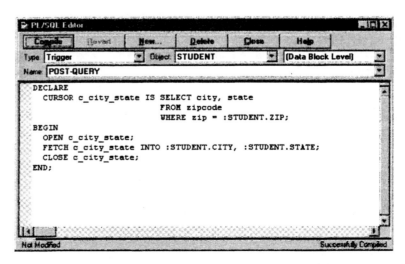

Figure 6.2 ■ The PL/SQL Editor showing a successfully compiled POST-QUERY trigger.

You have already worked with the PL/SQL Editor in previous Chapters, and have probably found that it is a rather simple, yet handy, tool for writing code. Now that your triggers are becoming more complicated, it is worth a bit more exploration.

THE PL/SQL EDITOR

Refer to Figure 6.2. The buttons across the top of the PL/SQL Editor's window are self-explanatory and do not require discussion. Just below the buttons are three list items: Type, Object, and one with no label. As you can see, these indicate the type of PL/SQL object that you are creating, along with the object to which you are attaching it. In this case, you are working with a trigger that is attached to the STUDENT block at the block level. The Name list item below indicates which trigger you are working with.

The PL/SQL Editor can also help you debug your code.

■ FOR EXAMPLE:

If there had been a mistake in your code, the PL/SQL Editor may have looked like Figure 6.3.

Note that the gray area below the trigger code lists error messages. In this case, the ZIPCODE table was misspelled, so the Form Builder could not find it in the database.

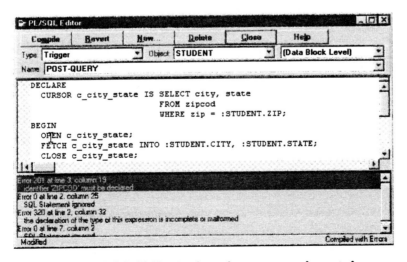

Figure 6.3 ■ The PL/SQL Editor showing errors in a trigger.

You will use the PL/SQL Editor in this Chapter to write triggers and also in later Chapters to write PL/SQL program units.

When the POST-QUERY trigger compiles correctly, run the form and issue a query.

f)   Were the CITY and STATE items populated?

Answer: No they were not.

g)   What was the error? Why did this happen? What should you do to the display items to correct this?

Answer: The error was FRM-40505 Unable to Perform Query.

If you looked at the Show Errors window, you would have been able to see the error in the SELECT statement. CITY and STATE are not base-table items in this block and should not be included in the query. They are non-base-table items, so their Database Item properties should have been set to No.

It is important to remember that, although CITY and STATE are being populated by values from the database, they are not base-table items in this block.

Run the form and issue a query to test the POST-QUERY trigger.

h)   Did it populate CITY and STATE this time? What happens when you scroll from record to record?

Answer: Yes, the CITY and STATE values change to correspond with the value in the ZIP item.

i)   If you were to create a new form based on the ENROLLMENT table, what are some display items you could create and populate with a POST-QUERY trigger?

Answer: You could create display items to show the student's LAST_NAME and FIRST_NAME and perhaps the COURSE_NO.

In these examples, you are using the POST-QUERY trigger to provide lookup values to make the form data more meaningful to the user. In the STUDENT form created above, the ZIP item was much more meaningful to the user when the CITY and STATE values were supplied along with it.

In the case of a form based on the ENROLLMENT table, what values from other tables might make the enrollment information more meaningful? The LAST_NAME and FIRST_NAME would make STUDENT_ID more meaningful. And perhaps the COURSE_NO would make the SECTION_ID more meaningful. You could include even more, like the DESCRIPTION of the course, the INSTRUCTOR_ID, and so on. In the following question, write a trigger that would populate LAST_NAME, FIRST_NAME, and COURSE_NO.

j) What would the code for the trigger be?

Answer: See below.

```
DECLARE
    CURSOR c_student_name is
            SELECT first_name, last_name
            FROM student
            WHERE student_id =
    :ENROLLMENT.STUDENT_ID;
    CURSOR c_course_no is
            SELECT course_no
            FROM section
            WHERE section_id =
    :ENROLLMENT.SECTION_ID;
BEGIN
    OPEN c_student_name;
    FETCH c_student_name INTO :ENROLLMENT.LAST_NAME,
    :ENROLLMENT.FIRST_NAME;
    CLOSE c_student_name;
    OPEN c_course_no;
    FETCH c_course_no INTO :ENROLLMENT.COURSE_NO;
    CLOSE c_course_no;
END;
```

Note that, in this case, the trigger had more than one cursor.

Save the form as R_POSTQ_VAL.fmb.

6.2.2 ANSWERS

a) What variable are you declaring to help check the validity of the ZIPCODE value? What is its data type?

Answer: The variable is v_invalid *and its data type is* Boolean.

b) Which line of code assigns a value to this variable? What cursor attribute are you using to assign the value?

Answer: See below.

The line of code is:

```
v_invalid := c_val_zip%NOTFOUND;
```

The cursor attribute is %NOTFOUND. As you know from your experience with PL/SQL, %NOTFOUND evaluates to TRUE if a cursor does not fetch a record from the database; it evaluates to FALSE if the cursor successfully fetches a record.

Here is where the actual validation in the WHEN-VALIDATE-ITEM trigger occurs. The cursor opens and begins trying to fetch rows. If it is unable to fetch a row that matches the criteria in the WHERE clause, it sets the %NOTFOUND attribute to TRUE.

c) What will be the value of the v_invalid variable if the cursor fails to fetch a row? What will this mean about the value the user has entered?

Answer: The value of v_invalid *will be* TRUE.

d) What two commands will the trigger issue if the value is invalid?

Answer: The trigger will issue a message to the user and RAISE FORM_TRIGGER_FAILURE.

FORM_TRIGGER FAILURE is a pre-defined, built-in Forms exception. It is used to halt Forms processing when an error has occurred. In this case, the user has entered an invalid value in the ZIP item. After receiving the message, the FORM_TRIGGER_FAILURE built-in exception will not allow the user to continue until they enter a valid Zip Code.

FORM_TRIGGER_FAILURE is not limited to WHEN-VALIDATE-ITEM triggers. It can be used in any Forms PL/SQL object. However, it cannot be used in PL/SQL objects that are stored in the database.

e) Why is the trigger fetching values into the CITY and STATE columns if the purpose is to validate the ZIP item? Won't the columns be populated by the POST-QUERY trigger?

Answer: See discussion below.

By fetching CITY and STATE into the form as you validate ZIP, you are killing two birds with one stone. As the user creates new records or edits existing ones, you will want to validate the ZIP value. You also want the CITY and STATE display items to change so that they correspond to the new ZIP value. The POST-QUERY trigger will not fire to populate these items while the user is editing items and tabbing around the form because there has not been a query.

f) Has the WHEN-VALIDATE-ITEM trigger fired? What two things about the form's behavior indicate that it has?

Answer: The message appeared on the hint line, and it is not possible to navigate from the ZIP *item.*

g) What Forms object could you attach to this item to help the user choose a valid Zip Code?

Answer: An LOV.

If the user is having trouble entering valid values, it might be helpful to provide an LOV for them to select from.

h) Could you write a Validation trigger to enforce this rule? What would the code be? The trigger code should not be overcomplicated. You should be able to do it in three simple statements.

Answer: See the code below.

```
IF :SECTION.LOCATION LIKE 'L5%'
   AND :SECTION.CAPACITY > 15
   THEN MESSAGE('Capacity must be less than 15 for
sections in the L5 building.');
   RAISE FORM_TRIGGER_FAILURE;
END IF;
```

Note that the trigger will check two of the items in the form and if both conditions are met, it will issue a message to the user and RAISE FORM_TRIGGER_FAILURE to halt processing.

i) If you use a WHEN-VALIDATE-ITEM trigger, which item should the trigger code be attached to?

Answer: It could be attached to the CAPACITY *or* LOCATION *item.*

j) If your answer to Question i was CAPACITY, when will the WHEN-VALIDATE-ITEM trigger fire?

Answer: It will fire after you change the CAPACITY *value and then navigate out of the item.*

k) If the user inserted a new row, what would happen if the user set CAPACITY
to 25 first and then set LOCATION to L501? Would the validation take place?
Why not?

Answer: No.

Because the trigger is attached to the CAPACITY column, it will fire only
after the user has changed CAPACITY and navigated out of it. It will not
fire when the user changes and navigates out of LOCATION. Therefore, if
the user changes the CAPACITY item first, then changes the LOCATION
item second, the trigger will not fire. This goes back to trigger scope; a
trigger will fire only within its scope, which in this case is within the validation of CAPACITY.

So, what could you do? You could copy the trigger and attach it to both
items, but that would not be very elegant. You could put the WHEN-VAL-
IDATE-ITEM trigger at the block level, but then it would fire for every
item, which would be inelegant and inefficient. Or, you could put a different trigger at the block level. Read the next question for more details
on what you could do.

l) Which Validation trigger could you create to make sure that the trigger fires
for each record? Which object should you attach it to? Create the trigger,
enter the code, and test the form.

Answer: You could create a WHEN-VALIDATE-RECORD *trigger and attach it to
the block.*

The WHEN-VALIDATE-RECORD trigger will fire once for the entire record
when the Validate Record event occurs. So, no matter what order a user
enters or changes the values in the block, the WHEN-VALIDATE-RECORD
trigger will fire and catch any invalid values.

6.2.3 ANSWERS

a) Why do you have to write a trigger to set these values? Why not make the
user input these values?

Answer: These are audit columns and should be maintained by the system.

The purpose of these columns is to keep a strict record of when, and by
whom, each record was updated or changed. If the audit trail is being
kept for security reasons, as well as for record-keeping reasons, then it
does not make sense to allow the user to edit the values.

The most secure method would be to populate these columns with database triggers. But, for the purpose of these Exercises, you will have the form populate them.

b) Should this trigger be assigned to the form or block level?

Answer: PRE-INSERT *triggers can be set at either the form or block level.*

The code you will write in this Exercise will be block-independent. That is, the block names will not be hard-coded into the trigger so that they can apply to any base-table block in the form. Therefore, if you put the triggers at the form level, their scope will be for all base-table blocks.

In this application, all of the base-table blocks will contain the audit items.

c) What two pieces of information will you need to get from the system to assign values for the audit columns?

Answer: You will need to get the user's name and the date.

d) Which built-in is being used to get the user's name?

Answer: The GET_APPLICATION_PROPERTY *built-in.*

e) How is the value of v_block assigned?

Answer: v_block *is assigned using the* :SYSTEM.CURSOR_BLOCK *system variable.*

System variables hold internal information about the form. SYSTEM.CURSOR_BLOCK holds the value of the current navigation block. There are many other system variables that you can reference to get all sorts of internal information like the name of the current item, if the form is in Enter Query mode or Normal mode, the current position of the mouse, and so on.

In this case, you want to get the name of the current block so that you can set the values for the audit items appropriately.

f) What parameters are being passed to the COPY built-in?

Answer: A value and a block.item *name.*

The COPY built-in takes a value and copies it somewhere else. Here, you are copying the value in the variable into one of the audit items. You could also use the COPY built-in to copy the value in one variable into another variable.

The value for each of the audit items could have been set without the COPY built-in using the following syntax:

```
:COURSE.CREATED_BY := v_username;
```

While this method would work, it is not block-independent since you had to hard-code the block name into the statement.

g) Did the trigger work? How do you know?

Answer: Yes, a Transaction complete one record applied and saved *message appeared in the hint line.*

Also note that the values appeared in the items in the form. This, however, is not an indication that the insert succeeded in the database. This merely indicates that the values were successfully populated in the items. The PRE-INSERT trigger fires before an insert. The code you have written in the PRE-INSERT only assigns values to items in the form; it does nothing to make sure that those values are inserted to the database. Once the PRE-INSERT trigger has completed, Forms continues with its default insert processing. Forms writes an INSERT statement that includes every data item in the block and sends it off to the database.

h) What trigger should you create to set MODIFIED_BY and MODIFIED_DATE every time a record is changed?

Answer: You should use a PRE-UPDATE *trigger.*

i) What will the code be for this trigger?

Answer: See the code below.

```
DECLARE
    v_block          VARCHAR2(30);
    v_username       VARCHAR2(30);
    v_date           DATE;
BEGIN
    v_username := GET_APPLICATION_PROPERTY(USERNAME);
    v_date := SYSDATE;
    v_block := :SYSTEM.CURSOR_BLOCK;
    COPY(v_date, v_block||'.MODIFIED_DATE');
    COPY(v_username,  v_block||'.MODIFIED_BY');
END;
```

Note that the only difference is that the CREATED_BY and CREATED_DATE items are not being populated here.

j) Could you reuse these triggers exactly as they are for forms with SECTION blocks? STUDENT blocks? Any block?

Answer: Yes you could.

Since you didn't hard-code the block names into the triggers, you have made them portable across forms.

Save this form as R_TRANS.fmb.

6.2.4 ANSWERS

a) Did the Key trigger respond when the key was pressed? Why didn't the form execute a query?

Answer: Yes, the trigger responded.

The MESSAGE statement that was written to the trigger was successfully executed. However, the form didn't execute a query. Key triggers, like On triggers, replace Forms default processing, so the original default processing will not occur. To augment the default processing of a keystroke, you must remember to manually enter the necessary code.

■ FOR EXAMPLE:

For the KEY-EXEQRY trigger to reproduce the default processing, the code must be as follows:

```
MESSAGE('You have pressed the F8 key to execute a query');
EXECUTE_QUERY;
```

b) Was the message text issued along with the query? Why not?

Answer: No it was not.

The WHEN-BUTTON-PRESSED trigger is not aware of the code that is in the KEY-EXEQRY trigger, so of course it will not fire the MESSAGE statement. The problem here is that the application will behave differently if the user executes a query by pressing the F8 key on the keyboard, or if they click the Execute Query button on the screen. In almost all cases, you will want the behavior to be the same no matter how the user chooses to issue a query. This is not only true for executing queries, but for all instances when you decide to use Key triggers. Question c will help you find a solution to this problem.

Change the code in the WHEN-BUTTON-PRESSED trigger to the following:

```
DO_KEY('EXECUTE_QUERY');
```

Run the form and test the Execute Query button.

c) What function did the DO_KEY built-in provide?

Answer: The DO_KEY built-in fired the KEY-EXEQRY trigger.

When executed, DO_KEY fires the Key trigger associated with the built-in it has accepted as its parameter.

■ *FOR EXAMPLE:*

If you issue the statement

```
DO_KEY('COMMIT_FORM');
```

the KEY-COMMIT trigger will fire.

If you issue the statement

```
DO_KEY('ENTER_QUERY');
```

the KEY-ENTQRY trigger will fire.

Study the code for the ZIPCODE block's KEY-DELREC trigger.

d) What function will this trigger perform?

Answer: See the discussion below.

The form will prevent the current record from being marked for deletion if that record has child records in another table.

Run the form. Click the Enter Query button on the toolbar to put the form into Enter Query mode. Issue a query for the Zip Code 06605. Click the Remove Record button on the toolbar.

e) Did the KEY-DELREC trigger fire? What built-in must the trigger associated with the Remove Record button use to make this happen?

Answer: Yes, the DO_KEY *built-in was used.*

This example illustrates the usefulness of the DO_KEY built-in. The default processing for the deletion of a record has been overwritten and replaced with a KEY-DELREC trigger. By using the DO_KEY built-in behind the toolbar buttons, the application is ensuring that any Key trigger logic will be fired.

You will use the DO_KEY built-in again when you create your own toolbar in Chapter 8, "Canvases and Windows."

LAB 6.2 SELF-REVIEW QUESTIONS

In order to test your progress, you should be able to answer the following questions:

1) Which of the following is true about POST-QUERY triggers?
   a) _____ They are not valid at the form level
   b) _____ They fire after a record has been fetched
   c) _____ You can attach them to record groups
   d) _____ a & b

2) Where could you attach a POST-QUERY trigger if you want it to populate a display item named STUDENT.LAST_NAME?
   a) _____ To the primary key item in the block
   b) _____ To the STUDENT block
   c) _____ To the LAST_NAME item
   d) _____ To any item in the form that will be queried

3) Which of the following is true about the PL/SQL Editor?
   a) _____ You can use it to write triggers and program units
   b) _____ It will check the syntax of your code
   c) _____ It will indent your code automatically
   d) _____ All of the above

4) When does the WHEN-VALIDATE-ITEM trigger fire?
   a) _____ In response to a Validate Item event
   b) _____ When an item is not valid
   c) _____ When the user navigates out of an item and that item's value has been changed
   d) _____ a & c

5)   Which trigger should you use to validate an entire record?

   a) _____ POST-VALIDATE-RECORD
   b) _____ WHEN-VALIDATE-RECORD
   c) _____ WHEN-NEW-RECORD-INSTANCE
   d) _____ a & b

6)   What is FORM_TRIGGER_FAILURE?

   a) _____ A built-in to respond to the failure of an event
   b) _____ A built-in you can use to crash the operating system
   c) _____ A built-in exception to help you handle errors
   d) _____ An event you can respond to with the ON-ERROR trigger

Quiz answers appear in Appendix A, Section 6.2.

L A B   6 . 3

FORMS BUILT-INS

LAB OBJECTIVES

After this Lab, you will be able to:

*   Use Forms Built-ins

The Forms built-ins are a set of PL/SQL functions and procedures that perform standard application functions. You have already used built-ins like EXIT_FORM and COMMIT_FORM in previous Labs.

In these cases, you simply typed the built-in's name, and in doing so, accepted its default functionality. But, like the PL/SQL functions and procedures you have written yourself, most built-ins can accept parameters. The parameters you pass a built-in will affect its behavior.

■ *FOR EXAMPLE:*

When you used the EXIT_FORM built-in, you didn't pass it any parameters. The code looked like this:

```
EXIT_FORM;
```

However, the EXIT_FORM built-in can also accept parameters that affect what the form does when it exits. It might look like this:

```
EXIT_FORM('DO_COMMIT');
```

By passing EXIT_FORM the DO_COMMIT parameter, you are telling the form to validate and commit any outstanding changes in the form as well as exit the form.

There are hundreds of built-ins in Oracle Forms, and you will learn and use many of them throughout the course of this book. In the next few sections, you will be introduced to some of the more common types of built-ins. A comprehensive list of all the built-ins and their individual functions and uses is provided by the Forms help system.

GET_ BUILT-INS

There are a number of built-ins that are prefixed with the word "GET_". You used the GET_APPLICATION_PROPERTY in Lab 6.1 to get the user's name and assign it to the CREATED_BY and MODIFIED_BY items. The code looked like this:

```
:COURSE.CREATED_BY := GET_APPLICATION_PROPERTY(USERNAME);
```

This specific built-in is used to get information about the application. There are other GET_ built-ins that you can use to get properties about other Forms objects such as items, blocks, canvases, and so on. It is also possible, and quite common, to assign the results of a GET_ built-in to a variable.

■ FOR EXAMPLE:

If you wanted to assign the user name to a variable called v_username, the code would look like this:

```
DECLARE
    v_user_name VARCHAR2(50);
BEGIN
    v_user_name := GET_APPLICATION_PROPERTY(USERNAME);
END;
```

SET_ BUILT-INS

There is another group of built-ins that are prefixed with the word "SET_". As you can imagine, you use them to set certain values.

■ FOR EXAMPLE:

You can use the SET_BLOCK_PROPERTY built-in to set properties about a block at run-time. The following two statements set the ORDER BY clause and the WHERE clause for a block called SECTION:

```
SET_BLOCK_PROPERTY('SECTION', DEFAULT_WHERE, 'INSTRUCTOR_ID = 101');
SET_BLOCK_PROPERTY('SECTION', ORDER_BY, 'SECTION_ID);
```

The SET_ built-ins are accepting three parameters: the name of the object to be adjusted, the name of the property to be set, and the value to give that property. There are SET_ built-ins for other objects in Forms, like windows, items, canvases, and so on.

FIND_ BUILT-INS

In both cases above, you used the SECTION objects' name in the SET_ statements. While this is correct, it is slightly inefficient since Forms must use resources to look up the object by name. Every object in Forms is assigned a unique object ID at run-time. Since you are referring to the SEC-TION block more than once, it is better to refer to it by its ID in the built-ins so that Forms can look up the object more efficiently. To get an object's ID, you must use one of the FIND_ built-ins. In this case, since you are working with a block, you would use the FIND_BLOCK built-in. You would use it to find the ID of SECTION, and then use that ID in the subsequent SET_ statements. The code would look like this:

```
DECLARE
    v_block_id  BLOCK;
BEGIN
    v_block_id := FIND_BLOCK('SECTION');
    SET_BLOCK_PROPERTY(v_block_id, DEFAULT_WHERE,
'INSTRUCTOR_ID = 101');
    SET_BLOCK_PROPERTY(v_block_id, ORDER_BY,
'SECTION_ID');
END;
```

The variable v_block_id is used to hold the result of the FIND_BLOCK built-in. Then, v_block_id is used in the subsequent SET_ statements to identify the object. Now, the SECTION object is only referenced by name once, in the FIND_BLOCK statement. The SET_ statements use the object ID for the SECTION block, which makes the code much more efficient.

LAB 6.3 EXERCISES

6.3.1   USE FORMS BUILT-INS

In this Exercise, you will use built-ins to manipulate the properties of a window at run-time.

Open the form EX06_03.fmb in the Form Builder. Create a WHEN-NEW-FORM-INSTANCE trigger at the form level.

LAB
6.3

a) How can you use the GET_APPLICATION_PROPERTY built-in to get the name of the current form module?

_____

_____

b) What built-in can you use to size the window MAINWIN to 200, 200? Try to do this using only one built-in statement.

_____

_____

c) How can you use the same built-in from Question b to set the title for MAINWIN? The title should be as follows:

'This is form... <FORM NAME> '

At the end of the title, you should insert the result of the GET_APPLICATION_PROPERTY built-in from Question a.

_____

_____

Run the form and test the built-ins.

d) What can you do to refer to MAINWIN more efficiently than by using its object name? Change the code in the WHEN-NEW-FORM-INSTANCE trigger to do this.

_____

_____

e) Would this trigger fire properly if MAINWIN did not exist?

_____

_____

Create a PRE-RECORD trigger for the ZIPCODE block and give it the following code:

    GO_ITEM('ZIPCODE.CITY');

Run the form and issue a query.

f) What was the error you received in the hint line?

_____

_____

LAB 6.3 EXERCISE ANSWERS

6.3.1   ANSWERS

a) How can you use the GET_APPLICATION_PROPERTY built-in to get the name of the current form module?

Answer: See the discussion below.

GET_APPLICATION_PROPERTY is a built-in function that returns a value, so in this case, its result should be assigned to a variable as is shown in the code below:

```
DECLARE
   v_form_name     VARCHAR2(50);
BEGIN
   v_form_name := GET_APPLICATION_PROPERTY(CURRENT_FORM_NAME);
END;
```

There are many GET_ built-ins that allow you to get properties for objects or information from the system. You can use GET_ITEM_PROPERTY, GET_CANVAS_PROPERTY, and GET_BLOCK_PROPERTY as well to find the current value of a property and then act on it. In this Exercise, you will get the current form name property for the application item and then display it to the user in the window's title. In the last Exercise, you used the GET_APPLICATION_PROPERTY to get the current user name and insert it into the database.

Note that the v_form_name variable is a VARCHAR2. This corresponds with the data type of the value that the GET_APPLICATION_PROPERTY returns. The built-in would have failed if you had set v_form_name to NUMBER, BOOLEAN, or another data type. This applies to all built-ins that accept and return values; you must always be conscious of the data type that the built-in is using so that you can write your code accordingly. You may have noticed that when you read about the GET_APPLI-CATION_PROPERTY built-in in the help system, there was information about the parameters the built-in accepts and the data types it returns. This type of information is available for all built-ins.

b) What built-in can you use to size the window MAINWIN to 200, 200? Try to do this using only one built-in statement.

Answer: See the discussion below.

You could have used the following built-in:

SET_WINDOW_PROPERTY('MAINWIN', WINDOW_SIZE, 200, 200);

The SET_ built-ins are similar to the GET_ built-ins in that you can SET_ properties for most Forms objects. You can use SET_ITEM_PROPERTY, SET_CANVAS_PROPERTY, SET_BLOCK_PROPERTY, and many others to set the value of a property.

Note that in the SET_WINDOW_PROPERTY example, the same rules regarding data types of values apply. The syntax for the built-in is as follows:

SET_WINDOW_PROPERTY(object name, property, value);

The object name accepts a VARCHAR2 parameter, so the value must be in quotes. The value in the example above was a NUMBER since you were setting the size of the window. However, the data type of the value can change depending on the type of property you are setting. In the next example, you will set the title of the window, which will require that you pass the built-in a VARCHAR2 value. What this discussion illustrates is that when you begin to use built-ins, it is important that you consult the help files often to confirm that you are using the proper syntax and that you are passing parameters using the proper data types.

c)   How can you use the same built-in from Question b to set the title for MAIN-WIN? The title should be as follows:

```
'This is form . . . <FORM NAME>'
```

At the end of the title, you should insert the result of the GET_APPLICATION_PROPERTY built-in from Question a.

Answer: See the discussion below.

Again, you would use the SET_WINDOW_PROPERTY to set the title. This statement would be as follows:

SET_WINDOW_PROPERTY('MAINWIN', TITLE, 'This is form '||v_form_name);

The syntax is the same as in the SET_WINDOW_PROPERTY statement that you used to set the window size. What is different are the values that you are passing to the built-in.

Note that you passed the v_form_name variable into the built-in. This is very common in that it keeps you from hard-coding values into the built-in.

Run the form and test the built-ins.

d)   What can you do to refer to MAINWIN more efficiently than by using its object name? Change the code in the WHEN-NEW-FORM-INSTANCE trigger to do this.

Answer: You can refer to it by object ID using the FIND_WINDOW built-in.

The FIND_WINDOW built-in will get the window's object ID for you. Then you can use the item ID in the SET_ built-ins instead of the item name. As you learned in the Lab text, it takes fewer resources to refer to an object by its ID than to refer to it by name, so whenever possible, it is more efficient to refer to an object by its ID.

Just like GET_ and SET_, there are FIND_ built-ins for virtually every object in Forms, all of which will return an object's system ID. To use the FIND_ built-ins, you must employ variables of specific types.

■ *FOR EXAMPLE:*

When you declare a variable to hold the system ID of a block, the variable must be of type BLOCK. So, if you want to FIND_ the ID of the ZIP-

CODE block and assign it to a variable called v_block_id, the code would look like this:

```
DECLARE
    v_block_id BLOCK;
BEGIN
    v_block_id := FIND_BLOCK('ZIPCODE');
    ...
```

Variables to hold the IDs of items would be of type ITEM, blocks of type BLOCK, and so on.

LAB 6.3

The code in the WHEN-NEW-FORMS-INSTANCE trigger should look like this:

```
DECLARE
    v_form_name       VARCHAR2(50);
    v_window_id       WINDOW;
BEGIN
    v_form_name := GET_APPLICATION_PROPERTY(CURRENT_FORM_NAME);
    v_window_id := FIND_WINDOW('MAINWIN');
    SET_WINDOW_PROPERTY(v_window_id, WINDOW_SIZE, 200, 200);
    SET_WINDOW_PROPERTY(v_window_id, TITLE, 'This is form
'||v_form_name);
END;
```

Note that a new variable called v_window_id has been created to hold MAINWIN's object ID. v_window_id is set using the FIND_WINDOW built-in. Then, the SET_ statement's v_window_id is used to refer to the window instead of its name. Note that the v_window_id variable is not in single quotes in the built-in statements.

e) Would this trigger fire properly if MAINWIN did not exist?

Answer: No it would not.

The FIND_WINDOW built-in accepts the MAINWIN window object's name. If this window did not exist in the form, you would see the following error when the trigger tried to fire:

```
FRM-41052 Cannot find window. Invalid id.
```

This type of error is not limited to the FIND_WINDOW built-in. You would receive similar errors if any built-in tried to refer to an object that did not exist in the form. To guard against this, it is wise to write the trigger so that it can alert you or the user to the absence of an object.

■ *FOR EXAMPLE:*

```
DECLARE
   v_form_name     VARCHAR2(50);
   v_window_id     WINDOW;
BEGIN
   v_form_name := GET_APPLICATION_PROPERTY(CURRENT_FORM_NAME);
   v_window_id := FIND_WINDOW('MAINWIN');
   IF ID_NULL(v_window_id) THEN
MESSAGE('MAINWIN does not exist. Error in WHEN-NEW-FORM-INSTANCE trigger');
   RAISE FORM_TRIGGER_FAILURE;
   END IF;
   SET_WINDOW_PROPERTY(v_window_id, WINDOW_SIZE, 200, 200);
SET_WINDOW_PROPERTY(v_window_id, TITLE, 'This is form '||v_form_name);
END;
```

The ID_NULL built-in evaluates whether or not the value v_window_id is null. If it is null, it means the MAINWIN window does not exist.

Create a PRE-RECORD trigger for the ZIPCODE block and give it the following code:

```
GO_ITEM('ZIPCODE.CITY');
```

Run the form and issue a query.

f) What was the error you received in the hint line?

Built-ins that have to do with navigation are deemed restricted. That is, they cannot be used in Navigational triggers. The PRE-RECORD trigger is a Navigational trigger, as is PRE-TEXT-ITEM, POST-BLOCK, POST-QUERY, and many others. You are unable to use restricted built-ins like GO_ITEM, GO_BLOCK, and so on in these triggers. As you have already seen, the help system will indicate whether a built-in is restricted or not under the "Built-in Type" heading. The help for triggers will also indicate what types of built-ins they can include under the "Legal Commands" heading.

LAB 6.3 SELF REVIEW QUESTIONS

In order to test your progress, you should be able to answer the following questions:

1) Which of the following is true about built-ins?
    a) _____ They are not valid in triggers
    b) _____ They fire at will
    c) _____ They are PL/SQL functions and procedures that provide standard application functionality
    d) _____ None of the above

**LAB
6.3**

2) What is true about the EXIT_FORM built-in?
    a) _____ You can pass it parameters
    b) _____ It gets a form out of Enter Query mode
    c) _____ It is not valid in WHEN-BUTTON-PRESSED triggers
    d) _____ a & b

3) Which built-in would you use to find the width of an item?
    a) _____ FIND_ITEM_PROPERTY
    b) _____ GET_APPLICATION_PROPERTY
    c) _____ GET_ITEM_PROPERTY
    d) _____ a & c

4) Which parameters can SET_ITEM_PROPERTY accept?
    a) _____ Item names
    b) _____ Object IDs
    c) _____ Property names
    d) _____ All of the above

5) Which of the following cannot be used in the SET_ITEM_PROPERTY built-in?
    a) _____ Variables as parameters
    b) _____ The :BLOCK.ITEM syntax
    c) _____ The Prompt property
    d) _____ Non-navigable items

6) What could you use to get an object's ID?
    a) _____ A GET_ statement
    b) _____ A system variable
    c) _____ A FIND_ built-in
    d) _____ a & c

Quiz answers appear in Appendix A, Section, 6.3.

C H A P T E R   6

TEST YOUR THINKING

1) Open the `R_STUDENT.fmb` form that you created in the "Test Your Thinking" section of Chapter 2 to complete this question. Add two display items called `CITY` and `STATE` to the form. Populate these display items with a `POST-QUERY` trigger. Validate `STUDENT.ZIPCODE` with a `WHEN-VALIDATE-ITEM` trigger.

2) Open the `R_INSTRUCTOR.fmb` form that you created in the "Test Your Thinking" section of Chapter 2 to complete this question. Add two display items called `CITY` and `STATE` to the form. Populate these display items with a `POST-QUERY` trigger. Validate `INSTRUCTOR.ZIPCODE` with a `WHEN-VALIDATE-ITEM` trigger.

3) Open the `R_CRSESECT.fmb` form you created in the "Test Your Thinking" section of Chapter 4 to complete this question. Add one display item to the `SECTION` block for the `INSTRUCTOR_NAME`. Populate this display item with a `POST-QUERY` trigger. The `INSTRUCTOR_NAME` item should contain both the `FIRST_NAME` and `LAST_NAME` of the instructor. The name should appear as follows:

```
Joe Smith
```

Validate `INSTRUCTOR_ID` with a `WHEN-VALIDATE-ITEM` trigger.

4) Open the `R_STUDENRL.fmb` form you created in the "Test Your Thinking" section of Chapter 4 to complete this question. Add two display items to the `ENROLLMENT` block: one for the `COURSE_NO` of the course, and one for the `LOCATION` of the course. Populate these display items with a `POST-QUERY` trigger.

Validate `SECTION_ID` with `WHEN-VALIDATE-ITEM` triggers.

LOVs AND ALERTS

CHAPTER OBJECTIVES

In this Chapter, you will learn about:

✔   Lists of Values (LOVs)   Page 226
✔   Alerts   Page 248

Lists of values (LOVs) and alerts are visual objects with which users can interact. They are different from items in that they appear in their own windows and are not positioned on a canvas.

An LOV is used to present a list of values from which a user can choose to populate items on a form. LOVs can be created manually or by using a wizard. In the Exercises in this Chapter, you will create an LOV and learn about the built-ins that you can use to display it.

Alerts are used to present an important message to the user. Alerts also have buttons so that the user can respond to the message that is being displayed. In the Exercises in this Chapter, you will learn how to create an alert and use the built-ins that you can use to display it.

L A B   7 . 1

LISTS OF
VALUES (LOVS)

> ## LAB OBJECTIVES
>
> After this Lab, you will be able to:
> * Create LOVs
> * Display LOVs

In Chapter 5, "Items," you used list items to present the user with a list of choices. LOVs also present lists of choices to the user, but the lists can be much longer, and they can display multiple columns instead of just one.

■ FOR EXAMPLE:

Figure 7.1 shows an LOV called Sections. It has three columns that display the section_id, course_no, and description values. The LOV was displayed when the user entered the SECTION_ID item and clicked the List of Values button.

To choose an item, the user can select the item in the list and click OK, or simply double-click the item. Once selected, some of the column values from the LOV will be returned to the form to populate text and display items. In this case, the section_id from the LOV value will be returned to the SECTION_ID item in the form.

LOVs serve a number of purposes. They make data entry easier, and they ensure the validity of data. The SECTION table has 78 section_ids. It would be unreasonable to expect users to memorize all of them along with their corresponding course numbers and descriptions. The LOV provides a quick and easy way for the user to reference the available

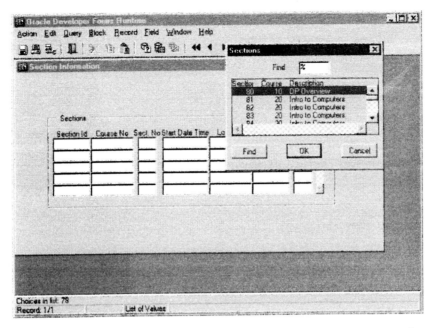

Figure 7.1 ■ An LOV showing section_id, course_no, and description.

section_ids and then select the one he wants. Not only does this help the user, but it also ensures that the value being put into the text item, and ultimately into the database, is valid. By offering the user the opportunity to choose from a list, you are lessening the chance that the user may enter the data incorrectly.

LOVs are usually assigned/attached to text items. In the example above, the LOV is attached to SECTION_ID. When the user navigates to this item, the LOV becomes available and the user can display it and choose from it. In the form shown in Figure 7.1, if the user is not in the SECTION_ID item, the LOV is not available and cannot be displayed. However, it is also possible to configure an LOV so that it is not attached to a specific item and is available no matter where the user has navigated. You will explore and experiment with both styles in the Exercises.

All LOVs are based on another Forms object called a record group. Record groups are logical objects, so they have no physical properties and are never displayed to the user. A record group is similar to a database table in that it stores an array of values in a column and row format. A record group can be based on a query or on a set of static values. The Sections LOV above was based on a record group that contained the following query:

```
SELECT s.section_id, c.course_no, c.description
FROM section s, course c
WHERE c.course_no = s.course_no
ORDER BY section_id
```

In the Exercises, you will use the LOV Wizard to create and configure an LOV. The wizard will also help you create the record group that will serve as the source of your LOV. Once created, you will explore the properties of both objects to further configure them. It is also possible to forego the LOV Wizard and build an LOV manually. Once you have created your LOV, you will experiment with different methods of displaying it.

LAB 7.1 EXERCISES

7.1.1 CREATE LOVs

Open the R_STUDENT.fmb form that you created in the "Test Your Thinking" section of Chapter 2, "Wizards and Files." You will use the LOV Wizard to create an LOV for the STUDENT.ZIP item. This LOV will display the ZIP, CITY, and STATE values from the ZIPCODE table.

a) Based on your experience with the Data Block and Layout Wizards, how do you think you can access the LOV Wizard?

_____

_____

b) As you go through and answer the questions on the wizard pages, what kinds of design-time operations will the wizard perform to create your list of values? Do not over-think this question; the answers are rather straightforward.

_____

_____

The LOV Wizard has 9 pages that you will walk through here. The headings in bold indicate the names of the pages according to the Forms help system. The headings will be followed by questions that refer to that page and the function it performs. After each set of questions, there will be a short statement describing how the page should be configured before clicking the Next button.

Please note that the LOV Wizard has a Welcome and a Finish page that will not be discussed here.

SOURCE PAGE

c) Are there any record group objects in the R_STUDENT.fmb form?

_____

_____

d) If there were existing record groups, would you be able to use one of them here as the source of your LOV? How?

_____

_____

Click the Next button to continue.

SQL QUERY PAGE

The SQL statement will be the basis of the record group, which will in turn be the source of the LOV. The LOV should display the ZIP, CITY, and STATE columns from the ZIPCODE table. The list should be ordered by STATE and then CITY.

e) What does the Build SQL Query button do? Do not use it to build the query, simply click the button to see what it does. Click Cancel when you are done.

_____

_____

f) Can you import an existing SQL statement? Where will Forms look for it? Do not import an SQL statement. Simply click the button to see what it does. Click Cancel when you are done.

_____

_____

g) What should the SQL statement be for this record group? Type it into the SQL Statement field.

_____

_____

h) How can you confirm that the SQL you have written is correct?

_____

_____

i) Should you put a semi-colon after the query?

_____

_____

Click the Next button to continue.

COLUMN SELECTION PAGE

Again, your LOV should display ZIP, CITY, and STATE.

j) Which columns from the record group should you include in the LOV?

_____

_____

Include the columns and click the Next button to continue.

COLUMN DISPLAY PAGE

Adjust the widths of the columns if you'd like, but remember that you can do this later after you have tested the LOV. Adjust the horizontal scrollbar so that you can see the Return Value field.

k) When the user makes a selection in the LOV, which of the LOV's columns should be *returned* to the form? ZIP, CITY, or STATE? In this case, *returned* means taken from the LOV and put into an item in the form.

_____

_____

l) Which item in which block should this LOV column be returned to?

_____

_____

m) How does the Look Up Return Item button help?

_____

_____

Make sure the proper return item is specified, and click the Next button to continue.

LOV DISPLAY PAGE

There will be no questions for this page. Simply follow the instructions below.

Title the LOV Zip Codes. **Leave the** Height **and** Width **coordinates as they are. Select** Yes, let Forms position the LOV automatically **and click the** Next **button.**

ADVANCED OPTIONS PAGE

There are 227 rows in the ZIPCODE table.

n) What would be the difference in behavior in leaving Retrieve Number of Rows at 20, or in switching it to 227?

_____

_____

o) How often do state names, city names, and their Zip Codes change? Do you think it is necessary for the form to issue the record group query to refresh the LOV every time it is displayed?

_____

_____

Leave Retrieve Number of rows **at** 20. **Uncheck** Refresh record group data **before displaying the LOV. Uncheck** Let the user filter records before selecting them. **Click the** Next **button to continue.**

ITEMS PAGE

So far, you have created a record group and created and configured an LOV.

> **p)** How can you indicate that you want the LOV to be attached to the STUDENT.ZIP item?

_____

_____

Click the Next button to continue to the Finish page. Click the Finish button to return to the Form Builder.

Rename the LOV ZIP_LIST. Run the form and issue a query. Slowly tab from item to item and keep your eye on the Forms Runtime's status line.

> **q)** What happens when you tab into the ZIP item?

_____

_____

Every operating system has a "List of Values" key. When the user presses this key, the LOV will open. On Windows operating systems, it is the F9 key.

> **r)** What happens when you press F9?

_____

_____

Note that the CITY column is a bit too wide and that the STATE column is not visible.

> **s)** What can you do to make the LOV easier to read?

_____

_____

7.1.2 DISPLAY LOVS

a) When you displayed the LOV in the previous questions, where was it displayed on the screen? Which of the LOV's properties determined that?

_____

_____

Set the LOV's `Automatic Position` property to No. Set the LOV's `X Position` and `Y Position` properties to 0, 0. Run the form, issue a query, and display the LOV.

b) Where is the LOV displayed? Are the X and Y positions relative to the canvas, the window, or the entire screen?

_____

_____

Exit the form and return to the Form Builder.

c) What is the property that will display the LOV as soon as the user navigates to the `STUDENT.ZIP` item? Do not set this property. Simply write its name as your answer.

_____

_____

Set `Auto Skip` to `Yes`. Run the form and issue a query. Tab to the `ZIP` item and display the LOV. Select any Zip Code value from the list and click the `OK` button.

d) Which item did the form navigate to after it closed the LOV? Why might `Auto Skip` be convenient for your users?

_____

_____

Look at the properties for the STUDENT.ZIP item and note the ones under the LOV category. Assume that the Validate from List property is set to Yes.

> **e)** What will happen if a user manually enters a value into STUDENT.ZIP that is not in the ZIPCODE table?

_____

_____

So far, you have been displaying the LOV by pressing the F9 key on your keyboard.

> **f)** What type of Forms item could you use to display the LOV?

_____

_____

Create a button and name it SHOW_LIST. Label it List. Make sure it is listed as the last item in the STUDENT block in the Object Navigator. Set its Mouse Navigate property to No. Create a WHEN-BUTTON-PRESSED trigger.

Type the following code into the PL/SQL editor:

```
LIST_VALUES;
```

Run the form and issue a query. Keep the cursor in the STUDENT_ID item. Click the SHOW_LIST button.

> **g)** Was the LOV displayed?

_____

_____

Navigate to ZIP and click the SHOW_LIST button again.

> **h)** Did it work this time? What does this tell you about the way the LIST_VALUES built-in displays LOVs?

_____

_____

Exit the form and return to the Form Builder. Select the WHEN-BUTTON-PRESSED trigger in the Object Navigator and right-click to open the PL/SQL Editor. Erase the code that is there and replace it with the following. Click the Compile button when you are finished.

```
DECLARE
    v_lov boolean;
BEGIN
    v_lov := SHOW_LOV('ZIP_LIST');
END;
```

Run the form and issue a query. Keep the cursor in the STUDENT_ID item. Click the SHOW_LIST button.

> **i)** Was the LOV displayed? What does this tell you about the way the SHOW_LOV built-in displays LOVs?

_____

_____

LAB 7.1 EXERCISE ANSWERS

7.1.1 ANSWERS

a) Based on your experience with the Data Block and Layout Wizards, how do you think you can access the LOV Wizard?

Answer: You can access the LOV Wizard by selecting Tools | LOV Wizard *from the Main Menu or by right-clicking on any object in the Object Navigator.*

Note that you do not have to select a specific type of object in the Object Navigator to access the LOV Wizard. However, if you want to reenter the wizard for an existing LOV you must select the LOV you wish to edit, then right-click.

b) As you go through and answer the questions on the wizard pages, what kinds of design-time operations will the wizard perform to create your list of values? Do not over-think this question; the answers are rather straightforward.

Answer: The wizard will create the objects that comprise an LOV and will adjust the properties of these objects.

As obvious as this seems, it is important to reiterate that the wizard is merely a user-friendly tool that saves you from having to create and configure objects manually. Any object you create, and any properties you configure using any of the wizards, can always be adjusted manually using the Form Builder.

SOURCE PAGE

c)   Are there any record group objects in the R_STUDENT.fmb form?

Answer: No, because you haven't done anything to create one.

A record group is like a database table in that it is made up of columns and rows. However, record groups belong to a form and are stored locally on a user's machine rather than in a database instance. The group's structure can be defined in three ways:

1)   By a query at design-time.
2)   Statically at design-time.
3)   Programmatically at run-time.

The LOV you create in this Exercise will have a record group based on a query.

d)   If there were existing record groups, would you be able to use one of them here as the source of your LOV? How?

Answer: Yes you would by selecting Existing Record Group *on the Source Page and choosing a record group from the list item.*

There are two reasons for basing an LOV on an existing record group. First, it allows you to have multiple LOVs based on the same record group. Second, it allows you to base the LOV on a static record group. A static record group is not based on a query. Instead, its source is an array of static values that you define at design-time.

The wizard only creates record groups based on queries; it cannot help you define static record groups. You would have to create and define the static record group manually and then reference it from the LOV Wizard's Source Page.

WHAT THE WIZARD WILL DO ON THIS PAGE: Since you selected New Record Group based on a query, the wizard will create a record group object along with the LOV object. The next few wizard pages will define some of the properties for the record group.

SQL QUERY PAGE

e)   What does the `Build SQL Query` button do? Do not use it to build the query, simply click the button to see what it does. Click `Cancel` when you are done.

Answer: It opens the Query Builder.

The Query Builder is a graphical tool for building SQL statements. It allows you to point and click at tables and their columns to specify the syntax of the SQL statement. It is useful for complicated statements that access multiple tables and columns, or require many joins. It is also helpful for those with poor SQL skills. The Query Builder is unnecessary for this LOV because the SQL statement is rather simple and can be typed in quickly.

f)   Can you import an existing SQL statement? Where will Forms look for it? Do not import an SQL statement. Simply click the button to see what it does. Click `Cancel` when you are done.

Answer: Yes you can. Forms will look for it in the filesystem.

g)   What should the SQL statement be for this record group? Type it into the `SQL Statement` field.

Answer: The SQL statement should be:

```
SELECT zip, city, state
FROM zipcode
ORDER BY state, city
```

h)   How can you confirm that the SQL you have written is correct?

Answer: You can click the `Check Syntax` *button.*

i)   Should you put a semi-colon after the query?

Answer: No you should not. If you put a semi-colon after the query, the wizard will return an `Invalid Character, Invalid SQL Statement` *error.*

WHAT THE WIZARD WILL DO ON THIS PAGE: The wizard will take the query you have written here and store it the record group's `Record Group Query` property. You can edit the query later either by reentering the wizard or by adjusting the `SQL Query Statement` property directly for the record group.

COLUMN SELECTION PAGE

Again, your LOV should display ZIP, CITY, and STATE to the users.

j) Which columns from the record group should you include in the LOV?

Answer: You should include all of them since the requirements call for the display of ZIP, CITY, and STATE to the users.

Why is this page necessary? Why wouldn't you want to display all of the columns you have included in the record group in the LOV? Think back to the Source Page where you were given the option to base an LOV on an existing record group. Essentially, the Source Page is indicating that you can define one query (record group) and use it as the basis for multiple LOVs. There may be columns in the record group that you choose not to display in an LOV.

■ *FOR EXAMPLE:*

Assume you build a record group called STUDENT_REC based on the following query:

```
SELECT student_id, first_name, last_name
FROM student
ORDER BY last_name;
```

There is a requirement that the application must have two LOVs: one that displays a student's student ID, last name, and first name, and another LOV that displays only the student's last name and first name. The columns for both LOVs exist in the STUDENT_REC record group, so you can use STUDENT_REC for both LOVs. The wizard's Column Selection page displays all of the columns included in the record group and allows you to indicate which columns each LOV should include.

WHAT THE WIZARD WILL DO ON THIS PAGE: The wizard will begin to populate the new LOV's Column Mapping Properties property. This property has multiple values, which are displayed and configured in the LOV Column Mapping dialog shown in Figure 7.2.

This property is one of the most important for an LOV because it not only defines which columns will be displayed, but also each column's return item (which item on the form the LOV column will populate) and the width and title for the LOV column.

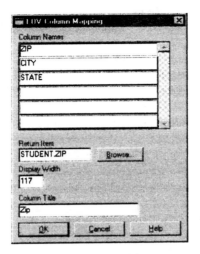

Figure 7.2 ■ The Column Mapping Properties property's LOV Column Mapping dialog.

The wizard configures column display, return items, column width, and the title for an LOV over a series of pages. Once completed, it gathers all of the information you have entered in the separate pages and configures the Column Mapping Properties property. If you were to build or edit an LOV manually, you would configure these same settings yourself in the Form Builder by clicking the Column Mapping Properties property for the LOV to open the LOV Column Mappings dialog.

COLUMN DISPLAY PAGE

k) When the user makes a selection in the LOV, which of the LOV's columns should be *returned* to the form? ZIP, CITY, or STATE? In this case, *returned* means taken from the LOV and put into an item in the form.

Answer: ZIP *should be returned to the form.*

l) Which item in which block should this LOV column be returned to?

Answer: ZIP *should be returned to the* STUDENT.ZIP *item.*

The Return Value field specifies which of the LOV columns and their subsequent values should be used to populate items on the form. On this form, the LOV is displayed to give the users a list of Zip Codes to choose from when inserting or updating a student record. So, the LOV's ZIP column's value should be returned to the form and it should populate the STUDENT.ZIP item.

The CITY and STATE columns are included in the LOV so that the Zip Codes make more sense to the user. But, since there are no CITY or STATE values in the STUDENT table and no CITY or STATE items on this form, it is unnecessary to set return item values for these LOV columns. This LOV only has one return item; however, it is possible and common for an LOV to have multiple return items.

m) How does the Look Up Return Item **button help?**

Answer: It presents a list of available items that can serve as return items.

WHAT THE WIZARD WILL DO ON THIS PAGE: The wizard will continue to populate the LOV's Column Mapping Properties property as it did on the Column Display page.

ADVANCED OPTIONS PAGE

There are 227 rows in the ZIPCODE table.

n) **What would be the difference in behavior in leaving** Retrieve Number of Rows **at** 20 **or switching it to** 227**?**

Answer: If the Retrieve Number of Rows *value is left at* 20, *Forms will only return 20 rows of the result set at a time. If it is set at* 227, *the entire result set will be returned to the LOV at once.*

The way you should choose to set this value depends on many things, including the number of records in the result set, the amount of traffic on your network, and so on.

A value of 20 could increase the speed at which the LOV gets populated, since only 20 rows will have to be fetched from the database at a time. But, it could degrade overall performance since there will have to be multiple fetches to return the entire result set to the LOV. On the other hand, a value of 227 may cause a delay in the initial population of the LOV because it may take a long time to fetch all of those records. However, it will reduce the amount of fetches required from the database, which could improve performance over the long run. The advantages and disadvantages to either choice depend on many factors.

As the text on the wizard page recommends, it is wise to accept the default for this setting. During the testing phase of your application, you can experiment with different values and consult with your DBA and network administrator to determine the best setting.

o) How often do state names, city names, and their Zip Codes change? Do you think it is necessary for the form to issue the record group query to refresh the LOV every time it is displayed?

Answer: They don't change very often and are unlikely to change during a user's session. Therefore, it is not necessary to refresh the LOV each time it is displayed.

If `Refresh record group data before displaying` LOV is checked, the record group's query will be issued each time the user displays the LOV. This will require resources from the database as well as resulting in increased traffic on the network. The values in the `ZIPCODE` table are fairly static and will not be changed or updated very often. Therefore, it is not necessary to refresh the record group each time the LOV is displayed.

However, what if you had created an LOV on `student_id`, `first_name`, and `last_name`? It is likely that the data in the `STUDENT` table will change during the course of a user's session, so it would be wise to refresh the LOV each time it is displayed despite the database and network resources required.

WHAT THE WIZARD WILL DO ON THIS PAGE: The wizard will set the `Record Group Fetch Size` property for the record group. It will also set the `Automatic Refresh` property for the LOV. It can also set the `Filter Before Display` property for the LOV. If set to `Yes`, this property will present the user with a small filter window to let them filter the values returned to the LOV.

■ FOR EXAMPLE:

Assume the user wishes to display the Zip Codes LOV, but they only want to see Zip Codes that begin with 07. If `Filter Before Display` is set to `Yes`, they will be presented with the dialog shown in Figure 7.3. Once they enter their filter criteria, the record group query will be adjusted and then issued. When the LOV opens, it will not include any records that are outside the filter criteria. This will not only make the list more focused for the user, but it will lessen the amount of rows that have to be fetched from the database.

ITEMS PAGE

So far you have created a record group and created and configured an LOV.

p) How can you indicate that you want the LOV to be attached to the `STUDENT` `.ZIP` item?

Answer: Move `STUDENT.ZIP` *from the* `Return items` *column to the* `Assigned items` *column.*

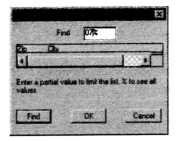

Figure 7.3 ■ Filter Before Display dialog for an LOV.

LOVs are usually attached (or assigned) to the text item or one of the text items that they are to populate. In this case, the Zip Codes LOV is returning a ZIP value to the STUDENT.ZIP item. It should be attached to the STUDENT.ZIP item so that when a user enters this item, the LOV becomes available.

WHAT THE WIZARD WILL DO ON THIS PAGE: The wizard will set the List of Values property for the STUDENT.ZIP item.

q)   What happens when you tab into the ZIP item?

Answer: The words "List of Values" appear in the Forms Runtime's status line.

List of Values appears on the status line whenever an LOV is available to the current text item.

r)   What happens when you press F9?

Answer: The LOV is displayed on the screen.

The LOV has some built-in features, which make it easier for users to work with them. The Find field at the top of the LOV lets the user enter criteria to filter the list.

The user can also single-click on one of the items in the list and start typing the value they are looking for. This will start automatically reducing the list to match the value(s) they are typing.

s)   What can you do to make the LOV easier to read?

Answer: You can adjust the LOV column widths or make the LOV itself bigger.

Both of these changes can be done either by reentering the wizard or by adjusting the properties directly in the Property Palette. It is probably easiest to make the CITY column a bit narrower by setting it to 85 in the Property Palette.

7.1.2 ANSWERS

a) When you displayed the LOV in the previous questions, where was it displayed on the screen? Which of the LOV's properties determined that?

Answer: It was displayed just below STUDENT.ZIP, *which is the item it is attached to. The LOV's* Automatic Position *property determined this.*

The Automatic Position property will relieve you from having to position the LOV yourself. It always positions the LOV just below the item that the LOV is attached to.

b) Where is the LOV displayed? Are the X and Y positions relative to the canvas, the window, or the entire screen?

Answer: It was displayed in the upper right-hand corner. The X Position *and* Y Position *properties are relative to the entire screen.*

Since the position properties are relative to the entire screen, you can position the LOV outside the canvas and window that contain the current items, or even outside the entire Forms Runtime MDI window. This can be helpful if you don't want the LOV to cover any of the items or objects on the form.

The item that an LOV is attached to also has LOV X Position and LOV Y Position properties. The item-level position properties override the LOV position properties. This can be helpful if the LOV is reused on multiple forms and you don't want the application to determine the position of the LOV automatically.

c) What is the property that will display the LOV as soon as the user navigates to the STUDENT.ZIP item? Do not set this property. Simply write its name as your answer.

Answer: The LOV's Automatic Display *property will display the LOV as soon as the user navigates into it.*

Set Auto Skip to Yes. Run the form and issue a query. Tab to the ZIP item and display the LOV. Select any Zip Code value from the list and click the OK button.

d) Which item did the form navigate to after it closed the LOV? Why might `Auto Skip` be convenient for your users?

Answer: It navigated to the PHONE item instead of returning to the ZIP item.

This could be helpful to users in that it saves them from having to tab out of the field after they have made their LOV selection. In most cases, you are assuming that after the user has selected from the LOV, she will not have to edit the value that has been returned to the item. Therefore, it is not necessary to return the LOV's item. The form should automatically skip to the next item to speed data entry.

e) What will happen if a user manually enters a value into `STUDENT.ZIP` that is not in the `ZIPCODE` table?

Answer: The LOV will open and the user will not be able to navigate out of the item until a valid value has either been entered or selected from the list.

f) What type of Forms item could you use to display the LOV?

Answer: You could use a button.

g) Was the LOV displayed?

Answer: No it was not.

Navigate to `ZIP` and click the `SHOW_LIST` button again.

h) Did it work this time? What does this tell you about the way the `LIST_VAL-UES` built-in displays LOVs?

Answer: See discussion below.

You may have already guessed that `LIST_VALUES` is a built-in that is used to display LOVs. In fact, it is the same built-in that was being used when you were pressing the F9 key in the previous questions.

`LIST_VALUES` will only work if there is an LOV attached to the current item. The cursor must be in an item that has an LOV attached to it for `LIST_VALUES` to work. In the instructions for this question, you were asked to set the `SHOW_LIST` button's `Mouse Navigate` property to `No`. Why was this necessary? If the cursor is able to rest on the button, then the button becomes the current item. Is the LOV attached to the `SHOW_LIST` button? No, it is attached to the `ZIP` text item. The `Mouse Navigate` property prevented the cursor from navigating to `SHOW_LIST` and allowed the `LIST_VALUES` built-in to open the LOV.

While this is acceptable behavior, it creates a small problem. The user must use the mouse to click the button to open the LOV. He cannot simply press the ENTER key to open the LOV, which may be more convenient during data entry. You can get around this by adjusting the WHEN-BUTTON-PRESSED trigger slightly.

■ FOR EXAMPLE:

Change the trigger code so that it now looks like this:

```
GO_ITEM('STUDENT.ZIP');
LIST_VALUES;
```

Run the form and issue a query. Tab through the items until the cursor rests on the SHOW_LIST button and press the ENTER key. The LOV should be displayed. The GO_ITEM built-in causes the form to navigate to the STUDENT.ZIP item so that the LIST_VALUES built-in functions properly.

Select the WHEN-BUTTON-PRESSED trigger in the Object Navigator and right-click to open the PL/SQL Editor. Erase the code that is there and replace it with the following code. Click the Compile button when you are finished.

```
DECLARE
    v_lov boolean;
BEGIN
    v_lov := SHOW_LOV('ZIP_LIST');
END;
```

i)   Was the LOV displayed? What does this tell you about the way the SHOW_LOV built-in displays LOVs?

Answer: See discussion below.

The SHOW_LOV built-in is also used to display LOVs, but its functionality is slightly different from that of LIST_VALUES. It does not require that the LOV be attached to an item and it allows you to call an LOV explicitly by name. Note that the parameter for SHOW_LOV is ZIP_LIST, the name of the LOV. Another interesting feature is that SHOW_LOV is a Boolean function that will return TRUE if the user picks a value from the LOV and FALSE if they press the LOV's Cancel button. This can be useful to augment processing depending on the user's behavior.

■ FOR EXAMPLE:

You can have the form issue messages depending on whether or not the user selects a value from the LOV. Edit the code for the WHEN-BUTTON-PRESSED trigger so that it appears as it does below:

```
DECLARE
     v_lov boolean;
BEGIN
     IF NOT SHOW_LOV('ZIP_LIST')
          THEN MESSAGE ('The user cancelled the
LOV');
     ELSE MESSAGE ('The user selected from the LOV');
     END IF;
END;
```

Run the form and issue a query. Experiment with selecting from the LOV and simply canceling it. Note the different messages that appear on the status line. The commands you put into the THEN and ELSE expressions can be as simple as these or more complicated, depending on how you want the form to react.

LAB 7.1 SELF-REVIEW QUESTIONS

In order to test your progress, you should be able to answer the following questions:

1) What is the difference between an LOV and list item?
   a) ____ LOVs open in a separate window, list items are positioned on a canvas
   b) ____ LOVs are suited for many rows, list items should be limited to 15 rows
   c) ____ LOVs show multiple columns, list items show only one
   d) ____ All of the above

2) Upon which Forms object are LOVs based?
   a) ____ Block
   b) ____ Record group
   c) ____ Query
   d) ____ Item

3) How can you create an LOV?
   a) ____ Manually
   b) ____ Using the Layout Wizard
   c) ____ Using the LOV Wizard
   d) ____ a & c

4) How can you size an LOV window?
    a) _____ Using the Property Palette
    b) _____ Using the Layout Editor
    c) _____ Using the LOV Wizard
    d) _____ a & c
    e) _____ a, b, & c

5) How do you populate a form item with a selection from an LOV?
    a) _____ Using a SELECT . . . INTO statement
    b) _____ Using a return item
    c) _____ You can't
    d) _____ Using a record group

6) An LOV must be refreshed each time it is displayed.
    a) _____ True
    b) _____ False

7) Which of the following built-ins will display an LOV?
    a) _____ LIST_VALUES
    b) _____ FIND_LOV
    c) _____ SHOW_LIST
    d) _____ a & c

8) What value will the SHOW_LOV built-in return?
    a) _____ The value selected from the LOV
    b) _____ TRUE if the user selects from the LOV, FALSE if they cancel the LOV
    c) _____ The position of the LOV
    d) _____ The LOV's object ID

Quiz answers appear in Appendix A, Section 7.1.

L A B   7 . 2

ALERTS

LAB OBJECTIVES

After this Lab, you will be able to:

• Create and Display Alerts

Alerts are windows that contain messages and buttons. They provide a convenient way to send a message to "alert" the user that something has caused an error, something they have done will have certain consequences, or that something has happened that they should simply know about. In previous Exercises and Chapters, you used the MESSAGE built-in to send messages to the user. It was convenient and easy, but had two limitations: there was no guarantee that the user would see the message, and there was no way for the user to respond to the message.

Alerts overcome these two limitations in that they appear in the middle of the screen and they require that the user react to them. They can also be configured to let the user make a decision as to how to proceed in response to the alert's message.

■ FOR EXAMPLE:

In Chapter 6, "Triggers & Built-ins" you used the MESSAGE built-in to send a message to the user reading, "This Zip Code does not exist in the database. Please re-enter another." There is a chance that the user may miss this type of message since it is a single line of text that appears at the bottom left-hand corner of the MDI window's hint line. You could use an alert instead to display the same message as shown in Figure 7.4.

Alert objects are displayed in the center of the user's screen so they are easy to see. Additionally, the user is not able to return to the form and continue processing until she presses the OK button to respond to the

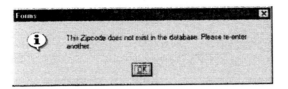

Figure 7.4 ■ An alert with one button.

alert. This ensures that the user will have to read and respond to the messages your application is sending them.

Alerts can have up to three buttons. This allows you to present the user with a message along with choices as to how they will respond to that message. So, the alert in Figure 7.4 could be edited slightly to offer choices as shown in Figure 7.5.

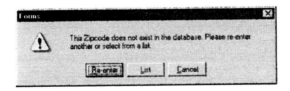

Figure 7.5 ■ An alert with three buttons.

CREATE ALERTS

Alerts are created and configured using the Object Navigator and Property Palette. They are fairly simple objects with only seven Functional properties. You will explore these in the Exercises. Like other visual objects, they have Color and Font properties as well.

Since an alert is a separate window, you do not position it on a canvas. Therefore, it is not visible in the Layout Editor, or anywhere else in the Form Builder at design-time. The only way to *see* an alert is to run the form and display it.

DISPLAY ALERTS

Alerts are displayed using built-ins in much the same way LOVs are displayed with the SHOW_LOV built-in. To display an alert, you would use the following built-in function:

```
SHOW_ALERT('ALERT_NAME');
```

You can pass the built-in the alert's name, as shown above, or the alert's object ID. SHOW_ALERT is a function that returns a number, so to simply display an alert called ALERT1, the code would be as follows:

```
DECLARE
    v_alert_button    NUMBER;
BEGIN
    v_alert_button := SHOW_ALERT('ALERT1');
END;
```

In the example above, there is no code to respond to the buttons: the alert is simply being displayed. This code could be used to display an alert that has only one button like the one pictured in Figure 7.4. When the button is clicked, the alert will close and control will be returned to the form.

When you create alerts that have more than one button, you need to write code to respond to the button that has been pressed. The SHOW_ALERT built-in returns a number that corresponds to the value of the alert button that was pressed. The three-button alert in Figure 7.5 would require that code be written so that the form could respond differently for each alert button. It would look something like this:

```
DECLARE
    v_alert_button    NUMBER;
BEGIN
    v_alert_button := SHOW_ALERT('ALERT1');
    IF v_alert_button = ALERT_BUTTON1 THEN
            --code to let the user enter another value
    ELSIF v_alert_button := ALERT_BUTTON2 THEN
            --code to display an LOV for zipcodes
    ELSIF v_alert_button := ALERT_BUTTON3 THEN
            --code to cancel
    END IF;
END;
```

The constants ALERT_BUTTON1, ALERT_BUTTON2, and ALERT_BUTTON3 correspond to the buttons in the alert.

As with LOVs, and other objects, you could use the FIND_ALERT built-in to get the alert's object ID.

Lab 7.2 Exercises

7.2.1 Create and Display Alerts

The purpose of this Exercise is to create an alert, learn how to display it, and learn how to write PL/SQL code to respond to its buttons. You will use form EX07_02.fmb, which has one block based on the ZIPCODE table and an Exit button. The block and its items are not important to this Exercise, since your goal is to focus on alerts.

Open form EX07_02.fmb in the Form Builder. Create an alert in the Object Navigator and name it EXIT_ALERT.

> **a)** Which of the alert's Functional properties have been set by the Form Builder?

_____

_____

> **b)** How do you think you can change the alert's Button Label 2 property so that it will not be displayed to the user?

_____

_____

Change the Message property so that it reads "You pressed the Exit button." Create a WHEN-BUTTON-PRESSED trigger for the ZIPCODE .EXIT button

> **c)** What code could you write behind the WHEN-BUTTON-PRESSED trigger to display this alert? For this question, your code does not have to respond to the alert buttons.

_____

_____

Run the form and click the Exit button. Note the alert's icon. You will need to know it to respond to Question e.

d) Can you return to the form without responding to the alert?

_____

_____

Click the alert's OK button, then exit the form using the toolbar's Exit but-ton to return to the Form Builder.

e) What icon was displayed inside the alert? Which of the alert's properties determined the icon?

_____

_____

Change the Message property to "Are you sure you want to exit the form?" Change the value of Button Label 1 to Yes and the value of Button Label 2 to No.

f) How should you change the code in the WHEN-BUTTON-PRESSED trigger so that the form will exit if the user chooses Button 1 from the alert? If the user chooses Button 2, send a message to the hint line that reads "You have chosen to continue."

_____

_____

Run the form and test the alert. Exit the form and return to the Form Builder. Set the Default Alert Button property to Button 2. Run the form and display the alert.

g) How did the Default Alert Button property affect the alert?

_____

_____

Exit the form and return to the Form Builder.

h) What built-in could you use if you needed to know an alert's ob-ject ID? Can you set any of the alert's properties programmatically?

_____

_____

i) How could you change this form so that the alert appears whether the user clicks the `ZIPCODE.EXIT` button or the `Exit` button on the toolbar? Do not make these changes to the form, simply write your answer below.

LAB 7.2 EXERCISE ANSWERS

7.2.1 ANSWERS

The purpose of this Exercise is to create an alert, learn how to display it, and learn how to write PL/SQL code to respond to its buttons. You will use form `EX07_02.fmb`, which has one block based on the `ZIPCODE` table and an `Exit` button. The block and its items are not important to this Exercise as your goal is to focus on alerts.

Open form `EX07_02.fmb` in the Form Builder. Create an alert in the Object Navigator and name it `EXIT_ALERT`.

a) Which of the alert's Functional properties have been set by the Form Builder?

Answer: The `Alert Style, Button 1 Label, Button 2,` *and* `Default Alert Button` *properties.*

Alerts are rather simple objects with relatively few properties. The Functional properties define the title, style, buttons, and the message for the alert. You will explore these properties in the rest of the Exercise questions.

The other properties are familiar to you in that they define the color and font of the alert. While it is possible to alter these properties, it is best if you leave them as their default values. A bright red alert with purple text might be more alarming for a user than necessary.

Note that there are no size or positioning properties for an alert. The alert is always displayed in its standard size in the center of the user's screen.

b) How do you think you can change the alert's `Button Label 2` property so that it will not be displayed to the user?

Answer: Make the `Button Label 2` *property blank.*

As you know, an alert can have as many as three buttons and as few as one. Alert buttons are only displayed if they have a label. By leaving an alert button's label blank, you are indicating to the form that you do not want this button to be displayed.

Button labels can be manipulated programmatically at run-time.

■ FOR EXAMPLE:

To set a button's label to Yes at run-time, you would use the following statement:

SET_ALERT_BUTTON_PROPERTY('EXIT_ALERT', ALERT_BUTTON1, LABEL 'Yes');

Change the Message property so that it reads "You pressed the Exit button." Create a WHEN-BUTTON-PRESSED trigger for the ZIPCODE.EXIT button.

> **c)** What code could you write behind the WHEN-BUTTON-PRESSED trigger to display this alert? For this question, your code does not have to respond to the alert buttons.
>
> *Answer: See the discussion below.*

The code would be as follows:

```
DECLARE
    v_alert_button    NUMBER;
BEGIN
    v_alert_button := SHOW_ALERT('EXIT_ALERT');
END;
```

In this example, all you are doing is showing the alert in response to the Button Pressed event. There is no need to evaluate which alert button was pressed since there is only one button on the alert.

This technique is useful if you simply want to display an important message to a user.

■ FOR EXAMPLE:

In Chapter 10, "Reusable Code," you will use an alert to tell the user that validation of an item has failed. No decision will be required of the user, so the alert will have only one button labeled OK. The code to call the alert will be similar to the code above since there will only be a need to display the alert, not evaluate any buttons.

Run the form and click the `Exit` button. Note the alert's icon. You will need to know it to respond to Question e.

d) Can you return to the form without responding to the alert?

Answer: No you cannot.

The alert is displayed in what is called a modal window. Modal means that the user cannot leave the window until she has exited it. You will learn more about modality in Chapter 8, "Canvases and Windows." In the case of alerts, users "exit" them by selecting one of their alert buttons. This makes alerts very useful when you want to require users to respond to a question or a message before allowing them to continue.

Click the alert's `OK` button, then exit the form using the toolbar's `Exit` button to return to the Form Builder.

e) What icon was displayed inside the alert? Which of the alert's properties determined the icon?

Answer: A red stop light. The `Alert Style` *property.*

The three alert styles, Stop, Caution, and Note, let you communicate the urgency of an alert's message to the user. Stop alerts should be used for the most urgent messages. Caution alerts can be used for those that are rather urgent and require the user to make a choice. In this Exercise, the message you will present to the user, "`Are you sure you want to exit the form?`", should have `Caution` as its `Alert Style`. Note-style alerts are for those messages that are important, but do not require a response. They will usually only have one button labeled `OK`. The alert you will use in Chapter 10, "Reusable Code," will have `Note` as its `Alert Style`.

Change the `Message` property to "`Are you sure you want to exit the form?`" Change the value of `Button Label 1` to `Yes` and the value of `Button Label 2` to `No`. Change the `Alert Style` to `Caution`.

f) How should you change the code in the WHEN–BUTTON–PRESSED trigger so that the form will exit if the user chooses `Button 1` from the alert? If the user chooses `Button 2`, send a message to the hint line that reads "`You have chosen to continue.`"

Answer: See the discussion below.

The code should be as follows:

```
DECLARE
    v_alert_button    NUMBER;
BEGIN
    v_alert_button := SHOW_ALERT('EXIT_ALERT');
    IF v_alert_button = ALERT_BUTTON1 THEN
        EXIT_FORM;
    ELSIF v_alert_button = ALERT_BUTTON2 THEN
        MESSAGE('You have chosen to continue');
    END IF;
END;
```

In this example, you are evaluating the v_alert_button variable to determine which button was pressed. The form will exit if the user selects Button 1 (Yes) and will send a message if the user presses Button 2 (No). Sending the message "You have chosen to continue" to the user is not really necessary. It was included in this example to show you how the user's response to the alert can be used to initiate other actions. If the alert had three buttons, another ELSIF statement would have been included to handle the additional button's response.

Run the form and test the alert. Exit the form and return to the Form Builder. Set the Default Alert Button property to Button 2. Run the form and display the alert.

g) How did the Default Alert Button property affect the alert?

Answer: It displayed the alert with Button 2 *selected.*

The Default Alert Button property determines which button the form should navigate to when the alert is displayed. This can be useful if the users will respond by using the keyboard, and if you think you can predict what their usual response will be.

■ *FOR EXAMPLE:*

If you can predict that your users will normally select Button 1, then you should set the Default Alert Button property to Button 1. That way, when the alert is displayed, the user can simply press ENTER to respond to the alert and close it.

Exit the form and return to the Form Builder.

h) What built-in could you use if you needed to know an alert's object ID? Can you set any of the alert's properties programmatically?

Answer: You could use FIND_ALERT *and* SET_ALERT_PROPERTY.

FIND_ALERT will find the alert's object ID, which you can then use in the SHOW_ALERT built-in or the SET_ALERT_PROPERTY built-in. You can use the SET_ALERT_PROPERTY built-in to set the title of the alert and the alert's message text programmatically.

■ FOR EXAMPLE:

The code to set an alert's title and message text at run-time could look like this:

```
DECLARE
    v_alert_id              ALERT;
    v_alert_button    NUMBER;
BEGIN
    v_alert_id := FIND_ALERT('EXIT_ALERT');
    SET_ALERT_PROPERTY(v_alert_id, TITLE, 'Warning');
SET_ALERT_PROPERTY(v_alert_id, ALERT_MESSAGE_TEXT, 'Are you sure you want to exit the form?');
    v_alert_button := SHOW_ALERT(v_alert_id);
    ...
END;
```

Note that, as always, you could also include the ID_NULL built-in to evaluate whether or not the alert object exists.

i) How could you change this form so that the alert appears whether the user clicks the ZIPCODE.EXIT button or the Exit button on the toolbar? Do not make these changes to the form, simply write your answer below.

Answer: You could use a KEY-EXIT *trigger to show the alert.*

If you moved the code to show the alert to a KEY-EXIT trigger, the alert would be shown whenever the user pressed the Exit key on the keyboard. It would also fire whenever the user clicked the Exit button on the toolbar. To get the alert to be shown when the user clicks the Exit button on the canvas, you would also have to change the code in the WHEN-BUTTON-PRESSED trigger to the following:

```
    DO_KEY('EXIT_FORM');
```

This way, when the user clicks the button, it fires the KEY-EXIT trigger as well.

LAB 7.2 SELF-REVIEW QUESTIONS

In order to test your progress, you should be able to answer the following questions:

1) How is an alert displayed to the user?
   a) _____ As a multi-line message on the canvas
   b) _____ As a single line of text on the hint line
   c) _____ As a separate modal window in the middle of the screen
   d) _____ As another forms module

2) How can you position an alert?
   a) _____ At design-time using its X Position and Y Position properties
   b) _____ Programmatically at run-time using SET_ALERT_PROPERTY
   c) _____ The position of an alert cannot be configured
   d) _____ a & b

3) How can a user respond to an alert?
   a) _____ By clicking one of its buttons
   b) _____ By correcting any errors on the form
   c) _____ A user cannot respond to an alert
   d) _____ By clicking the OK button on the toolbar

4) Which of the following statements will display ALERT1?
   a) _____ `v_alert_button := SHOW_ALERT('ALERT1', 200, 200);`
   b) _____ `SHOW_ALERT('ALERT1');`
   c) _____ `v_alert_button := SHOW_ALERT('ALERT1');`
   d) _____ `FIND_ALERT('ALERT1');`

5) Which of the following statements will correctly evaluate an alert button?
   a) _____ `IF v_alert_button = 1 THEN`
   b) _____ `IF ALERT_BUTTON1 = 'YES' THEN`
   c) _____ `IF v_alert_button = 'YES' THEN`
   d) _____ `IF v_alert_button = ALERT_BUTTON1 THEN`

6) How should you configure a simple informational alert?
   a) _____ Create a Stop alert with no buttons
   b) _____ Create a Caution alert with no message, but one button labeled OK
   c) _____ Create a Note alert with one button labeled OK
   d) _____ Create a Stop alert with three buttons

Quiz answers appear in Appendix A, Section 7.2.

CHAPTER 7

TEST YOUR THINKING

1) Open the R_STUDENRL.fmb file. Create an LOV for the SECTION_ID item in the ENROLL block. The LOV should display the section_id and its corresponding course_no and description. Return only the SECTION_ID to the form. The form should position the LOV automatically. Create a button to display the LOV using the LIST_VALUES built-in.

2) Open the R_INSTRUCTOR.fmb file. Create an LOV for the INSTRUCTOR_ID item in the INSTRUCTOR block. The LOV should display the instructor_id, first_name, and last_name, and return instructor_id to the form. last_name and first_name should appear together in one LOV column like this:

Smith, Joe

The form should position the LOV automatically. Create a button to display the LOV using the SHOW_LOV built-in.

CHAPTER 8

CANVASES AND WINDOWS

CHAPTER OBJECTIVES

In this Chapter, you will learn about:

✔	Canvas and Window Concepts	Page 262
✔	Content Canvases and Windows	Page 277
✔	Stacked Canvases	Page 287
✔	Toolbar Canvases	Page 298

So far, your forms have been limited to the windows and canvases that Forms has created for you. As your forms get more complex, you will want to add additional windows and canvases and display them in response to interface or internal processing events.

This Chapter will cover the fundamentals of canvas and window objects, as well as a variety of methods for displaying them.

L A B   8 . 1

CANVAS AND WINDOW CONCEPTS

LAB OBJECTIVES

After this Lab, you will be able to:

*   Understand Windows
*   Understand Canvases

For a canvas and its items to be visible, it must be assigned to a window. By the same token, for a window to be visible, it must contain at least one canvas. Therefore, canvases and windows rely on each other to make themselves and other Forms objects appear to the user. The forms you have created so far have had one window and one canvas. The window (WINDOW1) was created by default when the new form was created. The canvas was created by the Layout Wizard and automatically assigned to WINDOW1. A single form can contain multiple instances of both canvases and windows, which you can create and define yourself.

WINDOWS

Like any other physical object in Forms, windows have properties that determine their size and position. Under the Functional property category, they have a series of window-specific properties that determine whether or not the window can be minimized, resized, closed, and so on.

There are two styles of windows in Forms: document and dialog. Document windows are commonly used for data entry and query screens; they are the main windows in an application. Dialog windows are used to deliver messages, display lists, or present the user with a specific task. On Microsoft Windows operating systems, there is a third style of window

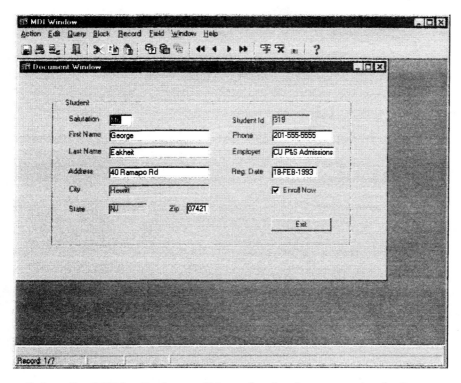

Figure 8.1 ■ **An MDI window with a single document window.**

called the Multiple Document Interface (MDI) window. The MDI window serves as a parent window to all of the other windows in a form. Figures 8.1 and 8.2 show examples of all three window styles. Note that the window titles in the figures indicate the window style.

Document and dialog windows are contained differently by the MDI window. Document windows are completely contained by their parent MDI window as illustrated in Figure 8.1. If a user were to drag the document window as far to the left as possible, it would disappear under the boundary of the MDI window. This is not the case with the dialog window (LOV) in Figure 8.2. It is not restricted by the MDI window's boundaries and can be moved completely outside of it.

Windows also have a modal property that helps determine how and when the user can leave the window. Navigation cannot leave a modal window until the user has completed whatever task the window calls for.

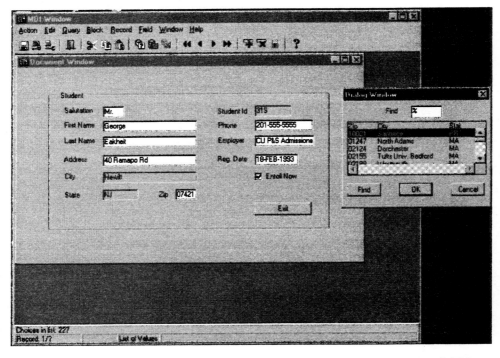

Figure 8.2 ■ A dialog window outside the boundaries of the MDI window.

■ FOR EXAMPLE:

In Figure 8.2, the LOV titled `Dialog Window` is modal. The user must either select from the LOV or click the `Cancel` button before going back to the window titled `Document Window`. The user cannot navigate to and from other windows. Modal windows give you the opportunity to present the user with a message or task and force them to respond to it before moving on.

If a window is modeless, the user can navigate to another window and leave the current window open and accessible. Modeless windows let you give your users the convenience of being able to switch from window to window.

Document windows are usually modeless (`Modal` property set to `No`) and dialog windows are usually modal (`Modal` property set to `Yes`). The `WINDOW1` object created by the Form Builder is a modeless document window.

DISPLAYING WINDOWS

There are a variety of methods for displaying and hiding windows at run-time. You can explicitly open windows by using window built-ins, you can set their properties, or you can simply navigate to them.

SHOW_WINDOW is a window-specific built-in that can be used to open all types of windows, be they modal or modeless, document or dialog.

■ *FOR EXAMPLE:*

You could open a window named MAINWIN with the following statement:

```
SHOW_WINDOW('MAINWIN');
```

Depending on the modality of MAINWIN and how its properties are set, the SHOW_WINDOW statement can produce different results in how the window is opened. It may display the window's content canvas or not. It may try to navigate to an item in the window or not. In the Exercises, you will experiment with some of the different outcomes of SHOW_WINDOW.

You can also open a window simply by navigating to an item in that window, or to a block that contains an item in the window. Keep in mind that for an item to "be in a window" it must be assigned to a canvas that is assigned to that window. If navigation has moved to a certain item and that item is not displayed or is not visible, Forms will make it visible. It will, among other things, display the canvas and window that item is assigned to. So by using built-ins to navigate to an item, you can open/display canvases and windows.

■ *FOR EXAMPLE:*

Assume you have the following code in a trigger:

```
GO_ITEM('BLOCK1.ITEM1');
```

Also assume that ITEM1 is on CANVAS1, which is assigned to MAINWIN. When Forms navigates to ITEM1, it must display it. So, if ITEM1 is not visible when the GO_ITEM built-in is executed, Forms will automatically show the canvas and window to make ITEM1 visible to the user.

There are numerous combinations of property settings and programmatic or navigational methods that affect the opening and closing of windows and their canvases. In the Exercises, you will experiment with some of these combinations.

CANVASES

So far, you have worked with content canvases to display and position the items in your form. Content canvases are the most common canvas type because every window must have one as its main canvas. In the Exercises in the rest of this Chapter, you will experiment with two other types of canvases: stacked and toolbar. Also, in the "Test Your Thinking" section, you will attempt to build a form with a tabbed canvas. In this Lab, you will focus on some concepts that are common to all types of canvases.

CANVAS VIEWPORTS (VIEWS)

The terms "canvas view" and "viewport" are synonymous; viewport will be used in this interactive workbook. The viewport refers to the area of the canvas that is visible to the user. What this means is that the canvas object itself is not always entirely visible; only the area defined by its viewport is visible. Returning briefly to the painter's canvas analogy, think of a painting with a wide wooden frame. The frame obscures the

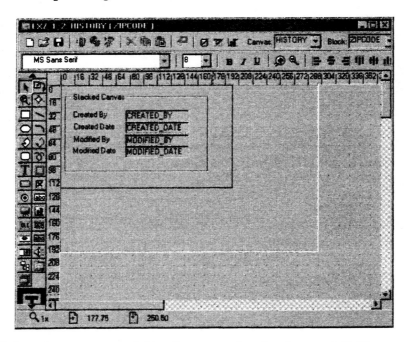

Figure 8.3 ■ A canvas and its viewport in the Layout Editor.

edges of the canvas, but the center of the canvas, the part with the painting, is visible. Think of the part that is visible as the viewport.

The size of the canvas and the size of its viewport are determined by properties. Figure 8.3 shows what a canvas and its viewport look like in the Layout Editor.

The viewport in Figure 8.3 is represented by the thin black line that surrounds the items and the frame. The canvas is represented by the larger rectangular area. The canvas ends where the surface of the Layout Editor appears to have raised dots. On a painter's canvas, the painting is rarely ever behind the frame, or in any way hidden from the viewer. This is not necessarily the case with Forms canvases. It is common to place some items outside the viewport so that they are not initially visible. Then, as the user scrolls or navigates the form, the viewport can move to expose different parts of the canvas. In the "Test Your Thinking" section of this Chapter, you will be asked to create a canvas whose viewport will move to show and hide items and create a scrolling effect.

DISPLAYING CANVASES

The rules for displaying and hiding canvases are similar to those for windows. A canvas can be displayed either by using built-ins to open it explicitly or by navigating to an item on the canvas. If you choose to display a canvas by navigating to it, you could use the same GO_ITEM built-in explained in the example above. If you choose to display a canvas explicitly, you could use the SHOW_VIEW built-in and pass it the canvas' name. The code would look like this for a canvas named CANVAS1:

```
SHOW_VIEW('CANVAS1');
```

LAB 8.1 EXERCISES

8.1.1   UNDERSTAND WINDOWS

Open the form EX08_01.fmb in the Form Builder. Run the form and issue a query.

a) Can you drag the window titled Main Window out of the MDI window? What does this tell you about its window style?

_____

_____

Click the `Alert` button.

b) Can you drag the alert out of the MDI window? What does this tell you about its window style?

_____

_____

c) Can you navigate to the form without closing the alert? What does this tell you about its modality?

_____

_____

Click the `OK` button to close the alert. Click the `Window` button.

d) What style is this window? Is it modal?

_____

_____

e) Have any properties been set for the MDI window? How can you tell?

_____

_____

Exit the running form and return to the Form Builder. Open the `WHEN-BUTTON-PRESSED` trigger for the `CONTROL.SHOW_HIST` button.

f) Is this built-in opening the window explicitly?

_____

_____

Comment out the current code in the `SHOW_HIST` button's `WHEN-BUTTON-PRESSED` trigger and then add the code shown below:

```
--GO_ITEM('CONTROL.HIDEWIN);
SHOW_WINDOW('SECONDWIN');
```

Run the form and click the `Window` button.

g) Did the window open? Are there any items visible? What does this mean about opening a window with navigation vs. doing it programmatically?

_____

_____

Reenter the `SHOW_HIST` button's `WHEN-BUTTON-PRESSED` trigger and change it back so it appears as it does below:

```
GO_ITEM('CONTROL.HIDEWIN);
--SHOW_WINDOW('SECONDWIN');
```

h) Which built-ins are being used in the `HIDE_HIST` button's `WHEN-BUTTON-PRESSED` trigger?

_____

_____

Comment out `HIDE_WINDOW('SECONDWIN');` in the `HIDE_HIST` button's `WHEN-BUTTON-PRESSED` trigger. Run the form and press the `Window` button. Now click the `Close` button.

i) Did navigation return to the `ZIP` item on the `MAINWIN`? Did the `SECONDWIN` close? What does this tell you about navigation in and out of modeless windows?

_____

_____

8.1.2 UNDERSTAND CANVASES

Open the `EX08_02.fmb` form in the Form Builder.

a) How many canvases are there and what are their names and types?

_____

_____

b) Which window is the ZIPCODE canvas assigned to? Which window is the HISTORY canvas assigned to?

_____

_____

c) How big is the HISTORY canvas? How big is its viewport?

_____

_____

Open the STACKED button's WHEN-BUTTON-PRESSED trigger.

d) How is the HISTORY canvas being displayed?

_____

_____

Run the form and test the Stacked Canvas button to see how the stacked canvas will behave.

LAB 8.1 EXERCISE ANSWERS

8.1.1 ANSWERS

Open the form EX08_01.fmb in the Form Builder. Run the form and issue a query.

a) Can you drag the window titled Main Window out of the MDI window? What does this tell you about its window style?

Answer: No you cannot. It is a document window.

Document windows are the most common windows in typical Forms applications. Most data entry and transaction-oriented work will be done on canvases that are displayed within document windows. In this form, and in most of the forms you will create using this book, you will only have one document window per module. However, it is common to build forms that have multiple document windows. These windows can be configured to be open simultaneously so that users can toggle back and forth between them, just like in MSWord and other typical windowing applications.

Click the Alert button.

b) Can you drag the alert out of the MDI window? What does this tell you about its window style?

Answer: Yes you can. It is a dialog window.

Alerts are good examples of simple dialog windows since they allow the user to read the alert message and then drag it completely out of the way to view the form before responding.

c) Can you navigate to the form without closing the alert? What does this tell you about its modality?

Answer: No you cannot. It is a modal window.

Dialog-style windows are often implemented as modal. They are windows that require some sort of response from the user before regular processing can continue. The alert in EX08_01.fmb will not let the user continue until they have clicked the OK button. In this case, the alert was merely informational. The response required can be seen as an "OK, I read the alert." But other alerts and modal dialogs require that the user make a decision or complete some tasks.

■ FOR EXAMPLE:

Figure 8.4 shows the LOV Column Mapping dialog from the properties of an LOV. This modal dialog requires that the user enter some information before continuing.

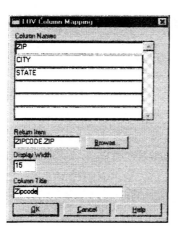

Figure 8.4 ■ The Lov Column Mapping dialog.

Click the OK button to close the alert. Click the Window button.

d) What style is this window? Is it modal?

Answer: It is a dialog window. No, it is modeless.

Although many dialogs are modal, it is not required that they be that way. In this case, the window titled Second Window is similar to a help window. No input is required from the user; it is merely displaying the history of the current record.

e) Have any properties been set for the MDI window? How can you tell?

Answer: Yes, the Title *property has been set.*

The MDI window is not visible in the Object Navigator, nor are its properties visible in the Property Palette. However, it does have properties and they can be adjusted programmatically using the SET_WINDOW_PROPERTY built-in. In this case, the PRE-FORM trigger sets three properties for the MDI window: Height, Width, and Title. Keep in mind that the MDI window is only available on Windows platforms.

Open the PRE-FORM trigger and look at the code. Note that the built-in refers to the MDI window a bit differently than it does other windows.

■ *FOR EXAMPLE:*

The statements in the PRE-FORM trigger look like this:

```
SET_WINDOW_PROPERTY(FORMS_MDI_WINDOW, WIDTH, 550);
```

FORMS_MDI_WINDOW is a Forms constant. It is not possible to refer to the MDI window by name in single quotes or with an object ID.

Exit the running form and return to the Form Builder. Open the WHEN-BUTTON-PRESSED trigger for the CONTROL.SHOW_HIST button.

f) Is this built-in opening the window explicitly?

Answer: No, the window is being opened by navigation.

This is a fairly straightforward method for opening a window and its canvas. Once you have told Forms which item it should navigate to, it does the rest of the work by opening the window and the appropriate canvas.

Comment out the current code in the SHOW_HIST button's WHEN-BUT-TON-PRESSED trigger and then add the code shown below:

```
--GO_ITEM('CONTROL.CLOSE_HIST');
SHOW_WINDOW('SECONDWIN');
```

Run the form and click the Window button.

g) Did the window open? Are there any items visible? What does this mean about opening a window with navigation vs. doing it programmatically?

Answer: Yes, the window opened. No, there are no items visible.

In Question f, navigation automatically opened the window and canvas. Here you can see that opening the window does not automatically display the canvas or its items. To get the canvas and its items to appear, you would have had to add another line of code to the trigger or adjust one of the window's properties.

■ FOR EXAMPLE:

To get the canvas and its items to open along with the window, you could change the code to the following:

```
SHOW_WINDOW('SECONDWIN');
SHOW_VIEW('SECONDCAN');
```

In this case, you are explicitly opening both the window and its canvas. The other option is to use properties to manipulate the window and canvas. In that case, you would set the SECONDWIN window's Primary Canvas property to SECONDCAN. By doing this, SECONDCAN will open automatically when SECONDWIN is opened.

Reenter the SHOW_HIST button's WHEN-BUTTON-PRESSED trigger and change it back so it appears as it does below:

```
GO_ITEM('CONTROL.HIDE_HIST');
--SHOW_WINDOW('SECONDWIN');
```

h) Which built-ins are being used in the HIDE_HIST button's WHEN-BUTTON-PRESSED trigger?

Answer: The GO_ITEM built-in, which is navigational, and the HIDE_WINDOW built-in, which explicitly closes the window.

i) Did navigation return to the ZIP item on the MAINWIN? Did the SECONDWIN close? What does this tell you about navigation in and out of modeless windows?

Answer: Yes, navigation returned to the ZIP item. No, the SECONDWIN did not close.

SECONDWIN is a modeless window. Therefore, simply navigating out of the window did not close it. Why is this? Modeless windows allow users to work on two or more tasks simultaneously. A user can be adding a student enrollment in one window and adjusting another student's address in another. The user would want to be able to go back and forth from window to window without having either close.

If SECONDWIN had been a modal window, then the behavior would have been different. The GO_ITEM built-in would have closed SECONDWIN without needing the HIDE_WINDOW built-in. Why is this? By definition, a modal window cannot be navigated out of or closed until its task has been completed or perhaps canceled. If the trigger is forcing navigation with the GO_ITEM built-in, then Forms will assume that the modal window's job is done and will close it.

The methods for opening and closing windows may seem a bit confusing. A good rule of thumb is to try to navigate to a window or a canvas to open it. If the window does not have any navigable items, or if you wish to simply open the window without navigating to it, use the SHOW_ built-ins.

8.1.2 ANSWERS

Open the EX08_02.fmb form in the Form Builder.

a) How many canvases are there and what are their names and types?

Answer: There are two canvases: ZIPCODE and HISTORY. ZIPCODE is a content canvas and HISTORY is a stacked canvas.

b) Which window is the ZIPCODE canvas assigned to? Which window is the HISTORY canvas assigned to?

Answer: Both canvases are assigned to MAINWIN.

A canvas must be assigned to a window to be visible. A stacked canvas must always be stacked on a content canvas to be visible. Therefore, both canvases are assigned to the same window. It is technically possible to display a stacked canvas in a window without a content canvas, but it is not recommended.

Canvases, be they stacked or content, do not have to be explicitly assigned to windows at design-time. Instead, they can be assigned programmatically at run-time.

c) How big is the HISTORY canvas? How big is its viewport?

Answer: The Height *and* Width *properties of the* HISTORY *canvas are* 200, 300. *Its view, or viewport, is* 122,200.

The properties that govern the size of the actual canvas are under the Physical category and are called Height and Width. The properties that govern the size of the viewport are under Viewport category and are called Viewport Height and Viewport Width.

In this case, as in many, the canvas is far larger than the viewport. It is quite common to place items on the canvas but not include them in the viewport.

Open the STACKED button's WHEN-BUTTON-PRESSED trigger.

d) How is the HISTORY canvas being displayed?

Answer: It is being displayed programmatically using the SET_VIEW_PROPERTY *built-in.*

The same rules that apply to windows apply to canvases. It is easiest to display a canvas using navigation, but it is possible and sometimes necessary to display a canvas programmatically. In this case, it was necessary to display the HISTORY canvas programmatically because it does not contain any navigable items. As an alternate and equally effective method to using the SET_ built-in, the SHOW_VIEW and HIDE_VIEW built-ins would have worked equally well here also.

LAB 8.1 SELF-REVIEW QUESTIONS

In order to test your progress, you should be able to answer the following questions:

1) Which of the following is not a window style?
   a) ____ Dialog
   b) ____ Document
   c) ____ Content
   d) ____ MDI

2) Which of the following is true about document windows?
a) _____ They have at least two content canvases
b) _____ They can be dragged outside the MDI window
c) _____ They are well-suited for data entry and query screens
d) _____ They cannot be opened at run-time

3) Which of the following is false?
a) _____ Alerts are dialog windows
b) _____ LOVs are dialog windows
c) _____ Dialog windows have at least one content canvas
d) _____ Dialog windows cannot be modal

4) What does the SHOW_WINDOW built-in do?
a) _____ It manages the MDI window
b) _____ It displays windows
c) _____ It responds to Open Window events
d) _____ a & b

5) What will happen if the GO_ITEM built-in is passed a non-navigable item?
a) _____ Navigation will not complete and the form will return an error
b) _____ Forms will navigate to it anyway
c) _____ Forms will open its window but not navigate to it
d) _____ All canvases will close

6) What are some of the methods for displaying a canvas?
a) _____ Navigate to an item on the canvas
b) _____ Use the SHOW_VIEW built-in
c) _____ Set the MDI Windows Visible property to Yes
d) _____ a & b

7) Which of the following is not true about the viewport of a content canvas?
a) _____ It is the same size as its window
b) _____ It cannot contain stacked canvases
c) _____ Items outside the viewport will not be visible at run-time
d) _____ It can be adjusted in the Layout Editor

Quiz answers appear in Appendix A, Section 8.1.

LAB 8.2

CONTENT CANVASES AND WINDOWS

> ### LAB OBJECTIVES
>
> After this Lab, you will be able to:
>
> * Create a Content Canvas and Window

While content canvases have viewports, they do not have properties to set the size of their viewports. The size of a content canvas' viewport is the same as the size of the window that it occupies.

■ *FOR EXAMPLE:*

Assume that CANVAS1 is the content canvas for WINDOW1. If WINDOW1's Height and Width properties are set to 200, 200, then this will be the size of CANVAS1's viewport. To set the size of a content canvas' viewport, you must either:

1) Use the Height and Width properties of the window it is assigned to.
2) Adjust it visually in the Layout Editor.

In the Exercise for this Lab, you are going to walk through the process of creating a content canvas and window. Your objective will be to duplicate the functionality of the form EX08_01.fmb.

First you are going to create a basic form using the wizards. Then you will create a second canvas and window. You will use these to display the values of the audit columns. You will then create a button to show this window and experiment with showing it and hiding it with navigation.

LAB 8.2 EXERCISES

8.2.1 CREATE A CONTENT CANVAS AND WINDOW

Use the wizards to quickly create a form based on the STUDENT table. Enforce data integrity should be **unchecked**. Include the audit columns in the block, but do not display them on the canvas. Give the canvas a Formstyle layout.

Rename the window to MAINWIN.

a) How can you create another content canvas? Should you use the Object Navigator or the Layout Editor?

_____

_____

Rename the canvas HISTORY.

b) Do you want HISTORY to be a content canvas for MAINWIN? Why not?

_____

_____

c) What steps should you take to create a window and assign HISTORY as its content canvas?

_____

_____

Rename the window HISTWIN. Users should be able to drag HISTWIN outside the MDI window, and they should not be able to access other windows while it is open.

d) Which of the HISTWIN window's properties should you set to make the above happen?

_____

_____

e) Should you assign the audit items to the HISTORY canvas or to the HISTWIN window? What's the easiest way to do this?

_____

_____

f) Can you view both canvases at the same time? How?

_____

_____

g) What should the item type for the audit columns be since you don't want users to be able to navigate to them or change their values?

_____

_____

Arrange the audit items and their prompts on the HISTORY canvas so that the layout is similar to that in Figure 8.5.

Create a non-base table block and name it CONTROL. Create two buttons in the CONTROL block and name them SHOW_HIST and HIDE_HIST. Position SHOW_HIST on the STUDENT canvas in the lower right-hand corner. Position HIDE_HIST on the HISTORY canvas below the items in the center. Set the Key Board Navigable and Mouse Navigable properties for both buttons to No.

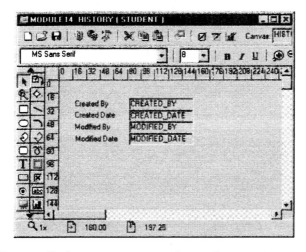

Figure 8.5 ■ The audit items arranged on the HISTORY canvas.

h) What navigation built-in could you use to open the HISTWIN window and its canvas?

---

i) Could you pass this built-in CREATED_BY as its parameter? Why not?

---

j) What is the only navigable item on the HISTORY canvas?

Create a WHEN-BUTTON-PRESSED trigger for the SHOW_HIST button with the following code:

```
GO_ITEM('CONTROL.HIDE_HIST');
```

Create another WHEN-BUTTON-PRESSED trigger for the HIDE_HIST button with the following code:

```
GO_ITEM('STUDENT.STUDENT_ID');
HIDE_WINDOW('HISTWIN');
```

Run the form and test the buttons.

k) Which object's X and Y Positions and Height and Width properties should you adjust to position and size the history information a bit better?

Try a Height of 130 and a Width of 190 to size the object. Adjust the X and Y Positions to taste, but try not to obscure any of the items on the STUDENT canvas.

Run the form to test the size and positioning properties.

Navigate to STUDENT.ADDRESS and click the SHOW_HIST button. Now click the CLOSE_HIST button. Note that navigation did not return to STUDENT.ADDRESS, but to STUDENT.ZIP.

l) When the Button Pressed event occurs, you want to capture the value of the current item so that you can navigate back to it when the HISTWIN window closes. What system variable can you use to do this?

_____

_____

Change the code in the SHOW_HIST button to use a global variable. The code should now look like this:

```
:global.last_item := :SYSTEM.CURSOR_ITEM;
GO_ITEM('CONTROL.HIDE_HIST');
```

m) How can you use the global variable in the WHEN-BUTTON-PRESSED trigger for HIDE_HIST so that it will return to the item that called it?

_____

_____

n) Will these windows, canvases, buttons, and triggers be useful in other forms that use the audit columns? Will the triggers work as they are written now?

_____

_____

Save the form as R_CONCANV.fmb.

LAB 8.2 EXERCISE ANSWERS

8.2.1 ANSWERS

a) How can you create another content canvas? Should you use the Object Navigator or the Layout Editor?

Answer: You should use the Object Navigator.

There is no tool on the Layout Editor's Tool Palette to create content canvases, so you must use the Object Navigator. It is possible to use the Layout Wizard, but that is probably more trouble than it is worth. Note that when you use the Object Navigator, its default behavior is to create canvases with Canvas Type set to Content.

Rename the canvas HISTORY.

b) Do you want HISTORY to be a content canvas for MAINWIN? Why not?

Answer: No you do not.

In this Exercise, you want to duplicate the look and feel of the EX08_01.fmb form that you experimented with earlier. In that form, there were two content canvases, each assigned to their own windows.

It is possible to assign two content canvases to the same window, but only one can be visible at a time. You would use either navigation built-ins or explicit canvas built-ins to switch from one content canvas to the other.

c) What steps should you take to create a window and assign HISTORY as its content canvas?

Answer: Create a window and then set the HISTORY canvas' Window property to the name of the window.

d) Which of the HISTWIN window's properties should you set to make the above happen?

Answer: Window Style should be set to Dialog and Modal should be set to Yes.

e) Should you assign the audit items to the HISTORY canvas or to the HISTWIN window? What's the easiest way to do this?

Answer: You should assign them to the canvas. Select all of the audit items in the Object Navigator and set their Canvas property to HISTORY.

Remember, items are assigned to canvases, and then canvases are assigned to windows.

f) Can you view both canvases at the same time? How?

Answer: Yes you can. You can open two instances of the Layout Editor.

You can have as many instances of the Layout Editor open as you'd like, which can make comparing canvases, especially stacked canvases, easier. You can also toggle from canvas to canvas using the `Canvas` list item on the Layout Editor's Utility toolbar.

In Lab 8.3, you will learn about another Layout Editor feature that allows you to view a content canvas with all of its stacked canvases stacked on top of it.

g) What should the item type for the audit columns be since you don't want users to be able to navigate to them or change their values?

Answer: The item type should be display item.

h) What navigation built-in could you use to open the `HISTWIN` window and its canvas?

Answer: You could use the `GO_ITEM` *built-in.*

You could also have used the `GO_BLOCK` built-in to navigate to the `CONTROL` block. `HIDE_HIST` is the first item in the block, so navigation would have succeeded.

i) Could you pass this built-in `CREATED_BY` as its parameter? Why not?

Answer: No, because it is a display item, it is not navigable.

The `GO_ITEM` built-in is only valid for items that are navigable. Display items are not navigable, so the navigation would have failed if you had tried to pass `CREATED_BY` into the `GO_ITEM` built-in.

j) What is the only navigable item on the `HISTORY` canvas?

Answer: The `HIDE_HIST` *button.*

Even though the `Keyboard Navigable` property was set to `No`, `SHOW_HIST` is considered a navigable item and the `GO_ITEM` built-in will succeed. Interestingly, as you learned in the previous question, this does not apply to display items since by definition they are non-navigable and have no `Keyboard Navigable` property.

Again, it would be possible to use SHOW_WINDOW instead of GO_ITEM. But since the HIDE_HIST button is a navigable item, it is easier to simply navigate to it.

Run the form and test the buttons.

k) Which object's X and Y Positions and Height and Width properties should you adjust to position and size the history information a bit better?

Answer: The HISTWIN *window's properties.*

Since the HISTORY canvas is a content canvas, its sizing properties are ignored by the Form Builder and do not affect the size or position of the canvas at run-time. This is because the content canvas inhabits the entire surface of its window. Therefore, the size and position properties that you set for the window, in this case HISTWIN, are what dictate the size and positioning of the canvas.

l) When the Button Pressed event occurs, you want to capture the value of the current item so that you can navigate back to it when the HISTWIN window closes. What system variable can you use to do this?

Answer: :SYSTEM.CURSOR_ITEM.

m) How can you use the global variable in the WHEN-BUTTON-PRESSED trigger for HIDE_HIST so that it will return to the item that called it?

Answer: See discussion below.

The code should be:

```
GO_ITEM(:global.last_item);
HIDE_WINDOW('HISTWIN');
```

The global variable created and assigned in the SHOW_HIST trigger is referenced in the HIDE_HIST trigger so that the form will know which item to return to.

Global variables are user-defined variables that, like other variables, can hold values that need to be referenced later on. However, global variables are special in four ways:

1) They don't have to be declared in a DECLARE statement of a PL/SQL block.
2) They are assigned as they are created.

3) They can be referenced outside the PL/SQL block they were created in.

4) If multiple forms are open, they can all reference the global variable.

■ FOR EXAMPLE:

In this case, the global variable is not declared in a DECLARE section of a PL/SQL block; it is assigned a value as it is created. It is created in one trigger and referenced in another.

n) Will these windows, canvases, buttons, and triggers be useful in other forms that use the audit columns? Will the triggers work as they are written now?

Answer: Yes they will.

All of the objects that create the Record History window could be copied immediately to another form that has the audit columns in its data blocks. A little work would be required to assign and position the audit items on the HISTORY canvas, but once done, the objects would be completely usable. Why does this matter? Now that you have designed a way to let the user view the contents of the audit columns, you can apply it to every form you create that includes the audit columns. This way, you won't have to redo it for every form.

In Chapter 9, "Reusable Objects," you will learn a way to group these objects so that you can move them from form to form quickly and easily.

Save the form as R_CONCANV.fmb.

LAB 8.2 SELF-REVIEW QUESTIONS

In order to test your progress, you should be able to answer the following questions:

1) Two content canvases cannot appear in the same window.
   a) _____ True
   b) _____ False

2) How can a content canvas be created?
   a) _____ By using the Object Navigator
   b) _____ By using the Layout Wizard
   c) _____ By using the Layout Editor
   d) _____ a & b
   e) _____ a, b, & c

3) Which of the following is true about a content canvas?

a) _____ It must be in a modal window

b) _____ It must be in a modeless dialog window

c) _____ It is contained by a window

d) _____ It can be visible without a window

4) Windows cannot be closed with navigation.

a) _____ True

b) _____ False

Quiz answers appear in Appendix A, Section 8.2.

LAB
8.2

L A B 8 . 3

STACKED CANVASES

LAB OBJECTIVES

After this Lab, you will be able to:

* Create and Display Stacked Canvases

Stacked canvases are never the sole canvas in a window. They are always stacked on top of other canvases, and partially or completely obscure those canvases when displayed at run-time. To stack a stacked canvas, you must position it relative to the content canvas that it is stacked upon. Figure 8.6 shows both a stacked and content canvas in the Layout Editor.

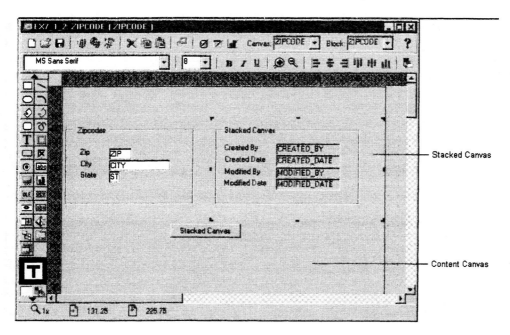

Figure 8.6 ■ A stacked canvas positioned on a content canvas in the Layout Editor.

The stacked canvas' viewport is what is visible here. The actual stacked canvas object might be much larger. In this example, we see only one stacked canvas, but it is possible to have multiple stacked canvases in a single window, stacked upon a single content canvas. They could be stacked on different portions of the content canvas, or they could be stacked on top of one another.

Stacked canvases have `Height` and `Width` properties just like content canvases. They also have properties to determine the size and positioning of their viewports. The viewport will be positioned in two ways.

1) Relative to the stacked canvas itself.
2) Relative to the content canvas it is stacked upon.

The `Viewport X Position on Canvas` and `Viewport Y Position on Canvas` properties determine where the viewport will be positioned on the stacked canvas itself.

A stacked canvas has two other properties called `Viewport X Position` and `Viewport Y Position`. These position the canvas relative to the content canvas.

■ FOR EXAMPLE:

If the `Viewport X Position` of a stacked canvas is set to `40` (in points), and its `Viewport Y Position` is set to `178`, that means that its upper left-hand corner will be at those coordinates on the content canvas as illustrated in Figure 8.7.

In form `EX08_02.fmb`, you saw how a stacked canvas could be shown and hidden programmatically. In this example, there is only one stacked canvas, but there could have been many stacked on top of one another to simulate pages. A wizard can also be built using multiple stacked canvases.

■ FOR EXAMPLE:

Assume you are going to create a wizard object to add student records and then add enrollment records for those students. The wizard will have three or more wizard pages to step the user through adding a student's name, address, employment information, enrollment information, and so on. These pages will be implemented as stacked canvases and will be positioned on top of one another. The underlying content canvas will contain the wizard's `Back`, `Next`, and `Finish` buttons. You will use navigation or `SHOW_VIEW` and `HIDE_VIEW` built-ins to switch from page to page.

**LAB
8.3**

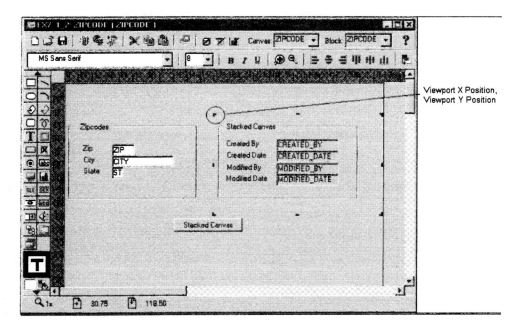

Figure 8.7 ■ Viewport X and Y Positions for the stacked canvas.

It is also common to use stacked canvases to simulate scrolling views. This can be useful if you have items that you'd like to display in tabular fashion but there are too many to comfortably fit on a normal-sized canvas. In the "Test Your Thinking" section, you will create a scrolling stacked canvas to accommodate all of the items in a SECTION block.

LAB 8.3 EXERCISES

8.3.1 CREATE AND DISPLAY STACKED CANVASES

In this Lab, you will create a stacked canvas called INSTRUCTOR. You will position INSTRUCTOR on a content canvas so that it covers some items. Then, you will use a button to programmatically show and hide the canvas.

Open form EX08_03.fmb in the Form Builder. Note that there are four blocks: SECTION, ENROLLMENT, INSTRUCTOR, and CONTROL. The SECTION and ENROLLMENT items are positioned on the SECTION content canvas. The INSTRUCTOR items have not been positioned yet.

a) What are three Form Builder tools you could use to create the stacked canvas?

_____

_____

The stacked canvas will ultimately lie on top of the content canvas.

b) With this in mind, which of the tools that you listed in Question a might be the best for creating and simultaneously positioning the stacked canvas?

_____

_____

Create the stacked canvas using the Stacked Canvas tool from the Layout Editor's Tool Palette. Make sure you completely cover the ENROLLMENT items on the content canvas, but do not obscure or cover the frame. Name the new stacked canvas INSTRUCTOR.

c) Are you able to see both the content canvas and stacked canvas in the Layout Editor? Is part of the content canvas obscured?

_____

_____

Select View | Stacked Views from the Main Menu. When the Stacked/ Tab Canvases dialog opens, de-select INSTRUCTOR and click the OK button.

d) Are you still able to see both canvases? What does this tell you about the View | Stacked Views feature?

_____

_____

Select View | Stacked Views from the Main Menu again. When the Stacked/Tab Canvases dialog opens, re-select INSTRUCTOR and click the OK button so that INSTRUCTOR is visible on top of SECTION.

In the Object Navigator, click the icon next to INSTRUCTOR to open another Layout Editor window.

>   **e)** How can you position the items in the INSTRUCTOR block on the INSTRUCTOR canvas?

> _____

> _____

Run the form and issue a query. The Change View button will not work yet, so use Block | Next Block from the Main Menu to test the stacked canvas. Exit the form and return to the Form Builder.

>   **f)** Which properties can you adjust to make the stacked canvas and its items look better? For example, isn't the stacked canvas set a bit lower than the content canvas?

> _____

> _____

>   **g)** Which of the stacked canvas' properties can you change so that the canvas is not visible when the form opens?

> _____

> _____

Open the WHEN-BUTTON-PRESSED trigger for the CHANGEVIEW button.

>   **h)** What trigger code could you write to change the canvas' Visible property? Your trigger should first evaluate whether or not the canvas is visible. If the canvas is not visible, use a built-in to show it. If it is visible, use a built-in to hide it. Use conditional logic and GET_ and SET_ built-ins to accomplish this.

> _____

> _____

Run the form, issue a query, and test the Change View button.

i) What are two other built-ins you could use to hide and show the canvas? These should not be GET_ or SET_ built-ins, and they should not cause navigation.

Run the form, issue a query, and test the Change View button. Exit the form and return to the Form Builder.

Replace the built-ins you used for Question i with GO_BLOCK('INSTRUC-TOR') and GO_BLOCK('ENROLLMENT') statements.

Run the form, issue a query, and test the Change View button.

j) How is the behavior of the form different now that you are using navigational built-ins instead of the built-ins you used in Questions h and i?

LAB 8.3 EXERCISE ANSWERS

8.3.1 ANSWERS

In this Lab, you will create a stacked canvas called INSTRUCTOR. You will position INSTRUCTOR on a content canvas so that it covers some items. Then, you will use a button to programmatically show and hide the canvas.

Open form EX08_03.fmb in the Form Builder. Note that there are four blocks: SECTION, ENROLLMENT, INSTRUCTOR, and CONTROL. The SECTION and ENROLLMENT items are positioned on the SECTION content canvas. The INSTRUCTOR items have not been positioned yet.

a) What are three Form Builder tools you could use to create the stacked canvas?

Answer: You could use the Object Navigator, Layout Editor, or Layout Wizard.

The stacked canvas will ultimately lie on top of the content canvas.

b) With this in mind, which of the tools that you listed in Question a might be the best for creating and simultaneously positioning the stacked canvas?

Answer: The Layout Editor.

By using the Layout Editor, you will be able to treat the stacked canvas like an item. You will be able to position the cursor where you would like the canvas to begin and stretch out the canvas until it reaches the size you desire.

Create the stacked canvas using the `Stacked Canvas` tool from the Layout Editor's Tool Palette. Make sure you completely cover the ENROLLMENT items on the content canvas, but do not obscure or cover the frame.

c) Are you able to see both the content canvas and stacked canvas in the Layout Editor? Is part of the content canvas obscured?

Answer: Yes, you can see both and yes, part of the content canvas is obscured.

Select `View | Stacked Views` from the Main Menu. When the `Stacked/Tab Canvases` dialog opens, de-select INSTRUCTOR and click the OK button.

d) Are you still able to see both canvases? What does this tell you about the `View | Stacked Views` feature?

Answer: No, you cannot see both.

The `View | Stacked Views` feature lets you view the size and position of the stacked canvases on their content canvases. The stacked canvas and its objects are accessible in this mode so that you can select and adjust their positions.

In the previous Lab, you learned that you can have two instances of the Layout Editor open. This can also be helpful in that it lets you see the stacked canvas on its own. Additionally, the Stacked Views mode shows only the stacked canvas' viewport.

Select `View | Stacked Views` from the Main Menu again. When the `Stacked/Tab Canvases` dialog opens, re-select INSTRUCTOR and click the OK button so that INSTRUCTOR is visible on top of SECTION.

In the Object Navigator, click the icon next to INSTRUCTOR to open another Layout Editor window.

e) How can you position the items in the INSTRUCTOR block on the INSTRUCTOR canvas?

Answer: Select all of the items in the Object Navigator and use the Property Palette to set their `Canvas` *property to INSTRUCTOR.*

Note that it makes no difference which instance of the Layout Editor you use to manipulate the items on the INSTRUCTOR stacked canvas. You can manipulate them using the Layout Editor that displays INSTRUCTOR in Stacked Views mode on top of the content canvas, or you can use the instance of the Layout Editor that displays the INSTRUCTOR canvas on its own.

Run the form and issue a query. The Change View button will not work yet, so use Block | Next Block from the Main Menu item to test the stacked canvas. Exit the form and return to the Form Builder.

f) Which properties can you adjust to make the stacked canvas and its items look better? For example, isn't the stacked canvas set a bit lower than the content canvas?

Answer: You can set the Bevel *property to* None *and re-arrange the items and their prompts.*

g) Which of the stacked canvas' properties can you change so that it is not visible when the form opens?

Answer: You can set the INSTRUCTOR *canvas'* Visible *property to* No.

As you noticed for the INSTRUCTOR canvas, if the Visible property is set to Yes and the form has not navigated to an item on a canvas that will cover INSTRUCTOR, then INSTRUCTOR will be visible. The layering of INSTRUCTOR on top of SECTION determines the stacking order of the canvases. Like default navigation, the stacking order of canvases is determined by the order of the canvases in the Object Navigator. Since INSTRUCTOR is listed after the SECTION content canvas, it appears on top. If there had been other canvases after INSTRUCTOR, those would have appeared on top.

■ *FOR EXAMPLE:*

Figure 8.8 shows the Object Navigator with two more stacked canvases added to this form. Note that CANVAS_3 and CANVAS_4 come after SECTION and INSTRUCTOR.

Figure 8.9 shows these same canvases at run-time, just after the form has been opened.

Note that because CANVAS_4 is the last canvas listed in the Navigator, it is displayed on top at run-time. The default stacking order of canvases is similar to default navigation in that it can be overridden programmatically at run-time.

Open the WHEN-BUTTON-PRESSED trigger for the CHANGEVIEW button.

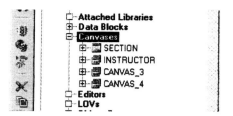

Figure 8.8 ■ Stacking order of canvases in the Object Navigator.

h) What trigger code could you write to change the canvas' `Visible` property? Your trigger should first evaluate whether or not the canvas is visible. If the canvas is not visible, use a built-in to show it. If it is visible, use a built-in to hide it. Use conditional logic and `GET_` and `SET_` built-ins to accomplish this.

Answer: See the discussion below.

The code for the trigger would be as follows:

```
DECLARE
  v_visible VARCHAR2(50);
BEGIN
  v_visible := GET_VIEW_PROPERTY('INSTRUCTOR', VISIBLE);
  IF v_visible = 'TRUE' THEN
    SET_VIEW_PROPERTY('INSTRUCTOR', VISIBLE, PROPERTY_FALSE);
  ELSE
    SET_VIEW_PROPERTY('INSTRUCTOR', VISIBLE, PROPERTY_TRUE);
  END IF;
END;
```

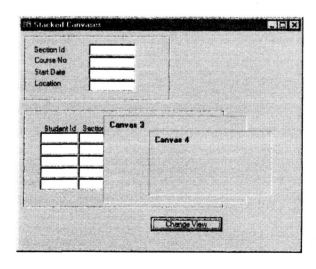

Figure 8.9 ■ Stacked canvases at run-time.

The GET_VIEW_PROPERTY statement returns TRUE if the canvas is visible and FALSE if it is not. The IF, THEN, ELSE statement evaluates the current state of the canvas to see whether it should be hidden or displayed.

Run the form, issue a query, and test the Change View button.

i) What are two other built-ins you could use to hide and show the canvas? These should not be GET_ or SET_ built-ins, and they should not cause navigation.

The SHOW_VIEW and HIDE_VIEW built-ins would work just as well and can simply replace the SET_VIEW_PROPERTY statements. The code would be as follows:

```
DECLARE
   v_visible VARCHAR2(50);
BEGIN
   v_visible := GET VIEW PROPERTY('INSTRUCTOR', VISIBLE);
   IF v_visible = 'TRUE' THEN
           HIDE_VIEW('INSTRUCTOR');
     ELSE
           SHOW_VIEW('INSTRUCTOR');
     END IF;
END;
```

Run the form, issue a query, and test the Change View button. Exit the form and return to the Form Builder.

Replace the built-ins you used for Question i with GO_BLOCK('INSTRUCTOR') and GO_BLOCK('ENROLLMENT') statements.

Run the form, issue a query, and test the Change View button.

j) How is the behavior of the form different now that you are using navigational built-ins instead of the built-ins you used in Questions h and i?

Answer: The cursor moves to the first item in the block that is being navigated to.

The GO_BLOCK built-in is similar to GO_ITEM in that it forces navigation. The form automatically navigated to the first item in the block being referenced in the built-in.

LAB 8.3 SELF-REVIEW QUESTIONS

In order to test your progress, you should be able to answer the following questions:

1) Which of the following is not true about creating stacked canvases?
   a) _____ You cannot position items on a stacked canvas only
   b) _____ You can create a stacked canvas visually in the Layout Editor
   c) _____ You can create a stacked canvas in the Layout Wizard
   d) _____ a & c

2) Where can stacked canvases be positioned?
   a) _____ On top of a content canvas
   b) _____ Outside the MDI window
   c) _____ Behind the MDI window
   d) _____ a & b

3) What is a stacked canvas' viewport?
   a) _____ The area that is visible at run-time
   b) _____ A graphic object used to frame objects
   c) _____ The logical container of a canvas
   d) _____ a & b

4) Which of the following built-ins can be used to display a stacked canvas?
   a) _____ GO_BLOCK
   b) _____ SHOW_VIEW
   c) _____ SET_VIEW_PROPERTY
   d) _____ All of the above

5) What can a stacked canvas be used for?
   a) _____ Partly or wholly obscuring other canvases and items
   b) _____ Creating wizard objects
   c) _____ Dynamically changing the look of the screen
   d) _____ All of the above

Quiz answers appear in Appendix A, Section 8.3.

L A B   8 . 4

TOOLBAR CANVASES

LAB OBJECTIVES
After this Lab, you will be able to:
• Create a Toolbar Canvas • Use the Toolbar in Another Form

A toolbar canvas properly positions toolbar items in a window. By specifying a canvas as either a vertical or a horizontal toolbar, Forms will position it horizontally along the top of a window or vertically along the left-hand edge of the window.

Toolbars, like all canvases, are made visible by assigning them to windows. Unlike other canvas types, toolbar canvases can be assigned to the MDI window. You will experiment with assigning a toolbar to both a normal window and the MDI window in the Exercises.

Since you are creating a toolbar, you must also create a group of items to place on it. In the Exercises below, you will create buttons. However, it is possible to include other item types on a toolbar. For example, the Utility toolbar in the Layout Editor includes two list items.

In the Exercises, you will create a simple toolbar that mimics some of the functionality of the default toolbar that Forms provides for all forms. Once the toolbar is created and configured, you will learn how to reuse the toolbar by copying it from one form to another.

LAB 8.4 EXERCISES

8.4.1 CREATE A TOOLBAR CANVAS

Create a new form and call it R_TOOLBAR.fmb. Create a canvas using the Object Navigator and name it TOOLBAR. Rename WINDOW1 to MAINWIN.

a) How can you change this canvas into a horizontal toolbar canvas?

_____

_____

This simple toolbar canvas will have five buttons: SAVE, EXIT, ENTER_QUERY, EXECUTE_QUERY, and CANCEL_QUERY.

b) What type of object will you have to create to logically contain these items?

_____

_____

Create a block and name it TOOLBAR. Create five buttons. Name them SAVE, EXIT, ENTER_QUERY, EXECUTE_QUERY, and CANCEL_QUERY. They should appear in this order in the block. Assign the buttons to the TOOLBAR canvas.

c) Do typical toolbars have text labels or iconic labels? Which property can you adjust to make your toolbar buttons typical?

_____

_____

Use the icons supplied by Oracle Developer. The item names are in CAPS and the corresponding icon names are in lower-case as follows: SAVE save, EXIT exit, ENTER_QUERY entqry, EXECUTE_QUERY exeqry, and CANCEL_QUERY canqry.

l) What built-ins can you use to respond to the rest of the buttons? Create a WHEN-BUTTON-PRESSED trigger for each button and use DO_KEY statements with the built-ins.

_____

_____

m) Does it make sense to have the SAVE button enabled during Enter Query mode? Why not?

_____

_____

n) What built-in could you use to adjust this at run-time?

_____

_____

Save the form as R_TOOLBAR.fmb.

8.4.2 USE THE TOOLBAR IN ANOTHER FORM

In this Exercise, you will copy the toolbar and its objects to the R_CON-CANV.fmb form. But, before you do, you will add another button to the toolbar. Open both R_TOOLBAR.fmb and R_CONCANV.fmb in the Form Builder.

a) What item on the R_CONCANV.fmb form could be better implemented as a toolbar item?

_____

_____

Minimize all of the objects for R_CONCANV.fmb for the time being. Create another button on the TOOLBAR canvas in R_TOOLBAR.fmb and position it to the right of Cancel Query. Name it SHOW_HIST. Adjust its size, navigable, and icon properties to match the other buttons on the TOOLBAR canvas. Set its Icon Filename property to srch_frw and set its Tool Tip to Record History.

This button will be used to open the HISTWIN window in the R_CON-CANV.fmb form.

> **b)** What code should you put in the WHEN-BUTTON-PRESSED trigger for the SHOW-HIST button?
>
> _____
>
> _____

Add the code and compile the trigger.

> **c)** Which objects should you drag from R_TOOLBAR.fmb to R_CONCANV.fmb so that it too can have a functioning toolbar? Copy the objects; do not subclass them.
>
> _____
>
> _____

> **d)** What should you do to make this toolbar available to the form? What else should you do to make it the only toolbar in the form?
>
> _____
>
> _____

Run the form and test all of the toolbar buttons.

> **e)** Was it convenient to have to drag these objects one at a time into R_CONCANV.fmb?
>
> _____
>
> _____

Save the changes to R_TOOLBAR.fmb. *Do NOT save the changes to* R_CONCANV.fmb. *If you already have, simply delete all of the* TOOLBAR *objects from* R_CONCANV.fmb *and re-save it.*

LAB 8.4 EXERCISE ANSWERS

8.4.1 ANSWERS

Create a new form and call it `R_TOOLBAR.fmb`. Create a canvas using the Object Navigator and name it `TOOLBAR`. Rename `WINDOW1` to `MAINWIN`.

a) How can you change this canvas into a horizontal toolbar canvas?

Answer: Change its `Canvas Type` *property to* `Horizontal Toolbar`.

b) What type of object will you have to create to logically contain these items?

Answer: You will have to create a non-base table block.

A toolbar is very similar to the forms you created for data entry and querying. It requires items that must be positioned on a canvas and contained in a block. The main difference is that there are no data items on a toolbar, only non-data items.

c) Do typical toolbars have text labels or iconic labels? Which property can you adjust to make your toolbar buttons typical?

Answer: Typical toolbars have iconic labels. You should adjust the `Iconic` *property.*

d) Should the user be able to navigate to these buttons with the mouse or keyboard? Which properties should you set to ensure that they can't?

Answer: No, set both `Keyboard Navigable` *and* `Mouse Navigable` *to* `No`.

In certain cases, you have seen that it is often necessary for a user to be able to navigate, at least with the keyboard, to a button. This is especially true if they are doing data entry and would like to use the ENTER key to initiate the Button Pressed event. However, it is never necessary to navigate to a button on a toolbar.

e) What Layout Editor feature can you use to quickly position all of the buttons next to each other? Note that if you used the Object Navigator to create the buttons, they may be currently positioned on top of each other. This should not pose a problem for you.

Answer: You can use `Arrange | Align Objects`, `Stack Horizontally`.

Stacking the buttons will put them next to each other as shown in Figure 8.10.

In many applications, you may have noticed that the toolbar buttons are spaced or separated into groups to make the toolbar more understandable.

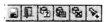

Figure 8.10 ■ A toolbar with buttons stacked horizontally.

■ *FOR EXAMPLE:*

You may wish to organize your toolbar so that the buttons are spaced by function. You could have two groups, one for the SAVE and EXIT buttons, and one for the QUERY buttons. The groups could be separated by blank space and even graphic objects as in Figure 8.11.

The graphic object is a line with its Bevel property set to Inset.

f) What property can you use to give each button a Tool Tip?

Answer: You can use the Tool Tips *property.*

While the button icons are usually quite descriptive, it is always helpful to include Tool Tips, especially for new users.

Run the form.

g) Which object is the toolbar attached to? Which of the TOOLBAR canvas' properties indicate this?

Answer: The TOOLBAR *canvas is attached to* MAINWIN. *The canvas'* Window *property indicates this.*

As you know, all canvases must be assigned to a window to be visible. The TOOLBAR canvas was attached by default to MAINWIN when you created it. Interestingly, all windows have a Horizontal Toolbar and Vertical Toolbar property. So, you could assign the toolbar canvas at the window level as well.

There are no other canvases in this form yet, but if there were, how do you think TOOLBAR would be positioned relative to those canvases?

■ *FOR EXAMPLE:*

Assume you have created a block based on the STUDENT table and have positioned all of its items on a content canvas called STUDENT. Both the STUDENT and TOOLBAR canvases are assigned to MAINWIN. How will the

**LAB
8.4**

Figure 8.11 ■ A toolbar with buttons separated by function.

TOOLBAR canvas behave? Will it stack itself on top of the STUDENT content canvas or will it position itself between the window's title bar and the STUDENT content canvas?

The TOOLBAR will position itself between the window's title bar and the STUDENT canvas. It will not behave like a stacked canvas and position itself on top of the STUDENT canvas. You don't have to be concerned about toolbars, be they horizontal or vertical, obscuring the content canvas.

In the next question, this will become a moot point because you will learn how to attach your custom toolbar to the MDI window.

h) Can you assign the toolbar to the module? How do you think this will affect the position of the toolbar?

Answer: Yes, using the form's Horizontal Toolbar *property. It will assign the* TOOLBAR *canvas to the MDI window.*

Assign TOOLBAR to the module and run the form again.

i) Where is the toolbar now? Is the original default toolbar still there?

Answer: It is attached to the MDI window. Yes, the original, default toolbar is still there.

Multiple horizontal toolbars are extremely common. Applications like MS Word can have as many as six horizontal toolbars. Even the Layout Editor has two horizontal toolbars. In this case, the toolbars have functionality in common, so it will not be necessary to have both.

j) What happened to the default toolbar?

Answer: The default toolbar has disappeared.

The TOOLBAR you have created is now the main toolbar for the application.

The &SMARTBAR value in the Menu Module property assigns a menu toolbar, also known as a smart bar, to the default Forms menu. The default menu and smart bar are objects that Forms attaches to every form at runtime by default. As you can see, you can override these default settings and use your own toolbars. In Chapter 13, "Forms Menus," you will learn how to override the defaults to create your own menus.

Use the wizards to quickly create a block based on the ZIPCODE table. Stop when you get to the Layout Wizard's canvas page.

k) Should you position the ZIPCODE items on the TOOLBAR canvas? If not, what type of canvas should you create for them?

Answer: No, you should not position them on the TOOLBAR *canvas. You should create a new content canvas for them.*

l) What built-ins can you use to respond to the rest of the buttons? Create a WHEN-BUTTON-PRESSED trigger for each button and use DO_KEY statements with the built-ins.

Answer: See the discussion below.

Use the following statements for each button:

```
1)  SAVE - DO_KEY('COMMIT_FORM');
2)  EXIT - DO_KEY('EXIT_FORM');
3)  ENTER_QUERY - DO_KEY('ENTER_QUERY');
4)  EXECUTE_QUERY - DO_KEY('EXECUTE_QUERY');
5)  CANCEL_QUERY - DO_KEY('EXIT_FORM');
```

**LAB
8.4**

Note that the CANCEL_QUERY button also uses the EXIT_FORM built-in because EXIT_FORM switches the form from Enter Query mode back to Normal mode.

m) Does it make sense to have the SAVE button enabled during Enter Query mode? Why not?

Answer: No, because you cannot commit records during ENTER_QUERY *mode.*

In fact, there are two other buttons that should not be enabled in Enter Query mode. The EXIT_FORM button should not be enabled because you should cancel the query before being able to exit the form. The ENTER_QUERY button should not be enabled either because you are in Enter Query mode already, which means there is no need to click the button again.

By the same token, the CANCEL_QUERY button should be disabled when the form is not in Enter Query mode.

Disabling and enabling buttons on a toolbar make an application much more user-friendly. The status of the buttons tells a user what she can and can't do at any given time.

Figure 8.12 ■ The toolbar in Enter Query mode.

Figure 8.13 ■ The toolbar in Normal mode.

n) What built-in could you use to adjust this at run-time?

Answer: You could use the SET_ITEM_PROPERTY.

In Question m, you learned that many buttons will have to be enabled and disabled depending on the state of the form. In Enter Query mode, the toolbar should look like Figure 8.12. In Normal mode, it should look like Figure 8.13.

You could add a series of SET_ITEM_PROPERTY statements to your triggers to enable and disable the buttons as the status of the form changes, but this would be a bit messy. You want to write the PL/SQL so that the SET_ITEM_PROPERTY statements can be reused instead of rewritten over and over again. In the "Test Your Thinking" section of Chapter 10, "Reusable Code," you will edit the WHEN-BUTTON-PRESSED triggers to call a program unit that will enable and disable certain buttons depending on the system mode.

Save the form as R_TOOLBAR. fmb.

8.4.2 ANSWERS

a) What item on the R_CONCANV. fmb form could be better implemented as a toolbar item?

Answer: The SHOW_HIST *button.*

Remember that eventually you will want both the TOOLBAR canvas and HISTORY canvas on all of your forms. Therefore, it makes sense to add the SHOW_HIST button to the toolbar.

This button will be used to open the HISTWIN window in the R_CON-CANV. fmb form.

b) What code should you put in the WHEN-BUTTON-PRESSED trigger for the SHOW-HIST button?

Answer: See the discussion below.

You will use the GO_ITEM built-in and add it to the trigger as shown below:

```
:global.last_item := :SYSTEM.CURSOR_ITEM;
GO_ITEM('CONTROL.HIDE_HIST');
```

Add the code and compile the trigger.

c) Which objects should you drag from R_TOOLBAR.fmb to R_CONCANV.fmb so that it too can have a functioning toolbar? Copy the objects; do not subclass them.

Answer: See the discussion below.

You should copy the following objects:

1) The TOOLBAR block.
2) The TOOLBAR canvas.

These two objects work together to make the toolbar visible and functional.

d) What should you do to make this toolbar available to the form? What else should you do to make it the only toolbar in the form?

Answer: Set the module's Horizontal Toolbar *property to* TOOLBAR. *Remove* &SMARTBAR *from the module's* Menu Module *property.*

Run the form and test all of the toolbar buttons.

e) Was it convenient to have to drag these objects one at a time into R_CON-CANV.fmb?

Answer: Not really.

You have created the toolbar to be a reusable object, but reusing it is a bit of a nuisance. In the next Chapter, you will create two more objects to include as part of the toolbar, so reusing it as you have here would become even more tedious. In the next Chapter, you will learn how to package the toolbar objects together so that you can move them as a single entity from form to form quickly and easily.

Save the changes to R_TOOLBAR.fmb. *Do NOT save the changes to* R_CONCANV.fmb. *If you already have, simply delete all of the* TOOLBAR *objects and re-save it.*

LAB 8.4 SELF-REVIEW QUESTIONS

In order to test your progress, you should be able to answer the following questions:

1) Which of the following is not true about toolbars?
   a) _____ They can be attached to the MDI window
   b) _____ They can be positioned vertically or horizontally
   c) _____ They can be attached to an LOV
   d) _____ They can have list items as objects

2) How can you completely hide a toolbar button?
   a) _____ Set its `Canvas` property to `Null`
   b) _____ Set its `Visible` property to `No`
   c) _____ Set its `Window` property to `WINDOW1`
   d) _____ a & b

3) Which of the following is true about toolbar buttons?
   a) _____ They can be enabled or disabled at run-time
   b) _____ They can be iconic
   c) _____ They can have `WHEN-BUTTON-PRESSED` triggers attached to them
   d) _____ All of the above

4) At what level in the Forms hierarchy can the triggers that respond to toolbar item events be?
   a) _____ Item level
   b) _____ Block level
   c) _____ Form level
   d) _____ All of the above

Quiz answers appear in Appendix A, Section 8.4.

C H A P T E R   8

TEST YOUR THINKING

1) Create four new iconic buttons on the toolbar in R_TOOLBAR.fmb for the following functions:

- New record
- Delete record
- Previous record
- Next record

Identify the built-ins to correspond to these buttons and add the code to the WHEN-BUTTON-PRESSED trigger. Save the form as R_TOOLBAR.fmb.

2) Implement the toolbar in R_TOOLBAR as a vertical toolbar. Save this form as R_TOOLBAR_V.fmb.

3) Use the wizards to create a form with tabbed canvases. This was not covered in the Lab sections of this Chapter, but you should be able to do it based on your knowledge of canvases. The form will be a master-detail-detail form based on the INSTRUCTOR, SECTION, and ENROLLMENT tables. The items from each block should appear on a different tab page. Arrange and align the items as you see fit.

4) Create a scrolling stacked canvas. First you must do some minor setup. Create a master-detail form based on the COURSE and SECTION tables. Include the audit columns in the blocks, but do not display them on the canvas. Add a display item called INSTRUCTOR_NAME to the SECTION block and populate it with a POST-QUERY trigger.

IMPORTANT: First use the wizards to position all of the items on a content canvas, as you would if you were creating a simple master-detail form. Do not try to create a stacked canvas using the wizard.

Once you have finished with the wizard and the items are positioned on the content canvas, use the Layout Editor to create a stacked canvas. Then, reassign some of the items in the SECTION block to this canvas. It should look like Figure 8.14. You will have to move the items to this canvas by adjusting their properties.

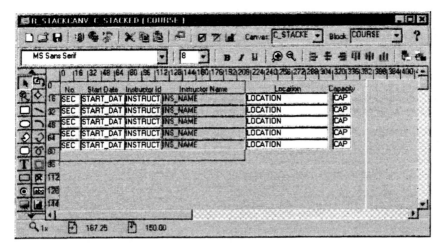

Figure 8.14 ■ Stacked canvas with some of the items from the SECTION block.

Note that, while the items are on the canvas, not all of them are within view. This is very important to simulate the scrolling effect. Also note that there is one item from the SECTION block that is not on the stacked canvas. Which item is it? Which canvas do you think it is on?

Use the Stacked Views feature to align and arrange the items. When the form is running, it should look like Figure 8.15.

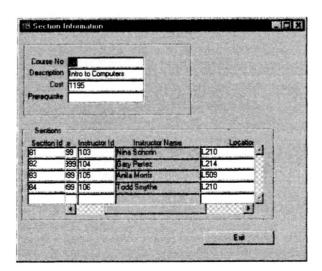

Figure 8.15 ■ A running form with a scrolling stacked canvas.

CHAPTER 9

REUSABLE OBJECTS

CHAPTER OBJECTIVES

In this Chapter, you will learn about:

✔ Subclassing   Page 314
✔ Visual Attributes and Property Classes   Page 323
✔ Object Groups and Object Libraries   Page 336
✔ Template Forms   Page 348

Reusing objects makes development easier and faster. If you create an object in one form and duplicate it in others, you save the time and hassle of having to recreate the same object over and over again. If the duplicates are linked to the source object so that they will change as their source changes, you have saved yourself time and hassle again by being able to maintain and update all of the objects at once rather than one by one.

Forms provides a number of facilities that make it easy and convenient to reuse objects. In this Chapter, you will learn about subclassing, which creates links between reusable objects and enables the inheritance of properties. There are a number of different ways to make use of subclassing. You can subclass entire objects and you can create groups of properties called property classes and subclass or apply them to objects. You can also store reusable objects in object groups, object libraries, and template forms to organize them and make access to them easier.

L A B   9 . 1

SUBCLASSING

LAB OBJECTIVES

After this Lab, you will be able to:

* Subclass Objects

To create one object based on another object, you can use either the Copy feature or Subclass feature. Copying an object creates an exact duplicate of an object that is independent of its source. The copied version of the object has no relationship or link to the source version. Each object can be edited or even deleted without affecting the other.

Subclassing, on the other hand, allows you to create an exact duplicate of an object and maintain a link between the source version and the subclassed (duplicate) version. The subclassed version inherits all of the properties of the source object. If the source is ever changed or edited, the subclassed version will inherit the changes.

■ *FOR EXAMPLE:*

In Lab 8.4, you created a non-base-table block called TOOLBAR that contained several button items. To reuse this TOOLBAR block, you could subclass it to other forms. By subclassing, exact duplicates of the TOOLBAR block will be created in the other forms. Since TOOLBAR contained several buttons, they will be duplicated as well. All of the properties for TOOLBAR and its buttons will be inherited by the subclassed versions of the objects. The link established between the source and the subclassed objects will ensure that if you add another button to the source TOOLBAR or change some of its properties, these changes will be propagated to the subclassed versions of the TOOLBAR.

The subclassed TOOLBAR does not have to remain an exact duplicate of the source. Its properties can be changed and manipulated. You are free to change the properties that have not been inherited, and you can also override the values of properties that have been inherited. Despite the changes to the subclassed object, the link will remain with the source and it will continue to inherit changes.

Any Forms object can be subclassed. In the previous example, by subclassing a block, you also subclassed its items and their triggers. By the same token, if you subclass a canvas, its frames and other graphic objects are subclassed as well.

There are two simple steps for subclassing objects in Forms:

1) Drag the source object from its form and drop it in the target form.
2) Select Subclass when prompted by an alert.

In the Exercises, you will experiment with this and another method for subclassing objects. You will also explore how the Form Builder indicates which objects have been subclassed and which of their properties have been inherited.

LAB 9.1 EXERCISES

9.1.1 SUBCLASS OBJECTS

Use the wizards to quickly create a form based on the ZIPCODE table. Include all of the columns in the block and leave Enforce data integrity **unchecked**. Name this new form R_TARGET.fmb. You will use this form to practice subclassing objects.

Open form EX09_01.fmb. Note that there is a window called MAINWIN and a form-level PRE-FORM trigger.

a) How can you create subclassed versions of MAINWIN and the PRE-FORM trigger in R_TARGET.fmb?

_____

_____

b) How does the Object Navigator indicate that there are sub-classed objects in R_TARGET.fmb?

_____

_____

c) Is there a way to determine the source of these subclassed objects?

_____

_____

d) How can you tell which of the subclassed object's properties are being inherited?

_____

_____

In the form EX09_01.fmb, change the PRE-FORM trigger's Execution Hierarchy property to Before.

e) Has this change been inherited by the subclassed PRE-FORM trigger in R_TARGET.fmb? How can this be useful?

_____

_____

Compile R_TARGET.fmb, then save it and close it.

In EX09_01.fmb, change the MAINWIN's Title property to "Changed while R_TARGET was closed."

Save and close EX09_01.fmb. Re-open R_TARGET.fmb.

f) Has the change to the Title property been propagated to the subclassed version of MAINWIN?

_____

_____

g) If you were to use the Forms Runtime to run the **previously** compiled version of R_TARGET.fmx, would the change have been propagated there?

_____

_____

Delete MAINWIN and the PRE-FORM trigger from R_TARGET.fmb. You should still have a window object named WINDOW1 in R_TARGET.fmb. If you do not, create one now.

Re-open EX09_01.fmb in the Form Builder.

h) How can you make the WINDOW1 object in R_TARGET.fmb a subclassed version of MAINWIN in EX09_01.fmb without using the drag-and-drop technique?

_____

_____

i) Would you still have been able to do this if EX09_01.fmb had been closed?

_____

_____

Save R_TARGET.fmb *as you will need it in the Exercises in Lab 9.2.*

LAB 9.1 EXERCISES ANSWERS

9.1.1 ANSWERS

a) How can you create subclassed versions of MAINWIN and the PRE-FORM trigger in R_TARGET.fmb?

Answer: Drag them from EX09_01.fmb *to* R_TARGET.fmb. *Choose* Subclass *when prompted by the alert.*

In this case, you were asked to create subclassed versions of the two objects in the R_TARGET.fmb form. By dragging and dropping and then choosing Subclass, you have created new subclassed versions of these objects that are linked to the source objects in EX09_01.fmb. The new objects have inherited properties from their sources, including their object names.

b) How does the Object Navigator indicate that there are subclassed objects in R_TARGET.fmb?

Answer: There is a red arrow over the object's icon.

This is very helpful in that whenever you open a form, you will immediately know which objects have been subclassed. This red arrow notation is also used to indicate which objects have property classes applied to them. You will learn about property classes later in this Chapter.

c) Is there a way to determine the source of these subclassed objects?

Answer: Yes, you can look at the subclassed object's Subclass Information *property.*

The Subclass Information property displays its value in the Subclass Information dialog as shown in Figure 9.1.

The Object Name list shows the name of the source object. The Module list item shows the name of the forms module that the source object belongs to.

d) How can you tell which of the subclassed object's properties are being inherited?

Answer: There is a small black check next to all of the properties that are being inherited.

In this example, only a handful of properties were set in the source object. The rest were left as their default values. The subclassed object inher-

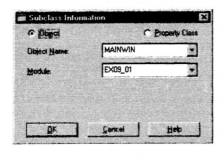

Figure 9.1 ■ The Subclass Information dialog for the MAINWIN object.

◦ Modal	No
▣ Hide on Exit	Yes
↳ Close Allowed	No
↳ Move Allowed	Yes

Figure 9.2 ■ The different icons that describe a property's state.

its all of the properties from the source, but only indicates the ones that have been changed from their defaults. These are the properties that are indicated with a black check mark.

There are four different icons that appear in front of a property in the Property Palette as shown in Figure 9.2.

The four icons indicate if and how the property has been changed and whether or not its value is being inherited.

The **small circle** next to the Modal property indicates that this property value has not been changed from its default value.

The **green box** next to the Hide on Exit property indicates that this property has been changed from its default value.

The **black check mark** next to the Close Allowed property indicates that the value in this property is being inherited from a source object, a visual attribute, or a property class.

The **black check mark with a red x** next to the Move Allowed property indicates that this property's value was inherited, but that the inheritance has been overridden by a change made at the object level.

In Chapter 3, "The Development Environment," you experimented with the Inherit button on the Property Palette's toolbar to return properties to their default values. The Inherit feature behaves a bit differently for a property that has had its inherited value overridden.

■ FOR EXAMPLE:

In R_TARGET.fmb, note that MAINWIN's Close Allowed property is being inherited. Change Close Allowed to Yes. Note that the black check mark is replaced with a black check mark with a red x over it, indicating that the inherited value has been overridden. Now click the Inherit button on the Property Palette's toolbar. What has happened? Here, the Inherit button re-establishes the link between the property and its inherited value, not its default value.

e) Has this change been inherited by the subclassed PRE-FORM trigger in
R_TARGET.fmb? How can this be useful?

Answer: Yes, the change has been inherited by the subclassed PRE-FORM *trigger.*

The ability to change the properties of a source object and have that
change be propagated to its subclassed objects is perhaps the most powerful feature of subclassing. In this case, the PRE-FORM trigger has only
been subclassed to one form. But imagine if your application had fifty
forms and all of them required this PRE-FORM trigger. If you had subclassed them, you would be able to edit and change all fifty simply by
changing the source object.

Compile R_TARGET.fmb then save it and close it.

f) Has the change to the Title property been propagated to the subclassed version of MAINWIN?

Answer: Yes, the change has been propagated.

In this case, the change was propagated as soon as you opened the
R_TARGET.fmb form, even though the EX09_01.fmb form was not open.
This is because the link does not require that both forms be open simultaneously for changes to be propagated. Therefore, you can make changes
to your source objects and know that the next time you open or compile
a form with subclassed objects, the changes will be propagated.

g) If you were to use the Forms Runtime to run the previously compiled version
of R_TARGET.fmx, would the change have been propagated there?

Answer: No it would not have.

If you had created any .fmx files before changing a source object, you
would have to recompile them for the changes to the subclassed object to
take effect. You could do this by using the Form Compiler utility to create
a new .fmx or by opening the form in the Form Builder and running it to
create a new .fmx.

h) How can you make the WINDOW1 object in R_TARGET.fmb a subclassed version of MAINWIN in EX09_01.fmb without using the drag-and-drop technique?

Answer: You can use its Subclass Information *property.*

In Question a you used the drag-and-drop method to subclass an object.
This created an entirely new object that was a duplicate of the source.
You can also use the Subclass Information dialog to subclass objects,
but the results are slightly different than dragging and dropping. You

would use the `Subclass Information` property if you wanted to make an existing object a subclassed version of a source object. In this case, a new version of the object is not created. Instead, the existing object inherits all of the properties in the source object that have been changed from their defaults. If the same properties have previously been changed in an existing object, they will be overridden by the source object's properties. Also, note that the existing object keeps its original name after it has been subclassed.

i) Would you still have been able to do this if `EX09_01.fmb` had been closed?

Answer: No you would not have.

The form that holds the source objects must be open when you perform the subclassing. This applies to the drag-and-drop method as well as using the `Subclass Information` dialog.

 Save `R_TARGET.fmb` *as you will need it in the Exercises for Lab 9.2.*

LAB 9.1 SELF-REVIEW QUESTIONS

In order to test your progress, you should be able to answer the following questions:

1) What are some of the advantages to subclassing?
   a) _____ It enables you to reuse objects
   b) _____ You can base multiple target objects on a single source object
   c) _____ A link is established between the source and the target
   d) _____ All of the above

2) How would you subclass a canvas from Form A to Form B?
   a) _____ Drag the canvas from Form A to Form B and click `Subclass` on the alert
   b) _____ Use the `Subclass Information` property
   c) _____ Copy the canvas from A to B
   d) _____ a & b
   e) _____ a, b, & c

3) How can you determine the source of a subclassed object?
   a) _____ By the icon in the Object Navigator
   b) _____ By the `Subclass Information` property
   c) _____ By the Windows Registry
   d) _____ All of the above

4) How does the Property Palette indicate that a property is being inherited?

    a) _____ A small circle

    b) _____ A green box

    c) _____ A black arrow

    d) _____ A black arrow with a red x over it

5) How does the Property Palette indicate that an inherited property value has been overridden?

    a) _____ A small circle

    b) _____ A green box

    c) _____ A black arrow

    d) _____ A black arrow with a red x over it

Quiz answers appear in Appendix A, Section 9.1.

L A B   9 . 2

VISUAL ATTRIBUTES AND PROPERTY CLASSES

LAB OBJECTIVES

After this Lab, you will be able to:

- Create and Apply Named Visual Attributes
- Create and Apply Property Classes

In Lab 9.1, you subclassed entire objects to promote inheritance. In this Lab, you will use visual attributes and property classes to promote the inheritance of a **group** of properties rather than an entire object.

VISUAL ATTRIBUTES

The visual attribute object contains all of the properties that determine font and color. These properties are useful in that they let you create and apply look and feel standards to multiple objects throughout your applications. A visual attribute called STD_TEXT_ITEMS might have its properties set as those in Figure 9.3.

If you were to apply this visual attribute to an item, it would inherit these property values, making its Foreground Color black, Font Name Arial, and so on. Visual attributes can be applied to physical objects like items, frames, canvases, windows, LOVs, and alerts. They cannot be applied to logical objects like blocks or record groups since those objects have no color or font properties. Although the block object has a visual attribute group property, it is ignored by the Form Builder.

Property Palette	
Visual Attribute: STD_TEXT_ITEMS	
General	
Name	STD_TEXT_ITEMS
Visual Attribute Type	Common
Subclass Information	
Comments	
Visual Attributes	
Character Mode Logical Attribute	<Unspecified>
White on Black	<Unspecified>
Color	
Foreground Color	black
Background Color	white
Fill Pattern	<Unspecified>
Font	
Font Name	Arial
Font Size	10
Font Weight	<Unspecified>
Font Style	Plain
Font Spacing	<Unspecified>

Figure 9.3 ■ Properties for a visual attribute.

PROPERTY CLASSES

Property classes are similar in principle to visual attributes, but they have a few more features that make them a bit more powerful.

1) Any property can be included in a property class, not only font and color properties.

2) Property classes do not have to be in the same form as the objects they are applied to.

3) Property classes can have triggers attached to them.

Visual attributes have a standard set of properties that cannot be changed. Property classes have no standard properties; you can add and delete whichever properties you like from a property class. This makes them more flexible in that you can include properties from the Functional, Database, Record, and other property categories.

Since a property class can include any property, its use is not limited to physical objects, as is the case with visual attributes. A property class can be applied to any object, including logical objects like blocks, record groups, and triggers.

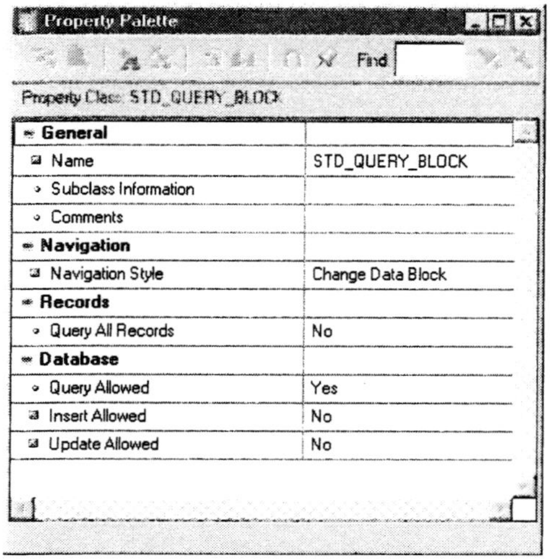

Figure 9.4 ■ **Property class for a query-only block.**

■ *FOR EXAMPLE:*

You could create a property class called STD_QUERY_BLOCK to set standards for blocks that are query-only. The property class might look like that in Figure 9.4.

LAB 9.2 EXERCISES

9.2.1 CREATE AND APPLY NAMED VISUAL ATTRIBUTES

Open R_TARGET.fmb. **Locate the** Visual Attributes **node in the Object Navigator and create a visual attribute. Name it** STD_TEXT_ITEM. **Set the** Font Name **property to** Arial **and the** Foreground Color **to red.**

a) How can you apply STD_TEXT_ITEM to ZIPCODE.ZIP?

_____

_____

b) Have the visual attribute properties been inherited? Is ZIPCODE.ZIP subclassed?

_____

_____

Look at the ZIPCODE.ZIP item in the Layout Editor to confirm that STD_TEXT_ITEM has been applied.

> **c)** How can you apply STD_TEXT_ITEM to all of the items in the ZIPCODE block? Do it in as few steps as possible.

_____

_____

Arrange the Form Builder so that both the Layout Editor and Property Palette are open, but do not overlap. View the properties for STD_TEXT_ITEM.

> **d)** What happens to the text items if you change the STD_TEXT_ITEM's Foreground Color property to blue? to green? to black?

_____

_____

Before you go on, make sure that the Foreground Color of STD_TEXT_ITEM is set to black.

Create a new visual attribute and name it STD_PROMPT.

> **e)** Which of STD_PROMPT's properties will let you define it specifically for prompts?

_____

_____

Set STD_PROMPT's Foreground Color to black, its Font Name to Arial, and its Font Weight to Bold.

> **f)** Can you set the Visual Attribute Group property for ZIPCODE.ZIP to STD_PROMPT? Which of ZIPCODE.ZIP's properties must you use to apply STD_PROMPT?

_____

_____

Apply STD_PROMPT to all the items in the ZIPCODE block.

g) Can you reuse STD_TEXT_ITEM and STD_PROMPT with the R_COURSE.fmb form that you created in Exercise 5.1.1? How? Do not actually take these steps. Simply write your answer.

_____

_____

Close R_TARGET.fmb. *You will not need it anymore.*

9.2.2 CREATE AND APPLY PROPERTY CLASSES

In this Exercise, you will create a property class that will be used to format the audit items. This property class will help you reuse the record history objects that you created in the R_CONCANV.fmb form.

Open the R_CONCANV.fmb form. Select the CREATED_BY item and view its properties.

a) Take a moment to consider the characteristics of all of the audit items and their relation to the Record History window. Which of their properties would you want to apply to all audit items on subsequent forms so that they could be a part of the Record History window?

_____

_____

Select all of these properties in the Property Palette. Click the Property Class button on the Property Palette's toolbar.

b) What object has been created? What are the properties of this new object?

_____

_____

Name the property class AUDIT_ITEMS.

c) How can you apply the AUDIT_ITEMS property class to the CREATED_BY item? Can you apply AUDIT_ITEMS to all of the audit items simultaneously?

_____

_____

d) If you make a change or add another property to AUDIT_ITEMS, do you think it will be propagated to the audit items that are inheriting from the property class?

_____

_____

Save R_CONCANV.fmb and keep it open in the Form Builder. The next few questions will guide you through using the property class in another form.

Quickly create a form based on the COURSE table. Include the audit columns in the block, but not on the canvas. **Leave Enforce data integrity unchecked.** Name the form R_TARGET2. R_TARGET2.fmb is a form you will use to practice subclassing.

e) Can you apply AUDIT_ITEMS to the audit items in R_TARGET2? Do you have to create an instance of AUDIT_ITEMS in R_TARGET2 first?

_____

_____

f) If you make a change to AUDIT_ITEMS in the source form, R_CONCANV, do you think it will be propagated to the audit items in R_TARGET2?

_____

_____

Save R_CONCANV.fmb *and close it. Save* R_TARGET2.fmb *and close it as you will need it in the Exercise in Lab 9.3.*

In the following questions, you will create another property class that will help you reuse the toolbar. This property class will be based on the module object in the R_TOOLBAR.fmb form.

Open R_TOOLBAR.fmb. Select the R_TOOLBAR module and view its properties.

g) Which of the module object's properties assign the toolbar to the module?

_____

_____

h) Which of the module object's properties indicate the menu module that should be used? How should the property be set so that the default smart bar is not displayed?

_____

_____

Create a property class in the Object Navigator and name it TOOLBAR_MODULE.

i) Which of the Property Palette's toolbar buttons can you use to add properties to the class? Do not use the Copy button.

_____

_____

Use this function to add the properties from your answers to Questions g and h to the TOOLBAR_MODULE property class. Also include the Console Window property and set its value to MAINWIN.

In Lab 9.3 you will use this property class and the other objects to reuse the toolbar in other forms.

Save the R_TOOLBAR.fmb *form.*

LAB 9.2 EXERCISE ANSWERS

a) How can you apply STD_TEXT_ITEM to ZIPCODE.ZIP?

Answer: By setting ZIPCODE.ZIP's Visual Attribute *property to* STD_TEXT_ITEM.

b) Have the visual attribute properties been inherited? Is ZIPCODE.ZIP sub-classed?

Answer: Yes, the properties have been inherited, but nothing has been subclassed.

The behavior of visual attributes is somewhat similar to subclassing in that properties from one object are inherited by another. However, there is no subclassed relationship here. If you look at the Subclass Informa-tion property for ZIPCODE.ZIP, you will not see any reference to the vi-sual attribute. The object's visual attribute properties are based on a named visual attribute. Or, put another way, the visual attribute is being applied to the object.

c) How can you apply STD_TEXT_ITEM to all of the items in the ZIPCODE block? Do it in as few steps as possible.

Answer: You can select all of the items in the block and set the Visual At-tribute property for them all.

This feature makes visual attributes a convenient way to standardize the look of a group of objects in a form. In this case, if the form had had two or three base-table blocks with multiple items in each, you could have formatted all of their visual attributes simultaneously.

d) What happens to the text items if you change the STD_TEXT_ITEM's Fore-ground Color property to blue? to green? to black?

Answer: The items' foreground color changes.

Since the visual attribute properties are being inherited by the items, any change to the visual attribute is immediately propagated to those items.

Before you go on, make sure that the Foreground Color of STD_TEXT_ITEM is set to black.

Create a new visual attribute and name it STD_PROMPT.

e) Which of STD_PROMPT's properties will let you define it specifically for prompts?

Answer: The Visual Attribute Type property.

There are three values for the Visual Attribute Type property:

1) Common, which for text and display items applies to the item it-self and its prompt. Common visual attributes can also be used for other interface objects like canvases, windows, and LOVs.

2)   `Prompt`, which applies only to the prompt properties of an item. A visual attribute of type `Prompt` will override any properties set by a visual attribute of type `Common`.

3)   `Title`, which applies to frame titles.

f)   Can you set the `Visual Attribute Group` property for `ZIPCODE.ZIP` to `STD_PROMPT`? Which of `ZIPCODE.ZIP`'s properties must you use to apply `STD_PROMPT`?

Answer: No you cannot. You must use the `Prompt Visual Attribute Group` *property.*

g)   Can you reuse `STD_TEXT_ITEM` and `STD_PROMPT` with the `R_COURSE.fmb` form that you created in Exercise 5.1.1? How? Do not actually take these steps. Simply write your answer.

Answer: Yes you can. You must copy or subclass it to the form.

An instance of a visual attribute must be in a form for it to be available to the objects in that form. It can either be copied or subclassed to the form. So, in this case, if `STD_TEXT_ITEM` and `STD_PROMPT` were subclassed to the `R_COURSE.fmb` form, they could be applied to its items. Also, both visual attributes would behave like any other subclassed object. If any changes were made to the source instances of `STD_TEXT_ITEM` and `STD_PROMPT`, they would be propagated to the subclassed instances of the visual attributes in `R_COURSE.fmb`. These changes would then be propagated to all of the items in `R_COURSE.fmb` that the visual attributes were applied to. This feature gives you the ability to easily enforce look and feel standards across your application.

9.2.2 ANSWERS

a)   Take a moment to consider the characteristics of the audit items and their relation to the `Record History` window. Which of their properties would you want to apply to all audit items on subsequent forms so that they could be a part of the `Record History` window?

Answer: See the discussion below.

The purpose of this property class is to size, position, and configure the audit items for the `HISTORY` canvas so that they can be a part of the `Record History` window. This way, each time you create a form and wish to include the audit items in the `Record History` window, you will simply have to apply this property class. The properties and values you should include are as follows:

Item Type		Display Item
1)	Canvas	HISTORY
2)	X Position	93
3)	Width	75
4)	Height	14
5)	Background Color	gray
6)	Foreground Color	black

You may want to adjust the value of X Position to suit the size of your HISTORY canvas. Unfortunately, since all of the items will have different Y Position values, you cannot add it to this property class. One workaround would be to create four property classes with four different Y Position settings.

b) What object has been created? What are the properties of this new object?

Answer: A new property class with a default name has been created. It contains only the properties that were selected.

To create a property class with multiple properties, this is the easiest way to do it. Not only were the properties added to the class, but their values were copied as well.

You could also create the property class in the Object Navigator and then copy and paste the properties from the source item into the property class.

c) How can you apply the AUDIT_ITEMS property class to the CREATED_BY item? Can you apply AUDIT_ITEMS to all of the audit items simultaneously?

Answer: You use the Subclass Information *dialog. No, you cannot apply* AUDIT_ITEMS *to more than one item at a time.*

In Lab 9.1, you used the Subclass Information dialog to subclass objects. Here you will use it to subclass property classes. In Figure 9.5 you can see that it looks only slightly different from the dialog you saw earlier.

Note that the Property Class radio button at the top of the dialog has been selected. As you did previously, you simply select the module name and property class to subclass.

Unfortunately, unlike visual attributes, you cannot apply a property class to more than one object at a time.

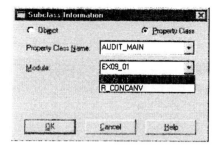

Figure 9.5 ■ The Subclass Information dialog for property classes.

d) If you make a change or add another property to AUDIT_ITEMS, do you think it will be propagated to the audit items that are inheriting from the property class?

Answer: Yes.

Again, the basic rules of subclassing apply here. Any change made to the source AUDIT_ITEMS property class will be propagated to subclassed versions.

e) Can you apply AUDIT_ITEMS to the audit items in R_TARGET2? Do you have to create an instance of AUDIT_ITEMS in R_TARGET2 first?

Answer: Yes you can apply it. No, you do not have to create an instance of AUDIT_ITEMS in R_TARGET2.

Property classes, unlike visual attributes, have a subclassed relationship with the object to which they are applied. If you apply a property class to an object, you will see a reference to it in the Subclass Information dialog. The object will also have a red arrow in front of it in the Object Navigator to further indicate that there is a subclassed relationship.

Because of this, the property class does not have to be in the same form as the object it is applied to. It can be subclassed from other modules just like any other object by using the Subclass Information dialog. This is different from the behavior of visual attributes, which have to be in the same form as the objects they are applied to.

f) If you make a change to AUDIT_ITEMS in the source form, R_CONCANV, do you think it will be propagated to the audit items in R_TARGET2?

Answer: Yes.

Basic subclassing rules apply here too.

g) Which of the module object's properties assign the toolbar to the module?

Answer: The module's `Horizontal Toolbar` *property.*

h) Which of the module object's properties indicate the menu module that should be used? How should the property be set so that the default smart bar is not displayed?

Answer: The `Menu Module` *property. In the property class, the value should be set to* `DEFAULT`.

i) Which of the Property Palette's toolbar buttons can you use to add properties to the class? Do not use the `Copy` button.

Answer: You can use the `Create` *button on the Property Palette's toolbar and select from the list of properties.*

This is an alternative method to copy/paste for adding properties to an existing property class. It is useful if you only wish to add one or two properties, but can become tedious if you wish to add more.

Save the R_TOOLBAR.fmb *form.*

LAB 9.2 SELF-REVIEW QUESTIONS

In order to test your progress, you should be able to answer the following questions:

1) Which of the following properties cannot be applied using a visual attribute?
   a) _____ `Foreground Color`
   b) _____ `Fill Pattern`
   c) _____ `Canvas`
   d) _____ `Font Weight`

2) Which of the following objects can inherit from a visual attribute?
   a) _____ Items
   b) _____ Canvases
   c) _____ LOVs
   d) _____ All of the above

3) A visual attribute can be subclassed to another form.
   a) _____ True
   b) _____ False

4) What are the three types of visual attributes?
   a) _____ Item, Frame, and Canvas
   b) _____ Item, Title, and Prompt
   c) _____ Object, Common, and Label
   d) _____ Title, Common, and Prompt

5) Which of the following is not true about property classes?
   a) _____ They can be applied to any object
   b) _____ They can contain visual as well as other properties
   c) _____ They cannot be applied to more than one item in the same form
   d) _____ Properties can be added or deleted from them

6) Which of the following cannot be done to properties in a property class?
   a) _____ Override them at the subclassed object level
   b) _____ Change them after the property class has been applied
   c) _____ Copy or paste them from another object
   d) _____ None of the above

7) How can you apply a property class to an object?
   a) _____ By dragging and dropping it on top of the object
   b) _____ By setting the property class' Target Objects property
   c) _____ By setting the target object's Subclass Information property
   d) _____ By making it available to the target form

8) Which takes precedence over the properties inherited from a property class?
   a) _____ Properties overridden at the object level
   b) _____ Form-level properties
   c) _____ Properties inherited from a visual attribute
   d) _____ a & c

Quiz answers appear in Appendix A, Section 9.2.

OBJECT GROUPS AND OBJECT LIBRARIES

LAB OBJECTIVES

After this Lab, you will be able to:

• Create and Reuse Object Groups
• Create and Utilize Object Libraries

Object groups and object libraries serve as containers to make reusing objects, either through subclassing or copying, much easier. An object group is an object within a forms module, while an object library is a module unto itself.

OBJECT GROUPS

In previous Labs, you created a group of objects that comprised a toolbar and a group of objects that comprised the Record History window. To reuse these groups of objects in another form, you had to drag each object one by one from the source form to the target form. An object group is a single object that allows you to store references to the two objects that comprise the toolbar. When you want to reuse the toolbar in another form, you simply drag the object group from the source form to the target and select Copy or Subclass. All of the objects are brought over to the target form in one simple step. This will become an extremely convenient feature when you begin to create reusable objects that are made up of five or more individual objects. Object groups are logical containers that are only visible in the Object Navigator. The object group for the toolbar might look something like that in Figure 9.6

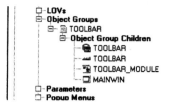

Figure 9.6 ■ An object group in the Object Navigator.

OBJECT LIBRARIES

As you create more reusable objects, you will want to store them in a central place so that you can access them easily. In the previous Labs, all of your objects were spread out across three or four forms. If you wanted to reuse a number of these objects, you had to open each form and then drag and drop each of the objects. An object library is a module, stored in a separate file, that can be opened and configured in the Form Builder. Library modules have an .olb extension. You can open object library modules in the LIBRARY window, view their objects, and copy or subclass their objects into forms modules. A typical object library would resemble that in Figure 9.7.

The object library can hold any type of object, including triggers, blocks, items, and even object groups. The tabs are user-defined and serve to make the library more organized. You can have as many or as few tabs as you'd like and name them as you please.

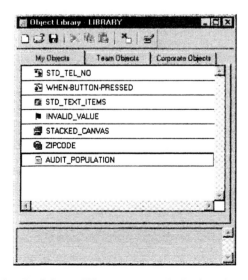

Figure 9.7 ■ A typical object library module in the LIBRARY window.

In the Exercises, you will create and configure your own object library. However, an extremely extensive object library has been installed along with Oracle Developer. It contains visual attributes, alerts, buttons, items, and so on. You are encouraged to use this library and its standard objects in your applications. It is called stndrd20.olb, and it can be found in the following directory:

\ORACLE_HOME\tools\devdemo60\demo\forms\stndrd20.olb

LAB 9.3 EXERCISES

9.3.1 CREATE AND REUSE OBJECT GROUPS

Open the R_TRANS.fmb form you created in Lab 6.2.3. Locate the Object Group node in the Object Navigator. Create an object group and name it AUDIT_POPULATION.

a) How can you make the form-level PRE-INSERT and PRE-UPDATE triggers children of the AUDIT_POPULATION object group?

_____

_____

Open R_TARGET2.fmb. Start dragging the AUDIT_POPULATION object group from R_TRANS.fmb into R_TARGET2.fmb.

b) Onto which two nodes in R_TARGET2.fmb can you drag and drop AUDIT_POPULATION? **Make sure you subclass the object group.**

_____

_____

c) Where were the trigger objects positioned? How will this be helpful when you create an object group for all of the objects that make up the Record History window?

_____

_____

d) Do the subclassed objects list the object group as their source? If not, what do they list and why?

_____

_____

e) If you were to change either the PRE-INSERT or PRE-UPDATE trigger in the R_TRANS.fmb form, do you think the changes would be propagated to R_TARGET2.fmb?

_____

_____

Close R_TARGET2.fmb *without saving. You will not need it anymore.*

Collapse all the nodes in the R_TRANS.fmb form so that the Object Navigator is easier to read. Open R_TOOLBAR.fmb. Create an object group called TOOLBAR.

f) Which objects should you drag into the TOOLBAR object group if you want it to contain all of the objects that make up the toolbar?

_____

_____

Drag the objects you listed for Question f into the TOOLBAR object group.

Collapse all the nodes in the R_TOOLBAR.fmb form so that the Object Navigator is easier to read.

Open R_CONCANV.fmb. Delete the SHOW_HIST button from the CONTROL block as you will not need it anymore. Create an object group called RECORD_HISTORY.

g) Which objects should you drag into the RECORD_HISTORY object group if you want it to contain all of the objects that make up the Record History window?

_____

_____

Drag the objects you listed for Question g into the RECORD_HISTORY object group.

Save R_TRANS.fmb, R_TOOLBAR.fmb, *and* R_CONCANV.fmb *to preserve the addition of the object groups.*

Create a new form in the Object Navigator. Subclass the AUDIT_POPULATION, TOOLBAR, and RECORD_HISTORY object groups into the new form.

h) Which property class should you apply to this new form to ensure that the toolbar is positioned on the MDI window?

i) How should the windows be ordered in the Object Navigator? Which window can you delete?

Quickly create a block based on the ZIPCODE table. Enforce data integrity should be **unchecked**. Include the audit columns in the block, but not on the canvas. Make sure you create a **new** canvas in the Layout Wizard.

j) Which property class should you apply to the audit items?

Open the HISTORY canvas. Arrange the audit items so that they are all visible and aligned.

Run the form and test that the toolbar works, the Record History window opens, and that the audit columns are populated when you insert and update records.

Close this new form without saving. You will not need it anymore.

9.3.2 CREATE AND UTILIZE OBJECT LIBRARIES

Open R_TOOLBAR.fmb, R_TRANS.fmb, and R_CONCANV.fmb in the Form Builder. Collapse all of their nodes to make the Object Navigator easier to read.

Locate the Object Library node in the Object Navigator. Create an object library and name it LIBRARY. Double-click the icon next to LIBRARY to open it.

> **a)** How many default library tabs were created for LIBRARY? How can you rename and label them? Use the following name and label combinations: OBJGROUP - Object Groups and SINGLEOBJ - Single Objects.

LAB
9.3

_____

_____

> **b)** How can you add the AUDIT_ITEMS property class from the R_CONCANV.fmb form to the Single Objects tab of LIBRARY?

_____

_____

> **c)** Were you asked to subclass or copy AUDIT_ITEMS into LIBRARY? Why not?

_____

_____

Collapse all of the nodes for R_CONCANV.fmb.

Save LIBRARY.olb since you cannot reuse any of its objects until it has been saved.

Create a new form, but do not create any blocks or objects.

> **d)** How can you reuse the AUDIT_ITEMS property class that is stored in the LIBRARY in this new form? Choose Subclass when reusing.

_____

_____

e) In the new form, what is the value of the `Subclass Information` property for AUDIT_ITEMS? Is there any reference to `R_CONCANV.fmb`?

_____

_____

Delete the subclassed version of AUDIT_ITEMS from your new form.

f) Can you edit the properties for AUDIT_ITEMS directly in LI-BRARY?

_____

_____

Drag AUDIT_ITEMS into the new form again so that you can edit it. Choose `Copy` instead of `Subclass`. Change AUDIT_ITEMS's `Comment` property to `"This object has been changed."` Drag AUDIT_ITEMS back to LIBRARY.

g) How should you respond to the alert you are presented with if you want LIBRARY to have the new changes?

_____

_____

h) If AUDIT_ITEMS were previously subclassed to other forms, would the changes to the `Comment` property be inherited by those forms?

_____

_____

Drag the AUDIT_POPULATION, TOOLBAR, and RECORD_HISTORY object groups into the `Object Group` tab of LIBRARY and save it. Close the forms R_TRANS.fmb, R_TOOLBAR.fmb, and R_CONCANV.fmb.

i) If you were to subclass these object groups from LIBRARY to other forms, do you think the subclassing behavior would be the same for them as it was for the AUDIT_ITEMS property class?

_____

_____

LAB 9.3 EXERCISE ANSWERS

9.3.1 ANSWERS

a) How can you make the form-level PRE-INSERT and PRE-UPDATE triggers children of the AUDIT_POPULATION object group?

Answer: You can drag them into the AUDIT_POPULATION object group.

Note that there are representations of the objects under the object group's Object Children node. If you click any one of the children, you can view and change its properties in the Property Palette.

b) Onto which two nodes in R_TARGET2.fmb can you drag and drop AUDIT_POPULATION? **Make sure you subclass the object group.**

Answer: You can drag the objects either onto the Module or Object Group node.

c) Where were the trigger objects positioned? How will this be helpful when you create an object group for all of the objects that make up the Record History window?

Answer: They were automatically positioned under the proper node in the Object Navigator.

This is helpful because it will save you a tremendous amount of time when copying or subclassing object groups from one form to another, especially when the object groups contain many objects of varying types.

d) Do the subclassed objects list the object group as their source? If not, what do they list and why?

Answer: No, they list the source object's name and its module.

The object group is only a logical container of objects; it is not considered the source module that holds the objects. Therefore, when you look at any subclassed object's Subclass Information property, you will see no reference to the object group.

e)   If you were to change either the PRE-INSERT or PRE-UPDATE trigger in the R_TRANS.fmb form, do you think the changes would be propagated to R_TARGET2.fmb?

Answer: Yes, because you subclassed, the changes are propagated.

f)   Which objects should you drag into the TOOLBAR object group if you want it to contain all of the objects that make up the toolbar?

Answer: See the list below.

1)   TOOLBAR block.
2)   TOOLBAR canvas.
3)   TOOLBAR_MODULE property class.
4)   MAINWIN window.

g)   Which objects should you drag into the RECORD_HISTORY object group if you want it to contain all of the objects that make up the Record History window?

Answer: See the list below.

1)   CONTROL block.
2)   HISTORY canvas.
3)   AUDIT_ITEMS property class.
4)   HISTWIN window.

The CONTROL block has also brought the HIDE_HIST button and its trigger into the object group. By the same token, if the HISTORY canvas had had any frames or other graphic objects, those would have been included as well.

h)   Which property class should you apply to this new form to ensure that the toolbar is positioned on the MDI window?

Answer: The TOOLBAR_MODULE property class.

i)   How should the windows be ordered in the Object Navigator? Which window can you delete?

Answer: The Layout Wizard will assign new canvases to the window that is listed first in the Object Navigator. Therefore, MAINWIN should be listed first. You can delete WINDOW1.

Since MAINWIN is going to be the window for the canvas that holds the data items, you want it to be listed first in the Object Navigator. This way, the canvas for the data items will not be assigned to HISTWIN.

j) Which property class should you apply to the audit items?

Answer: You should apply the AUDIT_ITEMS *property class.*

9.3.2 ANSWERS

a) How many default library tabs were created for LIBRARY? How can you re-name and label them? Use the following name and label combinations: OBJ-GROUP - Object Groups and SINGLEOBJ - Single Objects.

Answer: Two tabs were created by default. Library tabs have properties that you can use to set the name and label.

You can add as many library tabs to an object library as you'd like. In this Exercise, you will put Object Groups on one tab and Single Objects on another. You could organize the library differently with tabs for Items, Blocks, Physical Objects, Logical Objects, or whatever.

b) How can you add the AUDIT_ITEMS property class from the R_CONCANV.fmb form to the Single Objects tab of LIBRARY?

Answer: You can drag it into the object library.

c) Were you asked to subclass or copy AUDIT_ITEMS into LIBRARY? Why not?

Answer: No you were not.

Object libraries hold actual instances of objects, not just pointers to them. Also, since the object library is supposed to serve as the source for all of your objects, you would not want it to contain subclassed versions of objects. If you choose to use object libraries, they should be the source that all of your subclassed objects come from.

d) How can you reuse the AUDIT_ITEMS property class that is stored in the LIBRARY in this new form? Choose Subclass when reusing.

Answer: You can drag it from the object library into the form.

e) In the new form, what is the value of the Subclass Information property for AUDIT_ITEMS? Is there any reference to R_CONCANV.fmb?

Answer: The value is LIBRARY.AUDIT_ITEMS, *which has been subclassed from the object library, not the* R_CONCANV.fmb *form.*

It is important to emphasize that there is no link between an object in the object library and the object and module that it originally came from. The object library is now the source of the object, so the link and all references point to it.

f)   Can you edit the properties for AUDIT_ITEMS directly in LIBRARY?

Answer: No you cannot.

To edit or change an object that is in an object library, you must first copy that object into a form and then do the editing. When you have finished making the changes to the object, you must drag it back to the object library.

g)   How should you respond to the alert you are presented with if you want LIBRARY to have the new changes?

Answer: You should choose Yes.

You do this because you want to replace the existing version with the one you have just edited.

h)   If AUDIT_ITEMS were previously subclassed to other forms, would the changes to the Comment property be inherited by those forms?

Answer: Yes they would.

Drag the AUDIT_POPULATION, TOOLBAR, and RECORD_HISTORY object groups into the Object Group tab of LIBRARY and save it. Close the forms R_TRANS.fmb, R_TOOLBAR.fmb, and R_CONCANV.fmb.

i)   If you were to subclass these object groups from LIBRARY to other forms, do you think the subclassing behavior would be the same for them as it was for the AUDIT_ITEMS property class?

Answer: Yes it would. All of the subclassing rules would apply.

LAB 9.3 SELF-REVIEW QUESTIONS

In order to test your progress, you should be able to answer the following questions:

1)   Which of the following is true about object groups?
   a) _____ They can have multiple child objects
   b) _____ They can only contain objects of the same type
   c) _____ They are organized with tabs
   d) _____ They can only be subclassed, not copied

2) How do you add objects to an object group?
   a) _____ By setting the object group's `Child Objects` property
   b) _____ By setting the object's `Object Group` property
   c) _____ By dragging objects into the object group
   d) _____ None of the above

3) Why are object groups useful?
   a) _____ You can package related objects together
   b) _____ You can copy or subclass a group of related objects to another form in a single step
   c) _____ If subclassed, you can make changes to the objects in the object group that are propagated to target objects
   d) _____ All of the above

4) How are objects stored in an object library?
   a) _____ As pointers to objects in other modules
   b) _____ As actual instances of objects
   c) _____ As subclassed instances
   d) _____ b & c

5) How can you use an object library?
   a) _____ To organize the objects you wish to subclass or copy to other forms
   b) _____ As a central source for all of your Forms objects
   c) _____ As any area to edit and update reusable objects
   d) _____ a & b

6) What can you do with objects in an object library?
   a) _____ Copy them to other forms
   b) _____ Subclass them to other forms
   c) _____ Organize them any way you'd like
   d) _____ All of the above

Quiz answers appear in Appendix A, Section 9.3.

L A B   9 . 4

TEMPLATE FORMS

LAB OBJECTIVES

After this Lab, you will be able to:
*   Create and Use Template Forms

In the previous Labs in this Chapter, you learned how to reuse objects through subclassing, object groups, and object libraries. In each case, you were referencing an object in one form or library module and subclassing or copying it to another. This allowed you to pick and choose which source objects to include in target forms that either already existed or that were just being created. In each case, you had to drag and drop or otherwise manually reference the objects into the target forms.

Sometimes you will want to create entirely new forms that already contain a standard set of objects. When this is true, then you can create a template form. The template form would already contain all of these objects and would be what you would use as the starting point for your new forms. Using a template form will save you the time of having to manually add the objects to each new form you create.

◼ FOR EXAMPLE:

In the Exercises, you will create a template form to contain all of the objects for the audit population, the toolbar, and the Record History window. When you create forms based on this template, these objects will automatically be added to the new form.

Template forms are no different than any other form. They are created, configured, and saved in the Form Builder in same manner as regular .fmb files. When you want to create a new form based on a template form, you select File | New | Form Using Template from the Main Menu. A new form will open with all of the objects that are included in the template.

LAB 9.4 EXERCISES

9.4.1 CREATE AND USE TEMPLATE FORMS

Open the LIBRARY object library in the Form Builder. Create a new form and name it R_TEMPLATE.fmb. Subclass all three object groups from LIBRARY into R_TEMPLATE.fmb. You have just created a template form.

In R_TEMPLATE.fmb, delete WINDOW1 and apply the TOOLBAR_MODULE property class to the module. Make sure MAINWIN is listed first under the Windows node in the Object Navigator. Save and close R_TEMPLATE.fmb.

a) Why was it better to subclass all of the objects from the LIBRARY rather than from the individual forms (i.e., R_TOOLBAR.fmb, R_CONCANV.fmb, and R_TRANS.fmb)?

_____

_____

b) How can you use the Main Menu to create a new form based on the R_TEMPLATE.fmb template form?

_____

_____

c) What has the Form Builder named the new form? Why has it done this?

_____

_____

d) Are all of the objects from the template form in your new form?

_____

_____

Close the new form without saving as you will not need it anymore.

LAB 9.4 EXERCISE ANSWERS

9.4.1 ANSWERS

a) Why was it better to subclass all of the objects from the LIBRARY rather than from the individual forms (i.e., R_TOOLBAR.fmb, R_CONCANV.fmb, and R_TRANS.fmb)?

Answer: It was easier to take them all from one source rather than from three different ones.

Also, it makes sense for object maintenance. You will probably create many template forms, each with different combinations of objects. If you were to store the source objects in each template form, you would have to manage and edit them there as well. By storing them in the object library, you can manage all of your objects in one place regardless of how many template and non-template forms you create.

b) How can you use the Main Menu to create a new form based on the R_TEM-PLATE.fmb template form?

Answer: Select File | New | Form Using Template, *then select* R_TEM-PLATE.fmb.

After you click the OK button, a new form will open in the Form Builder. It will contain all of the objects that were a part of R_TEMPLATE.fmb. If you had chosen R_COURSE.fmb, your new form would have included a COURSE block and a COURSE canvas. So, any form can serve as a template form.

c) What has the Form Builder named the new form? Why has it done this?

Answer: It has given it a default name.

When you base a form on a template, the Form Builder automatically renames the form so that you will not accidentally overwrite the template.

d) Are all of the objects from the template form in your new form?

Answer: Yes.

LAB 9.4 SELF REVIEW QUESTIONS

In order to test your progress, you should be able to answer the following questions:

1) How are template forms used?
   a) _____ As starting "boilerplate" forms
   b) _____ As source forms for an object library
   c) _____ As areas to edit layout
   d) _____ a & b

2) What happens when you base a form on a template form?
   a) _____ Forms assigns a default name to the new form
   b) _____ Forms will overwrite the template form if you don't change the new form's name
   c) _____ All of the objects in your template form are included in the new form
   d) _____ a & c

3) What can template forms contain?
   a) _____ Any object
   b) _____ Only subclassed objects
   c) _____ Only objects subclassed from object libraries
   d) _____ Only object groups

4) How do you create a template form?
   a) _____ By setting the `Module Type` **property to** `Template`
   b) _____ By using the Form Builder like any other form
   c) _____ By saving a form with a `.tmp` extension
   d) _____ a & c

Quiz answers appear in Appendix A, Section 9.4.

TEST YOUR THINKING

Use the object library to subclass the TOOLBAR, AUDIT_POPULATION, and RECORD_HISTORY object groups to the following forms:

R_INSTRUCTOR.fmb

R_STUDENT.fmb

R_COURSE.fmb

R_CRSESECT.fmb

R_STUDENRL.fmb

In R_CRSESECT and R_STUDENRL, the Record History window objects should apply to the detail block.

C H A P T E R 1 0

REUSABLE CODE

CHAPTER OBJECTIVES

In this Chapter, you will learn about:

✔ Program Units   Page 354
✔ PL/SQL Libraries   Page 362
✔ Stored PL/SQL Objects   Page 374

So far, all of the PL/SQL logic you have written has been stored in triggers. This has been convenient and powerful because you were able to write custom code to respond to events. One of the limitations of triggers is that it is difficult to reuse them. Of course, you can subclass or copy them, but then you are creating multiple instances of the same code. It is far better to remove the code from a single trigger and store it somewhere where multiple triggers can access it.

In forms modules, this is done by creating program units. In Lab 10.1, you will create a single program unit that all of the WHEN-VALIDATE-ITEM triggers in a form can reuse. In Lab 10.2, you will store that same program unit in a PL/SQL library module so that triggers in other forms modules can reuse it. You will also learn how to write generic code so that a program unit can be useful in more than one situation.

L A B   1 0 . 1

PROGRAM UNITS

LAB OBJECTIVES

After this Lab, you will be able to:

• Create a Program Unit

Program units are Forms objects that contain PL/SQL code. They can be packages, procedures, or functions, and can accept parameters and return values. They are identical in structure and syntax to the packages, procedures, and functions stored in the database, except they are stored, compiled, and run within a Forms application.

Program units make the PL/SQL code within forms modules more reusable because they release the code from being bound to a single trigger and the events that the trigger responds to. Once code has been placed in a program unit, it is accessible from any trigger or other program unit in the form.

■ *FOR EXAMPLE:*

Assume you create a button called BUTTON_1 that displays a canvas called CANVAS_1 when pressed. The code in the WHEN-BUTTON-PRESSED trigger could be as follows:

```
SHOW_VIEW('CANVAS_1');
```

While this will work quite well, the limitation is that the canvas will only be displayed in response to the Button Pressed event for BUTTON_1. Now, assume that you also want to create POST-QUERY and POST-INSERT triggers to display the canvas each time the user issues a query and each time they insert a record. Since you cannot call the code in the WHEN-BUTTON-PRESSED trigger, you would have to re-write it in both the POST-QUERY and POST-INSERT triggers. You would then have three triggers with identical code. This would be difficult to maintain and hard to manage, especially if the code were more complicated than a single SHOW_VIEW statement.

The alternative is to create a program unit and call it from each of the three triggers. The program unit could be named DISPLAY_CANVAS and it could contain the following code:

```
PROCEDURE DISPLAY_CANVAS IS
BEGIN
   SHOW_VIEW('CANVAS_1');
END;
```

Each trigger would then contain the following statement to call DIS-PLAY_CANVAS:

```
DISPLAY_CANVAS;
```

The code is now in a central location and accessible to all three triggers in the form. It will also be accessible to subsequent triggers and program units created in the form.

Program units also make PL/SQL code more reusable because they can accept parameters. By doing so, the code in the program unit can be made more generic and therefore reusable.

■ FOR EXAMPLE:

Assume that your application has more than just CANVAS_1; assume that there is a CANVAS_2, CANVAS_3, and CANVAS_4. Instead of writing individual program units to display each canvas, you could make the code in the DISPLAY_CANVAS procedure more generic. The code could be as follows:

```
PROCEDURE DISPLAY_CANVAS (p_canvas_name VARCHAR2) IS
BEGIN
   SHOW_VIEW(p_canvas_name);
END;
```

The procedure DISPLAY_CANVAS now accepts a VARCHAR2 parameter and passes it to the SHOW_VIEW built-in. It is more generic because the canvas name is no longer hard-coded into the program unit. So, it can be used to show any canvas.

Figure 10.1 ■ The New Program Unit dialog box.

The code in the triggers or program units that call DISPLAY_CANVAS would be as follows:

DISPLAY_CANVAS('CANVAS_3');

The value passed to DISPLAY_CANVAS would change depending on which canvas needed to be opened.

When you create a program unit using the Object Navigator, you are first presented with the New Program Unit dialog as shown in Figure 10.1.

Here you name the program unit and select its object type. After clicking the OK button, the PL/SQL editor will open and it will have written a first cut of the program unit's specification section as shown in Figure 10.2.

Program units, like any other object in Forms, can be subclassed to other forms or stored in the object library, which further increases their reusability.

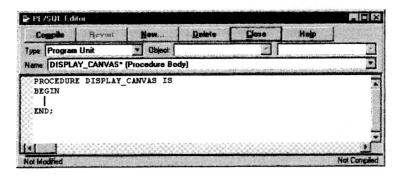

Figure 10.2 ■ The PL/SQL Editor with the specification section for a program unit.

LAB 10.1 EXERCISES

10.1.1 CREATE A PROGRAM UNIT

Open the form EX10_01.fmb in the Form Builder.

In this Exercise, you will create a simple program unit that changes the message text in an alert. You will show this alert whenever a WHEN-VALIDATE-ITEM trigger fails to validate a foreign-key item.

Note that there is an alert called VAL_ALERT already created in EX10_01.fmb. It has one button labeled OK.

Create a program unit and name it GET_ALERT_TEXT. The program unit will accept a VARCHAR2 parameter called p_item. p_item will be the name or description of the item being validated.

> **a)** How should you change the statements in the PL/SQL Editor so that this procedure will accept the p_item parameter?

_____

_____

> **b)** How can you declare three variables? They should be: v_alert_id of type ALERT, v_message of type VARCHAR2(200), and v_alert_response of type NUMBER.

_____

_____

Add the following code to the executable section of GET_ALERT_TEXT:

```
BEGIN
    v_alert_id := FIND_ALERT('VAL_ALERT');
v_message := ('This '||p_item||' does not exist in the database');
  SET_ALERT_PROPERTY(v_alert_id, ALERT_MESSAGE_TEXT, v_message);
  v_alert_response := SHOW_ALERT(v_alert_id);
END;
```

c) How is the p_item parameter being used in this procedure?

_____

_____

Open the WHEN-VALIDATE-ITEM trigger for STUDENT.ZIP.

d) How can you change this trigger so that the user sees the alert when validation fails? What value should you pass to the procedure?

_____

_____

Run the form and issue a query. Test the program unit and alert by entering an invalid Zip Code (e.g., 123). Exit the form and return to the Form Builder.

e) If you were to reuse this program unit in another form, which other object would you have to copy or subclass with it?

_____

_____

f) If GET_ALERT_TEXT had been part of a package called GEN-ERAL, how do you think you would have called it from the WHEN-VALIDATE-ITEM trigger?

_____

_____

Rename the form R_PUNIT.fmb _and save it._

LAB 10.1 EXERCISES ANSWERS

10.1.1 ANSWERS

Open the form EX10_01.fmb in the Form Builder.

a) How should you change the statements in the PL/SQL Editor so that this procedure will accept the `p_item` parameter?

Answer: See the discussion below.

The code so far should be:

```
PROCEDURE GET_ALERT_TEXT (p_item VARCHAR2) IS
BEGIN
```

The syntax for creating a program unit is identical to the syntax for creating a stored procedure in the database. The Form Builder automatically writes the specification section in the PL/SQL Editor. In this case, the procedure accepts one parameter called `p_item`.

b) How can you declare three variables? They should be: `v_alert_id` of type ALERT, `v_message` of type `VARCHAR2(200)`, and `v_alert_response` of type NUMBER.

Answer: See the discussion below.

The code so far should be:

```
PROCEDURE GET_ALERT_TEXT (p_item VARCHAR2) IS
     v_alert_id              ALERT;
     v_message               VARCHAR2(200);
     v_alert_response        NUMBER;
BEGIN
```

c) How is the `p_item` parameter being used in this procedure?

Answer: It is being passed to a character string variable, which is then referenced in the SET_ALERT_PROPERTY built-in.

`p_item` will be the description of the item that is being validated by the WHEN-VALIDATE-ITEM trigger. The message will tell the user that the value that has been entered is invalid. In this case, the value will be ZIP or ZIPCODE. `p_item` is concatenated to a string that will be the message text of the alert. This message text will then be applied to the alert using the SET_ALERT_PROPERTY built-in.

d) How can you change this trigger so that the user sees the alert when validation fails? What value should you pass to the procedure?

Answer: See the discussion below.

You should remove the line:

```
Message('This zipcode does not exist in the database');
```

and replace it with:

GET_ALERT_TEXT('Zipcode');

This example is rather simple, but it illustrates how the GET_ALERT_TEXT program unit could be reused and called from another WHEN-VALIDATE-ITEM trigger. If it were a COURSE_NO item being validated, the WHEN-VALIDATE-ITEM trigger would contain the following line:

GET_ALERT_TEXT('Course Number');

The code in the GET_ALERT_TEXT program unit would not have to change. It would accept the 'Course Number' character string as the value for p_item and set the alert's message text accordingly.

e) If you were to reuse this program unit in another form, which other object would you have to copy or subclass with it?

Answer: The VAL_ALERT object.

f) If GET_ALERT_TEXT had been part of a package called GENERAL, how do you think you would have called it from the WHEN-VALIDATE-ITEM trigger?

Answer: See discussion below.

The code would have been:

GENERAL.GET_ALERT_TEXT('Zipcode');

This is simply to illustrate that you would call a Forms-level packaged PL/SQL object the same way you would if it were stored in the database. All you have to do is prefix the name of the program unit with the name of the package.

LAB 10.1 SELF-REVIEW QUESTIONS

In order to test your progress, you should be able to answer the following questions:

1) What are program units?
   a) ____ Sub-modules within triggers
   b) ____ PL/SQL objects stored within modules
   c) ____ PL/SQL objects that respond to Forms events
   d) ____ b & c

2) Why are program units reusable?

a) _____ They are not bound to a single trigger and the events the trigger responds to

b) _____ They can be written generically so that they are more widely applicable

c) _____ They can be subclassed

d) _____ All of the above

3) Which of the following can be a program unit?

a) _____ Package specification

b) _____ Trigger

c) _____ Event

d) _____ None of the above

4) Where can program units be called from?

a) _____ Properties

b) _____ Triggers

c) _____ Other program units

d) _____ b & c

Quiz answers appear in Appendix A, Section 10.1.

L A B 1 0 . 2

PL/SQL LIBRARIES

LAB OBJECTIVES

After this Lab, you will be able to:

- Create and Attach PL/SQL Libraries
- Use Indirect References in Library Code

Some program units will be usable in more than one form, in which case, you have a few options for making them accessible to those forms. You could subclass or copy the program units to each form as you learned in Chapter 9, "Reusable Objects," or you could store the program units in a PL/SQL Library. PL/SQL Libraries should be used to store program units when these program units will be used by most, or all, of the forms in an application.

PL/SQL Libraries do not belong to forms modules. They are separate modules that can be created, edited, and compiled in the Form Builder. They can contain any number of program units, be they packages, procedures, or functions. Figure 10.3 shows a PL/SQL Library called COMMON in the Object Navigator. Note that it contains the DISPLAY_CANVAS program unit.

Before a form can execute the objects in a PL/SQL Library, the Library must be attached to the form. This can be done using the Object Navigator. Figure 10.4 shows the COMMON Library attached to a form.

PL/SQL Library modules are saved in two file formats: .p11 files, which contain the source code and executable code of the library and .p1x files, which contain only the executable code. Once a Library is saved as a .p11 file, you can use the Form Builder to attach it to as many forms as necessary. Continuing with the canvas example, if every form in your application needed to show canvases, then it would make sense to attach COMMON.p11 to all of those forms.

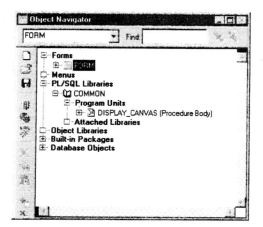

Figure 10.3 ■ A PL/SQL Library module called COMMON in the Object Navigator.

In addition to reusability, another advantage of PL/SQL Libraries is that they help make your application more lightweight and efficient. When you attach a PL/SQL Library to a form, the Library and its code are not stored within the form; the form simply knows that the Library exists and therefore can reference its subprograms. The forms module becomes significantly smaller because it does not have to store the PL/SQL code itself. In addition, if the same Library is attached to ten forms in your application, only one version of the Library file has to be deployed to the users. This will make the overall size of the application smaller.

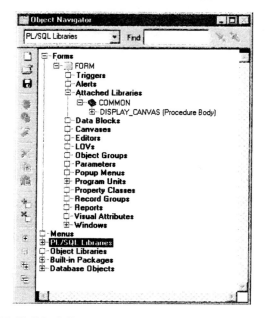

Figure 10.4 ■ A PL/SQL Library attached to a forms module.

INDIRECT REFERENCES IN LIBRARY CODE

In previous Labs and Exercises, you wrote PL/SQL statements that used bind variables such as:

```
v_student_id := :STUDENT.STUDENT_ID
```

and

```
v_item := :SYSTEM.CURSOR_ITEM;
```

These are known as direct references because you are *directly* using the name of a bind variable in your code. In the two statements listed above, you are assigning values to variables by making direct references to an item name and a system variable. You are able to successfully compile forms modules that contain statements like these because the compiler is able to locate an item called :STUDENT.STUDENT_ID in the form. However, you would not be able to successfully compile a PL/SQL Library if it contained direct references to bind variables. The Library module would not contain the item called :STUDENT.STUDENT_ID, so it would not be able to locate it and therefore would compile the Library with errors. To make reference to bind variables in Library code, you have to do so indirectly using the COPY and NAME_IN built-ins. In Chapter 6, "Triggers & Built-ins," you indirectly referenced the names of the audit items with statements that were similar to the following:

```
COPY(v_date, 'COURSE.CREATED_DATE');
```

v_date is being copied into the COURSE.CREATED_DATE item, but the item name is being referenced indirectly. The NAME_IN built-in allows you to indirectly reference bind variables and return their values. To indirectly reference the :SYSTEM.CURSOR_ITEM, you would write the following statement:

```
v_item := NAME_IN(':SYSTEM.CURSOR_ITEM');
```

LAB 10.2 EXERCISES

10.2.1 CREATE AND ATTACH PL/SQL LIBRARIES

Open the form P_PUNIT.fmb. In this Exercise, you will put the GET_ ALERT_TEXT program unit into a PL/SQL Library and then attach the Library to the R_PUNIT.fmb form.

Create a PL/SQL Library using the Object Navigator. Save the Library and name it COMMON.pll.

> **a)** How do you think you can add GET_ALERT_TEXT to COMMON .pll?
>
> _____
>
> _____

> **b)** What are two ways you can compile COMMON.pll from within the Form Builder?
>
> _____
>
> _____

Compile, save, and close COMMON.pll. Delete GET_ALERT_TEXT from the R_PUNIT.fmb form.

> **c)** How can you use the Object Navigator to attach the COMMON.pll library to R_PUNIT.fmb? What dialog has opened?
>
> _____
>
> _____

Browse the filesystem to locate COMMON.pll. Click Attach when COMMON.pll is in the Library field.

> **d)** How should you respond to the alert you are presented with? Should you remove the path or keep the path? How will Forms find the .pll if you remove the path?
>
> _____
>
> _____

> **e)** Can you open and edit GET_ALERT_TEXT through the Attached Library node in the Object Navigator?
>
> _____
>
> _____

Run the form, issue a query, and enter an invalid Zip Code to test that the code in the attached Library can show the alert.

Save the changes to form R_PUNIT.fmb.

10.2.2 USE INDIRECT REFERENCES IN LIBRARY CODE

In this Exercise, you are going to add the code in the triggers from the AUDIT_POPULATION object group to the COMMON.pll PL/SQL Library. Before you do, you will create program units based on the code that is in the PRE-INSERT and PRE-UPDATE triggers. You will also edit them so that there are no direct references to bind variables.

Open R_PUNIT.fmb. **Copy** the AUDIT_POPULATION object group from the LIBRARY object library into R_PUNIT.fmb. View the code for the PRE-INSERT trigger.

> **a)** Will the COPY statements be valid in the PL/SQL Library? Why or why not?

_____

_____

> **b)** Which statement will not be valid in the PL/SQL Library?

_____

_____

> **c)** How can you change it so its value is referenced indirectly?

_____

_____

Open COMMON.pll. Create a program unit and name it INSERT_AUDIT_ITEMS. It will not have to accept any parameters.

d) What will the code be for INSERT_AUDIT_ITEMS? Hint: It will be similar to the code for the current PRE-INSERT trigger. How will the code for the PRE-INSERT trigger have to change to call the INSERT_AUDIT_ITEMS program unit?

_____

_____

Create another program unit called UPDATE_AUDIT_ITEMS.

e) What should the code for UPDATE_AUDIT_ITEMS be? How should you change the PRE-UPDATE trigger?

_____

_____

Save COMMON.pll. *Also, make sure that you have changed the code in the* PRE-INSERT *and* PRE-UPDATE *triggers so that they call the program units.*

f) Have the two new procedures been added to the version of COMMON.pll under the Attached Libraries node in the Object Navigator?

_____

_____

g) What should you do with the AUDIT_POPULATION object group so that its version in the object library is current?

_____

_____

h) Can you add COMMON.pll to the object library? How about to your template form?

_____

_____

LAB 10.2 EXERCISE ANSWERS

10.2.1 ANSWERS

a) How do you think you can add GET_ALERT_TEXT to COMMON.pll?

Answer: You can drag and drop it onto COMMON.pll.

In this example, you are adding an existing program unit to a PL/SQL Library by dragging it and dropping it. It is also possible to create new program units directly within the PL/SQL Library using the Object Navigator's Create button. The New Program Unit dialog will open to let you name the program unit and choose its type, and then it will launch the PL/SQL Editor.

b) What are two ways you can compile COMMON.pll from within the Form Builder?

Answer: You can use CTRL-T, or from the Main Menu, you can select File | Administration | Compile file.

This will compile all of the PL/SQL objects in the PL/SQL Library. You can also use one of the compilation options under the Program heading in the Main Menu. The two options are Compile and Compile Selection. Under Compile there are two more options, Compile Incremental and All. The behavior of each is slightly different:

- Program | Compile | Incremental compiles all of the PL/SQL objects in the current module that have changed since the last compilation.
- Program | Compile | All compiles all of the PL/SQL objects in the current module.
- Program | Compile Selection compiles the currently selected PL/SQL object.

All will open the Compile dialog shown in Figure 10.5.

The Compile dialog gives you more control over the compilation than by pressing CTRL-T. It will allow you to interrupt and resume compilation using the buttons at the bottom of the window. Also, if there are any compilation errors, you can navigate directly to the offending PL/SQL object by clicking on the error.

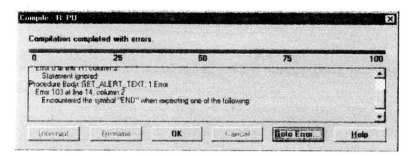

Figure 10.5 ■ The Compile dialog showing compilation errors.

It is important to note that these compilation options apply to forms modules as well as PL/SQL Library modules.

Compile, save, and close COMMON.pll. Delete GET_ALERT_TEXT from the R_PUNIT.fmb form.

c) How can you use the Object Navigator to attach the COMMON.pll library to R_PUNIT.fmb? What dialog has opened?

Answer: Select the Attached Libraries *node and click* Create. *The* Attach *dialog opens.*

The Attach dialog lets you search the filesystem, the database, or both for the PL/SQL Library. Unfortunately you cannot drag a PL/SQL Library in the Object Navigator and drop it on a form.

d) How should you respond to the alert you are presented with? Should you remove the path or keep the path? How will Forms find the .pll if you remove the path?

Answer: You should remove the path. Forms will find the .pll *using the* FORMSXX_PATH *Registry entry.*

As you learned in Chapter 9, "Reusable Objects," whenever Forms has to reference objects or code stored in other modules, it uses the Windows Registry to locate the modules. The Form Builder and Forms Runtime will look to the Registry for pointers to the files instead of using a hard-coded path to find them. This saves you from having to have identical directory structures on every machine that will run or edit this form.

e) Can you open and edit GET_ALERT_TEXT through the Attached Library node in the Object Navigator?

Answer: No you cannot.

The attached library is a read-only object that displays the names and specifications of the PL/SQL objects it contains. You cannot open or edit any of its objects. You can, however, drag objects out of the attached library and drop them on the `Program Units` node of a forms module or PL/SQL Library module.

10.2.2 ANSWERS

a) Will the COPY statements be valid in the PL/SQL Library? Why or why not?

Answer: Yes, they will be valid.

The COPY built-in makes indirect references to Forms items and variables. Therefore, it can be used in procedures and functions that are in an attached library.

b) Which statement will not be valid in the PL/SQL Library?

Answer: v_block := :SYSTEM.CURSOR_BLOCK; *will not be valid.*

Since this statement makes a direct reference to a system variable, it cannot be used in the PL/SQL Library.

c) How can you change it so its value is referenced indirectly?

Answer: Use the NAME_IN *built-in.*

The NAME_IN built-in will allow you to reference the system variable indirectly and then assign its value to a local variable. The statement will look like this:

```
v_block := NAME_IN(':SYSTEM.CURSOR_BLOCK');
```

Open COMMON.pll. Create a program unit and name it INSERT_ AUDIT_ITEMS. It will not have to accept any parameters.

d) What will the code be for INSERT_AUDIT_ITEMS? Hint: It will be similar to the code for the current PRE-INSERT trigger. How will the code for the PRE-INSERT trigger have to change to call the INSERT_AUDIT_ITEMS program unit?

Answer: See the discussion below.

The code for INSERT_AUDIT_ITEMS will be fairly similar to the code for the old version of the PRE-INSERT trigger. The only differences will be in the specification section and in how `:SYSTEM.CURSOR_BLOCK` gets referenced.

```
PROCEDURE insert_audit_items IS
    v_block          VARCHAR2(30);
    v_username       VARCHAR2(30);
    v_date           DATE;
BEGIN
  v_username := GET_APPLICATION_PROPERTY(USERNAME);
  v_date := SYSDATE;
  v_block := NAME_IN(':SYSTEM.CURSOR_BLOCK');

  COPY(v_date, v_block||'.CREATED_DATE');
  COPY(v_username,  v_block||'.CREATED_BY');
  COPY(v_date, v_block||'.MODIFIED_DATE');
  COPY(v_username,  v_block||'.MODIFIED_BY');
END;
```

The code for the `PRE-INSERT` trigger will be reduced to the following statement:

```
INSERT_AUDIT_ITEMS;
```

Create another program unit called `UPDATE_AUDIT_ITEMS`.

e) What should the code for `UPDATE_AUDIT_ITEMS` be? How should you change the `PRE-UPDATE` trigger?

Answer: See the discussion below.

```
PROCEDURE update_audit_items IS
    v_block          VARCHAR2(30);
    v_username       VARCHAR2(30);
    v_date           DATE;
BEGIN
  v_username := GET_APPLICATION_PROPERTY(USERNAME);
  v_date := SYSDATE;
  v_block := NAME_IN(':SYSTEM.CURSOR_BLOCK');
  COPY(v_date, v_block||'.MODIFIED_DATE');
  COPY(v_username,  v_block||'.MODIFIED_BY');
END;
```

Again, the only difference between this and the original PRE-UPDATE trigger is the specification section and the method of referencing SYS-TEM.CURSOR_BLOCK.

The code for the PRE-UPDATE trigger will be reduced to the following statement:

```
UPDATE_AUDIT_ITEMS;
```

f) Have the two new procedures been added to the version of COMMON.pll under the Attached Libraries node in the Object Navigator?

Answer: Yes they have.

As soon as you save changes to the COMMON.pll library, those changes are available to any form to which this PL/SQL Library is attached. If the form is open in the Object Navigator, the changes to the PL/SQL Library are seen immediately.

Also, other forms that have this PL/SQL Library attached do not have to be opened or recompiled to benefit from the changes. The PL/SQL Library is a separate module. You can edit and change the code in the PL/SQL Library without having to change code in the forms. This is as long as you have not changed the names of any of the program units or changed the parameters.

g) What should you do with the AUDIT_POPULATION object group so that its version in the object library is current?

Answer: You should move the modified version back into the object library.

The object group should still contain the PRE-INSERT and PRE-UPDATE triggers because they will be necessary to call the INSERT_AUDIT_ITEMS and UPDATE_AUDIT_ITEMS procedures. By keeping the object group and object library up-to-date, all of the forms, including template forms that have subclassed versions of the AUDIT_POPULATION object group, will inherit the changes.

All you have to do now is attach the COMMON.pll library to the forms that have subclassed versions of these triggers.

h) Can you add COMMON.pll to the object library? How about to your template form?

Answer: No, you cannot add an entire PL/SQL module to an object library. You can, however, add it to a template form.

LAB 10.2 SELF-REVIEW QUESTIONS

In order to test your progress, you should be able to answer the following questions:

1) Where are PL/SQL Libraries stored?
   a) _____ In an object library
   b) _____ Within a forms module
   c) _____ In the filesystem or database
   d) _____ The `Program Units` node of the Object Navigator

2) How do you make a PL/SQL Library accessible to a form?
   a) _____ Call it with the `FIND_LIBRARY` built-in
   b) _____ Attach it to the form
   c) _____ Simply make calls to its objects
   d) _____ a & c

3) When a PL/SQL Library is attached to more than one form, which of the following is true?
   a) _____ You must deploy a separate copy of the Library for each form it is attached to
   b) _____ A single copy of the Library can be shared by each form
   c) _____ The Library will be subclassed to the form
   d) _____ b & c

4) How can PL/SQL Libraries reduce the overall size of an application?
   a) _____ The PL/SQL objects are stored once in the Library rather than in each forms module
   b) _____ Only one instance of the Library file needs to be deployed with each application
   c) _____ The forms module and Library are compiled together to make them smaller
   d) _____ a & b
   e) _____ All of the above

5) Which of the following statements would not be valid in a PL/SQL Library?
   a) _____ `COPY(v_course_no, ':COURSE.COURSE_NO');`
   b) _____ `SET_ITEM_PROPERTY(v_item, foreground_color, 'blue');`
   c) _____ `v_value := NAME_IN(':SYSTEM.CURSOR_BLOCK');`
   d) _____ `:CONTROL.CURDATE := NAME_IN(':SYSTEM.CURRENT_DATETIME');`

Quiz answers appear in Appendix A, Section 10.2.

LAB 10.3

STORED PL/SQL OBJECTS

LAB OBJECTIVES

After this Lab, you will be able to:

*   Use Stored PL/SQL Objects

Forms modules can call PL/SQL objects that are stored in the database just as they do PL/SQL objects stored in attached libraries. Database-stored packages, procedures, and functions can be called from a Forms application, and they can also be passed parameters. The syntax for calling a stored PL/SQL object is no different than if you were calling a program unit in a form.

■ FOR EXAMPLE:

If you were to call a stored PL/SQL procedure called DELETE_STUDENT and pass it a value in a variable, the code in the Forms application would be as follows:

```
DELETE_STUDENT(v_student_id);
```

Forms will look for a PL/SQL object named DELETE_STUDENT and execute the first instance that it finds. First, Forms will search the forms module for a program unit named DELETE_STUDENT. If it doesn't find one, it will search any attached libraries. If it doesn't find one there either, it will then search the database.

Tremendous performance advantages can be gained from storing some of your application logic in the database. If, for example, the PL/SQL objects you have created are data-intensive, then it may be better to store the objects in the database. The database will execute the code more quickly and there will be less traffic back and forth across the network. Also, the code will be stored centrally in the database, which will make it accessible to other Forms and non-Forms applications.

Many PL/SQL objects can be written to successfully compile and run in both a Forms application and the database. As long as the PL/SQL object does not reference any Forms-specific PL/SQL statements like built-ins or bind variables, you can decide whether to store it in the database or in the form. It is not mandatory that PL/SQL objects be written to be so portable, but it can be helpful when doing performance tests.

■ *FOR EXAMPLE:*

If PL/SQL objects are portable, they can be moved back and forth from a form to the database with no changes to either the object itself or the form that is using it. Therefore, you can easily test an application to see where the code runs best.

PL/SQL objects can be moved back and forth between the database and a Forms application by dragging and dropping the objects in the Object Navigator from the forms module to the `Database Objects` node. This is often referred to as application partitioning, because you are "partitioning" the application by having some of the PL/SQL logic in the form and some in the database.

LAB 10.3 EXERCISES

10.3.1 USE STORED PL/SQL OBJECTS

In this Exercise, you will use a form to execute a PL/SQL function stored in the database. First you will test the function by running it in the form. Then you will store the function in the database and test it again.

Open form `EX10_03.fmb` in the Form Builder. This master-detail form is based on the `STUDENT` and `ENROLLMENT` blocks. The items in the `STUDENT` block are query-only.

There is a program unit called `COURSE_TAKEN` in the form. It evaluates the value in the `SECTION_ID` item to see if the course has already been taken by the current student.

Expand the nodes under the COURSE_TAKEN program unit and study the information under the Specification and Referenced By nodes.

    a) Which trigger calls this function?

    b) What parameters does the trigger pass to the function? What will the trigger do if the function returns TRUE?

Run the form and issue a query. Scroll through the student records until you find one that has two or three enrollments. Use the LOV for SECTION_ID to add another enrollment. Purposely choose a course that the student has already taken to test the function. Look at the hint line to confirm that the error message appears.

Exit the running form and return to the Form Builder.

    c) How can you use the Object Navigator to make this function a stored database function? Make sure you store it in the STUDENT schema.

    d) Do you have to change the code in the trigger that calls this function?

    e) What should you do with the version of the function that is stored within the forms module? Why?

Run the form again and test that the function still works.

LAB 10.3 EXERCISE ANSWERS

10.3.1 ANSWERS

a) Which trigger calls this function?

Answer: The `ENROLLMENT.SECTION_ID` *item's* `WHEN-VALIDATE-ITEM` *trigger.*

b) What parameters does the trigger pass to the function? What will the trigger do if the function returns `TRUE`?

Answer: It passes the `STUDENT_ID` *and* `SECTION_ID`.

If the function returns `TRUE`, the trigger will send a `MESSAGE` to the user indicating that the student has already taken this course.

c) How can you use the Object Navigator to make this function a stored database function? Make sure you store it in the `STUDENT` schema.

Answer: You can drag the function from the `Program Units` *node to the* `Database Objects` *node.*

You will have to have the `STUDENT` schema node expanded so that you can see the `Stored Program Units` node beneath it. The function will then be stored in the database as one of the objects owned by `STUDENT`.

d) Do you have to change the code in the trigger that calls this function?

Answer: No.

The code in the trigger does not have to change to call the function. The trigger does not have to know if the PL/SQL object it is calling is stored locally in the forms module, in a PL/SQL Library module, or in the database.

e) What should you do with the version of the function that is stored within the forms module? Why?

Answer: You should delete it.

As you learned in the Lab section, the running form will first search for the procedure in the current forms module. If it finds it, it will execute it there and will never reach the code that is stored in the database.

Run the form again and test that the function still works.

LAB 10.3 SELF-REVIEW QUESTIONS

In order to test your progress, you should be able to answer the following questions:

1) How do you call a stored PL/SQL object from forms?
   a) ____ Use the FIND_OBJECT built-in
   b) ____ Prefix the object name with DB_OBJ
   c) ____ Simply call it by name
   d) ____ Use the Database Objects node in the Object Navigator

2) Stored PL/SQL objects can accept and return parameters.
   a) ____ True
   b) ____ False

3) Which of the following statements would not be valid in both a client Forms PL/SQL object and a stored PL/SQL object?
   a) ____ SELECT LAST_NAME INTO v_ last_name FROM STUDENT;
   b) ____ OPEN CURSOR c_student;
   c) ____ FIND_ITEM(v_item);
   d) ____ END;

4) In what order does Forms search for PL/SQL objects?
   a) ____ Forms module, database, attached library
   b) ____ Database, attached library, forms module
   c) ____ Forms module, attached library, database
   d) ____ Database, forms module, attached library

Quiz answers appear in Appendix A, Section 10.3.

C H A P T E R   1 0

TEST YOUR THINKING

1) Attach COMMON.pll to the following forms:

   1) R_TEMPLATE.fmb*
   2) R_STUDENT.fmb
   3) R_COURSE.fmb
   4) R_INSTRUCTOR.fmb
   5) R_CRSESECT.fmb
   6) R_STUDENRL.fmb

   * This is optional. Attach COMMON.pll to R_TEMPLATE.fmb only if you plan to create more forms modules for the STUDENT schema.

   Make sure that the PRE-INSERT and PRE-UPDATE triggers have been updated in LIBRARY.olb so that all of their subclassed versions will be able to call the INSERT_AUDIT_ITEMS and UPDATE_AUDIT_ITEMS program units in COMMON.pll.

2) Edit all of the WHEN-VALIDATE-ITEM triggers in the following forms that could make use of GET_ALERT_TEXT:

   1) R_STUDENT.fmb
   2) R_COURSE.fmb
   3) R_INSTRUCTOR.fmb
   4) R_CRSESECT.fmb
   5) R_STUDENRL.fmb

   Make sure you subclass the VAL_ALERT alert to all of these forms.

3) Create a program unit that enables and disables the buttons on a toolbar depending on the mode of a form. Edit the WHEN-BUTTON-PRESSED triggers for the TOOLBAR buttons so that they call this program unit. Add this program unit to the COMMON.pll library.

C H A P T E R   1 1

MULTIPLE-FORM APPLICATIONS

CHAPTER OBJECTIVES

In this Chapter, you will learn about:

✔ Calling One Form from Another   Page 382

A typical application will contain more than one forms module. Users will use one form to accomplish one task, and another form to accomplish another task. If these tasks are related, you may want to have one form call the other. You may even want to pass information from form to from. In this Chapter, you will learn a number of different methods for calling forms. In the examples and Exercises, you will be using one forms module to call another. In Chapter 13, "Forms Menus," you will call forms from a menu system. While you are working through the Exercises in this Chapter, keep in mind that you will be reusing these methods in Chapter 13, "Forms Menus."

Throughout this Chapter, you will come across the terms "*calling* form" and "*called* form." Calling form refers to the form that is invoking another. Called form refers to the form that has been invoked. So, for example, if FORM_A calls FORM_B, then FORM_A is the calling form and FORM_B is the called form.

L A B   1 1 . 1

CALLING ONE FORM FROM ANOTHER

LAB OBJECTIVES

After this Lab, you will be able to:

*   Open Multiple Forms
*   Create a Parameter List and Pass it to a Form

There are three built-ins that call one form from another: OPEN_FORM, CALL_FORM, and NEW_FORM. To open another form, you simply issue one of these statements along with the form's name. The statement to open a form called COURSE would look like this:

```
OPEN_FORM('COURSE');
```

Since the full path is not included in the OPEN_FORM statement, the Forms Runtime will look for the COURSE.fmx file in the paths listed in the Registry. It is possible to include the full path in a built-in that calls another form, but it is not recommended because it makes the application less portable.

The form name is a mandatory parameter. However, each of the three built-ins can accept other parameters that, depending on how you set them, can affect the behavior and state of the calling form and called form. You will explore these parameters in the Exercises.

The built-ins themselves also alter the behavior of the calling and called form.

■ *FOR EXAMPLE:*

Assume that FORM_A is the *calling* form and FORM_B is the *called* form. The following is a description of what will happen when FORM_A issues different built-ins:

```
OPEN_FORM('FORM_B');
```

FORM_B will open, and FORM_A will remain active and accessible. The user will be able to navigate between both forms and access items in each.

```
CALL_FORM('FORM_B');
```

FORM_B will open as a modal form. The user will not be able to leave FORM_B until it has been exited or closed. FORM_A may be visible, but none of its items will be accessible.

```
NEW_FORM('FORM_B');
```

FORM_A will close and then FORM_B will open.

The EXIT_FORM built-in will exit and close the current form. The CLOSE_FORM built-in will also exit and close a form, but it requires a form name as a parameter.

```
CLOSE_FORM('FORM_B');
```

PASSING VALUES TO CALLED FORMS

There are two methods for passing values from a calling form to a called form: global variables and parameter lists. An example of each will be given here in the Lab text. However, in the Exercises in this Chapter, you will only experiment with parameter lists. The reason for this is that while global variables are useful and sometimes necessary, they should not be overused. They do not perform well on Windows platforms and can sometimes make an application unstable.

Global variables are user-defined variables that are visible to all objects in a Forms session. That is, any PL/SQL object within a single form or multi-form application can reference the value of a global variable.

■ *FOR EXAMPLE:*

Assume that FORM_A calls FORM_B. In a PL/SQL object in FORM_A, you could make the following two statements:

```
:global.username := GET_APPLICATION_PROPERTY(USER-
NAME);
```

You could then reference the value of :global.username in any PL/SQL object within FORM_B. If FORM_C and FORM_D were open as well, then those could also reference :global.username and they would all see the same value.

Global variables are simple to create and reference, and it can sometimes be useful to have them visible across all forms. However, there may be occasions when you want to pass values to other forms, but you don't necessarily want the same value to be available to all forms. In these cases, you would want to use parameters and parameter lists.

Parameters are values that you can create and set either at design-time using the Object Navigator or programmatically at run-time using built-ins. They are used to pass values to a form when it starts. In the calling form, the parameter can be defined and set programmatically. In the called form, the parameter must be created at design-time. To pass a parameter, it must first be placed in a parameter list.

■ FOR EXAMPLE:

Assume that FORM_A is the calling form and FORM_B is the called form. In FORM_A, you would use the following built-in to create a parameter list:

```
v_plist_id := CREATE_PARAMETER_LIST('forms_params');
```

v_plist_id is a local variable that would have been declared in the PL/SQL block. forms_params is the name of the parameter list that is being created; its object ID is being stored in v_plist_id.

Once you have created the parameter list, you would add parameters and their values to it.

```
ADD_PARAMETER(v_plist_id, 'P_1', text_parameter, v_value);
```

v_plist_id tells the ADD_PARAMETER built-in which parameter list to work with. P_1 is the name of the parameter being added to the list. text_parameter indicates the type of parameter. When passing parameters from form to form, they must be defined as text_parameters. v_value is the value you are assigning to P_1. This would have been declared and assigned earlier and could contain anything: an item's current value, a WHERE clause, etc. In the Exercises, the value of the parameter you create will contain a WHERE clause.

Now that the code has been written to create a parameter in FORM_A, FORM_B must be prepared to accept this parameter. Here you would use the Object Navigator to create a parameter with the same name as the parameter that will be passed in. So, in this case, the parameter in FORM_B must also be named P_1.

LAB 11.1 EXERCISES

11.1.1   OPEN MULTIPLE FORMS

In this Exercise, you will experiment with the three different built-ins for opening one form from another. You will use the form EX11_01 to open the form EX11_02.

EX11_01.fmb contains a STUDENT block. EX11_02.fmb is a master-detail form with a STUDENT block and an ENROLLMENT block. The STUDENT block is query-only.

Open EX11_01.fmb and EX11_02.fmb in the Form Builder.

a) When EX11_01 is running in the Forms Runtime, will it be able to run EX11_02.**fmb**? What must you do to EX11_02 so that the calling form can run it?

_____

_____

In EX11_01.fmb, create a WHEN-BUTTON-PRESSED trigger for the STUDENT.ENROLLMENT button.

b) What statement should you write in this trigger to open the form EX11_02? You want both forms to be open at the same time and you want both to be accessible to the user.

_____

_____

Run the form and test the button.

c) Can you navigate from form to form with the mouse? What happens if you click the ENROLLMENTS button again?

_____

_____

d) Does the MDI toolbar work for both forms? Do you have to exit both forms explicitly or does clicking the EXIT button close the entire application?

_____

_____

Exit the forms and return to the Form Builder.

Add the following parameters to the built-in. Position them just after the form name. Do not put them in single quotes.

NO_ACTIVATE, SESSION

Run the form and test the button.

e) What has the NO_ACTIVATE parameter done to the called form? What do you think the SESSION parameter has done?

_____

_____

f) How can you change the code in the WHEN-BUTTON-PRESSED trigger so that EX11_01 will close when EX11_02 is opened? The only parameter in the built-in should be the form name.

_____

_____

Add the following parameters to the built-in. Position them just after the form name. Do not put them in single quotes.

TO_SAVEPOINT, QUERY_ONLY

g) What effect will the QUERY_ONLY parameter have on the called form?

_____

_____

Run the form and click the ENROLLMENTS button to test your work. Confirm that the QUERY_ONLY parameter is effective.

h) How can you change the code in the WHEN-BUTTON-PRESSED trigger so that EX11_01 will stay open and EX11_02 will open as a modal form?

_____

_____

11.1.2 CREATE A PARAMETER LIST AND PASS IT TO A FORM

Open forms EX11_01.fmb and EX11_02.fmb in the Form Builder. In EX11_01.fmb, create a program unit that is a procedure and name it ADD_ENROLLMENTS. This program unit will not accept any parameters. You are going to create the parameter list and call form EX11_02.fmb from this procedure. It is being done here, rather than in the WHEN-BUTTON-PRESSED trigger, so that the code will be available to other Forms events rather than just the Button Pressed event.

Change the code in the WHEN-BUTTON-PRESSED trigger so that it has the following statement only:

```
ADD_ENROLLMENTS;
```

Add the following statements to the ADD_ENROLLMENTS program unit:

```
PROCEDURE ADD_ENROLLMENTS IS
   v_plist_id       PARAMLIST;
   v_where       VARCHAR2(50);
BEGIN
   v_where := 'STUDENT_ID = '||:STUDENT.STUDENT_ID;
   v_plist_id := CREATE_PARAMETER_LIST('forms_params');
ADD_PARAMETER(v_plist_id, 'P_1', TEXT_PARAMETER, v_where);
END;
```

a) What is the name of the parameter list? Which variable is holding its object ID?

_____

_____

b) What is the name of the parameter being added to the parameter list? What type of parameter is it? What will its value be?

_____

_____

Compile the procedure and run the form. Click the button **once.** Nothing should happen. Click the button a second time and note the alert messages. Exit the form and return to the Form Builder.

c) Can you create a parameter list twice? What code can you add to the beginning of ADD_ENROLLMENTS to check to see if the parameter list called `forms_params` already exists? Hint: Use a GET_ built-in to get the object ID of the parameter list, then evaluate the ID to see if it is null.

_____

_____

d) If the list exists and the value is not null, what built-in can you use to destroy the parameter list? Search the help system for the answer.

_____

_____

Add the following statements to the end of the ADD_ENROLLMENTS procedure:

```
COMMIT_FORM;
CALL_FORM('EX11_02', NO_HIDE, NO_REPLACE, NO_QUERY_ONLY, v_plist_id);
```

Check the answers section to confirm the code in ADD_ENROLLMENTS before continuing. Open form EX11_02.fmb.

e) How can you use the Object Navigator to create a parameter in form EX11_02.fmb? What should you name the parameter?

Create a WHEN-NEW-FORM-INSTANCE trigger in EX11_02.fmb and add the following code:

```
IF :PARAMETER.P_1 IS NOT NULL THEN
    MESSAGE('The parameter value is '||:PARAMETER.P_1);
END IF;
```

f) How is the parameter being referred to? Do you have to refer to the parameter list? Do you think the value of the parameter will be available to all triggers and procedures in EX11_02.fmb?

Compile form EX11_02. Run form EX11_01 and click the ENROLLMENTS button to test that the parameter is being passed properly.

Exit the running form and return to the Form Builder.

In EX11_02, edit the WHEN-NEW-FORM-INSTANCE trigger and enter the following code:

```
DECLARE
  v_where VARCHAR2(100);
BEGIN
  IF :PARAMETER.P_1 IS NOT NULL THEN
  v_where := :PARAMETER.P_1;
  SET_BLOCK_PROPERTY('STUDENT', DEFAULT_WHERE, v_where);
  EXECUTE_QUERY;
  GO_BLOCK('ENROLLMENT');
  END IF;
END;
```

g) What do the `v_where` variable and `SET_BLOCK_PROPERTY` built-in accomplish?

_____

_____

h) Why is the `GO_BLOCK('ENROLLMENT');` statement issued?

_____

_____

Compile `EX11_02.fmb` and run `EX11_01.fmb`. Issue a query or create a new record. Click the `ENROLLMENTS` button to test the `CALL_FORM` and parameter list.

i) In `EX11_01.fmb`, you issue a `COMMIT_FORM` statement just before you call form `EX11_02.fmb`. If you were creating a new record in `EX11_01.fmb` and you did not commit the form, would the query in `EX11_02` return any rows? Why not?

_____

_____

LAB 11.1 EXERCISE ANSWERS

11.1.1 ANSWERS

Open `EX11_01.fmb` and `EX11_02.fmb` in the Form Builder.

a) When `EX11_01` is running in the Forms Runtime, will it be able to run `EX11_02.fmb`? What must you do to `EX11_02` so that the calling form can run it?

Answer: No it will not. You must compile `EX11_02.fmb` so that the calling form can run it.

As you already know, an `.fmb` file cannot be run. The `CALL_FORM`, `OPEN_FORM`, and `NEW_FORM` built-ins will only run `.fmx` files.

b) What statement should you write in this trigger to open the form EX11_02? You want both forms to be open at the same time and you want both to be accessible to the user.

Answer: See the discussion below.

You would use the OPEN_FORM built-in. The statement should look like the following:

OPEN_FORM('EX11_02');

c) Can you navigate from form to form with the mouse? What happens if you click the ENROLLMENTS button again?

Answer: Yes, you can navigate from form to form with the mouse. If you click EN-ROLLMENTS again, another instance of the EX11_02 form will open.

Each time you click the ENROLLMENTS button, you will open another instance of the EX11_02 form. This can be useful if you want to allow users to work on multiple tasks simultaneously. When multiple forms are open, you can navigate between them using navigation built-ins.

■ FOR EXAMPLE:

If forms EX11_01 and EX11_02 are open, you can navigate from one to the other with the following statement:

GO_FORM('EX11_02');

The GO_FORM built-in is passed a name or object ID to open a specific form. Additionally, there are two other built-ins for navigating from form to form and their syntax is as follows:

NEXT_FORM;

and

PREVIOUS_FORM;

Note that these two built-ins do not refer to a specific form by name or object ID. Instead, NEXT_FORM and PREVIOUS_FORM navigate from form to form in the order that the forms were opened.

d) Does the MDI toolbar work for both forms? Do you have to exit both forms explicitly or does clicking the EXIT button close the entire application?

Answer: The MDI toolbar works for both forms. You must explicitly exit each form.

e)   What has the NO_ACTIVATE parameter done to the called form? What do you think the SESSION parameter has done?

Answer: NO_ACTIVATE *has opened the form, but it has not navigated to it.* SESSION *has opened another database session for the form.*

The OPEN_FORM built-in can accept as many as five parameters that affect how the called form will be opened. In Question e, three parameters were passed to the built-in: the form name, the Activate mode, and the Session mode. The two other parameters that can be passed to OPEN_FORM are Data mode and parameter list. The Data mode parameter indicates whether or not the called form and calling form will share data between attached libraries. The parameter list parameter indicates the name or ID of the parameter list that will be passed to the called form. An OPEN_FORM statement, including all of these parameters, would look like this:

```
OPEN_FORM('EX11_02', ACTIVATE, NO_SESSION, NO_SHARE_LIBRARY_DATA, 'parameter_list_name');
```

You are not required to include all of the parameters in an OPEN_FORM statement. If you leave any of them out, Forms will simply issue the built-in with the default values for each parameter.

■ FOR EXAMPLE:

The following statement:

```
OPEN_FORM('EX11_02');
```

will produce the same results as the statement:

```
OPEN_FORM('EX11_02', ACTIVATE, NO_SESSION, NO_SHARE_LIBRARY_DATA);
```

This rule applies to the NEW_FORM and CALL_FORM built-ins, as well as to any other built-in that accepts parameters. The on-line help system details the parameters for each built-in and its allowable values, along with the default value.

f)   How can you change the code in the WHEN-BUTTON-PRESSED trigger so that EX11_01 will close when EX11_02 is opened? The only parameter in the built-in should be the form name.

Answer: See the discussion below.

You would use the NEW_FORM built-in. The statement would look like the following:

```
NEW_FORM('EX11_02');
```

g) What effect will the QUERY_ONLY parameter have on the called form?

Answer: The called form will be in Query-Only mode.

NEW_FORM can also accept as many as five parameters, which are as follows:

```
NEW_FORM(formname, rollbackmode, querymode, datamode, parameterlist);
```

rollback mode lets you indicate how the form should roll back uncommitted changes in the calling form. The rollback mode parameter becomes important in applications with transactions that span multiple forms. It accepts the values TO_SAVEPOINT (the default), NO_ROLLBACK, and FULL_ROLLBACK.

The statement for Question g will open the form in Query-Only mode, which will prevent the user from issuing inserts, updates, or deletes. The form cannot be switched to Normal mode and will remain in Query-Only mode throughout the session.

h) How can you change the code in the WHEN-BUTTON-PRESSED trigger so that EX11_01 will stay open and EX11_02 will open as a modal form?

Answer: See the discussion below.

You would use the CALL_FORM built-in. CALL_FORM can accept as many as six parameters, which are as follows:

```
CALL_FORM(formname, display, switchmenu, querymode, datamode, parameterlist);
```

The display parameter indicates how the calling form should be displayed while the called form is active. It accepts one of two values: HIDE or NO_HIDE. If you want the calling form to be hidden while the called form is active, you would issue the following statement:

```
CALL_FORM('EX11_02', HIDE);
```

The switch menu parameter accepts one of two values: NO_REPLACE or DO_REPLACE. In Chapter 8, "Canvases and Windows," you learned that each module has a Menu Module property; the menu module assigned here is referred to as the form's default menu. It is possible for forms within the same application to have different menu modules assigned to them at run-time. The switch menu parameter lets you indicate whether or not the called form should use the default menu of the calling form.

■ FOR EXAMPLE:

At design-time, form EX11_01 was assigned menu module A; form EX11_02 was assigned menu module B. The following statement will cause the called form, EX11_02, to use the menu module of the calling form, EX11_01.

    CALL_FORM('EX11_02', NO_REPLACE);

The following statement will also call EX11_02 from EX11_01. However, in this case, the called form, EX11_02, will use its own default menu. In other words, it will replace the default menu of the calling form, EX11_01.

    CALL_FORM('EX11_02', DO_REPLACE);

11.1.2 ANSWERS

a) What is the name of the parameter list? Which variable is holding its object ID?

    Answer: The name of the parameter list is forms_params. v_plist *is the variable that is holding its object ID.*

b) What is the name of the parameter being added to the parameter list? What type of parameter is it? What will its value be?

    Answer: The parameter is called P_1, *and it is a* text_parameter.

The value of the parameter will be the value assigned to the v_where variable. This will contain the character string 'STUDENT_ID = ', concatenated to the current value of :STUDENT.STUDENT_ID.

c) Can you create a parameter list twice? What code can you add to the beginning of ADD_ENROLLMENTS to check to see if the parameter list called forms_params already exists? Hint: Use a GET_ built-in to get the object ID of the parameter list, then evaluate the ID to see if it is null.

    Answer: See the discussion below.

Forms cannot create two parameter lists of the same name, which is why you received errors when you clicked the ENROLLMENTS button the second time. Before you create a parameter list, you should check to see if one of the same name already exists and then destroy it if it does. In previous Labs, you used FIND_ built-ins to return the object ID of an object. There is no FIND_PARAMETER_LIST built-in; you must use the following built-ins instead:

```
v_plist_id := GET_PARAMETER_LIST('forms_params');
IF NOT ID_NULL(v_list_id) THEN
    --get rid of parameter list. See Question d
END IF;
```

d) If the list exists and the value is not null, what built-in can you use to destroy the parameter list? Search the help system for the answer.

Answer: See the discussion below.

The code should be as follows:

```
v_plist_id := GET_PARAMETER_LIST('forms_params');
IF NOT ID_NULL(v_list_id) THEN
    DESTROY_PARAMETER_LIST(v_list_id);
END IF;
```

DESTROY_PARAMETER_LIST erases the parameter list and any parameters and values that may have been added to it. Now you are free to re-create the parameter list and add new parameters to it.

In this example, the parameter list is being used to pass a WHERE clause from one form to another. You may want to perform this action multiple times within a user's session. Therefore, it will be necessary to destroy the existing parameter list before creating a new one.

Check the Answers section to confirm the code in ADD_ENROLLMENTS before continuing. Open form EX11_02.fmb.

The code for the procedure should be as follows:

```
PROCEDURE ADD_ENROLLMENTS IS
  v_plist_id           PARAMLIST;
  v_where   VARCHAR2(50);
BEGIN
  v_plist_id := GET_PARAMETER_LIST('forms_params');
  IF NOT ID_NULL(v_plist_id) THEN
      DESTROY_PARAMETER_LIST(v_plist_id);
  END IF;
  v_where := 'STUDENT_ID = '||:STUDENT.STUDENT_ID;
  v_plist_id := CREATE_PARAMETER_LIST('forms_params');
  ADD_PARAMETER(v_plist_id, 'P_1', TEXT PARAMETER, v_where);
  COMMIT_FORM;
CALL_FORM('EX11_02', NO_HIDE, NO_REPLACE, NO_QUERY_ONLY, v_plist_id);
END;
```

e)   How can you use the Object Navigator to create a parameter in form `EX11_02.fmb`? What should you name the parameter?

Answer: Select the `Parameters` *node and click the* `Create` *button. The parameter should be named* `P_1`.

f)   How is the parameter being referred to? Do you have to refer to the parameter list? Do you think the value of the parameter will be available to all triggers and procedures in `EX11_02.fmb`?

Answer: See the discussion below.

Parameters are referred to by the `:PARAMETER.PARAMETER_NAME` syntax. As you learned in the Lab, parameter `P_1` in `EX11_02` had to be created at design-time and it had to have the same name as the parameter being passed from the calling form.

Parameter lists are not visible across forms, so you are not required to make any reference to the list itself in the called form. Parameter lists are merely the vehicle that is used to pass parameters and their values from the called form to the calling form. Once the values have been passed, the list is of no use to the called form. It does, however, still exist in the calling form.

The parameter is now an object in form `EX11_02.fmb` and can be referenced by any trigger or PL/SQL object in the forms module. If you need to reference the parameter in an attached PL/SQL Library, you must do so indirectly by using the `NAME_IN` built-in. In this example, an indirect reference would be as follows:

```
NAME_IN('PARAMETER.P_1');
```

g)   What do the `v_where` variable and `SET_BLOCK_PROPERTY` built-in accomplish?

Answer: They set the `STUDENT` *block's* `WHERE` *clause.*

In this example, the calling form is passing a `WHERE` clause to the called form, setting the `WHERE` clause for a block in the called form, and then executing a query. For forms `EX11_01` and `EX11_02`, the result is that the same record is brought up in the called form and the user is given the opportunity to add detail records to it.

One caveat to this example is that, since the `WHERE` clause has been set, the user will only be able to access enrollment records for this `STUDENT`. This might be fine for this example, since you are calling this form explicitly to set enrollments for this student. However, if you wanted to give the user the ability to query other student records, you could reset the WHERE clause by adding another SET_BLOCK_PROPERTY statement as follows:

```
DECLARE
    v_where VARCHAR2(100);
BEGIN
    IF :PARAMETER.P_1 IS NOT NULL THEN
    v_where := :PARAMETER.P_1;
SET_BLOCK_PROPERTY('STUDENT', DEFAULT_WHERE, v_where);
    EXECUTE_QUERY;
    SET_BLOCK_PROPERTY('STUDENT', DEFAULT_WHERE, ' ');
    GO_BLOCK('ENROLLMENT');
    END IF;
END;
```

The form will execute the query using the WHERE clause that was passed into the form, and will then reset the block's DEFAULT_WHERE property immediately after the query has been executed.

h) Why is the GO_BLOCK('ENROLLMENT'); statement issued?

Answer: So that the form will navigate to the ENROLLMENT *block.*

The STUDENT block is query-only, so the user will not be able to change the record. Moreover, the purpose of this example is for the user to add enrollment records for this student, so it makes sense for the application to navigate to the first item in the ENROLLMENT block immediately.

i) In EX11_01.fmb, you issue a COMMIT_FORM statement just before you call form EX11_02.fmb. If you were creating a new record in EX11_01.fmb and you did not commit the form, would the query in EX11_02 return any rows? Why not?

Answer: No it would not. The changes to form EX11_01 *would not have been applied or committed to the database.*

The COMMIT_FORM statement, just before calling form EX11_02, applies and saves all the changes to form EX11_01. Therefore, there were no transactions that spanned both forms. However, there may be cases in which you want to spread transactions across multiple forms. To do so, you would take advantage of Forms' commit processing functionality.

**LAB
11.1**

■ FOR EXAMPLE:

The COMMIT_FORM statement applies and saves changes to the database in one step. Once you have committed changes with COMMIT_FORM, they cannot be rolled back. The POST built-in, on the other hand, applies changes to the database but does not commit them. These changes can then be committed or rolled back later on.

In this example, you could replace the COMMIT_FORM; statement with a POST; statement. The form will then post the changes and open form EX11_02. When a COMMIT_FORM is issued in form EX11_02, all of the changes, including the ones posted in EX11_01, will be committed to the database.

LAB 11.1 SELF-REVIEW QUESTIONS

In order to test your progress, you should be able to answer the following questions:

1) Which of the following built-ins would close the calling form before opening the called form?
   a) _____ OPEN_FORM
   b) _____ CALL_FORM
   c) _____ CLOSE_FORM
   d) _____ NEW_FORM

2) What is the syntax to open a form so that it is modal and so that the calling form is present but not visible?
   a) _____ OPEN_FORM('FORM_B', NO_ACTIVATE);
   b) _____ NEW_FORM('FORM_B, NO_DISPLAY);
   c) _____ CALL_FORM('FORM_B', HIDE);
   d) _____ OPEN_FORM('FORM_B', NO_SESSION);

3) Which built-in would allow you to programmatically move between forms but not open new instances of those forms?
   a) _____ OPEN_FORM
   b) _____ GO_FORM
   c) _____ NEW_FORM
   d) _____ FIND_FORM

4) How can you pass a parameter to another form?
   a) _____ Use a SYSTEM variable
   b) _____ Add it to a parameter list in the calling form
   c) _____ Create it at design-time in the called form
   d) _____ b & c

5) Which of the following is not true about parameter lists?

a) _____ They are not referenced in the called form

b) _____ They can contain only one parameter

c) _____ They are removed using DESTROY_PARAMETER_LIST

d) _____ They are populated with ADD_PARAMETER

Quiz answers appear in Appendix A, Section 11.1.

C H A P T E R   1 1

TEST YOUR THINKING

1) Add a button to the R_STUDENT.fmb form to call R_STUDENRL.fmb. Pass R_STUDENRL a parameter in a parameter list so that it immediately queries the corresponding student and enrollment records. Do not put the code in the WHEN-BUTTON-PRESSED trigger? Create a program unit similar to ADD_ENROLLMENTS from Exercise 11.1.2. Remember to add the appropriate triggers and objects to R_STUDENRL.fmb so that it can accept and process the parameter.

2) Add a button to the R_COURSE.fmb form and use it to call R_CRSESECT.fmb. Pass R_CRSESECT.fmb a parameter in a parameter list so that it immediately queries the corresponding course and section records. Do not put the code in the WHEN-BUTTON-PRESSED trigger. Create a program unit similar to ADD_ENROLLMENTS from Exercise 11.1.2. Remember to add the appropriate triggers and objects to R_CRSESECT.fmb so that it can accept and process the parameter.

Challenge

3) Edit R_STUDENT.fmb so that whenever a user saves a change to the form they are asked whether or not they would like to add enrollment records. If they respond Yes, then call the R_STUDENRL.fmb form. If they respond No, then simply commit the form. Take the following steps to accomplish this:

   1) Create another procedure in R_STUDENT.fmb that shows an alert similar to the one in Figure 11.1.
   2) If the user responds Yes to this alert, then call the ADD_ENROLLMENTS procedure. If they respond No, then do nothing.

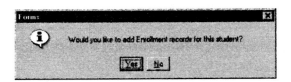

Figure 11.1 ■ Alert with two buttons to prompt user.

3) Call the procedure that shows the alert from a KEY-COMMIT trigger so that whenever a user attempts to save a change, they are prompted with the alert.

4) You can do any one of the following: leave the button you created in Question 1 as it is, change the WHEN-BUTTON-PRESSED code so that it calls the alert procedure, or delete the button.

4) Repeat the steps for Challenge Question 3 for the R_COURSE. fmb and R_CRSESECT. fmb **forms.**

C H A P T E R   1 2

ORACLE FORMS AND ORACLE REPORTS

CHAPTER OBJECTIVES

In this Chapter, you will learn about:

✔ Running Oracle Reports from Forms   Page 404
✔ Passing Parameters to Reports   Page 414

In many applications, you will want to display database data in report format as well as in data entry screens. The Oracle Forms and Oracle Reports products have been tightly integrated so that forms modules can use built-ins to call reports modules and even pass them parameters.

In this Chapter, you will learn two different methods for calling reports modules from forms modules. You will also learn how to pass user-defined parameters to influence a report's result set and how to pass system parameters to control how a report will be executed.

Since Oracle Reports is not within the scope of this interactive workbook, you will not be expected to create your own reports modules. Instead, you will use the pre-created reports modules that you downloaded from the companion Web site along with the forms modules you have been using for previous Exercises. These three reports modules should be in your `\guest\forms\exercises` directory. They are called `STUDENT.rdf`, `STUDENRL.rdf`, and `INSTSECT.rdf`.

L A B   1 2 . 1

RUNNING ORACLE REPORTS FROM FORMS

LAB OBJECTIVES

After this Lab, you will be able to:

* Run an Oracle Report with RUN_PRODUCT
* Run an Oracle Report with RUN_REPORT_ OBJECT

Before you learn the methods for calling reports from forms, it is best to get a brief overview of the Oracle Reports product and its modules.

In the simplest of terms, Oracle reports modules are SQL queries with formatting instructions. The two basic elements of a reports module are its query and its layout. The query specifies the data to be returned and the layout specifies how this result set should be formatted. Reports can be laid out in a number of different styles and can include color and graphics. In addition to the query and layout, you can also include triggers, program units, and attached libraries' in reports modules.

The Report Builder is used to design and build reports modules. It has a similar interface to the Form Builder in that it is a graphical development environment with an Object Navigator, Property Palette, Layout Editor, and PL/SQL Editor.

Reports modules can be run by themselves, using the Reports Runtime, or they can be called from forms. In the Exercises in this Chapter, you will call reports from forms. There are two Forms built-ins that can be used to call reports modules: RUN_PRODUCT and RUN_REPORT_OBJECT. They achieve almost the same result, but are implemented differently.

RUN_PRODUCT

The RUN_PRODUCT built-in is rather flexible in that it can be used to call any of the three types of Oracle Developer modules: forms, reports, and graphics. In this Lab, you will use RUN_PRODUCT to call reports modules only.

It is simple, as well, because it takes just one single statement to run a report. It can be called from a trigger or a program unit and does not require that any additional objects be created in the calling form. The syntax for RUN_PRODUCT is:

```
RUN_PRODUCT(product, module, commode, execmode, location, parameter_list, display);
```

A call to RUN_PRODUCT to run a report called COURSE would look like this:

```
RUN_PRODUCT(REPORTS, 'COURSE', ASYNCHRONOUS, RUNTIME, FILESYSTEM, 'NULL', NULL);
```

The built-in accepts a number of parameters, the two most important being the name of the product to be called and the name of the module to be run. You will explore the meanings of the rest of the parameters in the Exercises.

RUN_PRODUCT_OBJECT

This built-in is not as flexible as RUN_PRODUCT because it applies to reports modules only. Therefore, it cannot be used to call graphics modules or forms modules. It is also not as simple because it requires more work in the Form Builder at design-time. However, it is a more powerful method since it provides tighter integration between the calling form and the called report.

■ FOR EXAMPLE:

Assume you have a forms module called FORM_A. The syntax to run a report called COURSE from FORM_A using RUN_REPORT_OBJECT would be as follows:

```
DECLARE
    v_repobj_id        REPORT_OBJECT;
    v_repsrv_id        VARCHAR2(100);
BEGIN
    v_repobj_id := FIND_REPORT_OBJECT('COURSE');
    v_repsrv_id := RUN_REPORT_OBJECT(v_repobj_id);
END;
```

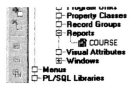

Figure 12.1 ■ A report object called COURSE in the Object Navigator.

For the FIND_REPORT_OBJECT to succeed, there must be an instance of a report object called COURSE in FORM_A. Report objects can be created in the Object Navigator. Figure 12.1 shows a report object called COURSE.

The report is still a separate module stored in a separate file. However, since it is represented in the forms module as an object, it will have properties that the forms module can act upon. Therefore, it is more tightly integrated with the forms module because it can be treated like an item, block, canvas, or any other Forms object.

The RUN_PRODUCT and RUN_REPORT_OBJECT built-ins work equally well, and each has its advantages. In the Exercises, you will experiment with both methods for calling a reports module.

LAB 12.1 EXERCISES

12.1.1 RUN AN ORACLE REPORT WITH RUN_PRODUCT

A reports module called STUDENT.rdf has been created for you already. You will not need to enter the Report Builder or in any way manipulate this reports module. You will simply be running it from within a form. However, you must make sure that the reports module (STUDENT.rdf) is in a directory that is pointed to by the REPORTXX_PATH Registry entry. If you have questions about the Windows Registry, refer to Appendix B.

Open the form EX12_01.fmb. Ignore the data items for now; they will become important in Exercise 12.2.1. Create a WHEN-BUTTON-PRESSED trigger for the STUDENT.REPORTS button. Put the following statement in the trigger:

```
RUN_PRODUCT(REPORTS, 'STUDENT', ASYNCHRONOUS, RUNTIME, FILESYSTEM, 'NULL', NULL);
```

Run the form and put it in Enter Query mode. Click the Reports button.

a) Can you navigate back and forth from the calling form to the reports module? What do you think the behavior would have been if `commode` had been set to SYNCHRONOUS?

_____

_____

b) Can you see the report and interact with it in the previewer? What do you think the behavior would have been if `execmode` had been set to BATCH?

_____

_____

c) Where will the Reports Runtime look for the reports module?

_____

_____

d) Is the form passing the report any parameters?

_____

_____

Exit the report and form and return to the Form Builder.

12.1.2 RUN AN ORACLE REPORT WITH RUN_REPORT_OBJECT

Open the form `EX12_01.fmb` in the Form Builder. Use the `Reports` node in the Object Navigator to create a report object based on an existing report called STUDENT.

a) How should you respond to the `New Report` dialog to base the report object on an existing report named STUDENT?

_____

_____

b) The RUN_REPORT_OBJECT built-in does not accept parameters like commode, execmode, etc. Where do you think you can set them instead?

_____

_____

c) Which property can you set so that the report output gets sent to the screen?

_____

_____

Set the Execution Mode **property to** Runtime **and the** Communication Mode **property to** Asynchronous.

d) What would the code be for the WHEN-BUTTON-PRESSED trigger to open this report with the RUN_REPORT_OBJECT built-in?

_____

_____

Run the form and test the report. Exit the form and return to the Form Builder.

e) What built-in do you think you could use to set the properties of the report object at run-time?

_____

_____

LAB 12.1 EXERCISE ANSWERS

12.1.1 ANSWERS

Open the form EX12_01.fmb. Ignore the data items for now; they will become important in later Exercises. Create a WHEN-BUTTON-PRESSED trigger for the STUDENT.REPORTS button. Put the following statement in the trigger:

`RUN_PRODUCT(REPORTS, 'STUDENT', ASYNCHRONOUS, RUNTIME, FILESYSTEM, 'NULL', NULL);`

Run the form and put it in Enter Query mode. Click the `Reports` button.

a) Can you navigate back and forth from the calling form to the reports module? What do you think the behavior would have been if `commode` had been set to SYNCHRONOUS?

Answer: Yes you can. The reports module would have been modal.

The `commode` parameter determines whether or not the user should be able to return to the calling module before the called module has been exited. When set to ASYNCHRONOUS, the user can navigate back and forth between both modules. When set to SYNCHRONOUS, the user must exit the called module, in this case the report, before returning to the calling module.

ASYNCHRONOUS mode can be useful in situations where a report is expected to take a long time to complete. The user can run the report and continue working in a forms module while they wait for the report to complete.

b) Can you see the report and interact with it in the previewer? What do you think the behavior would have been if `execmode` had been set to BATCH?

Answer: It would have run the report in the background.

BATCH mode is useful when the user does not want to view the report on-screen. Instead, they want to send the report results to a file or printer.

c) Where will the Reports Runtime look for the reports module?

Answer: It will look in the filesystem.

As you have learned in previous Chapters, Oracle Developer lets you choose between storing modules in the filesystem or in the database. The location parameter indicates where the Reports Runtime should look to find the module to be run.

In this case, since you have chosen filesystem and you have not included the full path with the report name, the Reports Runtime will search the directories indicated in the Windows Registry for the report file.

d) Is the form passing the report any parameters?

Answer: No it is not.

If you are not passing a parameter list to a report, you must indicate in the RUN_PRODUCT built-in that the value of the parameter list is 'NULL'. Note too that you must put the word NULL in single quotes ('NULL'). If you do not use single quotes, the trigger or program unit using RUN_PRODUCT will compile with errors. In Lab 12.2, you will learn how to pass parameter lists to reports.

The display parameter requires a value only if RUN_PRODUCT is being used to call an Oracle graphics module. In the remaining Labs and Exercises, always set this parameter to NULL. Note that this value does **not** require single quotes.

12.1.2 ANSWERS

Open the form EX12_01.fmb in the Form Builder. Use the Reports node in the Object Navigator to create a report object based on an existing report called STUDENT.

a) How should you respond to the New Report dialog to base the report object on an existing report named STUDENT?

Answer: You should select the Use Existing Report File *radio button and enter the name of the reports module in the* Filename *field.*

It is not necessary to include the entire path in the Filename field. The Reports Runtime will be able to find the reports module as long as it is stored in a directory that the Windows Registry points to.

The STUDENT report is now represented as an object in the form EX12_01.fmb. The reports module itself is not stored here, nor are any of the report objects. However, having this pointer to the report contained in the forms module makes it much easier to control the running of the report.

Incidentally, if you were to select Create New Report File, the Form Builder would launch the Report Builder and you would be able to create a new reports module.

b) The RUN_REPORT_OBJECT built-in does not accept parameters like commode, execmode, etc. Where do you think you can set them instead?

Answer: They can be set using the properties for the report object.

The report object has additional properties for other SYSTEM.PARAMETERS, like Destination Name and Destination Format. If the report is being sent to a file or printer, these properties determine how it should be named and how it should be formatted.

Destination Name and Destination Format can also be set using the RUN_PRODUCT built-in, but they would not be set using properties. They would have to be added to a parameter list, which requires coding.

Set the Execution Mode property to Runtime and the Communication Mode property to Asynchronous.

c) Which property can you set so that the report output gets sent to the screen?

Answer: The Report Destination Type *property.*

This property tells the Reports Runtime where to send the report. By choosing Screen, it sends the report to the previewer so that the user can view the report results. As their names imply, the values File and Printer would send the report output to a file or a printer, respectively. When selecting these options, you must also set the Destination Name property so that the report knows where to send the report.

d) What would the code be for the WHEN-BUTTON-PRESSED trigger to open this report with the RUN_REPORT_OBJECT built-in?

Answer: See the discussion below.

The code would be as follows:

```
DECLARE
    v_repobj_id                 REPORT_OBJECT;
    v_repins_id                 VARCHAR2(100);
BEGIN
    v_repobj_id := FIND_REPORT_OBJECT('STUDENT');
    v_repins_id := RUN_REPORT_OBJECT(v_repobj_id);
END;
```

As discussed in the Lab text, the FIND_REPORT_OBJECT built-in returns the object ID of the report object. RUN_REPORT_OBJECT runs the report and also returns a value. This value is the unique ID that the Reports engine has assigned for this job. This Reports engine could be on the user's machine or on a remote server somewhere in the network. You can use the ID returned by RUN_REPORT_OBJECT to get information about the status of a specific report job.

■ FOR EXAMPLE:

```
REPORT_OBJECT_STATUS(v_repins_id);
```

would return a VARCHAR2 value, indicating whether this job has finished, has been canceled, is still running, etc. This can be very helpful, es-

L A B   1 2 . 2

PASSING
PARAMETERS
TO REPORTS

LAB OBJECTIVES

After this Lab, you will be able to:

- Pass Parameters to a Report

Reports modules can be passed parameters using parameter lists. In fact, the methods for creating and using parameter lists are no different from what you learned in Chapter 11, "Multiple-Form Applications."

You first must create a parameter list in a form, add parameters to it, and then pass it to the called reports module. Both the RUN_PRODUCT_ OBJECT and RUN_PRODUCT built-ins accept parameter list names or parameter list object IDs.

■ FOR EXAMPLE:

If you had created a parameter list and stored its object ID in a variable called v_plist_id, the syntax to call a report named SECTIONS would be as follows:

```
RUN_PRODUCT(REPORTS, 'SECTIONS', ASYNCHRONOUS, RUNTIME, FILESYSTEM, v_plist_id, NULL);
```

or

```
v_repobj_id := FIND_REPORT_OBJECT('SECTIONS);
v_repins_id := RUN_REPORT_OBJECT(v_repins_id, v_plist_id);
```

For the report to accept the parameter, it must be created in the Report Builder at design-time. This requirement is identical to that when passing parameters from form to form using CALL_FORM, etc.

■ *FOR EXAMPLE:*

If a parameter called 'P_1' had been defined in the reports module at design-time, the ADD_PARAMETER statement in the forms module would look like this:

```
ADD_PARAMETER(v_plist_id, 'P_1', text_parameter, v_value);
```

PARAMETERS IN REPORTS MODULES

In the reports module, P_1 is referred to as a user parameter. What this means is that you, the programmer, have defined it. Reports modules also have a standard set of system parameters that have been pre-defined by the system. In the Exercises for Lab 12.1, you learned about DESNAME and DESTYPE, which are examples of system parameters.

When a user parameter is defined, the reports module will by default display its own parameter form to accept values for the user parameter. Figure 12.2 shows a Reports parameter form accepting a value for parameter P_1.

These parameter forms can be extremely useful when you are running a report on its own. However, in this case, you will be running the report from the form and passing it a value for P_1. Therefore, you do not want the report's parameter form to be displayed. You can use the system parameter PARAMFORM to suppress the parameter form. To do so, you would

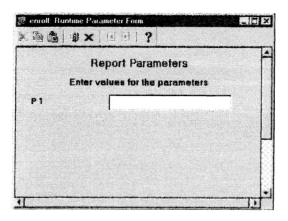

Figure 12.2 ■ A parameter form in an Oracle reports module.

add another parameter to the parameter list in Forms. The code would be as follows:

```
ADD_PARAMETER(v_plist_id, 'PARAMFORM', text_parameter, 'NO');
```

LAB 12.2 EXERCISES

12.2.1 PASS PARAMETERS TO A REPORT

In this Exercise, you will pass the value of the forms module's current STU-DENT_ID to a report called STUDENRL. The report will use this value in its WHERE clause to show the enrollment information of the current student.

Open the form EX12_01.fmb in the Form Builder. The name of the parameter in the STUDENRL report is P_1.

a) What would the code be to create a parameter list and then add the current STUDENT_ID to the list as a parameter? Remember to add code statements to destroy the parameter list if it already exists. Also remember to add a parameter to suppress the reports module's parameter form.

_____

_____

b) What would the RUN_PRODUCT syntax to call STUDENRL be?

_____

_____

Run the form and test the report. Issue a query for STUDENT_ID 248 to be certain that you are working with a student with enrollment records.

c) How would you have to change the WHEN-BUTTON-PRESSED trigger so that it would use RUN_REPORT_OBJECT instead of RUN_PRODUCT? Remember to add another report object to the form for the STUDENRL report.

_____

_____

LAB 12.2 EXERCISES ANSWERS

12.2.1 ANSWERS

Open the form EX12_01.fmb in the Form Builder. The name of the parameter in the STUDENRL report is P_1.

a) What would the code be to create a parameter list and then add the current STUDENT_ID to the list as a parameter? Remember to add code statements to destroy the parameter list if it already exists. Also remember to add a parameter to suppress the reports module's parameter form.

Answer: See the discussion below.

The code would be as follows:

```
DECLARE
        v_plist_id                  PARAMLIST;
BEGIN
        v_plist_id := GET_PARAMETER_LIST('rep_params');
        IF NOT ID_NULL(v_plist_id) THEN
            DESTROY_PARAMETER_LIST(v_plist_id);
        END IF;
        v_plist_id := CREATE_PARAMETER_LIST('rep_params');
ADD_PARAMETER(v_plist_id, 'P_1', text_parameter, :STUDENT.STUDENT_ID);
ADD_PARAMETER(v_plist_id, 'PARAMFORM', text_parameter, 'NO');
```

b) What would the RUN_PRODUCT syntax to call STUDENRL be?

Answer: See the discussion below.

The code would be as follows:

```
RUN_PRODUCT(REPORTS, 'STUDENRL', ASYNCHRONOUS, RUNTIME, FILESYSTEM, v_plist_id, NULL);
```

c) How would you have to change the WHEN-BUTTON-PRESSED trigger so that it would use RUN_REPORT_OBJECT instead of RUN_PRODUCT? Remember to add another report object to the form for the STUDENRL report.

Answer: See the discussion below.

The code should be as follows:

```
DECLARE
        v_plist_id                  PARAMLIST;
        v_repobj_id                 REPORT_OBJECT;
        v_repins_id                 VARCHAR2(100);
BEGIN
        v_plist_id := GET_PARAMETER_LIST('rep_params');
        IF NOT ID_NULL(v_plist_id) THEN
                DESTROY_PARAMETER_LIST(v_plist_id);
        END IF;
        v_plist_id := CREATE_PARAMETER_LIST('rep_params');
ADD_PARAMETER(v_plist_id, 'P_1', text_parameter, :STUDENT.STUDENT_ID);
ADD_PARAMETER(v_plist_id, 'PARAMFORM', text_parameter, 'NO');
v_repobj_id := FIND_REPORT_OBJECT('STUDENRL');
v_repins_id := RUN_REPORT_OBJECT(v_repins_id, v_plist_id);
END;
```

LAB 12.2 SELF-REVIEW QUESTIONS

In order to test your progress, you should be able to answer the following questions:

1) Where should you create parameter lists?
   a) _____ In the calling form
   b) _____ In the called form
   c) _____ In the reports module
   d) _____ None of the above

2) What should be true of the user parameter in a reports module that is being passed a value from a form?
   a) _____ It should have the same name as the parameter list
   b) _____ It should have the same name as the reports module
   c) _____ It should be a VARCHAR2 data type
   d) _____ It should have the same name as the parameter in the parameter list

3) What is wrong with the following statement:

   ```
   ADD_PARAMETER(v_plist_id, 'P_1', text_parameter);
   ```

   a) _____ 'P_1' should not be in quotes
   b) _____ The name of the reports module is missing
   c) _____ text_parameter should be in quotes
   d) _____ The value of the parameter is missing

4) What is wrong with the following statement:

`RUN_REPORT_OBJECT(v_repobj_id, v_plist_id, SYNCHRONOUS);`

a) ____ The built-in should be RUN_PRODUCT_OBJECT
b) ____ The report object should be referenced by module name
c) ____ RUN_REPORT_OBJECT does not accept parameter list IDs
d) ____ SYNCHRONOUS should be set with properties, not through the built-in

Quiz answers appear in Appendix A, Section 12.2.

LAB
12.2

C H A P T E R   1 2

TEST YOUR THINKING

1) Add a button to the R_STUDENT.fmb form that uses RUN_PRODUCT to call the STUDENRL.rdf reports module. This reports module was installed when you originally downloaded files from the Web site. STUDENRL.rdf displays a student record and the enrollments for that student. STUDENRL.rdf accepts a parameter called P_1 for the student_id. The user should be able to view the report in the previewer and return to the calling form before the report has been exited. Remember to suppress the report's parameter form.

2) Add a button to the R_INSTRUCTOR.fmb form that uses RUN_REPORT_ OBJECT to call the INSTSECT.rdf reports module. This reports module was installed when you originally downloaded files from the Web site. INSTSECT.rdf displays an instructor record and the sections that the instructor teaches. INSTSECT.rdf accepts a parameter called P_1 for the instructor_id. The user should be able to view the report in the previewer and return to the calling form before the report has been exited. Remember to suppress the report's parameter form.

CHAPTER 13

FORMS MENUS

CHAPTER OBJECTIVES

In this Chapter, you will learn about:

- ✔ Menu Modules   Page 422
- ✔ Menu Security   Page 435

Now that you have created a number of forms modules, it is time to learn how to tie them all together in an application with a menu system. So far, all of your forms modules have been run with the DEFAULT menu that is provided for each form. It has some basic but very useful functions for editing, navigation, querying, and so on. In this Chapter, you will learn how to create your own custom menus that go a little beyond the DEFAULT menu in functionality. In Chapter 11, "Multiple-Form Applications," you learned several built-ins for calling one form from another. You will use these same built-ins to call forms from a menu system. This will let you unite many of the forms you have created in previous Labs in a single application. You will also learn how to use menu modules to implement security features to control access to the application.

L A B   1 3 . 1

MENU MODULES

LAB OBJECTIVES

After this Lab, you will be able to:

*   Create Menus and Menu Items

MENU OBJECTS

Menu modules and their objects can be created in the Form Builder. There are four main components of a menu module: the menu module itself, the Main Menu, individual menus, and menu items.

Figure 13.1 puts these objects in the context of a running form.

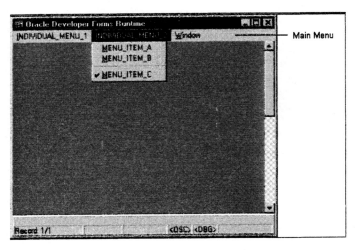

Figure 13.1 ■ **A sample menu module displayed in the Forms Runtime.**

The menu module itself, like a forms module, is not visible to the user. It is the logical container object that owns all of the other menu objects. The Main Menu is the horizontal bar across the top that contains the labels INDIVIDUAL_MENU_1, INDIVIDUAL_MENU_2, and Window. Each of these labels is an individual menu that contains a group of menu items. The menu items for INDIVIDUAL_MENU_2 are being displayed. The menu items are the most important objects in the menu module because they are what the users select to initiate actions.

MENU ITEMS

There are five types of menu items: plain, magic, check, radio, and separator. Plain menu items are the ones you will use most. They display text labels and have PL/SQL code behind them.

■ FOR EXAMPLE:

A plain menu item labeled Save might have the following code behind it:

```
DO_KEY('COMMIT_FORM');
```

As you can imagine, when the user selects this menu item, Forms executes the DO_KEY built-in and saves any changes.

Magic items are perhaps the most convenient menu items because some of them already have code associated with them; therefore, you do not have to write any code yourself. They can be used to perform functions that are common to most applications.

■ FOR EXAMPLE:

A magic item of type Copy has the code for copying text already associated with it. Therefore, at design-time, all you have to do is indicate that you want a certain menu item to be a magic item and Forms will associate the proper code with it.

Check and radio menu items allow you to create Boolean menu items that are often used to configure the state of the application at run-time.

■ FOR EXAMPLES:

The Form Builder uses check and radio menu items under View in the Main Menu. These items allow you to select the view style of the Object Navigator and whether or not to display PL/SQL objects. The View menu is shown in Figure 13.2.

Figure 13.2 ■ **The View menu in the Form Builder showing radio and check menu item types.**

In your applications, you could create a check menu item called Display Toolbar that would hide or display a toolbar.

Separators are the only menu items that do not have any commands associated with them. They are simply dummy items that you can use to separate menu items to make your menus more readable. In Figure 13.2, there is a separator between Visual View and Show PL/SQL only.

CREATING AND CONFIGURING MENU MODULES

The objects in menu modules are organized in a hierarchy and displayed in the Object Navigator as shown in Figure 13.3.

All of the objects in a menu can be created, deleted, and arranged in the Object Navigator and then further configured using the Property Palette. Although using the Object Navigator is a perfectly viable option for creating menu objects, it is not the easiest to follow. It is difficult to tell which menu items belong to which individual menus, especially when the menu module gets to be rather large.

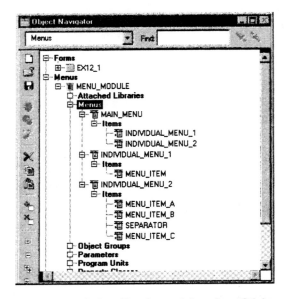

Figure 13.3 ■ **A menu module displayed in the Object Navigator.**

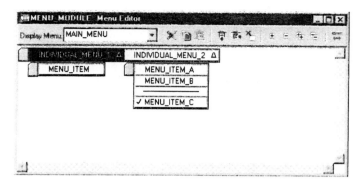

Figure 13.4 ■ A menu module displayed in the Menu Editor.

Luckily, the Form Builder also provides the Menu Editor for creating and defining menus. The Menu Editor offers a WYSIWYG view of the menu module. Figure 13.4 shows a menu module displayed in the Menu Editor. It is the same module that was displayed in the Object Navigator in Figure 13.3, but is clearly much easier to understand here.

ATTACHING MENU MODULES TO FORMS

A menu module cannot be run by itself. For a menu to be visible and accessible to the user, it must be attached to a forms module. When that form is run, the menu will be displayed to the user.

Menu modules have binary formats, .mmb files, and executable formats, .mmx files. When a menu is attached to a form, and that form is run, the Forms Runtime will search for and execute the .mmx version of the menu module. Therefore, you must explicitly compile a menu module using CTRL-T before using it. Simply running the form, whether you do it from the Form Builder or the Forms Runtime, will not automatically compile a menu module.

As you are working with and testing menu modules in the Form Builder, it is important to compile the menu module prior to each test. If you do not re-compile, the Form Builder will run an older version of the .mmx, which may not have your most recent changes.

LAB 13.1 EXERCISES

13.1.1 CREATE MENUS AND MENU ITEMS

The purpose of this Exercise is to create a menu module and experiment with some of the different types of menu items. You will begin by examining the DEFAULT menu provided by Oracle Forms. Then you will create and configure your own custom menu.

Open the form EX13_01.fmb in the Form Builder. Run the form.

a) What is the second individual menu in this menu module and what are its menu items? Can you guess their menu item types?

_____

_____

Close the form and return to the Form Builder. Use the Object Navigator to create a menu module. Name it MAIN and save it. Right-click the menu module and open the Menu Editor.

b) What objects have been created automatically?

_____

_____

c) How can you use the Menu Editor's toolbar to create a menu item for this individual menu?

_____

_____

In the Menu Editor, name the individual menu File and the menu item Exit. Look at the properties for each menu object.

d) What is the label property for the Exit menu item?

_____

_____

e) How can you make the menu item `Exit` a magic item that will quit the application?

_____

_____

Compile the menu module using CTRL-T.

f) How can you attach the R_MAIN menu module to EX13_01? Do you have to use its full path or just the module name?

_____

_____

Run the EX13_01.fmb form and test the menu. Exit the form and return to configuring the menu in the Form Builder.

g) How can you use the Menu Editor's toolbar to create another individual menu with two menu items? Make sure you create this new individual menu in the Main Menu at the same level as `File`.

_____

_____

Name the individual menu `Registration` and the menu items `Register Students` and `Enroll Students`.

`Register Students` and `Enroll Students` will be used to open the R_STUDENT and R_STUDENRL forms, respectively.

h) What should the menu item type be for `Register Students` and `Enroll Students`? Which property can you use to enter code to call them? For both menu items, use the CALL_FORM command and pass it only the forms module's name.

_____

_____

Compile the menu module. Run the EX13_01.fmb form and test the menu. Exit the form and return to configuring the menu in the Form Builder.

Change the menu item command for Register Students to:

```
CALL_FORM('R_STUDENT', HIDE, DO_REPLACE);
```

Change the menu item command for Enroll Students to:

```
CALL_FORM('R_STUDENT, HIDE, NO_REPLACE);
```

Compile the menu module. Run the EX13_01.fmb form and test the menu items under Registration.

i) What is different about the menu for each form? What has caused this difference?

_____

_____

Exit the forms and return to the Form Builder. Both forms should use the R_MAIN menu to change the menu item command for Register Students to:

```
CALL_FORM('R_STUDENT, HIDE, NO_REPLACE);
```

j) If you were to create another individual menu with menu items to call reports modules, what types of menu items would these be? What code would you put behind them to call the reports modules? Do not take these steps in the Menu Editor; simply answer the question.

_____

_____

Save R_MAIN.mmb *and* EX13_01.fmb.

LAB 13.1 EXERCISE ANSWERS

13.1.1   ANSWERS

Open the form EX13_01.fmb in the Form Builder. Run the form.

a)   What is the second individual menu in this menu module and what are its menu items? Can you guess their menu item types?

Answer: The second individual menu is Edit. *Its menu items are* Cut, Copy, Paste, Error, *and* Display List.

Cut, Copy, and Paste are magic items. Error and Display List are plain menu items with code behind them.

The menu you are exploring here is the DEFAULT menu that is attached to every newly created form. It is usually accompanied by the SMARTBAR, which you read a little bit about in Chapter 8, "Canvases and Windows." The SMARTBAR has been removed for this Exercise. The DEFAULT menu cannot be edited directly. You cannot make changes to a menu module called DEFAULT.mmb in the Form Builder. You must either use DEFAULT as-is or attach a different menu module to the form.

There may be some features within DEFAULT that you want to reuse. For that reason, a menu module called file menudef.mmb, which is identical in function to the DEFAULT menu, was installed along with your Oracle Developer files. You should be able to find it in the \ORACLE_HOME\ DEVDEM60\DEMO\FORMS directory. You edit this module directly or reuse some of its objects in other modules. For example, you may want to copy and paste the EDIT individual menu from menudef.mmb into your custom menu modules.

DEFAULT MENU FORM

You may have noticed that the form EX13_01.fmb has a block with one item that is not displayed. The only thing displayed on the canvas is a text message welcoming the user to the application. This type of form is often referred to as a default menu form. It is common to attach a functionless form like this one to a menu to serve as a starting point or splash screen. It can contain a simple message or an image to introduce the application, or it can contain functional items like buttons or display items.

Even though they are not used, the block and item are included in EX13_01.fmb because they are mandatory Forms objects; the form would not be able to run without them. The MENUITEM item is assigned

Figure 13.5 ■ A menu module in the Object Navigator with one Main Menu and one menu item.

to the MENUCANV canvas and its Width and Height properties are set to 0,0 so that it is not visible to the user.

It is not mandatory to have a functionless default menu form as your starting point. It is also common to attach a menu to a form that is always opened first by the user.

■ FOR EXAMPLE:

In the Student application, if it were the case that users began each session by entering or updating records in the STUDENT table, then it may have made sense to attach the menu module to R_STUDENT. fmb. This would then be the forms module that would be the starting point of the application.

b) What objects have been created automatically?

Answer: In the Object Navigator, there is a Main Menu called MENU1 *and an individual menu called* ITEM2. *In the Menu Editor, there is only an individual menu labeled* New Item.

Figures 13.5 and 13.6 show what you should be seeing now in the Object Navigator and Menu Editor.

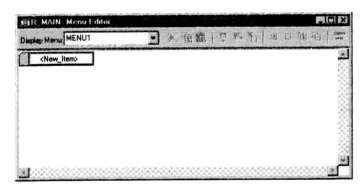

Figure 13.6 ■ A menu module in the Menu Editor with one individual menu.

c) How can you use the Menu Editor's toolbar to create a menu item for this individual menu?

Answer: Click the `Create Down` *button on the Menu Editor's toolbar.*

d) What is the label property for the `Exit` menu item?

Answer: The labels have been changed to `File` *and* `Exit`.

Note that changes have been made in the Object Navigator as well. This illustrates that it is much easier to label menu objects using the Menu Editor because it sets the name property as well. If need be, you can give menu objects two-word labels and Forms will automatically insert an underscore when it sets the object's name. For example, if you type `Save Form` into the label in the Menu Editor, Forms will set the name of this object to `SAVE_FORM`.

Hot keys can be set for the labels of menu items as well. The user can press the hot key associated with a menu item instead of clicking it.

■ FOR EXAMPLE:

The hot key for the `Exit` menu item is "E." If the user selects the individual menu `File` and presses "E," the menu module will respond as if the user clicked `Exit` with the mouse. The default behavior is that the first letter of the label is designated as the hot key for all menu items. This can be changed by inserting an ampersand into the label just before the letter that you wish to make the hot key. So, if you wanted "x" to be the hot key for `Exit`, you would write the label as follows:

```
E&xit
```

e) How can you make the menu item `Exit` a magic item that will quit the application?

Answer: You set its `Menu Item Type` *property to* `Magic` *and its* `Magic Item` *property to* `Quit`.

The `Quit`, `Cut`, `Copy`, `Paste`, `Clear`, and `Window` magic items already have code behind them that makes them easy and convenient to use. In this case, by selecting `Quit` as the magic item, you do not have to write any PL/SQL to exit or close the current form, as Forms will automatically execute the code built into the magic item.

f) How can you attach the R_MAIN menu module to EX13_01? Do you have to use its full path or just the module name?

Answer: You set the EX13_01 *module-level* `Menu Module` *property to* R_MAIN. *No, you do not have to include the full path.*

Again, Forms will search for the files it needs by referring to the Registry. As long as R_MAIN.mmx is in a path pointed to by the Registry, it will be able to find and run it. It is important to repeat that the menu module must have been compiled for it to be attached to the form at run-time. The Forms run-time will not be able to attach .mmb (binary) files, nor will it compile them automatically.

g) How can you use the Menu Editor's toolbar to create another individual menu with two menu items? Make sure you create this new individual menu in the Main Menu at the same level as File.

Answer: Select the File *individual menu and click the* Create Across *button. Then, click the* Create Down *button twice.*

The Menu Editor should resemble Figure 13.7.

h) What should the menu item type be for Register Students and Enroll Students? Which property can you use to enter code to call them? For both menu items, use the CALL_FORM command and pass it only the forms module's name.

Answer: The Menu Item Type *property should be* Plain. *The* Menu Item Code *property should be used to enter the code.*

Clicking the Menu Item Code property will open the PL/SQL Editor. In this Exercise, you will write simple CALL_FORM statements behind the menu items. However, if the application called for it, you could include entire PL/SQL blocks, calls to program units, or whatever code you'd like.

i) What is different about the menu for each form? What has caused this difference?

Answer: R_STUDENT displays the DEFAULT *menu, while R_STUDENRL displays the* R_MAIN *menu.*

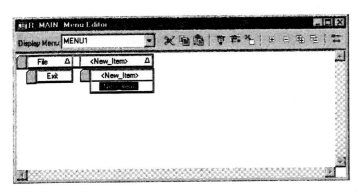

Figure 13.7 ■ The Menu Editor with a new individual menu and two new menu items.

The `switch menu` parameter of the `CALL_FORM` built-in determines which menu should be attached to the called form. Both `R_STUDENT` and `R_STUDENRL` have `DEFAULT` as the setting for their `Menu Module` property. The calling form is `EX13_01`, which has `R_MAIN` set for its `Menu Module` property.

`DO_REPLACE` in the call to `R_STUDENT` instructed the form to replace the menu of the calling form with the menu of the called form. Therefore, `R_STUDENT` (the called form) displayed `DEFAULT`, its own menu.

`NO_REPLACE` in the call to `R_STUDENRL` instructed the form not to replace the menu of the calling form with the menu of the called form. Therefore, `R_STUDENRL` (the called form) displayed `R_MAIN`, the menu attached to `EX13_01` (the calling form). `NO_REPLACE` is the default value of the `CALL_FORM` statement.

Exit the forms and return to the Form Builder. Both forms should use the `R_MAIN` menu, so change the menu item command for `Register Students` to:

> **CALL_FORM('R_STUDENT', HIDE, NO_REPLACE);**

j) If you were to create another individual menu with menu items to call reports modules, what types of menu items would these be? What code would you put behind them to call the reports modules? Do not take these steps in the Menu Editor; simply answer the question.

Answer: You could use either RUN_PRODUCT *or* RUN_PRODUCT_OBJECT.

Both built-ins would work equally well. However, to use `RUN_PRODUCT_OBJECT`, you would have to create a report object in `EX13_01.fmb`.

Save R_MAIN.mmb *and* EX13_01.fmb.

LAB 13.1 SELF-REVIEW QUESTIONS

In order to test your progress, you should be able to answer the following questions:

1) Which of the following is true about menu items?
  a) _____ They can have PL/SQL code associated with them
  b) _____ They can be manipulated in the Layout Editor
  c) _____ They can be used to call other forms and reports modules
  d) _____ a & c

2) The following statement is issued from a menu item in a menu module that is attached to FORM_A:

```
CALL_FORM('FORM_B', HIDE, NO_REPLACE);
```

What will the results of this statement be?

a) _____ FORM_B will open with FORM_A's menu; FORM_A will be visible and accessible

b) _____ FORM_B will open with its own menu; FORM_A will be visible but not accessible

c) _____ FORM_B will open with FORM_A's menu; FORM_A will not be visible

d) _____ FORM_B will open with FORM_A's menu; FORM_A will close

3) How do you associate a menu module with a form?

a) _____ Run the menu module and its child forms will be associated

b) _____ Attach the form to the menu module

c) _____ Attach the menu module to a form using the Menu Module property

d) _____ Run the form and issue a CALL_FORM statement to display the menu module

4) Setting a menu item's label to Sa&ve will make "a" the hot key for this menu item.

a) _____ True

b) _____ False

Quiz answers appear in Appendix A, Section 13.1.

L A B   1 3 . 2

MENU SECURITY

LAB OBJECTIVES

After this Lab, you will be able to:

*   Implement Menu Security

There may be instances in which you will want to restrict access to parts of your application from certain users. You will want to give some users access to all of the modules in an application, but then provide other users access to only a few modules in the application. Instead of creating two or more completely different menu systems for each group of users, you can create a single menu system and implement menu security by granting and restricting access to individual menus and menu items.

The menu security system is integrated with the database, meaning that you can base menu item access on database roles.

■ FOR EXAMPLE:

Assume that in the database you have created two roles: one called STU-DENT_USERS and one called OFFICE_USERS, with various users assigned to each role. STUDENT_USERS can only query the COURSE and SECTION tables to get information about courses. OFFICE_USERS can perform all DML operations on all of the tables in the STUDENT schema.

Also assume that you have created an application with a number of forms modules, one of which is a query-only master-detail form showing course and section data. When creating the menu module, you can set properties for the menu items so that the STUDENT_USERS role will only be able to access the menu item that calls the course and section master-detail form. You would use the same properties to indicate that the OFFICE_USERS role will be able to access all menu items in the application.

There are two simple steps for configuring menu security:

1) Indicate which database roles have access to the menu module.
2) For each individual menu item, indicate whether or not the roles specified in Step 1 should be granted access.

Both steps are taken using the properties that you will explore in the Exercises.

LAB 13.2 EXERCISES

13.2.1 IMPLEMENT MENU SECURITY

To practice menu security, you will need to create some sample database users and database roles. Before attempting the Exercises, you must complete the following two steps:

1) Run scripts to create sample database users and roles.

2) Build Forms schema objects and grant the sample database users access to them.

STEP 1—RUN SCRIPTS TO CREATE SAMPLE DATABASE USERS AND ROLES

Your \guest\forms\sql directory contains two files:

1) dba.sql

2) student.sql

Take the following steps to use these files to create users and roles:

1) Start an SQL*Plus session and connect as the SYSTEM user. You may have to ask your database administrator for help if you do not know the SYSTEM password.

2) Run the dba.sql file.

3) Wait for the script to finish. The script will issue some drop statements, which will result in error messages. Ignore these error messages.

4) When the script has finished, log into the STUDENT schema by issuing the following command from the SQL prompt. If **learn** is not the password you are using, then substitute the correct one:

```
conn student/learn
```

5) Run the `student.sql` file.

6) Wait for the script to finish. Exit SQL*Plus.

These scripts have created two users: `reg_user/reg_user` and `adm_user/`
`adm_user`. The scripts have also created two roles: `ADMINISTRATOR` and
`REGISTRAR`.

The `ADMINISTRATOR` role has been granted to `adm_user`. The `REGIS-`
`TRAR` role has been granted to `reg_user`.

STEP 2—BUILD THE FORMS SCHEMA OBJECTS AND GRANT ACCESS

There are a number of Forms schema objects that serve administrative purposes for the Forms environment. They create the database objects that will
let you store forms modules in the filesystem and let you use the menu security system. If you haven't done so already, you must take the following steps
to build the Forms schema objects.

1) From the Windows Start menu, navigate to the `Oracle Developer`
    `6.0 Admin` menu item.

2) Select `Oracle Developer Build`.

An SQL*Plus session will open and you will be required to enter the `SYSTEM`
password and database connect string. The script will run and create all of the
Forms schema objects.

Next, you must take the following steps to grant your users access to these
objects.

1) From the Windows Start menu, navigate to the `Oracle Developer`
    `6.0 Admin` menu item again.

2) Select Oracle Developer Grant.

An SQL*Plus session will open and you will be required to enter the `SYSTEM`
password and database connect string. You will then be prompted for the user
name to which you wish to grant access.

3) Enter the user name STUDENT each time you are prompted for a user
    name.

4) Repeat Steps 1 through 3 for ADM_USER and REG_USER.

You are now ready to use the Forms menu security system. If you ever want additional users to have access to the security system, you must repeat Steps 1 through 3 for each user.

Open the modules EX13_01.fmb and R_MAIN.mmb in the Form Builder. Select R_MAIN and view its properties.

a) What happens when you click the Module Roles property? What values should you enter?

_____

_____

b) Which property should you set to indicate that you would like to activate menu security?

_____

_____

Select both the File and Registration individual menus. You can do this in either the Object Navigator or Menu Editor.

c) What happens if you click the Item Roles property? How can you indicate that both roles should have access to both items?

_____

_____

Select the Exit menu item. Give both roles access to this menu item. Select the Register Students menu item. Give both roles access to this menu item.

d) How can you set the properties so that the ADMINISTRATOR role will have access to Enroll Students but the REGISTRAR role will **not** have access to Enroll Students?

_____

_____

Compile the menu module.

Press CTRL-J and re-connect as REG_USER/REG_USER. Run form EX13_01.fmb.

> **e)** Can you select the Enroll Students menu item? Why not?

_____

_____

Exit the form and return to the Form Builder.

> **f)** Which property could you set so that REG_USER would not be able to see Enroll Students without proper access? Do not do this in the Form Builder. Simply write down your answer.

_____

_____

Reset the properties for Enroll Students so that both ADMINISTRA-TOR and REGISTRAR have access to it.

Save R_MAIN.mmb *and* EX13_01.fmb.

LAB 13.2 EXERCISE ANSWERS

13.2.1 ANSWERS

Open the modules EX13_01.fmb and R_MAIN.mmb in the Form Builder. Select R_MAIN and view its properties.

a) What happens when you click the Module Roles property? What values should you enter?

Answer: The Menu Module Roles *dialog opens. You should enter the* ADMIN-ISTRATOR *and* REGISTRAR *roles.*

The Menu Module Roles dialog shown in Figure 13.8 is used to give certain database roles access to the menu system.

This property gives certain roles overall access to the menu module. Later, the role names entered here will be used to grant or deny access to individual menus and menu items.

Figure 13.8 ■ The Menu Module Roles dialog populated with role names.

b) Which property should you set to indicate that you would like to activate menu security?

Answer: The Use Security *property.*

The Use Security property enables or disables the menu security system. If it is set to No, menu security will not be implemented, even if it has been completely configured for all of the menu items in the module.

Select both the File and Registration individual menus. You can do this in either the Object Navigator or Menu Editor.

c) What happens if you click the Item Roles property? How can you indicate that both roles should have access to both items?

Answer: The Menu Item Roles *dialog will open.*

The Menu Item Roles dialog shown in Figure 13.9 displays the names of the roles that were entered in the Menu Module Roles dialog.

By selecting ADMINISTRATOR and REGISTRAR, you are giving both of these roles access to the File and Registration individual menus. What is important to note is that by selecting multiple items in the Object Navigator or Menu Module, you were able to assign roles to multiple items simultaneously. This can be a big time saver when you have many individual menus or menu items that need to be accessed by the same roles.

One caveat is that, while you were able to set the roles for more than one item at a time, you are not able to view the roles for more than one item at a time. If you wish to see which roles have already been assigned to a menu item, you must view its Item Roles property individually.

Figure 13.9 ■ The Menu Item Roles dialog displaying available roles.

Select the Exit menu item. Give both roles access to this menu item. Select the Register Students menu item. Give both roles access to this menu item.

d) How can you set the properties so that the ADMINISTRATOR role will have access to Enroll Students but the REGISTRAR will **not** have access to Enroll Students?

Answer: Select the Item Roles *property for* Enroll Students. *Select* ADMINISTRATOR *in the dialog but not* REGISTRAR.

By not selecting REGISTRAR for Enroll Students, you are denying access to this menu item to any user who has been granted the REGISTRAR role.

e) Can you select the Enroll Students menu item? Why not?

Answer: No, it is grayed out.

REG_USER has been granted the REGISTRAR role, so it has been denied access to this menu item. If you were to log in as ADM_USER, which has been granted the ADMINISTRATOR role, the Enroll Students menu item would be enabled.

f) Which property could you set so that REG_USER would not be able to see Enroll Students without proper access? Do not do this in the Form Builder. Simply write down your answer.

Answer: Display Without Privilege.

If the user does not have access to a certain menu item, and that item's Display Without Privilege property is set to No, then the item will be hidden completely instead of grayed out.

Reset the properties for `Enroll Students` so that both ADMINISTRATOR and REGISTRAR have access to it.

Save `R_MAIN.mmb` *and* `EX13_01.fmb`.

LAB 13.2 SELF-REVIEW QUESTIONS

In order to test your progress, you should be able to answer the following questions:

1) What must be done to the database for the menu security features to be functional?
   a) _____ Database roles must be created
   b) _____ Forms schema objects must be created
   c) _____ Application users must be granted access to Forms schema objects
   d) _____ All of the above

2) Which of the following is true about the `Module Roles` property?
   a) _____ It specifies access to the menu system by user name
   b) _____ It allows you to grant and revoke database privileges
   c) _____ It specifies access to the menu system by database role
   d) _____ It is part of the Menu Editor

3) How is a menu item displayed to a user who does not have access to it?
   a) _____ It is always grayed out
   b) _____ It is always hidden
   c) _____ It is visible but does not respond when selected
   d) _____ It can be either hidden or grayed out

Quiz answers appear in Appendix A, Section 13.2.

C H A P T E R   1 3

TEST YOUR THINKING

1) Add individual menus and menu items to R_MAIN.mmb so that it resembles Figure 13.10.

The following table indicates the function of each new menu item:

Menu Item	Function
Edit.Cut	Magic
Edit.Copy	Magic
Edit.Paste	Magic
Curriculum.Add Courses	Call R_COURSE.fmb
Curriculum.Add Sections	Call R_CRSESECT.fmb
Administration.Instructors	Call R_INSTRUCTOR.fmb
Reports. Students and Enrollments	Call STUDENRL.rdf
Reports. Instructors and Sections	Call INSTSECT.rdf

Use CALL_FORM to call all forms modules. The called forms should use the calling form's menu. The called form should be hidden while the calling form is active.

Use RUN_PRODUCT to call reports modules. The report should be displayed on the screen. Control should return to the calling form immediately. Do not pass any parameters or suppress the reports module's parameter form.

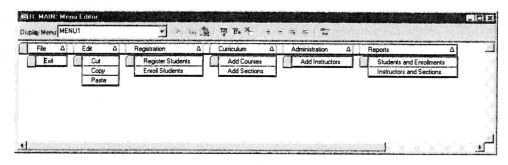

Figure 13.10 ■ Menu to build for this question.

2) Implement security for the menu.

The ADMINISTRATOR role should have access to all of the individual menus and menu items.

The REGISTRAR role should have access to all of the individual menus and menu items, except Administration and Add Instructors.

A P P E N D I X   A

ANSWERS TO SELF-REVIEW QUESTIONS

CHAPTER 1
Lab 1.1 ■ Self-Review Answers

Question	Answer	Comments
1)	d	
2)	b	PL/SQL is the language used in Forms triggers and program units.
3)	a	The direct result of clicking a button is the Button Pressed event, which is an interface event. If there is a WHEN-BUTTON-PRESSED trigger associated with the button, then this trigger will fire to respond to the Button Pressed event.
4)	d	
5)	c	

Lab 1.2 ■ Self-Review Answers

Question	Answer	Comments
1)	d	Blocks are logical containers of items. They are not physical objects because they do not have properties that would make them visible to the user.
2)	e	Modules, like blocks, are logical containers because they do not have properties that would make them visible to the user.
3)	a	
4)	a	
5)	d	Frames are graphic objects that are owned by canvases.
6)	a	All of the objects in a form are owned by the forms module. So, while Answers b, c, and d are also true, a is a more complete answer.

445

7)	d	At design-time, properties can be manipulated directly in the Property Palette. Some property values can also be manipulated in the Layout Editor. For example, if you drag an item from one place to another, you will be changing its X Position and Y Position properties. At run-time, PL/SQL code in triggers can be used to change property values programmatically.

CHAPTER 2
Lab 2.1 ■ Self-Review Answers

Question	Answer	Comments
1)	d	The Layout Wizard will help you create the first cut or rough draft of a canvas. You are free to edit this canvas by reentering the Layout Wizard or by using the Layout Editor and Property Palette.
2)	a	The main function of the Data Block Wizard is to create blocks and associate them with tables in the database. It also helps you create items in blocks and associate them with columns in the database.
3)	b	Reentering the Layout Wizard will allow you to change the prompt value for an item as well as edit many other item and canvas properties. While they are not listed as answers for Question 3, it is also possible to edit item prompts in the Property Palette and Layout Editor.
4)	c	Since neither the Data Block Wizard or Layout Wizard have anything to do with the module level of a form, they do not affect the module name.

Lab 2.2 ■ Self-Review Answers

Question	Answer	Comments
1)	d	
2)	c	
3)	e	Answer c is incorrect because icons are stored in .ico files, not as modules.
4)	c	Program Compile All will compile all of the PL/SQL in a form, but it will not create an .fmx file.

CHAPTER 3
Lab 3.1 ■ Self-Review Answers

Question	Answer	Comments
1)	c	
2)	d	

3)	d	Only object names can be changed in the Object Navigator. All other properties must be changed in either the Property Palette or Layout Editor.
4)	a	
5)	b	
6)	c	
7)	b	

Lab 3.2 ■ Self-Review Answers

Question	Answer	Comments
1)	c	
2)	c	
3)	d	Mass changes to properties can be done by selecting multiple objects in the Object Navigator and then changing their properties. It is not possible to delete item properties as Answer b suggests. However, in Chapter 9, "Reusable Objects," you will learn how to delete properties from objects called property classes.

Lab 3.3 ■ Self-Review Answers

Question	Answer	Comments
1)	c	
2)	a	
3)	b	
4)	e	
5)	b	
6)	d	

CHAPTER 4
Lab 4.1 ■ Self-Review Answers

Question	Answer	Comments
1)	b	
2)	d	The relation object is a logical object, so it cannot be displayed on a canvas.
3)	c	
4)	b	
5)	e	The relation object is always owned by the master block. The `Delete Record Behavior` property affects the way records are deleted.
6)	b	The `Deferred` property indicates whether or not the form should defer (wait) execution of the query for the detail block. If it is set to `No`, the query will not be deferred and the detail block will be populated along with the master block.
7)	c	

CHAPTER 5
Lab 5.1 ■ Self-Review Answers

Question	Answer	Comments
1)	c	
2)	c	
3)	a	It also lets you control the format in which information is entered into the form.
4)	d	Items can only be seen by the user if their Visible property is set to True and they are positioned on a canvas that is also visible.
5)	b	
6)	d	

Lab 5.2 ■ Self-Review Answers

Question	Answer	Comments
1)	d	Answer b is incorrect because while buttons have a Prompt property, it should not be used to communicate their function.
2)	b	
3)	a	
4)	a	
5)	d	
6)	d	

CHAPTER 6
Lab 6.1 ■ Self-Review Answers

Question	Answer	Comments
1)	a	
2)	a	Answer c is incorrect because the item-level WHEN-BUTTON-PRESSED trigger with Override set to Yes will cause the form to override or ignore WHEN-BUTTON-PRESSED triggers that are higher up in the hierarchy.
3)	d	Many item-specific triggers can be set at the block and form level as well to increase their scope.
4)	b	Answer c is incorrect because Post triggers do not replace default processing. They fire after the default processing has occurred.
5)	a	Answer c is incorrect because When triggers can also respond to internal processing events as demonstrated with the Validate Item event and WHEN-VALIDATE-ITEM trigger.
6)	b	
7)	b	
8)	b	WHEN-NEW-FORM-INSTANCE triggers can be created at the form and block level, but not the item level.

Lab 6.2 ■ Self-Review Answers

Question	Answer	Comments
1)	b	Answer c is incorrect because POST-QUERY triggers can only be attached at the block or form level. Moreover, no trigger can be attached to a record group or any other object that is not an item, block, or form.
2)	b	None of the other answers are true because POST-QUERY triggers cannot be attached to items.
3)	d	Although it was not mentioned in the Lab text, you probably noticed that the PL/SQL Editor formats your code to make it easier to read by indenting and coloring key words.
4)	d	
5)	b	
6)	c	

Lab 6.3 ■ Self-Review Answers

Question	Answer	Comments
1)	c	Answer a is only true if the built-in is restricted and the trigger fires because navigation has occurred.
2)	d	
3)	c	
4)	d	
5)	b	If you want to pass an item name to a built-in, you must use the following syntax: 'BLOCK.ITEM'. If you include the colon and exclude the single quotes as in Answer b, the built-in will not compile.
6)	d	If you answered a, you are half right. Up until now, you have only used FIND_ built-ins to get object IDs. However, later in the book, you will also use a GET_ built-in to get the object ID of a parameter list.

CHAPTER 7
Lab 7.1 ■ Self-Review Answers

Question	Answer	Comments
1)	d	
2)	b	
3)	d	
4)	d	
5)	b	
6)	b	
7)	a	
8)	b	

Lab 7.2 ■ Self-Review Answers

Question	Answer	Comments
1)	c	
2)	c	
3)	a	
4)	c	
5)	d	
6)	c	

CHAPTER 8
Lab 8.1 ■ Self-Review Answers

Question	Answer	Comments
1)	c	Answer c is incorrect because content is a type of canvas.
2)	c	Note that the answer says well-suited and not mandatory.
3)	d	Dialog windows are usually modal, although they do not have to be.
4)	b	
5)	a	
6)	d	Answer c is incorrect because the MDI window does not have a `Visible` property.
7)	b	

Lab 8.2 ■ Self-Review Answers

Question	Answer	Comments
1)	a	Two content canvases can be assigned to the same window, but they cannot appear at the same time.
2)	d	
3)	c	
4)	b	A window can be closed with navigation if its `Hide on Exit` property is set to `Yes`.

Lab 8.3 ■ Self-Review Answers

Question	Answer	Comments
1)	a	You can position items on a stacked canvas as you did in the Exercises for Lab 7.3.
2)	a	Stacked canvases are always positioned relative to a content canvas, not relative to a window.
3)	a	
4)	d	
5)	d	

Lab 8.4 ■ Self-Review Answers

Question	Answer	Comments
1)	c	Toolbars can only be attached to window objects or the MDI window.
2)	d	
3)	d	
4)	d	Answer c is incorrect because button items do not have a window property.

CHAPTER 9
Lab 9.1 ■ Self-Review Answers

Question	Answer	Comments
1)	d	
2)	d	Answer c is incorrect because copying an object does not create a subclassed version of that object.
3)	b	Answer a is incorrect because the Object Navigator only shows if an object has been subclassed, not what its source is.
4)	c	
5)	d	

Lab 9.2 ■ Self-Review Answers

Question	Answer	Comments
1)	c	Visual attributes only apply font and color properties, not physical properties like `Canvas`.
2)	d	Any object that has font and color properties can inherit from a visual attribute.
3)	a	
4)	d	
5)	c	
6)	d	
7)	c	
8)	d	Answer c is true because if the same property is set by both a visual attribute and a property class, the visual attribute's setting will take precedence.

Lab 9.3 ■ Self-Review Answers

Question	Answer	Comments
1)	a	
2)	c	
3)	d	
4)	b	Answer a is incorrect because an object group only contains pointers to objects, not actual instances of objects.

5)	d	Answer c is incorrect because an object cannot be opened or edited in an object library.
6)	d	

Lab 9.4 ■ Self-Review Answers

Question	Answer	Comments
1)	a	Answer b is incorrect because object libraries should serve as the source for template forms.
2)	d	Answer b is incorrect because Forms will automatically re-name a form that is based on a template form.
3)	a	
4)	b	

CHAPTER 10
Lab 10.1 ■ Self-Review Answers

Question	Answer	Comments
1)	b	
2)	d	
3)	a	
4)	d	

Lab 10.2 ■ Self-Review Answers

Question	Answer	Comments
1)	c	Answers a and b are incorrect because PL/SQL Libraries are separate modules.
2)	b	
3)	b	
4)	d	
5)	d	The statement :CONTROL.CURDATE directly references a block and item name, which would make it invalid in a PL/SQL Library.

Lab 10.3 ■ Self-Review Answers

Question	Answer	Comments
1)	c	
2)	a	
3)	c	
4)	c	

CHAPTER 11
Lab 11.1 ■ Self-Review Answers

Question	Answer	Comments
1)	d	
2)	c	Answer a is incorrect because the NO_ACTIVATE parameter will not make the calling form invisible. It will open the called form, but set the focus to the calling form.
3)	b	
4)	d	Answer a is incorrect because the value of a system variable only applies to a specific form.
5)	b	Parameter lists can contain more than one parameter.

CHAPTER 12
Lab 12.1 ■ Self-Review Answers

Question	Answer	Comments
1)	d	Answer a is incorrect because you cannot create reports in the Form Builder. You must do it in the Report Builder. It is only possible to invoke the Report Builder from the Form Builder.
2)	a	
3)	a	
4)	b	Answer a is incorrect because RUN_REPORT_OBJECT cannot accept report object names. Answer c is incorrect because RUN_PRODUCT_OBJECT is not a valid built-in. Answer d is incorrect because the single quotes have been left off the NULL parameter list value.

Lab 12.2 ■ Self-Review Answers

Question	Answer	Comments
1)	a	
2)	d	
3)	d	
4)	d	SYNCHRONOUS is not a parameter you can pass to RUN_PRODUCT_OBJECT.

CHAPTER 13
Lab 13.1 ■ Self-Review Answers

Question	Answer	Comments
1)	d	
2)	c	The switch parameter can sometimes be confusing. A good way to remember how to set the switch parameter

is to think of it as written in the following sentences: I want to **REPLACE** the calling form's menu. I do **NOT** want to **REPLACE** the calling form's menu.

3)	c	
4)	b	It will make "v" the hot key.

Lab 13.2 ■ Self-Review Answers

Question	Answer	Comments
1)	d	
2)	c	
3)	d	

APPENDIX B

THE WINDOWS REGISTRY

 Before continuing with Appendix B, please read the Introduction for information about the companion Web site and the Exercise files you will need to download to use this book.

The Windows Registry is a database that is maintained by the Windows operating system. It contains configuration information about your computer, the hardware it uses, and the software it runs. To complete some of the Exercises in this workbook, it is important to have a basic understanding of how Oracle Forms uses the Registry.

Whenever you install software, it is common for the installation process to add configuration information to the Registry. This way, when the software is running, it can look to the Registry for information like the working directory you have chosen for the product, the current version of the product, and so on. Oracle Forms and the other Oracle Developer modules use the Register similarly in that they often look to it for environment variables which, among other things, indicate where Oracle Developer modules are stored. The Registry contains far more complicated information about Forms and the rest of your computer as well, but that will not be covered in this appendix. If you are interested in learning more about Registry details, please refer to the manuals for your operating system. To complete the Exercises in this workbook, you only need to be concerned with how Forms looks to the Registry to find modules.

It is important to note that only Microsoft Windows 95/98 and NT have Registries. All other operating systems use other methods to manage and store environment variables.

EDITING THE REGISTRY

The easiest way to learn how forms uses the Registry is to look at Registry entries and edit them. You have often unwittingly edited the Registry when you installed software or adjusted system settings using the tools in the Windows Control Panel. You can also edit the Registry manually by using a GUI tool called the Registry Editor. To open the Registry Editor, take the following steps:

1) From the Windows Start menu, select the Run option to open the Run dialog.

2) Type the following command into the field labeled Open:

regedit

3) The Registry Editor should open as in Figure B.1.

Expand the HKEY_LOCAL_MACHINE folder to see its sub-folders. Working with the folders under HKEY_LOCAL_MACHINE will let you change Registry values for the local machine. So, any Windows user that logs into this machine will be affected by the Registry values set here.

Expand the SOFTWARE node and scroll down so that you can see the folder named ORACLE. Select the ORACLE folder, but do not expand it. The Registry Editor should now appear as it does in Figure B.2.

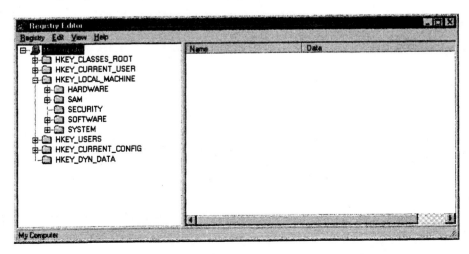

Figure B.1 ■ The Registry Editor with HKEY_LOCAL_MACHINE expanded.

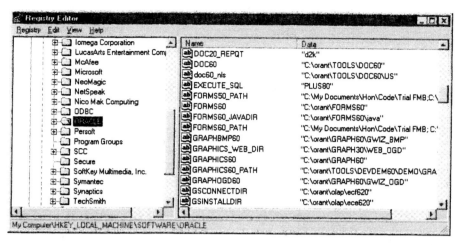

Figure B.2 ■ The Registry Editor with the ORACLE folder selected.

The hierarchy in the left pane of the window is displaying a list of Registry keys. HKEY_LOCAL_MACHINE and SOFTWARE are both Registry keys. The list in the right pane of the window is showing a list of Registry values. Scroll down in the right pane until you see a Registry value called FORMS60_PATH.

FORMS60_PATH

The FORMS60_PATH Registry value is a Forms environment variable that contains a list of directory paths. Whenever the Forms Runtime, Form Compiler, or Form Builder needs to find or reference a forms module, it looks to FORMS60_PATH to see which directory path that module might be stored in.

■ FOR EXAMPLE:

Chapter 11, "Multiple-Forms Applications," includes an example in which you run one form from another using the following command:

```
OPEN_FORM('STUDENT');
```

Note that this command does not include the path to the STUDENT module file. It simply uses the module's name. For Forms to open this module, it must search the directory paths listed in the FORMS60_PATH Registry entry until it finds the module STUDENT.fmx. If it cannot find STUDENT, you would receive the following error:

```
FRM-40010: Cannot read form STUDENT
```

What this could mean is that the STUDENT.fmx file is not in a directory that is pointed to by the FORMS60_PATH entry. (The error could also mean that the STUDENT module does not exist at all, or that STUDENT has been misspelled in the OPEN_FORM statement. For the sake of this appendix, assume that these are not the problems.) If you add the proper path to the Registry, you will not encounter this error.

When you download the Exercise files from the companion Web site, they are installed to a directory path called:

C:\guest\forms\exercises

If C: is not your drive letter, please be sure to substitute the drive letter you are using in the tasks that follow.

This is also the path you will use to save all of the files you will create throughout the Exercises. Therefore, you must add this path to the FORMS60_PATH Registry value.

At this time, you should only edit the FORMS60_PATH *Registry value. Changes to other Registry values could make your system unstable. If you are interested in exploring the Registry further, it is strongly recommended that you first read the manuals for your operating system.*

Take the following steps to edit the Registry:

1) Double-click the FORMS60_PATH value to open the Edit String dialog as shown in Figure B.3.

2) Use the cursor keys to navigate to the very front of the string. Be careful not to delete the entries that are already there. If you accidentally delete the existing entries, simply click the Cancel button and then re-open the Edit String dialog.

Figure B.3 ■ The Edit String dialog for editing Registry values.

3)   Type the following at the beginning of the string:

C:\guest\forms\exercises;

Make sure you include the semi-colon to separate your new entry from the one that comes after it. Again, if C: is not your drive letter, be sure to substitute the appropriate one.

4)   Click the OK button.

The Registry has been updated, so now Forms will be able to reference any modules that are stored in C:\guest\forms\exercises.

REPORTS60_PATH

The REPORTS60_PATH Registry value is the environment variable that stores directory paths that Oracle Reports uses to search for modules. You will not be building Oracle Reports in this book, but you will be calling them from forms. Therefore, you will need to adjust the REPORTS60_ PATH as well. Take the following steps:

1)   Double-click the REPORTS60_PATH value to open the Edit String dialog.

2)   Repeat Steps 2–4 above.

REGISTRY ADVANTAGES

The beauty of environment variables and how the Registry uses them is that you are saved from having to hard-code the paths to your files into your applications. The modules are able to find each other using the environment variables in the Registry without having to know the exact path. Therefore, you do not have to create identical directory structures on every machine that uses your application.

■ FOR EXAMPLE:

Assume you had used the following command to open a form:

OPEN_FORM('C:\applications\forms\modules\student.fmx');

By doing this, you would force every user and every developer who wanted to work with this form to have the same directory structure on their machines. This would seriously complicate the deployment and maintenance of your applications.

Thus, the Registry is important during development as well.

■ *FOR EXAMPLE:*

Chapter 9, "Reusable Objects," uses subclassing to have an object in one form reference an object in another form to inherit some of its properties. Subclassed objects maintain a link with their source objects. To maintain that link, the module containing the subclassed object uses the FORMS60_ PATH Registry value to find the module that contains its source objects.

This becomes even more important if you plan to share modules and objects with other developers. As long as the source and subclassed modules are saved in directory paths that FORMS60_PATH can find, you can easily share with other developers and still maintain the links established by subclassing.

INDEX

A

Advanced options page, LOV Wizard, 231, 240–41
Alerts, 25, 28, 248–58, 271
  creating, 249, 251–53
  displaying, 249–53
  as examples of simple dialog windows, 271
  with one button, 249
  with two buttons, 249
Alert Style property, 255
Attach dialog, 369
Attached Libraries node, Object Navigator, 372
AUDIT_ITEMS property class, 345–46
Automatic Display property, 243
Automatic Position property, 243
Automatic Refresh property, 241

B

Background Color property, 12
Base–table blocks, 14–16, 19, 107
Bevel property, 89
Binary files, 53–54
  compiling into executable files, 55–56
Block–level triggers, 28
Blocks, 25–26, 27
  and canvases, 27
  and items, 27
  physical properties, 25
Boolean menu items, 423
Built–ins, defined, 89
Buttons, 3, 144, 157–58
  creating, 147–48
  labels, 254
  putting simple code behind for, 148–50
Button tool, 134

C

Calculation Mode property, 139–40
CALL_FORM built–in, 392–93
Canvases, 11–13, 17–18, 24–25, 93, 262, 266–312
  and blocks, 27
  content canvases, 277–86
    creating, 278–85
  displaying, 267
  properties, 13
  stacked canvases, 287–97
  toolbar canvases, 298–310
  and triggers, 25
  understanding, 269–70
  viewports (views), 266–67
Canvases node, 67
Canvas page, Layout Wizard, 37–38
Canvas property, 133
Canvas viewports, 266–67
Character coordinate system, 49
Check boxes, 3, 22, 144–46, 165–68
  compared to check boxes in paper–based forms, 166
  creating, 155–56
  states, 165
Check Box Mapping of Other Values property, 166
Check menu items, 423
CLEAR_ALL_MASTER_DETAILS, 26, 119
CloseAllowed property, **MAINWIN**, 319
Collapse All button, Object Navigator, 74
Collapse button, Object Navigator, 74
Column display page, LOV Wizard, 230–31, 239–40
Column Name property, 137
Column selection page, LOV Wizard, 230, 238–39
COMMIT_FORM, 213
COMMIT_FORM statement, 397–98
Companion Web site, xiii
Compilation Errors window, 59, 61
Compile dialog, 368–69
Compile option, 59, 368
Compile Selection option, 368
Content canvases/windows, 266, 277–86
  creating, 278–85
Conventions, xvi
Coordinate System settings, 49
COPY built–in, 207–8
COURSE.fmb, 16
COURSE_INFORMATION, 26
COURSE_SECTION, 26
Create button, Object Navigator, 81, 183

CREATED_BY, 209
CREATED_DATE, 209

D

Database Item property, 136–37, 202
Database Objects node, Object Navigator, 81
Data block page, Layout Wizard, 38–39
Data Blocks node, Object Navigator, 67, 73–74, 76
Data Block Wizard, 32, 33–37, 42–43, 46–50, 126, 146, 197
   finish page, 38
   opening, 33, 42, 46
   pages, 33
   table page, 34–37
   type page, 34
   using, 42–43
Data Type property, 135
Default Alert Button property, 256
Default menu form, 429–33
DEFAULT.mmb, 429
DEFAULT_WHERE property, 397
Delete Record Behavior property, 120
DEMO_OBJECTS, 26
Development environment, 65–83
   Layout Editor, 93–104
   Object Navigator, 66–83
   Property Palette, 84–92
Dialog windows, 262–64, 271
Direct references, 364
Display items, 3, 22, 127
   creating/defining, 131–133, 138–141
   creating/defining without the wizard, 127–30, 133–39
Display Without Privilege property, 441
Document windows, 262–64, 270
DO_KEY built–in, 210–11

E

Edge Foreground, 101
Enter Query button, 122
Enter Query mode, Form Builder, 57, 61
.Err extension, 59
Events, 2–3
   and items/triggers, 4
Executable files, 53–54, 57
Execute Query button, 122, 197
Execution Hierarchy property, 183
EXIT_FORM, 213
Expand All button, Object Navigator, 74
Expand button, Object Navigator, 74

F

Fetch mode, Form Builder, 57, 61
Fill button, 101–2

Fill Color, 101
Filter Before Display property, 241
FIND_ALERT built–in, 250, 257
FIND_BLOCK built–in, 215
FIND_ built–ins, 215, 219–21, 394
FIND_WINDOW built–in, 220–21
Finish page, 38
   Data Block Wizard, 38
   Layout Wizard, 41–42
Firing, of triggers, 3
.fmb files, 53, 58–60
.fmx files, 53–54, 58–60, 320
Foreground Color, 101
Format Mask property, 136
Formatting toolbar, Layout Editor, 94–95, 97
Form Builder, 2, 4–7, 17–18, 27, 32, 46, 53–54, 58, 75, 119, 148–49, 157, 177, 252, 320, 404, 424–25
   View menu, 423–24
Form Compiler, 54, 59, 320
Form–level triggers, 28
FORMPL/SQL EditorTRIGGER FAILURE exception, 204
Forms, use of term, 16
Forms built–ins, 213–23
   defined, 89
   FIND_ built–ins, 215, 219–21, 394
   GET_ built–ins, 214, 217–18
   SET_ built–ins, 214–15, 218–19
   using, 216–17
Forms help system, 94, 173–74
FORMS_MDI_WINDOW, 272
Forms menus, 421–44
   menu modules, 421–34
   menu security, 435–43
Forms module, use of term, 16
Forms Runtime, 54, 177, 425
Forms triggers, 9
FORM_TRIGGER FAILURE, 204–5
Frames:
   and canvases, 18, 24
   defined, 13
Freeze/Unfreeze button, Property Palette, 90

G

GET_APPLICATION_PROPERTY built–in, 216–19
GET_BLOCK_PROPERTY, 217
GET_ built–ins, 214, 217–18
GET_CANVAS_PROPERTY, 217
GET_ITEM_PROPERTY, 217
Global variables, 382–83
GO_BLOCK built–in, 296
GO_BLOCK trigger, 221

GO_FORM built–in, 391
GO_ITEM built–in, 265, 267, 273–74
GO_ITEM trigger, 221, 283
Graphics, 93
GUI Design Essentials
  (Weinschenk/Jamar/Yeo), 125

H
HIDE_HIST trigger, 284
HIDE_VIEW built–in, 275, 296
HIDE_WINDOW built–in, 273–74
Horizontal Toolbar property, 334

I
ID_NULL built–in, 221, 257
Indirect references in library code, 364
Initial Value property, 135–36, 162,
  167
Interface event, 2
Interface object, 11
Internal processing event, 2–3
Item–level triggers, 28
Item Roles property, 440
Items, 3–4, 11–12, 17–18, 27, 125–69
  and blocks, 27
  buttons, 144, 157–58
    creating, 147–48
    utting simple code behind,
      148–50
  check boxes, 144–46, 165–68
    creating, 155–56
  controlling programmatically at
    run–time, 23
  display items, 127
    creating/defining, 131–33, 138–41
  and events/triggers, 4
  identifying type of, 22
  list items, 144–45
    creating, 150–52
  null–canvas, 133
  properties, 11–12
  radio groups, 144–45, 163–65
    creating, 153–55
  text items, 126–27
    creating/defining without the wizard,
      127–30, 133–38
Items page:
  Layout Wizard, 39–40
  LOV Wizard, 232, 241–43
Item Type property, 143, 153
Item types, choosing, 22–23

K
Keyboard Navigable property, 283
KEY-DELREC trigger, 197–99, 210–11
KEY-EXEQRY trigger, 197–98, 209–10
KEY-EXIT trigger, 257

Key triggers, 174, 175, 189, 209–11
  creating, 197–99
Knowledge requirements, xv

L
Label property, 157
Layout Data Block property, 24
Layout Editor, 13, 22, 23, 41, 50, 66, 77,
  85, 93–104, 109, 134, 147, 153, 249,
  267, 287, 292, 404
  arranging/sizing objects, 97–99
  Button tool, 99–100
  creating/formatting objects, 95–97
  Formatting toolbar, 94–95, 97
  Run Form Client/Server button, 60
  Size Objects window, 102
  toolbars, 93–94
  Tool Palette, 95
  Update Layout button, 102–3
  Utility toolbar, 94, 283
Layout Wizard, 32, 33, 37–42, 44–46, 48,
  50–51, 111, 138, 262, 292
  canvas page, 37–38
  data block page, 38–39
  Data Block tab page, 51
  finish page, 41–42
  items page, 39–40
  pages, 37
  records page, 40–41
  style page, 40
Line Color, 101
List Elements dialog box, 159–60,
  162
List items, 22, 144–45
  creating, 150–52
Lists of values (LOVs), 28, 226–47
  Automatic Display property, 243
  Automatic Position property, 243
  creating, 228–32
  displaying, 233–35
  LIST_VALUES built–in, 244–45
  LOV Wizard, 228–29, 235–43
    advanced options page, 231, 240–41
    column display page, 230–31,
      239–40
    column selection page, 230, 238–39
    items page, 232, 241–43
    LOV display page, 231
    source page, 229, 236
    SQL query page, 229–30, 237
  and record groups, 227–28
  SHOW_LOV built–in, 245–46
LIST_VALUES built–in, 244–45
List of Values property, 242
LOV Column Mapping dialog, 271
LOV display page, LOV Wizard, 231

LOV Wizard, 228–29, 235–43
  advanced options page, 231, 240–41
  column display page, 230–31, 239–40
  column selection page, 230, 238–39
  items page, 232, 241–43
  LOV display page, 231
  source page, 229, 236
  SQL query page, 229–30, 237

M

Magic menu items, 423, 429–31
Mandatory forms, 11–29
  base–table blocks, 14–16, 19
  canvases, 11–13, 18, 24–25
  elements, relating, 17, 20–21
  items, 11–12, 17–18
  modules, 16, 20
  non–base–table blocks, 14–16
  windows, 14
Mapping of Other Values property,
  161, 164, 166
Master block, and relation object, 118
Master–detail forms, 25, 107–24
  Copy Value from Item property,
  118–19
  creating, 110–12
  defined, 108
  Delete Record Behavior property,
  120
  master block, 115–18
    table based on, 115
  ON–CHECK–DELETE–MASTER trigger, 120
  ON–CLEAR–DETAILS trigger, 119
  ON–POPULATE–DETAILS trigger, 119–20,
  172
  purpose of, 115
  relation, 109
  relation object, creation of, 109
  SECTION block, 117–18
  wizards, 109, 115–16
  working with relations and, 112–15
Master–detail relation, 25
menudef.mmb, 429
Menu Editor, 27, 248, 425, 426, 429
Menu Module property, 334
Menu Module Roles dialog, 439–40
Menu modules, 421–34
  attaching to forms, 425
  creating/configuring, 424–28
  default menu form, 429–33
  menu items, 423–24
    creating, 426–28
    types of, 423
  menu objects, 422–23
Menu security, 435–43
  configuring, 436

defined, 435
forms schema objects, building, 437–39
implementing, 436–39
sample database users/roles, running
  script to create, 436–37
MESSAGE built–in, 209, 248
.mmb files, 58, 425
.mmx files, 425
Modal windows, 263–64
MODIFIED_BY, 208
MODIFIED_DATE, 208
Modules, 16, 20
Mouse Navigate button, 158
Multi Line property, 135
Multiple Document Interface (MDI) window, 263, 272
Multiple–forms, 381–402
  calling form compared to called form,
  382
  form name, 382
  global variables, 382–83
  opening, 385–87
  parameter list, 384–85
    creating/passing to form, 387–98
  parameters, 384
  passing values to called forms, 383–85

N

Name of Records Displayed property,
  138
NEW_FORM built–in, 392–93
New Program Unit dialog box, 356,
  368
NEXT_FORM built–in, 391
Non–base–table blocks, 14–16
Normal mode, Form Builder, 57, 61
Null–canvas item, 133
Number of Items Displayed property,
  138
Number of Records Displayed prop-
  erty, 140–41

O

Object groups, 336–37
  creating/reusing, 338–40
Object libraries, 337–38
  creating and utilizing, 341–43
  and **LIBRARY** window, 337
Object Navigator, 5–9, 22, 23–24, 46, 50,
  66–83, 88, 118, 128, 148, 197, 292,
  294–95, 336, 356, 369, 404, 424, 440
  Collapse All button, 74
  Collapse button, 74
  Create button, 81, 183
  creating/deleting objecs, 69–70
  cutting and pasting objects, 70–71
  database objects, viewing, 72–73

Database Objects node, 81
Data Blocks node, 67, 73–74, 76
dragging/dropping objects, 70–71
Expand All button, 74
Expand button, 74
hierarchy, 67
opening/identifying objects, 68–69
Run Form Client/Server button, 60
running/saving forms, 72
vertical toolbar, 67, 68
ON-CHECK-DELETE-MASTER trigger, 119, 120, 189
ON-CLEAR-DETAILS trigger, 26, 119
ON-DELETE trigger, 184
ON-INSERT trigger, 174
ON-POPULATE-DETAILS trigger, 119–20, 172–73, 189
OPEN_FORM built–in, 391
Oracle Developer 6.0 On–line Manuals, 162
Oracle Developer, 2, 53, 59, 157
Oracle forms, 2–10, 60
  button clicks, 7
  events, 2–3
  files, 53–64
    binary, 53–54
    compiling, 54
    compiling binary files into executable files, 55–56
    executable, 53–54, 57
    fmb and .fmx files compared, 54–55, 58
    running, 54
  how they work, 4–7
  items, 3–4, 22
  physical objects in, 25
  triggers, 2–3, 9, 24–25, 172–212
Oracle Graphics, 2
Oracle reports, 2
  running from forms, 404–13
  running with **RUN_PRODUCT** built–in, 406–7
  running with **RUN_REPORT_OBJECT** built–in, 407–8

P
Parameters:
  parameters in reports modules, 415–16
  passing to reports, 414–19
Pinning mode, 100
P_item parameter, 359–60
Plain menu items, 423, 429
.pll files, 58
PL/SQL, using in triggers, 175–76
PL/SQL Editor, 149, 158–59, 200, 201–3, 356, 404
PL/SQL libraries, 59, 362–73

advantages of, 363–64
creating/attaching, 364–66
defined, 362
editing/changing code in, 372
indirect references in library code, 364
  using, 366–67
modules, saving, 362
POST-BLOCK trigger, 221
POST-DATABASE-COMMIT trigger, 189
POST-FORMS-COMMIT trigger, 189
POST-INSERT trigger, 174, 354–55
POST-QUERY trigger, 184, 187–88, 190–91, 193–94, 199–200, 202, 204–5, 221, 354
PRE-CHANGE trigger, 174
Pre Compute Summaries property, 141
PRE-FORM trigger, 177, 272
PRE-INSERT trigger, 174, 189, 196, 207–8, 343, 371
PRE-RECORD trigger, 221
PRE-TEXT-ITEM trigger, 221
PRE-UPDATE trigger, 189, 343, 372
PREVIOUS_FORM built–in, 391
Primary Canvas property, 273
Program units, 354–61
  creating, 357–58
  defined, 354
  subclassing, 356
  syntax for creating, 359
Prompt Alignment Offset property, 139
Prompt Attachment Offset property, 139
Prompt property, 167
Properties, items, 11–12
Property classes, 324–25, 333
  creating/applying, 327–29
  with multiple properties, 332
Property Palette, 12–13, 22, 23–24, 49, 66, 78, 84–92, 404
  accessing, 88
  Canvas property, 133
  changing properties, 85–88
  Freeze/Unfreeze button, 90
  icons indicating property state, 319
  Item Type property, 143, 153
  Prompt Alignment Offset property, 139
  Prompt Attachment Offset property, 139
  property categories, 84
  viewing properties, 84–86
  Visible property, 133
Push buttons, 22

Q
Query All Records property, 141

Query Array Size property, 140–41
QUERY_MASTER_DETAIL trigger, 26, 119–20
Query triggers, 175, 187–88
  creating, 189–92

R
Radio Button node, 163
Radio groups, 3, 22, 144–45, 163–65
  creating, 153–55
  radio buttons in, 165
Radio menu items, 423
Real coordinate system, 49
Record Group Fetch Size property, 241
Record groups, and LOVs, 227–28
Record History window, 331–32
Records page, Layout Wizard, 40–41
Relation object:
  creation of, 109
  and master block, 118
Relations, 25, 107
Report Builder, 404
Reports Runtime, 404, 409
Reusable code, 353–61
  PL/SQL libraries, 362–73
  program units, 354–61
  stored PL/SQL objects, 374–78
Reusable objects, 313–52
  subclassing, 80, 314–22
    Subclass Information dialog box, 332–33
    subclass objects, 315–17
RUN_PRODUCT built-in, 404, 405
  running Oracle reports with, 406–7
RUN_REPORT_OBJECT built-in, 404, 405–6
  running Oracle reports with, 407–8

S
Sample schema, xv–xvi
SECONDCAN, 273
SECONDWIN, 273–74
Separators, 424
SET_ALERT_PROPERTY built-in, 359
SET_ALERT_PROPTERY built-in, 257
SET_BLOCK_PROPERTY, 218, 397
SET_ built-ins, 214–15, 218–19
SET_CANVAS_PROPERTY, 218
SET_ITEM_PROPERTY built-in, 89, 218
SET_VIEW_PROPERTY built-in, 296
SET_WINDOW_PROPERTY built-in, 218
SHOW_ALERT built-in, 250, 257
Show Errors window, 202
SHOW_HIST trigger, 273, 284
SHOW_LIST button, 245
SHOW_LOV built-in, 245–46, 249
SHOW_VIEW built-in, 267, 275, 296, 355

Size Objects window, 102
Software requirements, xiii–xiv
Source page, LOV Wizard, 229, 236
SQL, using in triggers, 175–76
SQL query page, LOV Wizard, 229–30, 237
Stacked canvases, 287–97
  creating/displaying, 289–92
  defined, 287–88
  INSTRUCTOR stacked canvas, 293–94
  viewport, 288
Stacked Canvas tool, Tool Palette, 293
Stored PL/SQL objects, 374–78
  calling, 374–75
  moving between database and Forms application, 375
  using, 375–77
Style page, Layout Wizard, 40
Subclass Information property, 91, 318, 321, 344
Subclassing, 80, 314–22
  Subclass Information dialog box, 332–33
  subclass objects, 315–17
Summary Function property, 139

T
TABLE_ITEM_PROMPT_ALIGNMENT, 26
Table page, 35–37
  Data Block Wizard, 34–37
Text Color button, 101–2
Text fields, 3
Text items, 3, 22, 126–27
  creating/defining without the wizard, 127–30, 133–38
  Enabled property, 134–35
Text Item tool, 134
Toolbar canvases, 298–310
  creating, 299–302
  TOOLBAR canvas, 305–6, 314–15
  using in another form, 302–3
Tool Palette, 99–100, 134, 147
  Layout Editor, 95
  Stacked Canvas tool, 293
Transactional triggers, 175, 189
  creating, 195–96
Triggers, 2–3, 9, 24–25, 172–212
  and canvases, 25
  categorizing, 173–75, 178–79
    by function, 174–75
    by name, 174
  and events/items, 4
  forms triggers, 9
  key triggers, 174, 175, 189, 209–11
    creating, 197–99
  On event triggers, 174
  Post event triggers, 174

Pre event triggers, 174
query triggers, 175, 187–88
creating, 189–92
scope, 172–73, 176–77
transactional triggers, 175, 189
creating, 195–96
using PL/SQL and SQL in, 175–76
validation triggers, 175, 188–89
creating, 192–95
When event triggers, 174
Type page, 34
Data Block Wizard, 34

U

Update Layout property, 24, 98, 102–3
Use Security property, 440
Utility toolbar, Layout editor, 94, 283

V

VAL_ALERT alert, 357
Validate Item event, 3
Validating an item, 3
Validation triggers, 175, 188–89
creating, 192–95
Value When Checked property, 165–67
Value When Unchecked property, 165–67
View menu, Form Builder, 423–24
Viewport Height property, 275
Viewports, 266–67
Viewport Width property, 275
Visible property, 133
Visual attributes, 323
behavior of, 330
creating/applying, 325–27
Visual Attribute Type property, 330–31
Common value, 330

Prompt value, 331
Title value, 331

W

WHEN-BUTTON-PRESSED trigger, 7–8, 144, 158, 173, 181, 198, 209, 251, 254–55, 272–73, 280–81, 294, 354, 387
WHEN-CHECKBOX-CHANGED trigger, 9, 23, 167
WHEN-NEW-FORM-INSTANCE trigger, 26, 55, 216, 220, 389
WHEN-VALIDATE-ITEM triggers, 4, 47, 176–77, 179–83, 188–89, 193–94, 204–6, 353, 357–58, 360
WHEN-VALIDATE-RECORD trigger, 206
WINDOW-CLOSED trigger, 3
Windows, 14, 262–69
content windows, 277–86
defined, 262
dialog windows, 262–64, 271
displaying, 265–66
document windows, 262–64, 270
modal windows, 263–64
Multiple Document Interface (MDI) window, 263, 272
styles of, 262
understanding, 267–69
Wizards, 32–52, 107, 288
Data Block Wizard, 32, 33–37, 42–43, 46–50
Layout Wizard, 32, 33, 37–42, 44–46, 48, 50–51
reentering, 43–45
Wrap Style property, 135
Www.oracle.com, 59
Www.phptr.com/phptrinteractive, 4
WYSIWYG, 12–13